W9-AYZ-623

IN A HOUSE OF HORRORS . . .

In a raspy, weak voice, the frail woman muttered the same words over and over. It was a plea for help; help that had come not an instant too soon for her.

But days too late for her sister.

"You have the power to take me away, haven't you?" she gasped in a desperate, plaintive manner. Her words brought a silent stream of tears from Margaret Conway, a woman who had sailed halfway around the world, only to find one of the Williamson sisters dressed out in a coffin and the other a hideous skeleton on the verge of death.

Again the raspy voice begged.

"You can take me? You can take me away? *Please*."

ALSO BY GREGG OLSEN

Mockingbird
Bitter Almonds
Abandoned Prayers

PUBLISHED BY
WARNER BOOKS

GREGG OLSEN

STARVATION HEIGHTS

THE TRUE STORY OF AN AMERICAN DOCTOR AND THE MURDER OF A BRITISH HEIRESS

WARNER BOOKS

A Time Warner Company

WARNER BOOKS EDITION

Copyright © 1997 by Gregg Olsen
All rights reserved.

Cover design by Tony Russo

Warner Books, Inc.
1271 Avenue of the Americas
New York, NY 10020

Visit our Web site at
http://warnerbooks.com

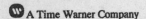 A Time Warner Company

Printed in the United States of America

First Printing: April, 1997

10 9 8 7 6 5 4 3

This is for the widows of Olalla . . .

Sally
Verna
Janetta
June
Cammie
Marie
Ethel
Myrtle
Becky

and for
Opal and Chuck

Some, as thou saws't, by violent stroke shall die,
By fire, flood, famine; by intemperance more
In meats and drinks, which on the Earth shall bring
Diseases dire, of which a monstrous crew
Before thee shall appear, that thous mays't know
What miser the inabstinence of Eve
Shall bring on men.

                If thou well observe
The rule of "Not too much" by temperance taught
In what thou eat'st and drink'st, seeking from thence
Due nourishment, not gluttonous delight,
Till many years over thy head return;
So mays't thou live, till, like ripe fruit, thou drop
Into thy mother's lap, or be with ease
*Gathered, not harshly plucked, for death mature.**

                        —John Milton,
                        Paradise Lost

*Epigram from the 1910 edition of Linda Burfield Hazzard's
Fasting for the Cure of Disease

STARVATION
HEIGHTS

PROLOGUE

THE OLDER BOYS ALWAYS BROUGHT IT UP to the younger ones.

Sit down, and I'll tell you the story of what happened here in the very spot you're sitting on. Cross my heart, hope to die, stick a rusty needle in my eye. I ain't lying. What I'm telling you is true.

Fourteen Boy Scouts and their Scoutmaster had gathered to camp in a clearing on a brambly hillside meadow not far from the shoreline of Puget Sound in Washington State. It was nearly autumn, 1946. The boys who comprised Fragaria Troop 528 were the sons of chicken farmers, berry growers, and shipyard workers. All were passing from boyhood to manhood.

None were unfamiliar with the place they camped, though they would not have thought to go there on their own. No one but the very stupid or the very brave ever did that. Even on a dare. Some folks who lived their entire lives in the community that was but a mere blip on most maps had never set foot on the property.

Those that knew the story best, those who could *tell* it best, would gather the others and speak in low, earnest tones. As the campfire burned to an ashy bowl of red-hot embers, the boys would ramble on, piling up horror upon horror, like cordwood stacked under a bloodred-barked madrona tree.

Like most places, Olalla had a bit of a past. Some of it was good, but that, of course, was humdrum, simply unsuitable for the milieu of a campfire. The proud history was the kind of talk a grandmother gives while her grandchildren squirm to break away from her sweetly uninspired dissertation about the good old days. Some of the past, however, was bad. And bad was always better.

Not much of a town anymore, but it's a true fact that there was a time when people from all over the world came here . . .

By the time the Scouts gathered to camp at the old Hazzard sanitarium, it had been decades since the town had seen its heyday. Good Lord, to walk its roads or along its beaches was to see nothing but reminders of a bygone era. By the 1940s, fate had reduced Olalla to a dwindling village, a place that inhabited only the faded memories of the greying and the bald. As old businesses along the waterfront burned down or fell into rotten disrepair, they were abandoned. No one ever rebuilt the pool hall, the bakery, the shingle mill, or the net sheds. No one reclaimed what the seawater had stolen, what the insatiable worms had gnawed to Swiss cheese. Many, many years later, old photographs would hang on the walls of the sole surviving waterfront business—a small grocery store and two-pump gas station. Illuminated under buzzing fluorescent lights, the black-and-white images would provide silent, yet convincing, testimony of what had once been.

As the tide from the Sound does to a child's aimless footprints on the beach, time washes away all traces of what had been.

No one could possess a shred of doubt that Olalla's most famous institution was the sanitarium up on the heights off Orchard Avenue. Nothing else even came close. Not the sawmills, the strawberry fields, the hotel on the little bay. But, of course, all—even the most famous—had been consumed by the years. All that was left of Dr. Hazzard's sanitarium were the ankle-deep walls of the foundation and the tower of a masonry incinerator that swelled from the ground like a huge grave marker. In a way, that's what it was.

The doctor locked her patients up and starved 'em. To skin 'n bone, I heard.

The half dozen or so little cabins that were reserved for some patients at the peak of the world-renowned institution's fame had rotted into the earth. The Pacific Northwest's legendary rains had gently turned the wooden floorboards into a soil so black it looked like a hole to another world. A perfect row of old firs and pines lined up like sentinels from the road.

Each one of them trees marks the spot where the old lady buried one of her victims.

Long before the Scouts and their Scoutmaster came to camp and told ghost stories, a great white, wood-frame building rose from the concrete outline that held it skyward. It was a magnificent structure for its time and place—a sanitarium of three stories, plus a basement. Dormer windows jutted over a porch that ran the full length; a dark, oak staircase in the grand foyer dominated the interior. There was even a kitchen, an office, and of course, the Treatment Room.

A stark white painted wooden archway over the north end of a circular driveway that looped from the road to the satiny oak of the building's front doors proclaimed to visitors that they had arrived at what the owners called Wilderness Heights.

All of what the place had been was the great dream of a woman, a doctor named Linda Burfield Hazzard.

There are bodies out here, buried all over the place. I heard a kid from up the valley found a couple of human skulls when he was diggin' a pit for baked beans . . .

Eleven years had passed since the sanitarium burned to the ground, even longer since the story began. The old lady had been dead since 1938, her husband, Samuel, followed her to the grave eight years later. The main house, overlooking a fern-glutted ravine still stood just south of where the old sanitarium had been. The cedar-shingled bungalow was empty at that time. A *For Sale* sign stuck in the dandelions alongside the driveway.

Many who passed by on Orchard Avenue remarked how the air always seemed a little colder around that place on the hill. Wind blew a little harder, too. At night, the sky's blackness seemed to hold no room for the cheer of the moon. The Scouts of Troop 528 unfurled sleeping bags into rows in the open field and lay as still as could be. The older ones insisted to the younger ones that at night, when the wind forced treetops to bend over backwards, the haunted screams of the dead could be heard.

It should not have ended that way. It wasn't supposed to end that way. But it did. Among the debris, hidden beneath tangled shields of blackberry vines and enormous bouquets of salal foliage, were secrets that time seized in its mighty, unforgiving grip. Only in the campfire-stoked stories of Boy Scouts, bedtime tales baby-sitters employ when they set out to frighten bratty charges, or in the sweet delight of grandpas who never grew up, would the stories live on.

I

Miss Claire &
Miss Dorothea

*Appetite is Craving; Hunger is Desire.
Craving is never satisfied; but Desire is
relieved when Want is Supplied.*

*Eating without Hunger, or pandering
to Appetite at the expense of Digestion,
makes Disease inevitable.*

—LINDA BURFIELD HAZZARD

It is a most beautiful treatment.

—CLAIRE WILLIAMSON

ONE

IT WAS A WORLD BOTH BUSTLING AND tranquil; a musky sweet-smelling blend of extremes. As hotel clerks, waiters, doormen, and gardeners went about their myriad duties, ladies in heavy, ankle-length satin dresses and mile-high hats of twisted taffeta and rosette-coiled velvet gossiped while demurely fanning themselves under the sparkle of a great glass dome amid enormous oriental urns planted with palms. Their chatter was frivolous and cheerful, like the chirping of songbirds gathering to feed on millet sprays and the dried discs of sunflowers.

The front desk calendar was inscribed: *September 1910.*

Across the lobby, Dorothea and Claire Williamson, splendidly attired in dresses pulled from one of the fourteen trunks that accompanied them around the world, gazed out a window. The evidence fall was lapping toward winter was everywhere on the grounds of the two-year-old Empress Hotel in Victoria, British Columbia. Small clusters of leaves had fallen in the cool, moist air; their bronze and gold remnants raked into ruffly heaps. New shrubbery framed the expansive lawns of the Canadian Pacific Railway-built hotel; ivy began its creep upward on the magnificently towering brick edifice. Plantings were crisp from the precise trim of a gardener's shears. There could be no disputing that the view of the green, well-tended grounds and the blue waters of the Inner Harbour was a soothing tonic for weary eyes.

Orphaned daughters of a well-to-do English officer in the Imperial Army Medical Service, Dorothea was born in Trichinopoli, India, Claire in London. And though schooled in Switzerland, England, and France and well traveled, the sisters, especially Claire, exhibited a childlike naïveté and innocence that sometimes left them a target of manipulation by those with dubious intentions. Hardly a week went by when there wasn't a banker or an investment expert with phony assurances that he had a plan for their money. Encounters with those who would do them financial harm only served to draw them closer to each other.

Suitors, however, were another matter. Neither sister had found a man that would make a husband worth leaving her sister all alone. And though Claire and Dorothea were unwed and beyond the age of thirty, neither quite considered herself a spinster. Yet, among the ladies in the lobby, they did not court the attentions of gentlemen. It was true they had had their admirers. But they were indifferent to such advances, and certainly they had no regard for the conventions of courtship.

Claire and Dora, as her sister called her, were likely the only women in the hotel with waists not bound and compressed like bunched-up necks of cloth sacks. Corsets, they told each other, were the devil's invention, cutting off circulation and choking digestive tracts. They preferred looser, one-piece undergarments. Clothing, they insisted, that wouldn't choke the very life out of them. To be fair, neither really had any need of corsets. Their figures were trim and youthful.

As they sat sipping tea, the sisters were a striking image: unblemished porcelain skin and blue-green eyes and the controlled posture of the upper class. Dora had auburn-hued hair with a few grey strands that she plucked from her scalp whenever they showed. Claire's face was more heart-shaped than round like her sister's, and her dark, wavy hair was the envy of the few who had seen it unfurled from beneath a hat. Claire, the younger of the two by four years, was slightly stouter in her bone structure than her sister. Both women had small, delicate hands that seldom went without the covering of gloves.

Dora cupped her hand over her mouth, turned away from her sister, and dramatically stifled a yawn.

"A bit more sugar, dearie," she said.

Claire nodded and moved a small tray with a silver pitcher and sugar bowl closer to Dora. Sugar, she thought, would provide a nice boost for the afternoon. A boost was decidedly in order. Neither sister had been sleeping well. Both longed to fall into the kind of slumber that would wash over them and give them the stamina needed to continue their journey. It had been such a long journey. They had come from Liverpool, England, by steamer, arriving first in Quebec, then Toronto, before making their way west across the Canadian Prairies to the Pacific Coast and Vancouver Island's Empress, a stately hotel that held its surroundings like a grand, decorated cake above the seawater in which the island seemed to float. It was the kind of fine establishment that travelers found unexpected in North America—a hotel with nearly the standards of the better places in Europe.

At each stop of their journey the sisters visited the distant relatives that made up all that was left of their family. Their father had died shortly after Claire's birth, their mother when Claire was only fourteen and Dora, eighteen. Scarlet fever drained the life out of two sisters, Ethel and Gertrude, when they were very young. Beyond each other, all Claire and Dorothea could embrace now were the odd collection of various aunts, uncles, cousins, and their beloved governess, Margaret Conway. They certainly, and they always said, *tragically*, had the money for such endeavors. Their Scottish-born grandfather, Charles Williamson, left his beloved Dorothea and Claire a fantastic fortune—worth more than a million American dollars. Most of it was in Victorian Government Inscribed Stock from Australia. Considerable land holdings in Canada, the United States, England, and Australia added a good deal more to their net worth. That two women controlled such extraordinary funds in 1910 was all the more remarkable.

While their fortune had afforded them world travel, wardrobes brimming with gowns from Paris, armloads of Irish linen and charming homes near London and Melbourne, it had not brought them the one thing they sought over everything else: a sense of well-being. If not their money, what would help them be happy, be well? It was a question often asked by the rich and unhappy, and it was a question Claire had frequently posed to her sister. Dora had no clear answers. She only knew they were not alone in their endeavors. Both Europe and America were dotted with centers for healing, institutions of physical culture, sanitariums, all promising robust health to those with brimming pocketbooks. By the time they visited North America, the sisters were like many other faddists for cures—they had been to several health institutes already. It was almost a hobby, a lifestyle, their great quest. And so they were drawn. Like a vapor-camouflaged island far away on the taut line of the horizon, always out of reach . . . always beckoning with the promise, the hope.

While on their travels, the women saw a small, but thoroughly intriguing newspaper advertisement in a Seattle daily newspaper. On September 2, 1910, Claire responded to the notice. She wrote a letter to Dr. Linda Burfield Hazzard, requesting the doctor's book, *Fasting for the Cure of Disease*. In her note, she exaggerated her sister's illness somewhat. It was true that Dora had not been feeling well, but she was hardly knocking on Death's door. Claire was given to overstating matters and emotions. She had been overindulged by a devoted sister who allowed her the leeway for slight embellishments. It mattered none to Dora. Her sister was the center of her world. Whatever it was Claire fancied, she only had to ask for it. Dora would cheerfully comply.

Claire described to the doctor how Dora had been on a partial fast since August 26 and had eaten nothing but fruit since then—with the exception of two small meals. Her glands were swollen and pain shot through her knees.

(Dora's) eyes just now are very bloodshot and seem to be eliminating a good deal of matter. Her period was due ten days ago, she has a very sharp pain over the right temple whenever she moves . . .

Five days after she sent the letter, a package arrived at the hotel front desk. It had been shipped from Dr. Hazzard's office in Seattle. In it was a slim but provocative volume penned by a woman who believed every ailment was caused by dietary factors. The idea was not entirely original, but Linda Burfield Hazzard presented her thesis in a convincing and revolutionary way. The sisters, especially Claire, couldn't wait. They were intrigued. Suddenly, sleep didn't seem so important.

Dora called for a waiter to have their tea sent up to their suite. They had some reading to attend to.

Their hotel suite was lovely, but a bit too snug. Dora Williamson had hoped for a little more room, perhaps two dressing tables. She remarked to her sister that she'd be more careful about their accommodations in the future. Even though only four years separated them, in Dora's mind it was she who had the role of the mother, Claire, the child. Claire happily accepted the role. She found her place in telling Dora how they could not have survived the loss of their parents without her maturity and unflappable resolve. It was Dora who reminded her sister that they should rely only on each other. No financial advisors. No husbands. Just the two of them.

It was also Dora who made the arrangements when it came to the details of their lives. At least Claire allowed her to believe so. When disappointment was the result of such efforts, Dora took the blame.

"I hadn't wanted to stay at that hotel in the first place. I suppose I shall recover from the draftiness of the place. Dora, it isn't your fault. It really isn't."

Claire studied Dora's face as she surveyed their room at the Empress. She could see Dora's dissatisfaction. To ease her sister's sense of responsibility, Claire spoke up quickly and cheerfully reminded her older sister of their circumstances.

"We are not in England . . . this, my dear, is North America. This was a colony, for goodness sake!"

Dora clasped her hands against her cheeks and laughed. With that, the hotel was suddenly fine. Besides, they had more important concerns.

As Dora breathlessly read the doctor's book aloud, Claire brushed out her long, burnished hair.

With each word, Dora's voice singsonged with bursts of enthusiasm. Every so often, Claire would stop her brushing and turn from the looking glass to tell her sister how she agreed with every word.

It should not require an exhaustive argument to establish the fact that disease has its origin in impaired digestion.

Upon this fundamental truth and its development the treatment known as the fasting treatment, depends on its entirety; and long experience at varied hands has demonstrated that, whatever the manifestation, the only disease is impure blood and its sole cause impaired digestion.

Dr. Hazzard's thesis was to "rest" the digestive system and allow the "impurities" to pass out of the body. The "natural cleansing process" would in time, she reasoned, strengthen the body.

A fresh foundation is there to work upon—a new and thoroughly cleansed body, ready to take up its labors, and with proper hygienic and dietic care, to carry them on indefinitely.

Already vegetarians, the Williamsons embraced natural methods of healing as superior to modern medicine. They thought little of traditional doctors and their drugs.

"Such medicine is for fools," Dora said.

Claire knew exactly what was next. In many ways the two were like twins. Everyone thought so. They always knew what the other was thinking. And they seldom, if ever, disagreed.

As they clouded their tea with sugar and milk poured from Canadian Pacific Railway silver service, each sister entertained the possibility of submitting to Linda Hazzard's fasting treatment. It was so intriguing, so promising. A poor diet was always suspect in health problems. The fasting treatment might finally provide their long-sought key to lifetime good health. Turning the pages, Dora found a small brochure tucked into the book touting the sanitarium known as Hazzard's Institute of Natural Therapeutics. The sanitarium was in the country, west of Seattle across Puget Sound. The sanitarium's address was in a village called Olalla. Its very name was melodic. *O-la-lla.* Like a song, maybe sung by a seabird. The place sounded lovely, a location blessed with fresh air, sparkling salt water, and a forested covering that would surely keep the environs cool in the hottest of summers.

"Dare we do it?" Claire asked, already knowing Dora's answer, already knowing her sister's desire.

Dora smiled and grabbed Claire's hand and squeezed.

"Dare we not!"

Dora closed the pages of *Fasting for the Cure of Disease* and watched Claire spin her long hair into a spiral to coil it away in the confines of a sleeping cap.

Neither sister was seriously ill, if at all. But the two women persuaded each other that treatment was in order. Claire had told her older sister about Dr. John Harvey Kellogg and his celebrated sanitarium in Michigan, but the two had decided it was too far and inconvenient a trip. Besides, the sisters preferred coastal, over inland, travel. To their way of thinking, treatment was both a medical necessity and the basis for a holiday.

Dorothea had foolishly convinced herself she suffered from swollen glands and "acute rheumatic pains in her knees." To add more credence to Claire's misguided notion she also was in dire need of treatment, a London osteopath told her that her uterus had dropped back on her spine and her ovaries were badly inflamed. Until that diagnosis, all Claire believed she had was a delicate stomach.

Dr. Hazzard, they read, was the only licensed fasting specialist in the entire world. Through the years of her practice, Dr. Hazzard had stood before patients and the medical establishment with the announcement she had discovered the basis for all ailments—mental, physical, and moral.

"Overeating", the doctor wrote, *"is the vice of the whole human race."*

THERAPY IN THE COUNTRY SOUNDED LIKE THE right prescription, and, with the decision made, the practical issue of just when they could take the treatment was considered. After visiting North America, the sisters had plans to travel back to Australia and on to London, places where they had family homes. Claire planned to set sail for London on May 18, 1911. She had enrolled in a kindergarten instruction course. Her sister, not overly enchanted with the prospect of being alone, decided she'd travel to Australia to visit a distant aunt. Dora knew she could not stay with Claire during the training.

They were voyages neither would take.

The night of September 7, 1910, fueled by excitement and heavily sugared tea, the sisters took turns reading from the doctor's book as they tended to their immediate and secret plans. Under the advice of an osteopathic physician they had visited in Victoria, they decided to winter in California, and visit the doctor the following spring when the northwest weather would be warmer. Claire carefully composed a letter in a graceful and fluid handwriting. She told the doctor that Dora was not well enough to make the trip to Seattle just yet. She needed sunshine. There was hope for improvement. Dora had been employing the enema nightly and was feeling somewhat invigorated, but still not well enough for a trip to drizzly Seattle.

She enclosed a $1.25 payment for the book.

THEY WERE STRONGER THAN THEY LET ON. EVEN as they reminded themselves and their American family members of their abdominal troubles, and the scads of other things that they said ailed them, they still looked as though they could take on the world. In many ways, they did just that. They had been traveling for six months when they arrived in Riverside, California, in November 1910. They booked rooms at the exclusive Arrowood Hotel and proceeded to soak in mud baths, lie on sheet-covered mattresses for massages, and drink gallon after gallon of water—water therapy. Even though Dora was feeling fit as could be, her sister was eager to correspond with the fasting specialist from Seattle. She wanted help for herself this time.

Claire Williamson imagined her uterus dragged like a dead dog on a leash, pressing on her spine, inflaming the tissues. It had been that way on and off since she was twenty-seven. Relief was intermittent, sometimes lasting months or more. But it was the pain and the indignity of the potential treatment that was most excruciating. She felt she had no choice but to seek treatment with a doctor in Riverside. Like the one who administered care to Dora in Victoria, the woman was an osteopath. And while the doctor seemed competent enough, she didn't exude the kind of knowledge possessed by the Seattle doctor who had written that little green book on fasting. No, not at all.

When Claire posed a question concerning the internal massage Dr. Hazzard had advocated, the Riverside doctor agreed to perform it, but it didn't seem as though she was expert at it. Claire also wondered about the wad of cotton batting, soaked in boric acid and glycerin, that she was to insert into her vagina for twenty-four hours at a time, three times a week, to relieve the congestion that was giving her so much discomfort.

The glycerin and boric acid was an antiseptic measure as well.

"This is the only way to strengthen the ligaments and muscles sufficiently to support the uterus," the doctor told her.

Beyond the fact that it hurt, a kind of wincing sting she had never known, Claire felt the procedure was unlikely to fix her uterus.

Claire tested the doctor again on other health matters. None of the answers brought the kind of response she sought. And questions about therapeutic fasting brought only vagueness.

Answers did not match what Claire had learned from the book.

Claire, more so than Dora, was disappointed that a stop in Seattle had not been possible. She, more than her sister, had studied the book and memorized its contents. But on November 23, 1910, when she daintily dipped her pen into the black pool of ink and wrote a letter to Linda Hazzard, she always referred to herself as a "we" or "our." The only time she slipped into the singular was when she inquired directly about her own health.

Five days later, a letter from the Hazzard Institute of Natural Therapeutics in Olalla, Washington, arrived in Riverside. It was addressed to Claire. When she tore it open she rapidly scanned each page before settling down to read it to her sister. Dr. Hazzard's words were precise and direct.

My experience tells me at once that the fast properly entered into and conducted will relieve permanently the conditions you describe as existing in your own case at present . . .

The only way she could truly know, would be a personal examination.

*I think I may speak without undue egotism in placing the
matter before you because of the years that I have been
advocating and practicing this method of cure . . .*

The doctor glossed over her treatment, the enema, the fast,
hot baths, internal massage. All of it had been outlined in
Fasting for the Cure of Disease. All of it made perfect, utterly
perfect, sense.

*. . . will put you on the road to recovery . . . after the fast
proper.*

Dr. Hazzard closed her letter by telling Claire to discontinue
the use of the cotton batting immediately. Though it may provide temporary support, in the long run, she wrote, it would
serve no purpose but to irritate the uterus. She enclosed an
invoice for $5, for her letter of advice.

THE WILLIAMSON SISTERS CONTINUED THEIR
attentions to questions of their health, the source of their discomfort. They had money, and with it came the expectations,
the *right*, to feel better. Time and again, they asked, why was it
that they didn't feel as good as others?
    Or if they *did* feel as good as others, why didn't anyone else
complain of ailments as they did? When was it that it started?
    Dora and Claire suspected they knew the answer. They had
talked about it so often.

GEORGE AND ROSOLIDA D'ALMEIDA WILLIAMSON
were making their home in London when Claire was conceived.
It was a difficult time for the young mother and father. George
had been injured in India, which necessitated their return to
England. Even worse, he had strained his heart by walking up a
steep hill near their home. Rosolida regretted the timing of the
pregnancy. Her husband was dying, and though she loved Dora
and had longed for another child—a playmate for her eldest
daughter—she had to nurse her husband. He had to get well.
The stress of the pregnancy and her husband's ever-weakening
state was too much for the woman to bear without breaking
down. She cried and fretted all the time.

In 1877, two months after Claire was born, George Williamson died. He was only thirty-nine.

Claire had never suffered any serious illness, and when pressed for the disclosure of such, she found nothing in her background. She simply suffered from a delicate constitution.

"Being rich is the cause of all their problems," a cousin of lesser means had told others in the family. "Claire and Dorothea are ill because they can afford to be ill."

As a child, Claire suffered from nervous exhaustion, which took the form of "morbid cravings for food."

Doctors prescribed small meals every two hours and a full meal at bedtime. The food regimen appeared to work. By eating late at night, she woke up in the morning without a headache.

"I was very nervous and continually crying, which I have been told," she said later, "was due to the circumstances of my birth."

IN A RESPONSE TO ANOTHER OF CLAIRE'S MISSIVES, Dr. Hazzard returned correspondence on December 13, 1910. Her sanitarium was not ready yet, but would be open to receive patients in a few weeks, no later than the very early part of the new year. She told the sisters to keep up the employment of the enema and to switch to a diet that would consist of vegetable broths.

Breads made from yeast are tabooed entirely, and only corn bread unraised may occupy their place . . .

Dora made a face while her sister read out loud.

"No breads at all?"

"None. At least no breads that taste good."

Dr. Hazzard closed with a statement the sisters would insist to each other was more than a mere promise. It was a prophecy.

. . . you should have decided and favorable results in the future.

Two

CLAIRE AND DORA HAD KEPT SECRETS
before. As sisters who had suffered the loss of their parents,
they had come to rely on each other with a binding intimacy.
Their closeness frequently excluded family and friends from
knowing their full plans. It wasn't that they were snobbish and
didn't wish to disclose how they spent their inheritance. In fact,
the sisters were quite generous in that regard. No trip they
took—no matter where they went—was complete without the
gathering of souvenirs for giving to friends and family who
hosted them whenever they arrived. Some gifts were trinkets
costing very little; most, however, were quite expensive. If an
item caught their fancy, they bought it.

The Williamson sisters simply didn't see a need to offer
every detail of their lives, their private affairs.

"It is a personal matter, uncle."

"Personal business must be attended to in Victoria."

*"Private matters concerning father's estate are taking us
away on business."*

Though vague, their comments were never offered in a manner seeming any less than straightforward. Never did relatives
feel a need to press for more detail. At least none tried.

So as they made arrangements to travel again, Dora and
Claire had kept their pact that when they took Dr. Hazzard's
treatment, they would not tell any of their relatives. None
would understand. They might even ridicule their supposed
folly. They planned to move on from Riverside to stay a couple
of weeks in El Toro, with their aunt and uncle, Capt. George
Huddy and his wife Elizabeth, followed by a couple of days in
Santa Barbara, before moving on to gather their trunks at the

Custom House in Los Angeles for the train ride north. They wanted to be in Seattle by the first of March to enjoy the marine climate of an early spring. In mid-April Dora planned to set sail for Australia and Claire had booked passage to return to England.

But each day the mail drop brought disappointment. Dora and Claire wanted to see the sanitarium prospectus that the doctor had promised to send in one of her earlier letters. They held hope that they would be able to stay in the country when they took the cure.

On January 14, 1911, the sisters sent another note to Linda Hazzard. Dora was feeling great and Claire, who was following the regimen outlined in previous correspondence, was feeling much more herself. The corn bread and broth were fine, but Claire felt the regimen was difficult to follow outside of a sanitarium setting. There were too many temptations at her aunt's, too many distractions. Too much good food and no sympathizers to the sisters' way of thinking when it came to natural ways of healing.

Disappointment flushed over Dora's face as her sister read the latest letter from the fasting specialist, which arrived the second week of January. The sanitarium was still unable to receive patients. It was possible, however, that if work progressed rapidly, a transfer could be made to Olalla after treatment was started in Seattle. The doctor's fees would be $60 per patient per month. The fee included daily office visits. More would be charged if additional consultation was needed. Arrangements could be made to house the women in a furnished apartment near Dr. Hazzard's offices at the Northern Bank and Trust Building in Seattle.

The doctor wrote:

> It is possible I think from your description of both of your cases that there will be no excessive weakness or difficulty in the conduct of the fast, hence you should both be able throughout to come to me daily.

Discouragement lingered. Not about the treatment, no far from that. Claire and Dora embraced the idea of the fast and were elated Linda Burfield Hazzard, the author of the book both had practically memorized, would be taking personal charge of their cases. They were discouraged because they would have to take up residence in an apartment, not a charming sanitarium cottage in the wilderness at Olalla.

Claire composed a note back to the doctor on January 27, 1911. Yes, they would be coming and would she be so kind as to send them addresses of some apartments that would be suitable? Though they couldn't be in the country, they still sought a quiet location, as far out of town as possible. They wondered if the doctor could assist them in securing a nice sunny apartment for $60 per month, paid weekly, in case they found it unsuitable and desired to relocate.

> . . . *would require two bedrooms, a sitting-room and bathroom. We understand by apartments that they are what we should call in England a flat . . .*

The Buena Vista was a lovely name for an apartment house. It meant "beautiful view." Built on the corner of Boylston and Olive Streets in downtown Seattle, it was hardly out in the country. Appropriately enough, however, some rooms did face west to gorgeous views of Puget Sound and the Olympic range. Dr. Hazzard secured a two-bedroom apartment for the Williamsons, with the provision that if they didn't find it to their liking, they could easily move elsewhere.

"*The building is situated away from the car lines and is yet convenient when one needs to use them,*" the doctor wrote of the apartment in a letter dated January 31, 1911.

Dr. Hazzard also professed disappointment that her Olalla sanitarium was not ready. The winter rains had delayed construction, and she couldn't even imagine it opening before June, possibly even later. She told the women to write to a Mrs. Arthur, and that she could make satisfactory arrangements for their stay. The rent would not be greater than $50 for the month. If there were any problems, the women were to cable her at once. The sisters hoped they would never have to bother the doctor with such concerns as their personal comfort. Goodness, if the rooms were not to their liking, they'd simply endure it.

Linda Burfield Hazzard, it seemed, was the kind of woman who tolerated nothing less then the best for her patients. Her concern touched the Williamsons. Beyond her obviously great intellect, Dr. Hazzard was a woman of great compassion.

She might even become a new friend. In a country where they had few intimates, the idea made the sisters nearly breathless with their anxiousness.

"I feel a little foolish to say it, Claire, but I venture to say Dr. Hazzard has taken a personal interest in our case," Dora said.

THE SISTERS PLANNED TO BE IN SEATTLE ON Sunday, February 26, and hoped to see the doctor Monday morning—if she could find the time on her schedule.

"She probably has a very full roster of patients, Dora."

"Possibly, but I feel she will want to see us right away. Perhaps she could clear her schedule whilst we get settled at the Buena Vista?"

"Perhaps," Dora replied, knowing that her sister's lack of patience and skepticism permeated everything she did. She wondered if once on the program, Claire would feel the fast wasn't quick enough. The thought of a "slow" fast made her laugh.

The two planned to stop in Portland to see their uncle John Herbert on their way to Washington. Claire withdrew $250 in traveler's checks, Dora, $100. It was more money than they usually carried. Still, no matter who inquired of their ultimate plans, no mention was to be made of a visit to Seattle. They told everyone they were going to Canada.

"Business, you know," they chimed in perfect unison.

Claire tried to explain her position in a letter to the doctor written on February 7, 1911.

. . . Unfortunately we cannot tell them we are going to stop in Seattle to do a fast as already they disapprove of our way of living, in fact, we are not mentioning it to anyone.

Both were having a difficult time remaining on the clear broth and corn-bread diet as prescribed by the fasting specialist.

Neither felt they had any choice but to eat as their host families did. That meant that while they could reduce portions, they were still unable to get entirely away from plates of brown bread, crackers, eggs, puddings, milk, and stewed fruit. As vegetarians they were able gracefully to decline meat when it was offered at the table.

While Dora was content to bide her time and enjoy the excursion up north, Claire was frustrated. She talked about her stomach discomfort with the kind of regularity that bordered on annoying.

> *I would gladly stop eating anything as I feel as if I had a liver attack and get constant indigestion, so I'm counting the days until we arrive in Seattle and I can eliminate this matter collected in me.*

THREE

SEATTLE'S MARINE AIR REMINDED THE
sisters of the seaside near Brighton and in Hove, Sussex
County, England, where they had a lovely south-of-London
summer residence. They also adored how the Pacific
Northwest's largest city was young and growing. And though
three hundred thousand made Seattle their home, it was still at
the beginning of its evolution to greatness. Granted, it was
nowhere near as wealthy as London, and what sophistication it
held was new. Its elegance was crisp and untattered. Seattle was
a shiny silver piece, not a tarnished tiara. All about was activity.
Cable lines for the electric streetcar crocheted a steel spiderweb
over main city arterials. Buildings rose from brick-paved streets
far broader than those across the Atlantic. There was more
room. Room to grow. Wagons drawn by horses shared the road
with the automobile. Transition and growth. Forward-moving.
Forward-thinking. All of it appealed to Claire and Dora.

The sisters had been waiting for the moment for weeks,
months, really. At 11 A.M., February 27, 1911, the Williamson
sisters finally found themselves standing in Linda Burfield
Hazzard's office in the Northern Bank and Trust Building.

Dr. Hazzard stood up from behind a monolithic desk and
extended her hand with a rapid, pistonlike movement. It was a
strong and authoritative gesture. Men usually reserved the
handshake for themselves. But it was the movement, more so
than its meaning, however, that startled Claire.

The doctor pushed her hand forward like a sword.

"I see you are English," she said, brightening a bit with a
smile. "I am English, too."

The sisters nodded in unison.

Linda Burfield Hazzard was a striking woman. Not pretty, not dainty. It was a look more handsome than beautiful. With the exception of her jawbone, which was somewhat pronounced and angular, she might have blended into a crowded downtown Seattle street in the unremarkable way most people do. But Claire and Dora Williamson could immediately see there was something extraordinary about the woman standing before them. It was her bearing. Her manner. It suggested the confidence and intelligence of a woman who had definitive and immediate answers, regardless of the questions. She had no time for nonsense.

Whether Linda Hazzard had a full schedule of patients to see or merely paperwork to complete, she donned a white dress that looked more a nurse's uniform than what a doctor might wear. As the doctor continued with her pleasantries, she welcomed Claire and Dora into a back room for some treatment.

The forty-three-year-old doctor told them she was from western Minnesota, born to an American father and a Canadian and English mother.

"I was raised in a home of refinement, under sheltered and orthodox methods," she told them, in a manner that suggested frequent repetition of the same words. It sounded as though the statement had been written on a calling card.

Dr. Hazzard was first a nurse, and later, in 1898, an osteopath. She had been a prominent fixture in Minneapolis society—so few women had embarked on medical careers. The Williamson sisters knew nothing of the doctor's origins, only the hyperbolic greatness and revolutionary treatment as it was offered in the pages of the brochure and book that had brought them to their meeting.

Claire was enthralled, Dora less so. Claire had been so good in persuading Dora what to do, what to buy over the years, that she was easily persuaded by others. It was Claire who always purchased from the street peddler. Dora never bought off the street if she could get it at a reputable shop.

THE LIST WAS ASTONISHING IN ITS BREADTH. Cancer, toothache, psoriasis, heart trouble, tuberculosis, epilepsy, insanity—all had been cured by the fasting specialist from Seattle. In the annals of medicine, her followers would assert, had there ever been a doctor with such a remarkable record of success? The woman who stood alone among all others was not one to deny herself an opportunity to recite her achievements. She did so frequently, before new patients, family members, civic groups, and the newspapermen who dogged her for interviews whenever her name made the papers.

When Linda Burfield Hazzard recounted tales of her patients and their remarkable recoveries, she spoke with an ear-ringing voice and presence so commanding that be it before a group of a hundred or two, there would be no others in the room. Dr. Hazzard lectured with the kind of conviction usually reserved for the clergy. And in an odd sense, that was what she was. She was a believer in the new gospel of good health. Science bore it out. Dr. Hazzard was a missionary of medicine.

One case she frequently recalled was that of Mrs. J. B. Barnett, a sixty-five-year-old woman from Kansas City, Missouri. In many ways it was typical of the doctor's medical epics. Mrs. Barnett had never been well, suffering from "chronic constipation and aggravated bilious attacks," until she undertook the fasting treatment. She was afflicted with an unshakable and debilitating melancholia resulting in mild suicidal tendencies; she had been a burden to her family for years.

The doctor outlined the treatment.

"On arrival the two-meal regime was immediately begun on the strictly vegetarian basis that the treatment is based upon; and, by the way, the patient had been an enormous meat eater."

Meat eater was a term the doctor used with considerable and unbridled disdain. She said the phrase sharply, a bit louder than the other words and with a slight knowing shake of the head.

Meat eaters are foolish, disgusting, suicidal!

"After a week of this, one meal was dropped, and the daily repast fixed at the regular six o'clock dinner hour of my family. She began also to have the foulest discharges from the bowels, and each enema brought away quantities of old fecal matter with quantities of bile, blackish in color."

At this point, listeners would usually shift uncomfortably in their seats. Linda Hazzard was a doctor, but her candor was unsettling—if not a little too descriptive—for such a private concern.

"A few days of this and the meal was cut down to a little fruit. The last solid food given was a bowl of lima bean broth, after which the patient went forty-eight days until any solid food again was given, of which forty-five days were absolute fast. I call this bean broth a solid food, for it is a great strength giver, and is my standby in many instances when breaking a fast. The fast developed no unusual symptoms, except that the discharges were continually foul and very black."

Very black, very foul.

"During the whole time Mrs. Barnett was able to be about the house, and when elimination finally gained the day and her vitality began to increase the old lady did lots of work that served to keep her occupied and content. From the second week of dieting the mental state showed improvement. At the third week the patient sat down of her own accord and wrote a long, cheerful, rational letter to her daughter—a thing she had not done in four years. The little household duties that she performed were things that she could not do and showed no desire to do in all the history of her loss of mental power, and from the fourth week of her fast this desire was present, and she was able to have it gratified as her strength returned.

"Hunger manifested itself about the forty-third day, and the tongue showed clean on the forty-fourth, but we waited until the morning of the forty-sixth before feeding a small bowl of diluted bean broth, which tasted like the nectar to a system renewed—as it seemed to her own people—*miraculously*."

Mrs. Barnett left Seattle completely recovered, mentally and physically—miraculously.

Another case the doctor liked to invoke concerned twenty-eight-year-old Amelia Larsen, a Swedish hired girl. Again the culprit was poor nutrition. She was another sufferer of the taste of the beast.

Meat again!

Miss Larsen also suffered melancholia with somewhat violent tendencies. In fact, as Dr. Hazzard related it years after the girl had left her care, if it hadn't been for a devoted sister, she would have been consigned to the unspeakable horror of an asylum.

A devoted sister like Claire. A sister like Dora.

"The physician last called in had recommended that she be confined, when the sister, as her last hope, brought her to my home. I took the case, and found on examination that the pulse was continually at 128, and the temperature varied from above to below normal with no apparent cause. The patient was put immediately on a liquid diet, the daily enemas were of course rigorously plied, and hot towel packs were used on the spine to control the circulation and to steady the pulse. After a short time these were discontinued, for this symptom showed a constant improvement from the first.

"The enemas brought away black, foul-smelling discharges, as in all cases of this nature, and these continued long into the fast. The girl showed a vast amount of vitality, and about two weeks after accepting the case, when the fast began, she walked to my home, a distance of two miles, took her treatment, and returned to her own rooms without fatigue, and this she kept up throughout the whole fast of forty-two days. In the latter part she was able and desirous of increasing the amount of exercise.

"In this case, as in the previous one, the mental condition showed improvement from the very first, and, on the thirtieth day of the fast, Amelia sat down and helped her sister with some dressmaking, doing the work well and cheerfully. After this she did daily work about the house, and practically shouldered all the household duties. Hunger returned the forty-first day, and we broke the fast the morning of the forty-third. Two weeks later the two sisters sailed from Montreal for their home in Sweden, and Amelia has written me, since her arrival there, a most interesting letter that shows in every way that she is sane and rational, and happy."

A MAN AND A LITTLE BOY LEFT DR. HAZZARD'S office, smiling at the quaint sisters with the genteel English accents. Dora fussed with her unwinding hat trim while her sister took in every bit of the surroundings. The office was tidy. A colored map of the human body hung on the wall opposite the windows to the street. A few glass beakers of the sort a chemist might use poked from a wooden box. The sisters realized that the woman before them was as unorthodox in her method as her

manner. Dr. Hazzard made no further inquiries into their current state of health. There was no questionnaire. No physical
exam. The doctor merely greeted them, shook their hands and
proceeded to outline the treatment for the fast.

"We have no time to lose. You must begin the treatment right
away."

"Are we going to the country, the sanitarium today?" Claire
asked. "We do so love the country."

"We love animals," Dora added. "Are there farm animals
there? Horses, I hope."

Dr. Hazzard shook her head.

"The sanitarium is not quite ready as yet. I should think it
will be ready in a few weeks. Construction has been hampered
by the rain."

The sisters were disappointed, but the doctor allowed no
pause for a response.

"We will begin treatment here. When the sanitarium is ready,
we will arrange for a private launch and transfer treatment there."

Claire looked at Dora and nodded.

"I suppose that will be fine . . . though we had been looking
so forward to the country."

Dr. Hazzard smiled understandingly.

"Yes, my dears, there are animals there. Horses, too. Olalla is
lovely in the spring."

Though the doctor was only ten years older than Claire, her
authority, her role as a great doctor, brought her the kind of
respect and awe due a parent.

Linda Hazzard stepped toward an open door in the back of
her office.

"Come. We will begin at once."

"Not tomorrow?" Claire asked.

"As I said, you haven't time to wait. Your conditions are
quite serious."

"Will there be an exam?" Dora asked, a bit surprised that a
pen had not been lifted to take notes as she inquired about further details of their health.

"No. Not necessary," the doctor said. "It is no use to do an
examination for any organic disease until the fast has proceeded
for some time."

The doctor's persuasive delivery made her unusual course make sense. After all, the sisters had written numerous letters describing their health. Surely Dr. Hazzard knew all that could be gleaned from those.

The women were led into the room for an osteopathic treatment. First Dora, then Claire. The doctor asked the sisters to shed their outer clothing, and instructed them to lie on a linen-covered table while she prepared to hammer her fists against their backs, heads, and foreheads.

Claire, ever the eager one, was first. She whimpered as the doctor pummeled her.

"Feeling better, dear?"

The younger sister nodded. The treatment, though far different than her experience with the London osteopath, did take her mind off her stomach for a moment. Perhaps that was the intention, she thought.

Dora, always worried about her younger sister, made vocal note of her concern.

"Dearie, did it hurt?"

"Not really," Claire answered, wincing a bit. "I think it was a good treatment."

After the doctor performed the same treatment, though a bit harsher on Dora, she decreed that three or four weeks of the fast, coupled with vigorous exercise, would eliminate the poisons from their bodies.

"You shall be in complete and perfect health."

As they stood to leave, Claire and Dora noticed an imposing man with black hair and an enormous moustache standing by a window in the waiting area. Linda Hazzard motioned in his direction.

"Ladies, my husband, Samuel."

Sam Hazzard was handsome, a little over six feet tall and broad-shouldered. A big man, there could be no doubt. He had hands the size of washboards.

"My pleasure," he said, brushing past as he made his way to a desk in the corner. "I trust you ladies had a satisfactory treatment."

Dora blushed and nodded. Claire merely smiled.

Like his wife, Sam Hazzard bore the kind of confidence of someone who knew exactly where he fit in. And quite possibly that was an accurate assessment. The West Point man was the sanitarium business manager, the promoter for his wife's long-dreamed-of enterprise. It was his pamphlet tucked inside the fasting book that inspired the sisters to come to Seattle for treatment. But as his wife quickly announced to the refined English ladies, Samuel was also a gifted musician and teacher. He was affiliated with the Columbia College of Music, where he offered tutoring and individual instruction.

There was something about Sam Hazzard that indicated a darker, unsavory side. Dora picked it up before Claire. The air around the doctor's husband wafted an odor of alcohol, slight, nearly imperceptible, yet it was there, nevertheless. The whites around his grey-blue eyes were flecked with the vermilion of broken capillaries.

Though neither sister knew it at the time, the imposing man's troubles were rooted deeply in the past.

LINDA HAZZARD WAS THE COCKSURE VOICE OF experience. She stood before the sisters with complete confidence in her dietary regimen. It was so simple, yet so effective. She told her new patients that they were to prepare a vegetable broth by boiling tomatoes in a quart of water. When it reduced to about a pint of tomato stock it was ready.

"How are we to season it?" Claire asked.

"No seasonings, except the very smallest bit of butter, the size of your thumbnail. No more."

"No salt?"

"No, dear. No salt, no sugar either."

"How much are we to drink?" Dora inquired.

"I'm getting to that," the doctor smiled. "The fast calls for a cup of this broth twice a day. Later, we will vary the stock to include an asparagus broth, and some orange juice will be allowed in the mornings."

Dr. Hazzard instructed the sisters on the necessity of an exercise program that included vigorous walks several times a day.

"Your bodies are full of poison," she explained. "You need to walk it out. No matter how difficult it may be as the fast continues, you must persevere and walk. Walk! Walk! Walk!"

The sisters were excited, though Dora, in particular, had hoped the fast included more variety. She felt her sister had involved her in the program, and while she was ready and willing, she might not have done so on her own. And as they left for their apartment, the doctor told them she would see them in her office every day except Saturday and Sunday for enemas and osteopathic massage.

"Remember, girls, your bodies will be clean and you will be in perfect health!"

That afternoon as the sun began to lapse behind the snowy Olympics, Dora and Claire unloaded their trunks into their apartment on the third floor at the Buena Vista. Disappointed the respite in the country sanitarium had been delayed, but quite pleased with the doctor's plans for treatment, the Williamson sisters told each other they were well on their way to good health. Clouded by giddy enthusiasm, neither sister could have predicted the events that would ultimately take them to Olalla.

OVER THE COURSE OF THE NEXT FEW DAYS, THE sisters would hear more of the doctor's heroics. While most stories were recent cases involving patients she treated in Seattle, occasionally she would recall cases from Minneapolis. Dr. Hazzard spoke fondly of a boy named Edward Anderson, whom she had treated in 1905.

The story made Claire cry. Dora listened politely.

Edward Anderson was only seventeen when a doctor solemnly informed his mother that there was no hope. *No hope.* The words ached in her heart. *Ed was dying.* It was to be a slow, bit-by-bit demise, a kind of easing toward death that would steadily sneak up like a foggy moon behind the distant tree line. Like most of Minneapolis, Mrs. Anderson had read of Linda Burfield's controversial fasting practice and the personal scandals that made her the source of gossip and derision. Everyone had read about her, even laughed at her. Some felt sorry for Dr. Burfield. All had opinions. Mrs. Anderson knew all of that, yet none of it would concern her enough to stop her from taking the only step she could. When a son lays pale, helpless, and drained, preconceived judgments are hurled out like buckets of smelly rubbish. Mrs. Anderson summoned the fasting specialist to her home at 2517 Riverside Avenue on the evening of December 19, 1905.

Linda Burfield Hazzard drew Claire and Dora close, the three of them filling a divan at the apartment. It was almost as if the doctor was a schoolteacher, and they were young children gathered for story time. She lowered her voice so each word would emerge from her in a soft, dramatic fashion. The sisters were riveted.

"Oh please continue, doctor. Do tell us what happened to the sweet boy!" Claire pleaded.

Slightly annoyed at the interruption, the fasting specialist continued.

"I found him suffering from a characteristic case of inflammatory rheumatism, and in a most precarious state. The boy's physician had thrown up his hands, and had told the distracted mother that the disease had affected the heart and that it was only a matter of a day or two at the most. All that he could do was to ease the pain with opiates and give the young man a pleasant passage into eternity. The mother had heard of my work through one of my former patients, and, as a last resort, came to me."

Last resort. Certainly a familiar term; almost always born of desperation. The fasting specialist had been visited by scores, by hundreds, as a last resort. She would later laugh at the folly of those who had been brainwashed by the purveyors of surgery and drugs. She held little sympathy for them; they had been warned that Nature's remedies were unquestionably superior to the attempts "doctors" had invented. She felt she could save many, many lives if patients sought her out for the *first* course of treatment.

The Anderson boy was such a case, so typical, so potentially tragic. He had been bedridden for five weeks, a victim not only of his disease, but of the futile treatments applied. His left arm, wrist, and hand were swollen to the puffiness of a bee sting. The boy's ankles and joints were inflamed. His face was flushed; his breath labored and short. The doctor's thermometer rose to 105 degrees.

No doubt it was only a matter of time.

The fasting specialist ridiculed the conventional doctor's course of treatment for Edward. Claire shook her head disapprovingly, mirroring Linda Burfield Hazzard's disposition.

"The foundation I had to work on was flimsy in all respects, for the five weeks since the beginning of the attack were worse than lost—at least to me. I found that in the two weeks just preceding, the heart action had been stimulated with doses of digitalis and strychnine; food had been forced on the rebellious stomach as many times daily as the boy could be induced to swallow it; and, when the pain had become too great, or delirium had intervened, codeine and other opiates had been used unsparingly. In addition to all this, in five days' time, two quarts of brandy had been poured into the drugged interior. The boy could neither lie down nor sit up, and his position was a painful compromise."

She worried that the boy would die, but felt compelled to take instantaneous and decisive action.

Edward Anderson was placed on an immediate fast. Dr. Burfield stopped the drugs, the brandy, the *insanity* of a prescribed treatment that only attempted to cover the symptoms, not attack the root of the disease. She massaged the boy's hot and limp frame and employed the "internal bath"—the enema—to eliminate matter from the lower bowel. Within an hour, improvement came. The pulse and temperature crawled toward the normal ranges.

When the doctor left the Riverside Avenue address, the boy in the back bedroom was resting more comfortably than he had in days.

And though Mrs. Anderson had sought out Dr. Burfield, she was still apprehensive about the course of treatment. He was a growing boy. He needed nourishment. The fasting specialist pressed on; as far as she could see there was no choice but to take the drastic measures. Over the next days, the fever, the pain, the swelling ceased. By the third day of the fast, he was able to sleep fully and restfully.

On December 28, Dr. Burfield broke Edward's fast with two servings of tomato broth—morning and evening. As he regained strength, the amount of food was increased.

Ed Anderson, as far as his family was concerned, was a miracle boy, and his savior was Dr. Burfield. She alone had delivered him from certain death. No matter her critics, no matter the scandals that popped up like crocuses through the snow, she brought medical salvation to the desperate.

Linda Burfield Hazzard would frequently recall this case. It was one of many she would never forget. One of the Williamson sisters would never forget it either.

The doctor even wrote a letter about the case a half dozen years after the fact:

> One month from the date of my first call, the boy came across town to my office, a distance of six miles by car, with a walk of four blocks at the end of the line. Within a few days judicious building-up exercises were begun, and in six weeks from the 19th of December the patient was back at work in one of the down-town business houses. So far as I can learn, he has since adhered strictly to the diet and exercise advised, and, when I last saw him, he had developed into a sturdy, robust youth with seemingly perfect health.

NELLIE B. SHERMAN HAD A HIGH FOREHEAD AND haggard eyes set so uncomfortably close together they pinched her nose to a yelp. At forty, she already had the kind of loose, wrinkled mouth that suggested a paper sack that had been opened and closed many, many times. Wee fissures radiated from Nellie's lips.

A nurse since graduating from Homeopathic Hospital in Boston fourteen years before, Nellie had found herself in Seattle starting over when her late-in-life marriage to a jealous man named Frank Otis ended in time to save her life in 1908. In a hideous routine that played far too many times, within three weeks of their wedding, Frank Otis had beat Nellie and accused her of adultery with a number of different men. The reality was that there had been no others. Nellie Sherman had waited a lifetime for Frank Otis, and when the marriage shattered, she expected to live her life alone. The marriage had lasted but a year.

Nellie met Dr. Hazzard on the morning boat from Olalla to

Seattle. The nurse had come from her bungalow near Alki Point, West Seattle, to Olalla to care for various members of the Lillie clan. On the deck of the *Virginia* one morning, Linda Hazzard sought out the petite woman in the nurse's uniform. The doctor confided her plans for a world-class sanitarium at Wilderness Heights, as if it were information she seldom imparted. She needed believers in nature cures to help her build it. Nellie was interested and flattered. It seemed the two women shared many fascinations, many beliefs. They both shared an interest in horoscopes and matters of the spiritual, as well as the physical world. Nellie had fancied herself a medium of sorts. Séances were not otherworldly parlor prattle; she held such incarnate gatherings at her home in West Seattle and at the Lillie farm in Olalla. Nellie also relied on her spirit guides whenever she made an important decision. She once had a "spirit miner" check into the potential success for a copper mine in which she had considered purchasing shares.

As the steamer eased into a slip alongside Colman Dock, the doctor asked if the nurse would consider assisting with a case involving two sisters.

Nellie didn't take the time to consult her spirit guides that day. She told herself she could do that later.

"Yes," she answered quickly. "I'll handle the case for you, though I have other commitments that will tax my time."

"It is two English girls at the Buena Vista," Dr. Hazzard told the nurse as they crossed over the gangway. "They're in a bad way. I'm afraid it shouldn't be long."

PAULINE FEIN'S FATHER, CHARLES, WAS A MAN OF tragic mystery. He went to work in Tacoma one day and never returned to the family farm at the edge of Olalla Bay. Not a soul ever heard from Charles again. Some locals wondered if financial burdens had been too much and he had escaped his responsibilities; others wondered if he had met with foul play. No one ever knew. It left Pauline and her mother, Gladys, and the smaller kids to make do on their own. Pauline, born in 1907, trained at St. Joseph's Hospital in Tacoma to become a nurse.

It was during her nursing student days that Pauline called Dr. Hazzard with the request for a tour of her sanitarium.

Pauline had heard the rumors about what had happened there. A person would have to have been deaf and blind to miss the hissings of the gossip line that ran between Olalla and Fragaria and back again. Everyone knew something had happened up there, years before, but no one seemed ready to challenge the woman who ran the place. No one would say anything to her face. None of their business. Not at all.

Pauline led a group of young women to the sanitarium's big oak front doors. It was a field trip of sorts.

"She had a sanitarium and we were nurses and we wanted to see what her place looked like, what she did. We were wondering what was going on in it. It was legitimate as far as we knew. She had patients there. She showed us all she did, which was mostly giving people enemas, flushings, and things like that and feeding them certain foods, which didn't amount to much at all probably. It was all clean. It was fixed all up like a ward would be. We weren't there very long.

"Dr. Hazzard was very glad to show us around, very pleased that we came to see her. She thought that it was wonderful that someone was interested in what she was doing. That's what always stuck in my mind all these years."

FOUR

AT LAST, THE TREATMENT. FINALLY, THE promise of unsurpassed health. Claire could barely contain her joy over their good fortune to be treated by Linda Burfield Hazzard. Though the country sanitarium was not yet ready to receive them as patients, the sisters were delighted they still had the fasting specialist to care for them personally. Visits to Dr. Hazzard's offices assured personal attention, five days a week.

Their flat, as they still referred to their modest accommodations, was functional and clean. Upon entering, off to the right was a narrow hall and private bathroom. In back was the bedroom Dora claimed. Claire's bedroom was through another doorway that could be screened off with a dark curtain. A small kitchen was located off Claire's room. And though the two could converse while in their beds, neither could be seen by the other.

And so the sisters played a waiting game. Each day they would ask each other if that would be the day they would be cured of their maladies. The wall supporting the uterus would strengthen, the irritated stomach would be soothed, its lining smooth and fresh, and strength overall would take the place of weakness.

Each day, after the broth, after their enemas, they would play the game.

"Though we feel weak, we are getting better," Dora confided to Claire one afternoon. "I notice I am getting cleaner."

"I am, too," Claire answered, managing a smile.

Dora could never figure out quite when the moment came, but at some point during the early days at the Buena Vista she developed a stronger feeling of belief in the treatment than she had at first. The days of the treatment had brought her a weariness, but also a kind of euphoria unknown to her. The treatment was making sense to her in a way she could not fully understand.

"I do believe we are better now, even with the fast just begun, than we were when we first arrived in Seattle," she told Claire.

Claire, who had always been partial to the treatment, far more so than her sister, concurred. Dora's acceptance served to fuel her desire to make a go of the treatment. She wanted to see it to the end. To achieve unsurpassed health.

"I believe you are right," Claire answered.

Letters written to friends and family members highlighted their good health. None, however, detailed exactly what treatment they had turned their bodies over to, or under whose care they had placed themselves.

The Williamsons decided their perfect health would be their testament to Dr. Linda Burfield Hazzard's beautiful treatment.

Almost from the first week at Buena Vista, something seemed amiss. Even though neither sister had fainted once in their lives, fainting became so common around the Buena Vista that neither seemed to give it a second thought. Dora heard her sister fall to the floor in the kitchen one afternoon, but she didn't feel well enough to get up to look after her.

Many came to the Buena Vista to see the sisters during their treatment. All were sent by Linda Hazzard. A young nurse named Sarah Robinson assisted briefly, though it was not the kind of work to her liking and when she found a good excuse, she departed for another job. Another visitor, a more frequent one, was a personal friend of Linda Hazzard's—a young amiable fellow named James Watson Webb. Webb always arrived with stacks of books on Spiritualism and Theosophy in tow. He watched as Dora tottered on the brink of consciousness, while he read select passages aloud to her. Claire seemed to sleep most of her days away.

"Look how much better I am," Dora said one time as she stood up to walk to greet Webb. "I can walk! I can walk!"

The instant she stepped forward in her joy of getting better, she keeled over and fell flatly against the hardwood floor.

Over time, more than the exercise, more than the scant nourishment of the fast, the internal bath became the most taxing ordeal. The sisters were required to take six quarts of warm water after stripping down to their chemises and doubling up in what the doctor termed the "knee chest" position.

"Knee chest, ladies! Knee chest!"

At the beginning of the fast, the internal bath took just under a half hour. As the days passed the duration increased. One hour. Two hours. Three hours. *All day?* The enemas were a painful blur. Dora even fainted in the midst of one. After that, canvas yardage was stretched over the rim of the bathtub in a hammock which allowed the sisters to continue even when supporting their own weight knee chest-style was too difficult.

Dr. Hazzard insisted that without the aid of the internal bath they would not achieve their desired results.

"We must eliminate the poisons, dear girls!"

AS THE SPRING WEATHER DRENCHED THE MUDDY roads of Seattle, sending coffee-colored water roaring down to Puget Sound, the sisters became anxious about their recovery. Though they didn't doubt the fasting treatment or their doctor, they doubted themselves. It was a slow, sinking feeling that made them question whether they would be cured as quickly as they had hoped. Perhaps they suffered a greater illness than which they had been aware. Dr. Hazzard had given the women the name and telephone number of a nurse who could be called upon in the event they felt they needed more care.

Dora took it upon herself to make the call. By then, Claire was too weak to do much of anything. Dora could see the treatment had weakened her sister to an extent that she had not expected. It frightened her a little. She dialed a number for a nurse named Nellie Sherman.

"Nurse Sherman," she began, her voice slightly quavering with hunger and worry, "Dr. Hazzard suggested you might come to care for us. My sister is very ill. I'm afraid we can't manage on our own."

"I'm sorry. I'm too busy now to take on your case."

Dora Williamson implored her to come if only for a day or two.

"I'm certain we will be well soon, but for now we cannot manage."

The nurse said she had other affairs and couldn't break away. She apologized again and suggested they seek out another nurse.

"We know of no other. Dr. Hazzard said you would come. Please."

Nurse Sherman very reluctantly agreed. She would call on them, but not for any length of time.

"Come at once, *please*." Dora used both hands to lift the telephone receiver back to its hook on the wall. It weighed less than a pair of coddled eggs, yet it seemed beyond her strength. Her bony hands caught a shard of metal from the hook and she started to bleed. Blood polka-dotted the floor.

"Oh, look at the dreadful mess I have made. Dr. Hazzard shall be completely disappointed in me," she told her sister.

BUENA VISTA NEIGHBOR MARY FIELDS COULDN'T sleep. The noise coming from the Williamson girls' apartment was not only disturbing in its volume, but its nature was even more unsettling. Though she could not make out words, Mary Fields clearly understood the message. The girls were groaning and moaning in obvious agony. Soft, then louder, soft again. Mary tried a pillow over her head to muffle the noise. It still did not abate it enough to give her the respite from the noise to fall asleep. Part of the problem was the way the two apartments had been arranged. Mary had a wall bed, which she raised into a closet out of view during the day. The closet wall, where Mary's head would rest when she lay down, separated the head of Dora's bed in her apartment.

The Buena Vista was modern, but it was not soundproof. The tenants in the apartment below announced the status of their marriage through the ceiling, through the floorboards above. An air shaft separated Mrs. Fields's room from the Williamsons' apartment, and her hall window faced the English ladies' kitchen. With such an arrangement it was natural that there would be some spilling over of sound. At first she could hear the women talk, their voices childlike in excitement. Other times talk overlapped as if three or more were carrying on in the apartment.

But as the weeks went by, it was the nightly noises that alarmed her.

"It seemed as though somebody was in great distress," she said later.

The change in sisters' physical appearance was so sudden, it jarred a number of the residents at the Buena Vista. Claire and Dora's weight had dropped shockingly so. Mrs. Fields estimated that, though clothing obscured their figures somewhat, Dora likely weighed about one hundred pounds and her sister Claire, slightly more robust, weighed in the low one-twenties. As the days and weeks passed they shed their weight, pound by pound, day after day and began to take on a hideous appearance. Mrs. Fields began to avoid them. Deep, dark lines etched the area around their mouths, their rheumy eyes were hollow and under-scored with a dark smudge of skin. Their hands were bony, knuckles raising the skin up like rows of four tiny tentpoles.

But mostly, for Mrs. Fields, it was Claire's smile that haunted and repulsed her.

"Her lips were so thin. When she smiled her upper lip would draw back and her lower lip would be a line," she subsequently recalled.

When white-uniformed Nellie Sherman assisted the girls down the length of the hall for air on the little porch near the fire escape, Mrs. Fields watched from a crack in her door. She didn't want to come out to say hello.

Though in the beginning both girls appeared to suffer the same weakness and frailty, it was Claire Williamson's struggle to the sun porch that was the most disturbing to neighbor Mary Fields.

"She became so weak she could hardly walk even with Miss Sherman's assistance. She would assist herself by placing her hand against the wall. She had to pass my door unless she went down a flight of stairs, and come up another way, and she would have to put her hand against the wall as a child walking, and the last time I saw her in the hall it was very distressing to me to talk to her, she was so thin."

MISS CLARA CORRIGAN MOVED INTO THE BUENA Vista a few weeks after the Williamson sisters took up resi-

dence there. She was a busy young woman, working and trying
to make her way in the world. While she didn't have time to get
too tangled in the lives of her neighbors, she tried to be amiable.
It was in that respect that she met the nurse who was caring for
the sisters.

One afternoon, while acting on Miss Sherman's invitation to
stop in and meet the English ladies, Clara Corrigan came calling on Apt. D-8. When she was led into the apartment she saw
Claire lying on a couch as Dr. Hazzard bent over her.

"Osteopathic massage treatments," Nurse Sherman whispered, before making introductions. Dora was in bed.

The sight of the sisters' emaciated bodies overwhelmed her.
She hesitated in stepping closer, so horrified at their appearance. They looked like pictures she had seen of starving
Hindus. Their skin was tight, drawn over their bones like wet
sheets drying on a line.

Dr. Hazzard smiled at her and continued the treatment. Her
fists slammed against Claire Williamson's thighs, stomach,
back, and forehead. She kneaded the weakened woman's torso
like a baker might handle a lumpy batch of bread dough. Claire
groaned a little from the force of the doctor's actions, not from
the certain pain of it.

It seemed she was used to it.

Clara Corrigan finally spoke up.

"That seems a very severe treatment," she said.

"On the contrary," Dr. Hazzard answered, without looking
up. "It does her good, it promotes circulation."

The skin looked red where she had slapped Claire.

Miss Corrigan stepped to Dora's bed to speak with her,
though she really wanted to get a better look at how the other
patient was feeling. She wondered if Dora had already had her
treatment and if she was feeling better. Dora, however, was
sleeping.

As she continued her treatment, Dr. Hazzard spoke with her
nurse about a patient who died over at Olalla. Miss Corrigan
couldn't make out all of what was being said. She gathered that
after the patient had died, Dr. Hazzard had performed an
autopsy.

One sentence came through loud enough as to have been

amplified by a megaphone. Dr. Hazzard was miffed because she had been without a large enough vessel for the patient's remains.

"I must bring home a larger kettle today," she said, indicating to Miss Corrigan that she dismembered the deceased at Olalla.

Dr. Hazzard turned her attention to Dora. She stepped in front of Miss Corrigan in such an abrupt manner that it was clear she meant to convey that there was only room for her in the little bedroom.

Dr. Hazzard spoke in low, sweet tones.

"Let go. Relax," she instructed the frail woman. "You are getting on all right, let go, that is what you want to do."

The doctor told her patient to show her tongue.

Dora obliged.

"Your tongue is not clean. *You* are not clean. You are not fit to take food yet; your tongue will have to be clean, and your breath must be sweet."

Miss Corrigan could take no more. She excused herself and returned to her apartment, haunted by what she had seen and heard. She felt such sorrow for the Williamsons. They were so desperately ill, she supposed it was possible such severe treatment was of some benefit to them. Yet they were so thin, so frail, so very helpless.

After she was certain Dr. Hazzard had left the Buena Vista, Clara Corrigan returned to Apt. D-8. She had come to offer help.

"Miss Claire, would you like a sponge bath?"

Claire smiled weakly and spoke softly.

"I believe I would."

With the tenderness of a mother bathing a sickly child, Clara ran a warm sponge over the patient's body and followed it with a gentle rubbing of alcohol. She could see where the doctor had slapped her, leaving red patches the size of her fists.

"Doesn't the treatment hurt?"

Claire shook her head.

"No. No. It is a most beautiful treatment."

Afterward, when Miss Corrigan told a friend of the Williamson sisters' condition, she made mention of the tight, rigid cavity that had become Claire's stomach.

"The skin was drawn tight over it and there was no more flexibility in the skin of the abdomen than there is in a chair," she said.

Clara Corrigan returned to the English sisters' apartment the following evening. No matter how hideous the sisters looked, they were sick, and if she could help in any way, she would. Nurse Sherman had business to take care of downtown and asked Clara to stay with the English girls. The nurse reported Claire was not eating, but Dora was to be fed a tablespoon full of orange juice every hour. Before she left, Miss Sherman had the apartment neighbor help her carry Dora to the bathroom and back to bed.

After the nurse left, Miss Corrigan asked Claire why she wasn't taking nourishment.

"It causes me distress about now, though it will pass," she said. Her eyes were tired and glassy. "The poison is still in my system. I simply can't tolerate food."

Miss Corrigan goaded her to eat, but the patient steadfastly refused. Claire had full confidence Dr. Hazzard's treatment would bring her renewed and vigorous good health.

Her sister was another matter. There was no conversing with Dora that evening. Her mind wandered aimlessly. She wasn't quite delirious, but she was foggy in her thinking. Miss Corrigan told her to rest, and she'd wake her for her next sip of orange juice.

"Sleep, my dear, sleep."

WHILE CLARA CORRIGAN AND MRS. ARTHUR, THE landlady, had actually visited inside the sisters' apartments, it was Mary Fields who had a ringside seat to what was going on. The juxtaposition of their apartments made one thing very clear to her: The kitchen was seldom used by the nurse or the women who lived there.

Mrs. Fields pulled Clara Corrigan aside one evening when she passed by her doorway.

"They do not seem to be cooking in there. Never is there the smell of food, the clatter of dishes or tinware. Have you noticed?"

Clara Corrigan had.

"The girls won't eat," she said. "The doctor says that after the fast their appetite is to return, then they will. But I don't know."

Mrs. Fields wasn't so sure, either. She had another friend that had been on such a fast, and that man was dead because of it. She wanted to find out what was going on in the apartment next door.

Mary Fields tried to speak to Nurse Sherman about the Williamson case on several occasions, but where the nurse had been friendly with other residents at the Buena Vista, she was somewhat curt to her. Mrs. Fields didn't know Nellie Sherman, and she assumed that it was simply her manner. Later, she would wonder if it was because she had known Dr. Hazzard. Mary Fields had met the doctor at the S.E. Harrison home, Old Hickory Hut, on South Alki in Seattle. Mr. Harrison, Mary's friend, was a patient of the fasting specialist. When he died it was noted that it was due to a lack of nourishment. Harrison had been starved.

She saw the girls occasionally when they walked the halls for exercise. They were friendly, always offering a greeting. Once, after Dora was no longer able to exercise, Mary Fields saw Nurse Sherman leading Claire Williamson on a walk. Claire had a strange and disturbed look on her face. Her eyes were sunken, and wide.

"She tried to speak with me, but the nurse didn't give her time to say anything. She just pulled her along in the hall. Miss Claire turned her head about to speak with me," she said later.

DURING THE TREATMENTS, LINDA HAZZARD would talk about a great many subjects. Her practice, other patients, the construction of the Olalla sanitarium. Conversations were one-sided. Dr. Hazzard chattered on as she pushed, rubbed, and kneaded the women's torsos. Claire and Dora murmured approval and interest in what was being told to them. The Williamson sisters enjoyed listening to the doctor.

She was not only a gifted practitioner of natural cures, but Dr. Hazzard was a kindhearted woman as well. She was so attentive, so considerate that the sisters came to feel a fondness for their doctor. Though a little more than a decade separated all of them in age, Dr. Hazzard seemed nearly a mother to them.

The fasting specialist offered to help them in any way she could. She paid particular attention to Claire.

"I know it must be difficult to handle your affairs in a strange city in a strange country."

"Indeed, it is," Claire answered one afternoon as she languished like a damp rag doll in her bed.

Sometimes the doctor's message took on the kind of demanding tone a mother might use on a spoiled child. Claire considered her increased assertiveness a measure of growing concern.

"You must never talk of business with your sister," the fasting specialist would say. "It would not be good for you to consider such matters at this time," Dr. Hazzard said.

Yet oddly, nearly every evening Dr. Hazzard would bring up the subject to Dora and Claire.

"Are there any business matters troubling you?"

Dora did not answer.

Dr. Hazzard asked again.

"I am not going to think about it," Dora finally answered.

"Is there anything that you need to discuss, dear? Tell me about it. What is it?"

"There is nothing. I don't think of business. I put it right away from me."

Shortly after Nellie Sherman arrived, about mid-March, Dr. Hazzard began to increase her inquiries into the Williamsons' personal and business matters. When the girls became too weak to write letters, Dr. Hazzard arranged to have her attorney's secretary come to the Buena Vista apartment to take dictation. The first letters concerned missing luggage from California. Other letters were written to bankers.

Dr. Hazzard continued to press for more information on financial affairs of the sisters.

"Is there anyone in your family, any relations, who have authority over you?"

The sisters said no.

"We have always managed our affairs ourselves."

"No one?"

"No. My sister and I have been alone for so long we have managed just beautifully," Dora said.

The fasting specialist continued her work, but in the coming days she made other requests of the Williamsons.

"I would like to store your valuables," she told them one evening. "I have a safe in my office, and I could care for them while you get well."

The Williamson sisters saw nothing sinister about the suggestion, but they simply didn't see a need for such measures. They were perfectly satisfied that there was no risk to their security at the Buena Vista.

"I do not see how anyone could get into our apartments," Dora told her bedridden sister.

"I agree," Claire answered. "It seems we are perfectly safe here. There is no reason for any such worry."

But as the days passed, Dr. Hazzard persisted in stressing the necessity of securing their expensive belongings.

After the third request, Dora finally gave in to the doctor's suggestion.

"It might be a good thing to have it in a safe," she said.

"And your rings, too," the doctor said. She slipped the diamonds off Dora Williamson's thin fingers and smiled sweetly.

"Any land deeds, dear?"

"Yes," Dora told her, "I have deeds to land in Vancouver."

"Very well. I'll secure those as well. I'll store the lot in my office safe for a few days before I take them to the bank."

NELLIE SHERMAN APPEARED TO BE THE KIND OF expressionless woman who could command any situation, medical or otherwise. She didn't flinch at her chores and, though she would have rather attended to other business than the Williamson girls, once she reluctantly committed herself she had no choice but to do the best she could. But if she had the kind of professional manner that usually didn't portray fear or concern, it was slipping away during the days and nights at the Buena Vista. The results of the fasting treatment were troubling her.

She knocked on Clara Corrigan's door one evening in the middle of the month.

"Miss Corrigan, I hate to be a bother." Her expression was anxious. The tone of her voice suggested particular worry. "I have something to show you. Will you come to the girls' apartment?"

Clara agreed and followed Nurse Sherman to the bathroom in the Williamsons' apartment. Nellie pulled on the chain and the light came on swinging slightly and bouncing shadows across the bathtub where she had bent down to retrieve something. The stretched canvas was over the tub, indicating that an enema had been administered to one of the sisters.

Nellie held up a pail two-thirds full of water. Inside the liquid were numerous milky white particles.

"What do you think it is?" she asked. "It's the water from Miss Claire's enema."

Clara didn't know.

"Did you ever see anything like it before in an enema?"

"No, I never have," Clara answered flatly. She tilted the pail slightly to see its contents under more light. She shook her head. She was mystified.

"What do you suppose it could be?" Nellie Sherman asked once more.

"I'm sure I don't know. I have no idea."

"Well, it can't be food, because there was no food in her stomach. It looks so peculiar to me."

Clara left the apartment. She was shocked by what she had seen; disgusted, too. What was the white material swirling in the water? Was it part of Miss Williamson's innards? Was her diet causing her body to consume itself?

The poor girl; I hope she'll be all right.

The next evening a worried Nurse Sherman arrived at Clara's apartment. Clara invited her inside. Both women were at a loss about what they had seen floating in the pail the night before. Both were worried.

"I don't know what to make of these girls," the nurse said. "Miss Claire is getting weaker every day and cannot retain food in her stomach. She is in such a queer condition of health."

"How is Miss Dora?" Clara asked.

"Not much better, really. She is getting weaker every day. I'm not sure either will live. Claire has fasted over thirty days, and Dora over forty."

Thirty. Forty. The number of days without food was alarming.

As Nellie Sherman ran her hands through her hair, she talked about the effect Dr. Hazzard's treatment was having on the English ladies.

The words were indelibly etched in Clara Corrigan's memory.

"I'm not sure it is working. I think the girls may die."

THOUGH CLAIRE LOST THE MOST WEIGHT AND appeared to be the weaker of the two, it was Dora who began showing signs of mental weakness. Dr. Hazzard came early one afternoon when Nurse Sherman reported Dora's mind had wandered in a rambling and confused measure of delirium.

Confined to her own bed, Claire couldn't get to her sister to help her. She lay there as still as she could, straining to hear what was being said beyond the drawn curtains.

"Doctor, she's been like this all morning," Nurse Sherman said, as Dr. Hazzard began to pat Dora's face.

"Dear, listen to me. You must come out of this. Now!"

Dora murmured something incomprehensible.

"It's your brain, dear," she declared. "Your trouble is not your body, but your brain. There's been a reason why doctors haven't been able to figure out what is wrong with your health . . . it is your brain."

Dora looked up and nodded.

"Yes, my brain."

THE WILLIAMSON SISTERS WERE IN DIRE SHAPE, and Nellie Sherman knew it. Though she had never done so in her long nursing career, she went to another doctor for a second opinion. She felt she had no choice. She went to the Seattle offices of Dr. Augusta Brewer. It was, she felt, the safest tack to take. There was good reason for such a supposition. Dr. Brewer was not only a good friend of Nellie's, she already knew the Williamsons.

Augusta Brewer, an osteopath of impeccable credentials, had treated Claire with some spinal treatments in July of 1910.

When Nellie Sherman arrived at the doctor's office on March 29, she did so with the idea that she would get some medical books that she could study for clues on how to help the girls get over the hurdle that was before them. She didn't want Dr. Hazzard to know that she was there, and she knew her friend would never tell her.

The look on her face could not hide her genuine worry.

"The girls are so weak from hunger," the nurse said, nearly succumbing to tears.

Dr. Brewer reached out her hand.

"What are they eating?"

"Only a broth. A broth made from the boiling of tomatoes and asparagus tips."

"Nothing more?"

"Oh. A half cup of orange juice."

"Give them more food, Nellie. They ought to have more food."

"I have tried. I tried to give them some milk and raisins, but they wouldn't take any of it."

"Why not? Are they not hungry?"

"Augusta, they won't take any more unless Dr. Hazzard tells them to. They are absolutely under her dominion."

"This is very wrong. This treatment is wrong. Nellie, you know I do not approve of Linda Hazzard's methods. She is not a graduate of any osteopathic school. She doesn't know what she is doing! She is not equipped to handle these kinds of cases!"

Linda Hazzard, not *Dr.* Hazzard . . . Augusta Brewer was one of the many who refused to give the fasting specialist the title of doctor.

"I don't know," Nellie offered, more composed. "She has cured many, many people. I know that."

"Think what you wish, but do something to help the girls. Feed them at once!"

DOROTHEA KECK RAN A SMALL NEIGHBORHOOD grocery store at 608 East Pike Street, only two blocks from the Buena Vista. She knew Miss Sherman from her occasional visits the spring of 1911. She knew that the Williamsons were patients of the nurse working under the direction of Linda Burfield Hazzard. Tomatoes and asparagus were the only groceries Nellie Sherman purchased.

On April 19, Nurse Sherman arrived for her last visit. She had called a few days before to request that the last bill would be made ready as they were transferring the sisters to the sanitarium at Olalla. Mrs. Keck made out the bill. It came to just under $5.

"How are the girls?" the lady grocer asked as she counted out change.

"Mrs. Keck, I don't know. I'm worried about them. Claire had a very bad fainting spell. I just revived her from it before I came down. Whenever she has a spell, it gives Dora a setback, to see her sister in such a condition."

Mrs. Keck shook her head in sympathy.

"Cannot you give them something to eat? Something to keep them up when Dr. Hazzard is not there?"

"Oh, no, Mrs, Keck, they would not take a glass of water unless Dr. Hazzard said so. You would think she had hypnotized them."

"Oh dear."

Nellie went on to tell the woman that the sisters had wasted away to the point where neither could walk anymore. They had to be carried.

"The only good of it is that they are as light as children by now," she said.

The grocer didn't know what to say.

Nellie Sherman looked weary as she turned to leave, offering a comment that would stick with Dorothea Keck for the rest of her life.

"If I knew what I was undertaking with the Williamson girls, I would never take another case like it. It's not worth it."

IT WAS DARK ON APRIL 21, 1911, WHEN LINDA Burfield Hazzard arrived at the Buena Vista to help Nellie Sherman pack the Williamson sisters' belongings. Ambulances would be called and a special launch to Olalla was arranged for the following morning. Mrs. Arthur came up to Apt. D-8 to gather the sisters' soiled laundry. Dr. Hazzard presided over the packing while Dora and Claire rested in their beds.

At 11 A.M., a small crowd gathered around the twin ambulances. Clara Corrigan, Mary Fields, the Arthurs and their children were among the onlookers as the sisters were carried out by stretcher. Dora's face was completely covered with a white dressing of cotton bandages; it appeared her hands were bound in the manner of an Egyptian mummy.

Claire murmured and tried to speak as she was carried away.

Mr. Arthur called out to the emaciated ladies.

"Good-bye, Miss Claire, Miss Dora."

Claire didn't answer, and Dora likely didn't even hear him.

Dr. Hazzard looked up from her patient as she hovered over Claire's stretcher.

"Tell Mr. Arthur 'good-bye,' " she said, her voice warm and pleasant.

"Good-bye," Claire replied softly. "We will be back soon."

The man nodded and exchanged forlorn looks with his wife. Neither of the Arthurs expected they'd ever see Claire or Dora Williamson again.

"Poor dears," Mrs. Arthur said.

Mary Fields shook her head. She was heartsick about the sisters' condition, but relieved they were leaving the Buena Vista. She took one last look at Dora on the stretcher. Her eyes were closed, her head bandaged. Her appearance was horrifying. She looked like a skull with a bandage wrapped about it, circles cut out of the fabric for her eyes. She fixed Claire's weight at less than seventy pounds; Dora slightly heavier.

She didn't expect to see them again, either.

FIVE

WRAPPED IN SCRATCHY, DARK BLUE wool blankets, the sisters waited in the ambulances. In and out of consciousness they passed. Dr. Hazzard, dressed in her white doctor's garment with a black coat slung over her back and buttoned at the neck to a capelike affair, soothed them with words that promised every concern would be taken care of once they arrived at the still-unfinished sanitarium.

"Mother Lillie, a kindly old neighbor, will be there to assist Nurse Sherman. You will grow to love her as I do. A very dear old woman indeed."

Dr. Hazzard spoke in sweet, comforting tones as she pulled the blanket up tightly to cover the length of Claire's neck.

Claire tried to speak, but the doctor put her fingertips on her patient's mouth.

"You'll be fine, dear."

Claire managed a slight, though ghastly, smile.

"Soon," the doctor said. "Very soon."

Passersby peered into the back of the ambulances. Out of kindness for the delay, the driver tried to talk with Dora. And the minutes on the dock passed. One hour, then two. Finally, John Arthur, Dr. Hazzard's attorney, breezed onto the dock with a carrying case of papers and the red and perspiring face of a man who had hurried to make his arrival.

"Doctor, in which ambulance is she?" he asked, his voice still resonating with a crisp preciseness that was a legacy from his youth in England.

"Miss Claire is in the second one. I've informed her that you were coming. She is quite lucid. Dora, I'm afraid, is another matter. Take care of the business, and we will be on our way to Olalla."

John Arthur disappeared into the back of the ambulance. He pulled out a sheet of paper and a fountain pen and handed it to Claire, who heaved for breath under the covers that pressed on her chest like a pile of stones. She could barely speak and needed help with her writing. At Mr. Arthur's direction, the sickly woman wrote a letter to her longtime nurse and companion, Margaret Conway in Brunswick, Victoria, Australia. The attorney's presence was more than that of a concerned observer. His signature at the bottom of the notice was absolutely necessary. It was not a letter at all. It was a codicil to Miss Claire's will.

The thirty-three-year-old woman's penmanship, once clear and precise, was erratic and sloppy.

Dear Margaret:

In the event of my death, my books and jewels are hereby given to you for disposition by you according to your own judgement and discretion. This is intended as a bequest to you, as if contained in a formal will and to be treated as a codicil to my will already made. I also hereby give twenty-five pounds sterling per year to the Hazzard Institute of Natural Therapeutics in Olalla, Kitsap County, State of Washington, U.S.A.; to be also treated as a codicil to my said will. My remains are to be cremated under the charge and direction of Linda Burfield Hazzard of said Olalla. This letter is also intended as directions to my solicitors in London.

—*Claire Williamson*

Linda and Sam Hazzard stood outside, assuring onlookers that the patients were doing well.

Finally, just as the launch arrived, John Arthur finished his business with Claire and exited the back of the ambulance.

"I'll have papers for you tomorrow afternoon," he called over his shoulder as he headed for the electric car.

YEARS AFTER, NELS CHRISTENSEN, MANAGER OF the West Pass Transportation in 1911, recalled what happened on that day. He knew the fasting specialist and held her in high, irreproachable, esteem. She traveled on his boat whenever she went from her Seattle office to her Olalla country home and soon-to-be-built sanitarium.

"I made a special trip the day the two girls were taken over to her place for treatment," he remembered. "And the two girls were brought down to my boat in two ambulances. I helped carry them aboard on two stretchers. I was very much surprised when I took one end of the stretchers; it seemed to me it was though the girls didn't weigh more than fifty or sixty pounds at the most. They were so weak and so sick, neither one of them could stand up."

BY THE SPRING OF 1911, ELECTRICITY STILL HAD not come to Olalla, the small, rain-soaked town that rimmed the shore of Puget Sound like the soggy, grey edge around a bowl of oatmeal.

Rain sprayed the boardwalk and slickened the wood. Lacking the sumptuous trim of those worn by ladies in the city, frayed, plain hemlines functioned as mops as fabric dragged over the wet surface. And though they hadn't actually nailed it into place, the women of Olalla laid claim to the construction of the boardwalk. First, they raised money for the lumber through basket socials at the schoolhouse, and with that accomplished, they hauled lunches and kegs of beer to their men as they hammered planks into place. The boardwalk, the women told each other, was proof that their salt water-sprayed town was more than an outpost for the drunken and lost. It was a civilized community.

The West Pass steamer, the sternwheeler *Virginia*, filled the air with a stream of black-and-white vapors. Three women had made the two-hour trip from Seattle to the shores of Kitsap County. Two of the women had been told they would be docking at Olalla. Located midway down the passage, Olalla was known for a razor-edged, shell-encrusted shoreline of oysters and clam beds so rich, it took a circuitous route and thick shoe leather to walk its beaches. Olalla was a place where Coastal Indians and white settlers fished the same waters, overloading nets with salmon and heaping baskets with shellfish.

It was, however, the tangled vines of wild strawberry plants that webbed its hillsides and gave the town its name.

"Mamook Olallie!" an Indian had called out in 1881 to L. P. Larson, a thirty-two-year-old Swedish beach logger and the first white settler in the area. The Indian had asked Larson if he had picked berries, but the man misunderstood the Chinook jargon. He thought he was being told the name of the place.

In time, Finnish and Swedish homesteaders arrived to carve a village out of a land so thick with trees that lanterns were sometimes needed during daylight. As Olalla grew, it became a primary stop for the "Mosquito Fleet"—so called because of the scores of tiny steamers crisscrossing the points along the inland waterways between rivals Tacoma and Seattle. Before 1911, there had been no dock. Those meeting a steamer found it necessary to row across the bay on a scow.

No one knew it at the time, none could even have dreamed it. But Olalla, a village of only 357 souls, would forever be changed that spring day the sternwheeler brought those three women from Seattle: Claire and Dorothea Williamson, and their doctor, Linda Hazzard.

After two months of treatment, the sisters rested weakly on cots like damp loaves of bread. Dr. Hazzard commanded the attention of all on the boat. Just before the landing at Finney Creek, but a mile from Olalla, she sharply called to Mr. Christensen that she had a change in plans. They would not be off-loading at Olalla.

"I spoke with John Karcher before we left the dock. He is meeting us at Finney Creek."

The shift was odd. The Olalla landing was superior in nearly every regard. The shoreline at Olalla was of lesser grade. The Finney Creek landing road took the kind of steep route better suited for a goat herd than the infirm drawn by horses. Finney Creek was the site of the village of Fragaria, named for the Latin word for wild strawberries. It was isolated. It was, by far, less populated than Olalla.

John Karcher, a fifty-seven-year-old carpenter and rancher, had a spring wagon waiting. Hay and blankets had been smoothed out to form mattresses. In an instant, the sisters were loaded into it, and the horses were called into action.

"We are in Olalla, dear," Dr. Hazzard told Claire as she brushed loose hairs from her forehead.

She said nothing to Dora.

Sword ferns brushed the wagon wheels as they cut through the muddy road. Unripe salmonberries draped over branches like green beaded garlands. Along the creek bed, and toward the main road, the wagon lumbered on. The sisters remained still, among sacks of potatoes and hay. Their destination was the sanitarium on a tree-shrouded, forty-acre tract dubbed by its owners as Wilderness Heights.

A murmur, a voice confused in delirium, could barely be made out. Claire reached out for her sister's hand. The bounce of the wagon had jostled a renewed alertness into her half-dead body.

"The country! We are here! Oh, Dorie!"

Dora was unable to move her lips to form a response.

"It will be all right. We'll be well soon," Claire said softly as she gripped her sister's hand.

Dr. Hazzard turned away from her frail patients and yelled at Mr. Karcher.

"Hurry! The sisters are ill! I must attend to them at once!"

THE SISTERS WERE CARRIED INTO THE HAZZARD home through the back door. No one spoke as their stretchers turned and twisted as they passed through a small kitchen, which opened to the dining and living rooms. On the right side of the house was Sam and Linda's room, and inside of that, a little bathroom. Just into a small hallway was a staircase.

Up the fourteen fir risers of a narrow staircase was little more than an unfinished attic. At one end was what would be Claire's room, a small sleeping place with a window taking in the sight of a logged-out field. A wooden screen separated it from the outside landing where Dora would sleep.

THE MORNING AFTER THE SISTERS' ARRIVAL, Samuel Hazzard appeared at Claire's bedside. He said his wife had thought it prudent for him to step in and assist the ladies with any correspondence that needed to be done. Dora was still out of her head, but Claire was strong enough—trusting enough, really—to take the suggestion as a genuine offer for help. She tried to lift her head from the pillow to talk more directly to the man who had knelt on the floor and looked up at her, a pencil and sheet of paper poised in his hand. Claire murmured some vague comments about her happiness at being at Olalla.

Sam offered to type her words in letter form.

"That is very kind of you, sir," she said, before slipping off to rest her eyes. Later, when Claire inquired of the letter, Sam said his typewriter was in need of a new ink ribbon. He would get to it as soon as a replacement could be brought home.

LINDA BURFIELD HAZZARD WAS A WOMAN OF dreams and undeniable vision. She was on a mission of great importance; her fervor no less deep than a tent-bound preacher on an endless circuit of the indistinguishable small towns and villages that pockmarked the West. She had a great dream. Her sanitarium would rival the best in the world, surpassing even Kellogg's Michigan enterprise. Patches of stony earth had been cleared for the cabins, five to start, twenty more to follow. Later, when funds permitted, a great white structure would rise in the forest. It would be a part of nature, with a feeling of home. Hospitals were artificial and detrimental. She could *see* something while husband Sam and grown son Rollin could only voice enthusiasm: Three stories, a hundred beds, a staircase sweeping from the lobby to the top floor. Elegance and refinement. The woods hinted at a great future. Huckleberry bushes with their dark green waxy leaves could be trimmed in to shrubbery.

So lovely with the black and blue berries that cluster at branch tips. So very pretty.

Though they could be burned out and then hitched to a team to yank roots from the soil, tree stumps were too difficult to remove in every instance.

"Sam," she instructed, with a voice that carried over the ravine and toward the Bay, "I want you to hollow the stumps into wondrous, natural seats. Resting places provided by nature!"

The lady with the plans stood still for a moment to watch a goldfinch ride the waves of a breeze. Up and down, the little bird's feathers were the brightest hue against the rich green surroundings.

IT WAS GOOD THAT LINDA HAZZARD WAS A woman of great inner strength. She was strident. She was tough. No one doubted she was an extraordinarily motivated woman. It was necessary that she be all of those things, too. She needed to summon every ounce of her strength when it came to her twenty-two-year-old son by her first marriage. Rollin Burfield was the bane of his mother's existence. He knew it. She knew it. In time, all of Olalla knew it.

Rollin was a shorter man, the kind who overindulges his ego to compensate for his small stature. He had the kind of bland, but well-proportioned features that often passed for handsomeness. Since his mother dreamed big, Rollin likely figured ideas of grandeur were his birthright. He wanted to bask in the applause of an audience, first on the stage, later in the movies. After joining his mother and Sam in Seattle, Rollin became a company player specializing in juvenile roles at several Seattle stock houses. By the time 1910 rolled around, the roles were waning. He did not have the physical presence to make the transition to leading man.

Rollin Burfield would not be relegated to character roles. Linda agreed. Her son was far too talented for that. Those who didn't see it . . . well, it was their unfortunate loss.

From the move to Olalla and the years beyond, Linda Hazzard had to put up with the demands of her banty son, whose hands were out more often than a snotty kid's tongue. She had given Rollin slack, and he used it to make her life miserable. Rollin needed money. For this. For that. Rollin was going to be this and that. Everything was for Rollin, and in the beginning there was no telling his mother that her son was the consummate financial leech. In later years, however, she would wise up.

When Claire and Dora arrived at Olalla, Rollie was there to help his mother do what needed to be done.

When Claire begged for food, Rollie parroted the doctor's line.

"Just a bit longer, hold on, Miss. If you eat now, you'll die. Soon you'll be in perfect health."

NEARLY FROM THE MOMENT THEY ARRIVED AT
Olalla, Dr. Hazzard had insisted the sisters remain separated.
The nurses were told the girls needed to focus all of their atten-
tion on their treatments. Each other was a distraction.
Distraction could lead to a slower recovery.

Dora had been told that Claire was too weak to see visitors.

"Surely she can see me?" she pleaded.

"In time. Not yet. She's simply too weak for the strain."

Claire, on the other hand, had been told Dora was completely
demented. *Altogether out of her head.* Claire's heart ached at the
news.

"I am hopeful she will come out of this, but it is very delicate.
We must wait for the poisons to leave the body, thus restoring
the mind," Dr. Hazzard told her.

Neither sister, of course, knew what had been told to the
other. One afternoon when the house seemed so very quiet,
Dora pushed herself onto the fir-planked floor and crawled to
her sister's bedside.

"Claire! Can you hear me?"

The skeleton stirred. Dora gasped at the sight. Her sister
looked dreadful.

"Dora! You mustn't!" Claire's eyes were wild, full of disgust
and fear. She pushed at her sister's hand. "You did not have to
come. You *mustn't* come!"

Dora wanted to cry, but she was unable to conjure the
strength for such an emotion. She doubted whether she had
tears within her eyes.

"I want to be with you, dearie."

"*Go! Please, now!*"

Dora complied. Like a yellow potato drawn across a stone,
the skin on her knees rubbed off as she crawled back to her bed.
Dora looked at the bloody circles seeping through her night-
dress and pulled the blanket over her legs. In a moment, she fell
into the sweet darkness of sleep.

*WILLIAM BLOOMQUIST WAS NEVER AFRAID OF HARD
work. He cleared his Olalla acreage with a stump puller driven
by a sweaty old horse. Trees burned in massive piles, smoke
sending a cue skyward that another man had taken the chal-*

lenge of turning raw land into fields of Van Dieman strawberries. Years later, the family farmed chickens. The Bloomquist farm was just up a dirt lane from the Hazzard place.

Born in 1913, Ernest Bloomquist was the proverbial gleam in his old man's eye when Dr. Hazzard proclaimed herself the martyr of the great fasting movement. Long after, Ernie would recall how his father had taken the starvation doctor's treatment to cure ulcers that had been unsuccessfully treated by a Tacoma physician.

"She fasted him about twenty or thirty days—it wasn't as much as some of the others—some of them went sixty days without any food. Then she would build them back on soups, lots of vegetables. She wouldn't let them drink anything else but goat milk—she had a lot of goats there that they milked. I never was a patient, I only know what she did to my father. He had to eat certain vegetables. No eggs. No meat. She was death on meat. Or fats. Her main idea was to take all that weight off you until you are skin and bones and there isn't anything left, and after you are just about ready to die, then she'd bring you back on certain vegetables.

"My dad lost a tremendous amount of weight. Some of those were awful thin that used to walk past our place. My father wasn't as thin as some of them, but he got to the point where he couldn't hardly walk around. He got over the stomach ailment that he had. Dr. Hazzard cured him. She really did."

Six

LINDA BURFIELD HAZZARD HAD HER ADMI-
rers. Particularly so among the young ladies of Olalla. She was
an elegant presence, a lady of considerable refinement in a
place where a course of yards of cotton was purchased to
replace a garment that had long since given up the ghost. She
usually wore the latest in dresses, a hat and gloves, and often a
fur. A favorite was a fox stole that she draped over her shoulders with a dramatic flourish and fastened with an oversize gold
clasp. For many years, Linda had a cocker spaniel whose reddish gold coloring matched her fox as though the dog was an
accessory dyed to match. With her little dog on a leash, off the
doctor would go to catch the launch for Seattle.

Sam Hazzard seldom went to the city with his wife. Instead,
he would leave her off at the boat and head back up the hill to
do whatever it was he did when she wasn't around to delegate
chores she considered essential.

In the evening, Sam would return to the landing to pick up his
wife.

And across the waters, as the boat let off passengers on
Vashon Island, her voice could be heard.

"Sam, you heathen, you better be there!"

Again, she'd call for good measure.

"Sam!"

Folks in Olalla and Fragaria always knew when Doc Hazzard
was on the boat. And as he had been told, Sam was there. No
one knew what would happen if Linda had to wait—even for a
minute. No one wanted to know.

A WORLD AWAY FROM THE WINDSWEPT SHORES of Colvos Passage, Margaret Conway and her sisters gathered together in a home near Melbourne, Australia. It was a happy time. They were bound by sisterhood, but separated from each other because of vast distances and obligations made when they were all many years younger. It had been six years since Margaret and her sisters had been together; six years that to aching hearts felt an eternity.

More than any time in their lives, over the years that had kept them apart, the sisters' faces and bodies had changed. Tiny wrinkles accentuated their smiles, soft pillows of flesh cushioned their midsections and thighs. They were no longer young. Each had moved from mature woman to older lady. Yet they were far from unattractive. Margaret had steel grey eyes. It was no matter the color was often considered cold, her eyes were not. Her hair, once dark, had softened to a becomingly tawny shade of grey. Her face was rounded and sweet.

Like her mother and her grandmother, Margaret had been a nursemaid to wealthy English children. Margaret knew many women outside of her family that had followed the same road in life. They were women more like her than her mother and grandmother. Though she loved children, she had never had any of her own. Margaret Conway had never married. Even so, she always believed she was lucky, far luckier, than most. When the Williamson family needed a nursemaid for their daughter Dorothea, they called upon Margaret. She was a young woman then, barely twenty.

Margaret came to care for Dora when the little girl was only one year old. She left her home; she left her sisters. She found her calling. The night before Margaret Conway came, Mrs. Williamson gave birth to a baby girl named Gertrude. Tragically, Gertrude was sickly from the start. Nearly seven months passed with Mrs. Williamson bearing the burden of her sick baby, before Margaret cared for the frail little thing.

At three and a half, little Gertrude contracted scarlet fever and died. This was the second Williamson daughter to die young. Another had died in India.

Before the two surviving Williamson sisters came of age, they were orphaned. Rosolida, who could never shake the devastating loss of her husband, followed George to the grave. The cause of her death was never known. The girls always thought their mother died of a broken heart.

While the loss of their parents was devastating, it was hardest on Claire. She was afraid to go anywhere. Everything frightened her. As a little girl her eyes were frequently cast downward and her face blushed with color. She embarrassed easily and cried often. When strangers came calling, Claire would run for the dark envelope that was made of the folds of Miss Conway's skirt. When a tea party invitation was issued, Dora would be elated to attend, Claire did not want to go. It was Margaret Conway who would try to soothe her fears and persuade her to go. After the tears, after the worries were chased away, Claire would attend. In time, she outgrew her debilitating shyness. She had her nursemaid to thank for that, and she knew it. Because of the death of their parents, Margaret Conway had become far closer, far more important to their lives. She was like a mother to the sisters.

From childhood, they called her "Tooddy"; after their mother's death, she called them "my girls."

Beyond the occasional cold or attack of grippe as they grew up, the sisters generally enjoyed good health. When Claire was seven she complained of feeling poorly, and her mother treated her with a course of burgundy by giving her a tablespoonful every morning for two or three weeks. At nine, Claire suffered the only serious illness of either child: Diphtheria kept her bedridden for five days.

However, both could, and did, take part in any sport that caught their fancy. Tennis was a favorite of Dora's. During the warmer summertime weather, or on trips to the south of France, Claire loved to swim in the sea.

In all their lives there were only two times when the sisters and their nurse had been apart when they needed one another. Living in Australia at the time, Dora suffered some vague infirmity associated with "female troubles." Since Margaret was away with her family, the burden of her care rested on Claire, then twenty-one. The stress was great—perhaps too great. While Dora got better, Claire suffered problems of her own.

Margaret Conway recalled Claire's illness years after it had passed into memory.

"The way the old family doctor described it to me was that if she had been a workingwoman, he could have fixed some little appliance that would enable her to do her work in an ordinary way. He said thousands of women go around in that way, but as she had the means and was not obliged to work he recommended her to keep quiet and let nature assert itself. She used to lie down a great deal, but she was not suffering."

A year later, Claire's tipped-back uterus was fine.

MARGARET CONWAY MISSED HER GIRLS THROUGH-out the second of the two times they would be separated. While the trip had been planned, and she was able to see her sisters, it still seemed a very long time to be away.

Claire and Dora had tired of England. They had wondered if it might be that they would enjoy living in British Columbia. Victoria or Vancouver had been visited by friends who remarked that they both had gorgeous settings, glorious seaside summers, and vast expanses of wilderness at their boundaries. The Williamsons said they would look about the region for six months and when they found the perfect place to settle they would send for their beloved Tooddy.

On May 6, 1910, Margaret boarded the steamer *Empress of Ireland* in Liverpool to see her girls to their staterooms. Two days later, she set sail herself for Australia to reunite with her own sisters. Though thousands of miles separated the sisters and their nurse, each mail brought letters of their travels. Dora's notes chattered on about their voyage and the people they met along the way. Claire's were more detailed, almost a diary of her thoughts and experiences. One letter noted how the girls had found property in both Vancouver and Victoria and purchased a great many household goods. They would, in fact, be settling in British Columbia.

Margaret had half hoped that Claire and Dora would not find North America to their liking. And though she knew that her place would be wherever they selected as a home, she allowed herself the secret hope the sisters would consider Australia. Margaret wanted to be near her own family.

Another letter brought both worrisome news and the announcement of a change in plans. Dora was suffering from a bout of rheumatism and the sisters had decided to winter in California. After that, Dora was going to Australia and Claire was bound for England to train to become a kindergarten teacher. Naturally, she didn't need the money. Claire only sought a sense of purpose.

Over the course of the winter months, letters continued to come to Margaret in Australia. Claire and Dora wrote of new friends and reunions with relatives in Riverside and El Toro, California. The rheumatism was a memory, and the sisters wrote that they planned to return to British Columbia for a short time before sailing for England and Australia.

No mention was made of Seattle or Linda Burfield Hazzard.

THE SIX-MONTH VISIT THAT EXTENDED TO NEARLY a year was coming to an end. Though she had longed for her sisters and Australia, Margaret Conway was glad for the day when Dora's steamer would reach port.

On April 30, 1911, a cablegram arrived.

Come SS Marama May 8th, first class. Claire.

Though it was only a few simple words, Margaret Conway didn't make much of them at first. She placed the cablegram on a table and turned to her sisters to make the announcement.

"Dora must have sailed later than she had planned. She's coming on the SS *Marama* May 8."

The conversation continued, but there was something about two words on the cable that gave her pause. She picked up the small slip of paper and read it again:

First class.

Why did Claire write that? The choice of words was odd. Why would Claire include the reference to first class? The very idea of it ate her. A woman of means, a woman born into wealth, Claire was not the type to flaunt it in that way. It just was. Margaret pondered the words a bit more. She couldn't let it lie; she decided to make inquiries.

She telephoned the steamship company's offices and learned that the *Marama* was not sailing to Sydney, but *from* Sydney on May 8.

"I don't understand," she said, halting her words for a moment. Something was so strange. She knew the girls so well. Something was wrong with Dora and Claire. The cable, she felt, was a call for help.

"Reserve me a first-class berth," she ordered.

"We have none."

"Reserve me a second-class stateroom then."

Again, none were available.

"Third-class. I must go!"

The man drew a breath. "I'll have to inquire of our office in Sydney."

Margaret's repetition of her quandry betrayed her impatience.

"*Third-class. I must go!*"

Perhaps the man didn't understand the necessity of the trip? She knew something was amiss. Couldn't he hear it in her voice? Couldn't he make room for her?

"I must sail on the *Marama*. It is urgent. Do the best that you can for me, but I leave on that boat!"

The man on the other end of the line sighed. He promised he would do what he could.

"We shall do our best," he said.

AT 420 FEET IN LENGTH, THE OIL-BURNING steamer, the Union Steamship Company's SS *Marama,* was a serviceable, if not particularly noteworthy, passenger vessel. The New Zealand-based ship was slower than most traversing the Sydney–Vancouver route and as such, left passengers precious little time for lingering in Fiji and Hawaii. The schedule for mail and perishable goods deliveries could not be impeded. Some ports were only seen by moonlight from the ship's rail.

A week after Margaret successfully pleaded—*begged*—for a spot on the passenger list, the *Marama* left a black trail of steam and smoke from its single stack over the South Pacific as it sailed for British Columbia. Miss Conway sat in a cramped inside cabin and buried her hands in her face and thanked God she made it aboard. The girls who needed her were not born of her womb, but no one could deny they belonged to her. No mother loved her children in a greater measure than she did

Dora and Claire Williamson. Whatever was wrong, she was sure she could fix it. It had to be so.

IMPRESSIONS AS INTENSE AS THOSE LEFT BY LINDA and Sam Hazzard never fade. Hugh Buchanan, born in 1920, is one who could never forget how things were between the doctor and her husband. The Buchanans raised chickens like many in the area during those early years, farming anywhere from twenty-five hundred to five thousand egg-layers at any given time at their place in Fragaria. Since Hugh's father, Art, was a close friend of the Hazzards, trips up the hill to the sanitarium were frequent. Each time, young Hugh was afforded a glimpse into the relationship of Olalla's most famous couple. Sam, it seemed, was a bit of a loner. Linda ran the show.

"I do recall that Doc Hazzard would come in and want to speak to Sam and she was very emphatic about what she wanted to say to him. It didn't seem like there was anything affectionate there. I didn't hear any strong language or bad language or anything. She was a strong woman. I believe she could knock a man down if she wanted to. That kind.

"Sam always seemed like he was in the midst of writing, maybe a book or articles. He was very philosophical, he would sit back and light that pipe, you know, and it seemed like every word that issued out of his mouth were gems of wisdom to me. That kind of a guy. But who knows? I didn't know everything about him."

SEVEN

THE SS *MARAMA* PUFFED INTO POSITION AS it sliced a shimmering line through the warm waters of Honolulu's aquamarine harbor. The Hawaiian Islands were as Margaret Conway had been told: dark green, nearly black, sandy discs trimmed in the creamy white of sand. The islands drifted like great umbrella tops floating in a sea of incomparable beauty. But as Margaret looked off the ship she scarcely allowed herself a moment to soak in the beauty of the sights surrounding her. Her mind was knotted with apprehension over the fate of the girls. She was determined to reach Victoria in time to help Claire and Dora. As the sunshine warmed her face and the breath of the wind mussed her hair, she could think of nothing else that spring day, May 23, 1911.

She could also hear the girls telling her over and over:

"Don't forget to go to the Punch Bowl, Tooddy. The view is among the best in the world. If you get there, you must, you simply must see it."

Before going to take in the view as the girls had made her promise if she ever took passage to Honolulu, Margaret Conway made an inquiry at the agent's office.

"Mail for Miss Margaret Conway?"

"Indeed. A cablegram as well," the man said, fishing through a stack of papers. Margaret tore open the cable first. It was a Commercial Pacific cablegram dated May 17, 1911. It had been dispatched from Seattle, Washington, less than one week before. Relief bathed her face as she read:

Margaret Conway arriving SS Marama Honolulu. Ask agent for letters. Both quite well.—Williamson.

"Is there another letter?" she asked. "The cable says 'ask agent for letters.' "

"Sorry. Just the one."

The letter had been written on May 2, 1911. The return address was in care of a person and a place Margaret had never heard mention of before. Linda Burfield Hazzard, Olalla, Kitsap County, Washington, U.S.A. It was Claire's handwriting that had formed the words on the four pages contained within the envelope. The structure of the writing was alarming. Words collided into each another. Lines rode over each other like the waves of the sea. Claire's penmanship, once delicate and clear, was a fright of sloppiness. Margaret was unnerved.

My dear, dear Tooddy,

How we are looking forward to your arrival it would be hard to say. I felt I couldn't wait any longer for you and as we are going to stay here until sometime in July it seemed the best thing to do. In fact, I had other reasons as well as I will be able to tell you when you come.

As Margaret continued to read, it was the omissions from the text that concerned her. What was it that Claire was unable to say in the letter? Was Dorie all right? Was there some indelicate problem that could not be committed to paper? The nurse with the round face and wide grey eyes read on. She learned that her beloved Claire and Dora had fallen into ill health until they discovered Linda Burfield Hazzard—the only "licensed fasting doctor in the world." Margaret had never heard of a fasting doctor, and frankly, didn't know what to make of it. The girls had chased peculiar cures so many times, it was practically a parlor game.

Claire wrote of the doctor and her husband:

She is a wonderful woman as rightness is her religion and all the high principled absolutely genuine people who keep near their ideals she is the greatest. She has gone through a terribly hard life and fearful struggles besides suffering terribly from an organic trouble caused by drugs and it is marvelous what she accomplishes by fasting and

*living most abstenioususly on vegetables and salads . . .
she comes from Irish and English parents and though she
has always been brought up in the U.S. is much more Irish
and English in her tastes than American. She is quite a
lady and is married for the second time to Mr. Hazzard
who is one of the most clever and cultivated gentlemen we
have ever met in any country. He is American and has held
very important positions, he has such a wonderful fund of
information it is always an education to hear him talk.*

Margaret stopped as she pondered the contents of the letter.
She was thankful that her girls had found such kind people
to care for them. She still was unsure of the treatment, but she
didn't have the education, didn't have the kind of life experience that Claire and Dora had. Though she lived with them, and
was close to them, she was a servant. She didn't live within
their world, merely on its lovely periphery.

She read on. The letter made mention of cabins the Hazzards
would be building at Olalla. Two were being readied for the
sisters.

*They are to have verandas in front where we can sleep
out if we like. We shall be able to do our cooking and
everything up there, or if we want anything more we can
do it at their house as the cabins are only higher up still in
a lovely position.*

Claire Williamson had warned the American way of life was
far different than life in Australia or England. The Wild West
was strange, and its people exceedingly interesting. She cautioned Margaret to keep an open mind and to be ready to listen
to the local people and their views.

*Dorie and I are going to make the most of our time here
and can learn all we can from these people. I am going to
study Botany and other things as we can do it out of doors
if we get good weather . . .
Darling, will you be a vegetarian whilst here to please
me? You can have salt and pale roasted coffee and extras*

*if you find them necessary and delicious bread unfer-
mented I hope much lighter than in England. The nurse
who eats meat and fish likes it immensely. So . . .*

Claire closed with a hint of what Margaret felt had troubled
her enough to allude to it in the first paragraph. Something was
gravely wrong with Dora.

*. . . the Dr. had a long talk with me last night about
Dorie, she may take months to get her brain right which
you know has been so weak the last few years her memory
going so completely. I will tell you details when you come
and I conceive the Dr. will tell you about us . . .*

Margaret Conway was breathless with worry. Goodness,
what in the world was wrong with Dora's brain? What was this
talk of staying in a sanitarium until July? In cabins? She had
never heard of such things in all her life.

She put the letter and cablegram in her pocketbook. There
would be no trip to see the volcanic crater called the Punch
Bowl. If the girls asked her about it, she would tell them the
view had been as lovely as they described. Instead, Margaret
planned to shop for Hawaiian curios for Dora and Claire.
Perhaps hatpins with little colored seashells affixed to the heads
could be had? They were so pretty. They were within
Margaret's modest means, and she knew they would be just the
right cheer for the girls. Never far in the back of her mind, it
relieved her that the cablegram had been sent on May 17—
fifteen days after the letter. Dora must have taken a turn for the
better.

The cablegram indicated "both quite well."

MARGARET CONWAY GRIPPED THE HANDRAIL AS
she and other passengers poured down the *Marama's* gangway
in Vancouver on June 1, 1911. The air was warm and moist.
Grey-winged gulls circled and screamed from a chalky white
sky. Miss Conway's clothing was heavy for the season; summertime in Canada was winter in Australia. She wished she had
packed more appropriately, but there hadn't been time.

Anxiousness and the warm air caused her face to glow and wisps of escaping hair from under her hat to paste against her scalp.

As Margaret prepared to climb aboard the omnibus, a handsome man approached. He identified himself as Samuel Hazzard. Margaret Conway was at once both surprised and pleased. He wore the clothes of a gentleman; a dark summer suit of worsted wool and shoes that glistened black in the sunlight. Even though he was nearly a perfect stranger, she was glad someone was there to meet her. She knew he was the man mentioned in Claire's letter; the husband of the fasting doctor. Sam said he had taken two rooms at the Babington Hotel and that after a night of rest he would accompany her on a four-hour boat trip to Seattle. Once there, they would take a launch to Olalla.

"How are the girls?" Margaret asked, catching her breath, as they boarded the omnibus.

"Miss Dora is all right," Sam said, the warm smile of his greeting dissolving in the damp air. "But I will tell you of Miss Claire presently."

Margaret settled her round frame into a seat, her heart heavy with concern. Now Dora was doing better, and it was Claire who was enduring the worst of it. She worried if Claire's uterus had been giving her pains, or if she had suffered an attack of rheumatism as her sister had the year before.

"Miss Conway, I have something I must tell you," he said in a manner that would later haunt Margaret as unbecomingly and peculiarly casual. There was nothing in his tone to suggest that what would follow was no greater than a trivial disclosure between parties who had just met.

"Yes, sir?"

"Miss Claire has died, and Miss Dora is helplessly insane. I am sorry."

Claire dead? Sam Hazzard's words stung at her heart. An ambush. His message was so unexpected that for an instant she didn't allow herself the certainty that she heard Mr. Hazzard correctly. It could not be that dire. She had just received a letter from Claire. The girl was ill, but improving. The old nurse felt the world drifting to darkness, and she held tight to her seat. Her

heart pressed against her rib cage. *Dead? Insane?* Margaret
Conway knew something was wrong, but never in her life
would she have conceived a seriousness as grave as presented
en route to the hotel.

"It was an awful shock," Margaret later recollected. "I knew
nothing of the Hazzard Institute. I was unprepared for such a
terrible announcement."

All she could do was sit and cry. She was in such a state she
could not even ask any more questions. It was likely that was
just as well. After the shocking announcement, Sam Hazzard
buried his face in his work. He looked up only fleetingly, once
offering his handkerchief.

*JACK EATON WAS SIX YEARS OLD WHEN HE STARTED
first grade at the Fragaria School in 1932. He was the only
one in his class. He remained the sole member of his class
until he graduated. Fragaria was a tiny school with only
seven or eight pupils during those Depression era years. And
though there were few, all knew that the boogeyman in southern Kitsap County was not a man, after all. It was a woman
who lived down a long, dirt road in the place called
Starvation Heights.*

*More than sixty years later, Jack Eaton could still picture the
woman he only knew by a reputation forged of childhood
rumors. He never spoke to the fasting specialist.*

*"I never even got close enough to call her anything. I was
scared to death of her. We had heard wild tales about her. I
remember her real well. She had the most beautiful white hair
of anybody in the whole world. She wore it shoulder length. I
can see her now.*

*"We used to walk down the road to go down to old Charlie
Nelson's store—I was seven, eight years old—we'd go by the
Hazzard place, and if my mom wasn't with us, we'd run like the
devil to get by it. We were scared to death that old woman was
going to come out and get us. If she'd be walking up the road,
we just got off it and let her go by. Then we went on. I stayed
away from that lady.*

*"We heard there were stories that she had dead people in her
house and that whole place was buried with dead people that*

she killed. Maybe it was, I don't know. There was all kinds of stuff going on down there. It scared the hell out of me."

Jack Eaton has still never set foot on the property once owned by Linda and Sam Hazzard. Though he still lives barely a mile away and has been everywhere in Olalla, he could not imagine a time when he would visit the place.

EIGHT

THE STEAMER AIMED AT SEATTLE VOL
L-eyed over a choppiness which Margaret Conway conceded was
only a partial source of the monstrous sickness that had bored
through her knotted stomach. The tottering motion of the seawater and the heartache over Claire's sudden death had melded in a
way that made her lean slightly forward, grab ahold of the rail,
and prepare for the possibility that she would spew a trail of
vomit into the grey-blue of Puget Sound. She waited and
watched. Seals coughed out barks from jammed rookeries along
uneven basalt shorelines spattered white with colonies of barnacles. An eagle dived from the sky and grabbed a bit of flashing,
the silver of a salmon, from below the surface of the cold water.
Despite all that, nothing was lovely. Everything was dour.
Memories brought tears.

Sam Hazzard seemed oblivious to Margaret's anguished
state. He was as handsome as he was unconcerned, a self-
absorbed man who made no effort to console the heartbroken
Australian. Instead, Sam fidgeted with a small, perfectly
squared in its edges, stack of papers and a book he had brought
on board to fill the hours. He commented on his reading every
so often, and promised Miss Conway they would arrive in
Seattle shortly, then off to Olalla.

Margaret Conway had never felt so alone in all her life.

In Seattle, Sam led the shattered and dazed woman to the
offices of his wife. Margaret had never been to America before,
but she paid little attention to her new surroundings. Her mind
was filled with thoughts of Claire. Sam told her to wait there
while he met Dr. Hazzard on the wharf as she disembarked
from the launch from Olalla. Margaret numbly complied. In

some ways, she was thankful. The time alone would help her regain her composure. She sat and waited.

But as her eyes wandered over the doctor's desk, something caught her attention. She was uncertain what it was. What had she seen? She continued reviewing the contents of the room, wondering about the doctor's practice, just what her renowned fasting treatment actually entailed. Again, she returned her gaze to the great oak desk that stood in the room like a monolith. This time, what caught her eye was a blue leather writing pad. It seemed familiar. She stood and leaned forward to inspect it further.

It couldn't be.

But it was.

It was Claire's. It was positioned among the bric-a-brac of table fittings as if it belonged to the person who sat behind the desk. But it was Claire's. Margaret Conway was about to reach for it, when a loud voice cut through the room.

"Miss Conway, I am Linda Hazzard."

Startled, Margaret settled back into her chair. The Williamson girls' closest companion moved her lips to speak, but Dr. Hazzard apparently would have none of that. She had seized her office's quiet air and was not about to share it with anyone else. She did not offer condolences; she did not extend her hand in greeting. Later, Miss Conway would say she was very thankful that she did not touch the doctor's hands.

And in time, no matter how much would pass, she would never forget the words the doctor used or what she showed her.

"She began to tell me at once that the girls had come to her in a very bad state of health; in fact, when Claire came to her office—the first time she saw her—she was purple in the face and in a shocking state of health and she dropped into a chair and said, 'Mrs. Hazzard, I have come to you to be cured or to die.' "

As Dr. Hazzard further described the sisters' decline, Margaret fumbled for something on which to write. She wanted to make note of what was being told to her. Relatives would inquire, and she was in such a dizzy state she felt she might forget what was being said in that office in the Northern Bank and Trust Building.

"There was no hope for either one of them," she said, stopping for a moment as her eyes traced the thin line that was the direction of the Australian woman's gaze.

Margaret was studying the desk top once more.

"You can use this pad, it is Claire's."

"Yes, I know."

Though neither woman realized it at the time, the exchange was like a challenge of sorts. A war was about to be waged. And the good Lord willing, no prisoners would be taken.

Margaret ran her hand over the supple blue leather that bound the pages of the treasured little book. Why did the doctor have this writing pad? Why indeed?

Next, as if there could possibly be more upsetting revelations, the doctor told Margaret of the postmortem examination she had conducted on Claire's remains.

"Miss Williamson's liver was so hard I could not get a knife to penetrate it . . .

"The blood in one of the heart's valves was so dry it powdered in my fingers . . .

"Her intestines were so small, so infantile, you could not have passed a lead pencil into them . . .

"The only organ that was sound," the doctor concluded, as she straightened up her desk, "was her lungs."

As Margaret tried to grasp the meaning of each detail the doctor set before her, her mind seized with grief and horror. When Dr. Hazzard launched into a litany of her credentials, her patients being the "highest class of people," her success with those other doctors had written off, Margaret Conway barely listened. Her attention snapped into place when Linda Burfield extended a strange offer.

"Would you like to see Claire?"

"See her?" Margaret was confused.

"Yes, I have her beautifully embalmed."

Margaret was shocked and a little repulsed. The dead were not embalmed in England or Australia. Indeed, they were buried almost immediately after death. Margaret Conway was unaware any such thing was even possible. Claire had been dead for days, for weeks.

"I suppose," she muttered.

THE ROOM WAS TENEBROUS AND UNDENIABLY foreboding. A single beam of light cast a meager glow onto a casket partially draped in a dreary swirl of black crepe. Dr. Hazzard had led the Williamsons' nurse, a woman who had been fighting back tears since they first met, the First Avenue entrance to the undertaking parlor of Edgar Ray Butterworth & Sons. They had taken an elevator to the Blue Room on the fifth floor. And there they stood and looked at the body.

Dr. Hazzard remarked once more about the superb embalming, how lovely Claire looked in death.

"Despite her grave and fatal illness," she added.

Margaret did not look closely at first. She was too overcome with emotion. Finally, she pulled herself together and looked at the corpse laid in state in a white, plush casket.

It seemed a complete stranger. Margaret felt it was the result of the embalming process. The woman's hands did not look like Claire's. Her hair was a couple of shades fairer than Claire's. There were no grey strands at the temples. The forehead appeared to be somewhat similar, but even that was not certain. The only thing Margaret Conway recognized was the loose gown the body had been attired in.

It was indeed Claire's dress.

"It was Miss Claire's wish to be cremated," the doctor explained as they left to return to her office. "She desired to have her ashes buried at Olalla."

Margaret said nothing. This day had been too much. There was no need to refute what she felt couldn't be true. So much had happened. She wondered if Claire had been in her right mind when she made such a proclamation. She had never professed a belief in cremation. She preferred burial in Australian or English soil. Never in a land she did not know.

"Did you recognize her?" the doctor asked, as they walked up the street.

"No, not really. I suppose the forehead looked a little like hers," Margaret said.

COLVOS PASSAGE CUT A MILE-WIDE SWATH BE-tween the orchard-dotted hills of Vashon Island to the east and the steep and rugged banks of Kitsap County to the west. The contrast was noticeable. As the fleet of steamers made their stops, it was Vashon that showed its country wealth. Cove, Lisabuella, and other settlements along its shore were gateways to an island paradise. Farmers coming from the markets in Seattle returned to homesteads with pockets of money and stories to tell. The lumberjacks and fishermen who came ashore at Fragaria or Olalla had emptier pockets and fewer stories to tell. Alcohol sweetened their breaths and warmed cold fingers.

Margaret Conway could not have imagined a more horrific day than the one that, mercifully, would be passing into evening in a few hours. It was almost six. Soon, the launch would stop at Olalla, and she would find Dora and take charge of her case. The purported insanity, first alluded to by Claire herself in her letter, and by repeated and insensitive musings from Dr. Hazzard, surely was in error. Dora simply could not be insane. Margaret promised herself over and over, she would not lose Dora, too.

DOUGLAS FIRS WITH FIFTEEN-FOOT GIRTHS OF crinkled grey bark darkened the lane crawling over the hill to the Hazzard property and site of the sanitarium. Stumps taller than a man and wider than a railroad car punctuated a few of the clearings. Black smoke choked from a slash burn. Gloomy was a word Margaret would later ascribe to the place. Dark, lonely, isolated were other words that would come to mind when she mined her memory for a recollection of her first impressions of Olalla.

It was seven that evening when they arrived at the lane that led to the main house, which sat alone on the top of the hill. The house was shingled in cedar with an open veranda that wrapped around two sides. Trees were so close on the west side of the house they threatened to brush against the eaves with their branches. A single window indicated an upper story, or attic room. It was not fancy, but as Margaret reasoned, it did not need to be. It was merely a country home.

"Dora's cabin is over there," Dr. Hazzard announced. Her index finger was a stiff arrow pointing up the hill.

She motioned past a sturdy, little barn to a narrow cabin perched on an incline not far from the veranda. It was no bigger than a chicken house and looked to be built with the consideration a rancher might have for a small flock of white leghorns. One paneless window and a somewhat roughly fashioned plank door. It couldn't be a home for a person. Certainly not the sick; never the wretched, the insane. *Not Dora.* The cedar was old-growth, knot-free, and not yet faded by showers and sunshine to the silver tone that the very lazy or too busy firmly insist makes painting unnecessary.

"She moved in a couple of days ago," the doctor continued. "Before that she shared our home. Hurry along, she's been waiting for you all day."

Margaret nodded and without hesitation started up the slope on a path tracing the rim of a great fern- and bramble-covered ravine. She could hear the faint sound of water draining through the chasm. Closer to the cabin, she could see the figure of what appeared to be a child, a young girl, waiting by the door.

The girl's face was turned away from the sun as it dropped behind the shadowy green of a maple grove.

It wasn't a child, of course. It was Dorothea Williamson.

Trembling, Margaret pulled her beloved Dorie close to her body and held her. As she did, Dora turned her face just as the final flicker of sunlight evaporated into darkness.

Margaret would never forget what she saw. She would try to eliminate the sight from her mind over and over. At night, she would imagine an English wildflower field running for miles to the sea. She would envision kittens and lambs; a newborn baby. Anything lovely, precious. Anything that would help her forget the face she stared into that first night in Olalla. She would think of Dora as she was: her flawless skin, her blue-green eyes, and her beautiful auburn hair.

"It was ghastly, ghastly," she later explained of that first encounter, tears spilling down her face, overcome with the memory. "I was looking at a death's-head, a skull with skin drawn tightly over the bones. Over it all was a bluish tint."

She held Dorie tightly. Closely, so she could comfort her; closely, so she could hide her horror.

In a raspy, weak voice, the frail woman muttered the same words over and over. It was a plea for help; help that had come not an instant too soon for her.

But days too late for Claire.

"You have the power to take me away, haven't you?" she gasped in a desperate, plaintive manner. Her words brought a silent stream of tears from Margaret Conway, a woman who had sailed halfway around the world with the great hope that all would be well when she arrived, only to find Claire dressed out in a coffin and Dora a hideous skeleton on the verge of death.

Again, the raspy voice begged.

"You can take me? Tooddy, you can take me away? *Please*."

Margaret said she would do everything in her power to help her get well so they could leave. She turned her head from Dora's shoulder to the fresh air of the country. An odd smell permeated Dora's dress and Margaret could not stomach it. She did not consider it especially foul, but sort of a sweet, musky kind of stench that she associated with death. Though she never said so out loud, she later told others what she thought of it.

"I don't know why," she said later in her straightforward, simple manner. "I don't know whether death has a particular smell."

AND SO THEY SAT, THE NURSE AND THE GROWN woman she had taken care of since childhood. It was the two of them, and the world had gone darker than a cavern a hundred miles deep into the earth. Nothing would ever be so lovely, so frivolous and fancy as it had been. The laughter and excitement of plans made by inseparable sisters over tea at the Empress Hotel would seem so distant, so cherished, a memory.

First father, then sisters Ethel and Gertrude, then mother. And now Claire, just thirty-three. All gone. Though Dora had felt so very solitary in her misery, she knew she had Margaret. Tooddy would be with her always.

THE NIGHT OF MARGARET CONWAY'S ARRIVAL, the Hazzards graciously invited—*insisted*—the Williamson family nurse stay in their home while she visited at Olalla. Margaret could occupy the attic bedroom—the one in which Claire had drawn her last breath. It would not benefit Dora's treatment to have her old nurse by her side, doing for her what she should accomplish on her own. Margaret hated leaving Dora in that little cabin in the woods by herself. But the young woman seemed in agreement with the plan. Margaret found Dora's allegiance to the treatment and the fasting specialist disturbing. The treatment had killed Claire, for goodness sake. It had left Dora in a state very near death herself. And as Margaret understood the whole turn of events, it was Claire who had sought the advice and treatment of the fasting doctor—not Dora. Dora merely went along with the plan because her sister had wanted the treatment so very badly. It was Claire, after all, who had the tilted-back uterus. Dora's rheumatism had not been a problem for some time.

While grief continued to squeeze her chest to the point of breathlessness, she could not let Dora see her anguish. *Dora*. Even calling this grotesque creature by that name seemed inconceivable. She looked nothing like the girl that she had tended to since infancy. Margaret wanted a better look at Dora's gaunt body, hidden under the bunched folds of her loose-fitting dress.

"Dorie, let me see the all of you," Margaret asked quietly the morning after she came to Olalla.

"*No!*"

The answer was clipped and firm, nearly shockingly so in its abruptness. It was not like Dora to speak in such a manner.

Margaret moved closer. "What is it, dear? I want to help you."

"Nurse told me not to let you look upon my body. You would be horrified by my appearance. I am getting better, so there is no point in you looking on me and upsetting yourself over it. I am getting better daily."

Margaret was overwhelmed by Dora's change in attitude. When she first saw her on the cabin porch Dora had implored her to take her away. But no more. Only a day later, Dora asserted the bizarre fasting treatment was working—she was on the mend. It was such a startling about-face that it left Margaret Conway confused and worried. Was it because Dora had abdicated her will to Claire so many times as she adored and, even, coddled her, that her own desires were weak and tenuous to the point of incredible fragility? She knew the doctor had paid Dora a visit at the cabin and no doubt had persuaded her that all would be well. Dr. Hazzard was a clever woman. Perhaps she had clearly seen the roles the sisters had played?

Or maybe the worst of it was true? Dora, in fact, was insane.

Margaret Conway was ostensibly a servant who was hired only to do as she was told—perish the notion she should think for herself. She was not educated. She did not have money, though she had been around the Williamson fortune all her life, and had seen how the specter of wealth influenced those around the sisters. Her life was to serve. She had envisioned her role as a gardener tending the lovely flowers that were Dora and Claire. She was not to tell them how to grow, but only to ensure that the little rosebuds bloomed. None of what she had thought of herself was realistic in Olalla.

Margaret Conway resolved that no matter that Dora was her mistress, she would do the thinking for both of them. When the time was right, when Dora could survive the move, she would get them out of Olalla.

NINE

ANOTHER HAD BEEN THERE, HAD STOOD IN that very spot. Margaret Conway did not know it at the time that her rounded frame heaved in misery beside the white coffin holding the body Linda Burfield Hazzard steadfastly asserted was Claire's. Indeed, Margaret would later reason, there were a great many things which she had not been privy to when she first encountered Sam and Linda Hazzard. But Claire and Dora's uncle, John Herbert, had also made the journey to Seattle to view Claire's remains in the dank confines of the Blue Room at Butterworth & Sons. Mr. Herbert also had worries about what had truly happened on the forest-slathered slopes above Olalla Bay, at the place Dr. Hazzard referred to as her sanitarium at Wilderness Heights.

The worries came abruptly following the startling news of the death of his late sister's youngest surviving daughter.

Word came by cable a few minutes before noon on May 22, 1911.

> *Your niece Claire Williamson is dead.*
> *Would like you to come*
> *to Seattle to attend the funeral on Thursday.*
> *Dora is with me.*
> *—Dr. Linda Burfield Hazzard*

By three o'clock that Tuesday afternoon, John Herbert was seated on the express train headed north from his home of the past three years, Portland, Oregon. He could not imagine what tragic and sudden illness had befallen his niece. He had last heard from the girls on March 5, and all seemed fine. He also did not know what to conclude about the Seattle connection. Claire and Dora were supposed to be en route to Europe and Australia. Seattle? What had happened there to keep them from their plans? What, of course, more than anything, had caused Claire to die?

It was nightfall when he arrived in Seattle. Darkness had dropped like a lid over a box formed by the Cascade and Olympic Mountains as they jutted snowy and skyward. John Herbert found the Northern Bank and Trust Building, but Dr. Hazzard had left for the day. He checked into a hotel to watch the hands of the clock crawl in circles until morning. No sleep could be summoned that long, long night.

FOR A MOMENT, A SURGE OF ANGER DISPLACED the numbness of shock and grief. In the offices of the fasting specialist, as a nurse attended to another patient, Linda Burfield Hazzard leaned forward and explained that Claire had died on Saturday, May 19.

"I beg your pardon?" Mr. Herbert remarked with amplified incredulity. "Why wasn't I notified sooner than yesterday? Didn't you know the girls had an uncle in Portland? This is a great shock to me. I did not even know they were in this country, doctor. I hadn't known they were sick."

Dr. Hazzard let the man continue. She let him say what he needed and when he finished venting, she spoke. By this time, the nurse had left the patient and moved closer, joining the conversation.

"We did not know your address, Mr. Herbert," Dr. Hazzard said.

"You could not ascertain it? You could not ask Dora my address?"

"No, Mr. Herbert, we could not. The girls did not wish anybody to be informed of their treatment or whereabouts."

John Herbert was red-faced. He was mystified. Anger had been replaced by embarrassment. He hadn't meant to press so hard, and if in fact his nieces had not wanted their whereabouts known, then it was not Dr. Hazzard's fault. He didn't know if he believed everything that was being said, but he was doing his best to get through a difficult time.

"Did Claire know previous to her death that she was dying?"

"Yes, she did. She had known it about a week before. I told her I couldn't save her. Nothing could be done."

Dr. Hazzard told him that Claire had made all the necessary arrangements for handling her affairs. She had even transferred various funds to pay for her own funeral. She had also made the financial arrangements to pay her bill to the sanitarium, though the doctor made a point of stating that she did not know how much money Claire had arranged for her services.

"Why, doctor, under these circumstances, knowing my niece had an uncle in Portland who could be got in a very few hours . . . why didn't you send for me?"

"As I said, it was your nieces who made that decision."

John Herbert refused to believe it. It seemed unnatural and inhuman that he hadn't been notified prior to her death. It also hurt him. He wished he could have been there for his sister, who had never seen her daughters grow to maturity.

"What caused her to die?" he asked.

"I will show you." Linda Hazzard stood and led him through a door to an inner office. She explained she had executed Claire's postmortem exam and determined the cause of death. From a place out of view, the doctor lifted a bunched-up dingy white cloth that had been tied with a string to create a small pouch. She loosened the string and arranged its contents on a table.

"Mr. Herbert, these are Claire's organs. This is her stomach; this her liver; this her intestine . . ."

The man's eyelids slammed shut for a moment. He was not an anatomist. He did not know exactly what he was being shown. It was all so terrible, so ghastly. The objects were dark, wrinkled, and the apparent source of a stinky, though somewhat sweet odor.

The doctor went on, paying no attention to her caller's utter shock and disgust.

". . . You can see she was suffering . . . notice how shrunken, how very small each organ is . . ."

John Herbert looked up to see the nurse nod her head in agreement.

Dr. Hazzard stated that it was her opinion that powerful drugs administered when she was a child had been the culprit.

"She died of cirrhosis of the liver."

He was speechless. What more to say? What in God's name was going on? Words eluded him. The uncle observed the doctor poke the intestine with the sharp end of a pencil. He felt a pain in his own abdomen and finally found his voice to hastily change the subject.

"What treatment were the girls undergoing?"

"Mr. Herbert, I am a fasting specialist licensed by the state of Washington. Claire and Dora came to me to take the fasting cure—through the abstinence of food, the controlled abstinence."

"How is Dora?"

Dr. Hazzard's grey eyes met the man's worried stare with fierce directness.

"Dora is mentally incompetent, unable to care for herself or her business."

She put her fingers to her lips as if to stifle the shock. She promised to tell him more on the boat to Olalla. He was told to meet her with his bags at three that afternoon.

As a stream of passengers loaded aboard the *Virginia* under the shadow cast by the enormous clock tower at Colman Dock, the doctor and the uncle stood on the bow and discussed the matter at hand. There could not have been a more busy, more inappropriate place for such a discussion. Colman Dock was the center of all cross-Sound transportation. Hundreds used the boats that came and went at all hours of the day. People laughing. People running to avoid missing a particular launch. And there the doctor and the uncle stood in the midst of chaos and the scream of steam whistles while the most tragic of matters were broached. Mr. Herbert had to strain to hear everything being told to him.

Dora Williamson, the doctor stated, was so mentally incompetent, such a danger to her business affairs, she had been forbidden to write letters as well. Dr. Hazzard insisted Dora's mental state was so impaired that it would be nearly life-threatening for her to engage in anything of the kind. Too much of a strain. Too hard for her to handle the responsibility of such communications. Dr. Hazzard had full control of the matters at hand.

"Do not discuss business with her. It would be very dangerous to her to do so."

It was Linda Burfield Hazzard's experience that such cases often progress to the point of hopelessness. Dora had already crossed that line. Sadly, it was only a matter of time. All that could be done, was being done.

"I do not expect her to last much longer," she said, looking out across the Sound before returning her gaze to the sisters' uncle. Her words had cut through the din of the harbor and the whistle of the *Virginia* as it left its trail of steam and smoke heading toward points on Vashon Island and Kitsap County.

Dr. Hazzard explained how she was certain Dora's mental troubles had been brought about by the onset of menopause.

Mr. Herbert was unfamiliar with the term, and when the doctor explained the change of life, he pressed for no additional explanation. It was too delicate an area to make further inquiry.

As the two-hour journey over Puget Sound came to an end, the doctor told the uncle that his niece had wanted her remains cremated and her ashes buried outside a little house they had built and named for her.

"Dora," she added, "wants to stay at the sanitarium for the remainder of her life."

"UNCLE JACK?" A SOFT VOICE WITH THE LILTING accent of an Englishwoman called from the folds of a makeshift bed on the porch.

It was Dora. The sight of her sickened John Herbert, but the warm smile on his face conveyed deep feelings of love as he reached out to greet her. She stood and, as was his custom from the time they were small children, the uncle's great bear hug lifted her off the ground.

Her lightness stunned him. *So easy. Like a bundle of kindling.* He judged Dora to weigh no more than fifty pounds. He loosened his grip, fearing he would snap her bones like bunches of straws. As they spoke and the tears fell over Claire's death, John Herbert studied Dora's face and hands. The thought could not be purged from his consciousness.

Dora was as weak and thin as could be without being dead.

But she seemed lucid. It was true she was in great pain over her sister's death, but she seemed able to cope with it. Maybe the doctor was erring on the side of caution. Maybe she would be all right?

Dr. Hazzard hurried from the door and interrupted the reunion with a reminder Dora could take only so much excitement for one day. The dear girl needed her rest. After the funeral, she promised, she and her uncle would have more time together.

"Dora, keep your promise to me and go to sleep now."

"It seems so early."

"Now, now. Your promises are very important, are they not? Sleep, dear."

Dora curled into a ball and closed her eyes.

"*Sleep, dear*."

At seven the following morning, the Hazzards and Mr. Herbert left the shores of Kitsap County for the 1:30 P.M. services that would mark Claire Williamson's untimely passing from this world. The one who longed to go more than any who boarded that boat was left behind in restless sleep on the porch. Dora had been told that she was not in the condition to make the trip to Seattle. Her good-bye prayers for her sister would have to be offered from Wilderness Heights.

JOHN HERBERT WAS OVERWHELMED WITH SHOCK. The body in the funeral parlor did not resemble his sister's daughter, Claire. Not in the least. Given a moment to grasp composure, he whispered his concern to Dr. Hazzard as they stood next to the coffin and looked upon the corpse. He wondered if there had been a mix-up of some fantastic sort.

"This doesn't look like my niece," he said.

Dr. Hazzard looked at the girl's uncle and tilted her head. Sympathy poured from her eyes like a fountainhead.

"Oh, dear Mr. Herbert, it is Claire. It is your niece."

Long after the sun set on that day, and hundreds of days since it, John Herbert remembered the details of the dead woman he had seen at Butterworth & Sons. It wasn't Claire.

"The color of the hair was different from anything I had seen before, the length of the face was different, the condition of the face, cheeks, and hands was not in accordance with the condition as told to me by Mrs. Hazzard."

The body was not as emaciated as had been indicated. It was not anywhere near what he had seen of Dora's body. And *she* was *alive*.

That evening Sam and Linda gathered with Mr. Herbert in the dining room. Sam brandished a document of which he thought John should be made aware.

"Miss Claire wrote this," Sam said, sliding two sheets of paper across the dark walnut surface of the dining table. It was addressed to her relations and friends and dated April 23, 1911, Olalla, Washington.

For some time past both my sister, Dora, and I have realized that we were decidedly unwell and that immediate attention to the condition of health in which we found ourselves was necessary and imperative. As you know, our tendency in late years has been toward the natural methods of the preservation of health and the prevention and cure of disease. Knowing also the benefits that came as a result of experience at "Broadlands," we turned our minds to the fast and its accompaniments as the most rational application of the methods of nature, and after long correspondence we came to Seattle, arriving there on March 26th, last, and placed ourselves under the care of Dr. Linda Burfield Hazzard, who has made a specialty of the treatment of disease by fasting for the past fifteen years.

When we interviewed Dr. Hazzard she told us frankly that the fast is not a cure-all, but that barring the presence of organic defects it will benefit, and relieve and ultimately cure functional troubles. She made the fact plain to us that often times organic disease lurked in the system and was undiscoverable until the fast had been entered upon, and that no one could determine its presence or absence when internal defects existed. That there was danger of organic disease in my own case I had sometimes thought especially after thoroughly grasping the fact that the administration of drugs in infancy causes contractions and adhesions throughout the entire alimentary canal, and I had been given quantities of medicine in my younger days.

I find now that symptoms have developed in my case that

*are not favorable to encouraging and that there is a chance
of my not recovering, I am writing this statement to say that
both Dora and I entered on this course of treatment only
after thorough investigation, that we continued it voluntarily, and that if death occurs, I believe that it is inevitable
and that it would have come in any circumstances as the
result of organic disease that is incapable of repair.*

*Our care has been most considerate that I can imagine,
and Dr. Hazzard has brought us to her own home where
we have everything that sympathy and love could add. I
have taken care of the necessary business that will have to
be handled in the event that our fears are realized, and yet
I feel that I shall live to destroy this statement.*

*Asking that you will feel that all we have done has been
for the best, and that you will understand that, on the other
hand, everything that professional knowledge and womanly tenderness can suggest has been done for us, I am
content to leave the matter as it is.*

*I might add to the above, the fact that I have been under
the care of Mr. May of Russell Square, London, England
for nearly two years and was told by him that I could have
lived but a little time had I not come for treatment, since
the only organs that I possessed that were functioning
properly were my lungs and heart.*

The dead girl's uncle looked up from his reading to speak.

"Mr. Hazzard," he said, "this is typed and unsigned."

Sam explained at the first it had been partly written by Claire,
but she became too fatigued to continue drafting it in her own
hand. She dictated the remainder. He punched the keys on the
typewriter to create the document. He promised to look for the
original.

"It must be somewhere among my papers."

That night as he tossed under the thin blankets in the small
bed in the attic bedroom, the uncle's mind continued to ponder
the contents of the letter. A few aspects about it were unsettling
in ways that he could not fully appreciate. Beyond the fact that
it was unsigned, he began to doubt Claire had written any of it.
And if indeed the letter had been written three weeks before

Claire's death, why did the language exactly match the diagnosis that Dr. Hazzard would make at her postmortem? He recalled how as the doctor had spread open the cloth she conclusively announced the only normal organs Claire had were her lungs and heart. All others had become shrunken and contracted from the drugs doctors had employed when she was a child.

It seemed so incredible. How could Claire have known all of that before she died?

He also recalled how Dr. Hazzard had insisted Claire had known for a week or so that she was dying. Yet the letter indicated Claire had considered death a very real possibility as early as April 23.

The next morning, as he prepared to leave for the launch to Seattle, John Herbert inquired once more if the original had turned up.

Sam shrugged his shoulders slightly.

"No. I have not been able to find it. I will keep looking, though."

With a few hours before his train departed for Portland, Mr. Herbert made his way to the home of John Arthur. Dr. Hazzard had told him that Mr. Arthur was a friend of the girls as well as their attorney. He was handling all the necessary arrangements. John Arthur was gracious and kind to the uncle and insisted that all was being done in Dora's best interest.

EVEN FOR THE UNTRAINED, THERE WAS NO MIStaking that Dora was physically weak. But as far as the uncle could determine, Dora seemed *mentally* sound. He wondered if she had been distraught by her sister's death, or if there had been a mental defect that he had been oblivious to over the years. Perhaps such conditions had tainted more than one limb of the family tree.

He later recalled his youngest sister and a bout of nervous trouble that she had battled.

"Her nerves were weak, and at the time she was in that condition her child was put into the care of another sister for safekeeping, because my sister was not in a fit condition to look after the child."

He had never seen such tendencies in either of his nieces. As the train ran the tracks southward, he put the thoughts out of his mind as he drifted off to the peace and quiet of slumber. Despite his worry, Dora seemed to be in a place suited to the kind of convalescent care she needed to get better. He knew how much she adored nature, and he recalled her nearly childlike joy over seeing a fawn and its mother in the orchard. She would rest. She would get well.

But she would have to live without her sister. Like the curl of smoke from a candle, Claire was gone forever.

HOW TO FIGURE IT? Some looked the other way because they thought they didn't understand what the doctor was trying to do with her "great institution" in the woods of Olalla. Some didn't know what the word institution meant. All the talk about osteopathic manipulations and natural therapeutics was beyond their vocabulary, beyond their understanding. They were more concerned with tide and dinner tables.

Others shared a different, a more hardheaded view. They knew that whatever it was that was going on at the Hazzard sanitarium was simply none of their concern.

"Don't stick your nose in that woman's business, she's liable to slice it off!"

As an Olalla boy, Ed Fein also looked the other way. The reality was, he couldn't have done anything for the Williamson sisters, anyway. After all, he was born the same year the Hazzard affair would make world headlines.

"We used to see them sitting down, lying down, all along the road. Her patients. People going to the store, and they couldn't walk any farther. Most of them couldn't talk. That's a fact. I ain't kiddin' ya. Some days the road was full of them," he recalled many years later.

Ed never said a word to anyone who could stop what was happening, he was only a kid. Still, he was certain there were other victims.

"I know damn well that people didn't leave. It was impossible to live through the ways of that witch. Everybody talked about it. She starved people and got their money. So if you really want to make a deal of it, I suppose you'll find some skulls down there in that goddamn canyon."

TEN

GOD KNEW IT TOOK PLACE LIKE CLOCK-
work and so quite naturally folks stood around and watched.
Around eleven o'clock each morning, Dora Williamson's
unearthly stick figure staggered and tumbled down the root-
corkscrewed pathway that led from her little cabin to the main
house. To Margaret Conway's utter horror, the pathetic scene
was an event that was apparently repeated daily, like some
gruesome matinee. Down to the ground Dora would fall, on to
her hands and knees, lingering on the soil long enough to give
the viewers on the Hazzards' porch enough pause to be somewhat concerned. Did the tiny English lady have the strength to
get up once more?

She always managed somehow. Slowly she stood to wipe the
soil off her dress, smooth the wrinkles in the fabric, before
gamely carrying on. Though Dora Williamson was a shadow of
what she once had been, within her weakened grip she held
tightly to vestiges of her dignity and pride. She was a surgeon's
daughter. She was an heiress, educated in Europe. Her appearance, as repulsive as it was to the eyes of those who gaped at her
from the porch, was still of great importance. A little brush off
of the dirt, her head held as high as her strength allowed, and
again she would tumble to the earth.

Once Miss Conway ran from the porch to help. Dora bristled
with anger when her old nurse stooped to lift her from the path.

"I much prefer to do this on my own, Tooddy. I am not an
invalid! Now get on with yourself!"

Margaret never offered again.

And so it went each day on the wooded hillsides of Olalla.
Each morning, Sarah Robinson, a twenty-six-year-old nurse

hired from Seattle, set a kettle on the kitchen stove to warm the water. A lamp stove was set in the bathroom for warmth and a canvas cradle, similar to the one at the Buena Vista, was stretched across the great white bathtub. Positioned overhead, a graniteware pail was filled with warm water that flowed through several feet of tubing. The enemas were a necessity, for in time, it was the only way the patients were able to eliminate any bodily waste. It was as if their bodies had completely ceased functioning at their most basic levels.

After the procedure, Dora was given a sponge bath and a thorough rubbing of coconut oil.

Margaret Conway was not invited into the bathroom. More than two hours often passed before Dora would emerge from the treatment and her first meal of the day was served. A tiny cup of vegetable broth, a few peas, or a mashed tomato. Dora had an impossible time with the peas. Though they were cooked properly, she was unable to eat them. She was too weak to chew.

As seconds slipped into excruciating minutes, then five, sometimes ten, Dora struggled with a single pea as she tried to remove the skin with her fingernails.

Margaret loathed Dora's mealtime.

"She did not seem to know how to eat, and she was so cold, she wanted it so hot and she was crying all the time. Her meals were a terrifying object to see her trying to eat. She wanted the food and could not eat it and she cried over it and then it would get cold and then she wanted it hot again so it would be warmed up to practically the boiling point two or three times during that time she was taking that little quantity of food."

Throughout the course of the day, Dora's mouth dribbled like a chipped teapot. She could not expectorate, she could only wipe her mouth with her tiny twig fingers. Margaret kept a steady supply of freshly laundered Turkish towels and each day her beloved Dora required between twenty and thirty.

DORA WAS FRAIL, BUT SHE WAS NOT BLIND. While she only saw the doctor in the evenings and on weekends, the contact was far greater than her daily visits at the Buena Vista.

Linda Hazzard had one peculiarity that she took great pains

to hide. For such a powerful woman, the very idea that she could be bothered by anything struck Dora as ludicrous. But in time, the most curious aspect of the doctor's personality became evident.

It happened every night.

"Is the lamp on? Do you need the lamp on?" the doctor would call before stomping up the staircase in the evening. At first Dora thought the questions were out of concern for her patients. In time, she understood differently. Dr. Hazzard was afraid of the dark.

Nurse Sarah Robinson confirmed it.

"She has to sleep with a lamp going in her room. All night it has to burn."

THOUGH MISS ROBINSON HAD BEEN KIND, THERE was relief when she departed Olalla in the middle of June. Margaret saw her chance and insisted on taking charge of Dora and her case. Dr. Hazzard reluctantly agreed, provided her orders were followed to the absolute letter. Each morning before Dr. Hazzard left for the launch to Seattle, Margaret inquired about the day's menu. In time, Margaret wondered why she had bothered to ask. It was always the same. Two meals a day consisting of broth, water, a supposed serving of mashed vegetables.

It was clear Dora was wasting away. Margaret tried to persuade her to eat more than the two meals. She tried to get her to eat something before her morning enema and bath. But as weak as she was, Dora was willful. She was impressed with the idea that she must not consume more than two meals a day. The doctor talked about it so often that Dora had accepted it as her own belief.

It took some time, even some pleading, but Margaret finally persuaded Dora to drink a little fruit juice before her morning enema. Margaret also saw that the enema and sponge bath were given promptly at noon. Dinner was served promptly at half past five. Never again did Dora have to wait for her food, such as it was.

It was also around that time that Margaret finally got a close look at the ravages Dr. Hazzard's treatment had inflicted on

Dora's body. Smoky flames from a pair of table candles and the yellow light cast by a gas lantern dangling from a bent nail in the ceiling deepened the hollows of Dora's face and elongated the painfully visible bones of her fingers. Later, when Margaret described Dora in her gaunt nakedness, it was all the old nurse could do to keep her voice from splintering into a thousand tears. Her hands trembled as she spoke.

"There was practically no flesh at all. All her joints were quite sticking out beyond the limbs. The joints were great protuberates and the abdomen was a cavity sunk right in and appeared to rest on her backbone. Her spine protruded, and she could not sit down without being seated on a cushion without great pain."

WHEN ALONE, DORA WOULD TELL MARGARET little things about how it had been at the sanitarium the weeks before her arrival. She told Margaret how she and Claire had been out of their minds with hunger.

"For a time, all we could speak about was the food we were not allowed to have."

Dora had dreamed of raspberry jam and butter on hot, fresh brown bread. Even though the weakness that consumed her body had dulled her senses, Dora could almost taste the food of her dreams. She also wanted eggs and coffee. Claire didn't fantasize about breads or the like. She wanted something more substantial. Her mind fixed on a meal in which a knife and fork were required. She wanted to chew and then swallow. She wanted to feel food move down her throat and into her stomach.

Once she asked for chicken—though she had been a vegetarian for years.

Yet though they grew weaker, even the teacup-sized servings of broth brought delirious anticipation.

Later, one incident would remain etched in Dora's mind. Her thoughts drifted to one of the rare times she and Claire were allowed time together at Olalla. They lay next to each other on Claire's bed one spring afternoon. Though sun streamed through the window, for warmth they snuggled together like twin babies nested in a crib.

Miss Robinson called up the stairs that it was mealtime.

"Tomato broth's ready, Miss Claire! Miss Dora!"

Claire began to squirm excitedly, almost as a half-starved mongrel would as he raced for table scraps thrown from the kitchen window. In a way, Dora thought, Claire had been reduced to something like a dog.

Maybe she had as well? What did Claire see when she looked at her sister?

Claire told Dora to leave her at once. She was too embarrassed about the ravenous manner in which she consumed her meals. There was nothing refined, nothing dainty about it. It was the picture of a famished woman, dribbling broth down her face . . . licking her cup . . . sucking the spots where the hot liquid splashed on her dress . . . all to capture every precious drop.

"I cannot eat with you here, Dorie." Claire pushed at her older sister as Nurse Robinson's footsteps resonated up the stairwell. "I must be alone."

"All right," Dora said, managing the strength to move her sapling-thin limbs. "I will go way off now, and you shall have your food quickly."

Days later the Williamsons compiled a list of all the foods they wanted and took it to Dr. Hazzard.

"You will have *none* of this," she snapped as she scanned what would have passed for a reasonable shopping list for a vegetarian diet.

"No. No. No."

As if suddenly aware of the sharpness of her own voice, the doctor hastily mellowed. She reached for Claire's and Dora's bony hands and gave each a tender squeeze. Her lips forged a slight smile.

"Dears, I tell you, the broths are working! When I look in your eyes I see it so clearly."

MARGARET CONWAY CONSIDERED DR. HAZZARD'S diet about as good as feeding Dora a slow-acting poison. It would ultimately and undoubtedly lead to death—as she believed had been done to Claire. With the sanitarium's apparent henchwoman Nurse Sherman or even somewhat sympathetic Sarah Robinson gone, Margaret Conway knew it was her opportunity to take charge and make some changes in her own quiet way. She did not wish to antagonize Linda Hazzard. She felt it was crucial to appear as though she was following the regimen.

But, of course, she did not. Not on her life. Not on Dora's. When the others were out of view, Margaret pretended to follow the routine as outlined in her morning meetings with Linda. With no one watching, however, Margaret secretly spiked the broths with extras she felt would give Dora a little sustenance.

Lord, she was thin.

Margaret opened a can of Madrona-brand tomatoes, dumped them into a kettle, added a portion of water, and boiled it for a broth. That was to be all Dora was allowed—not the tomatoes, but the juice. When Margaret was certain no eyes were upon her, she added some rice or a little flour into the foaming red boil.

The girl needs food! She is starving, and she doesn't even realize it!

Though she hated to, she was forced by the doctor's iron-forged edict to double strain the mixture. Dora could not masticate and choked on the slightest sediment. Margaret hoped that the particles of rice or flour were small enough as to be unnoticed. Most of the time her change in recipe went over well.

But one time, when she put some cream into the broth, Dora gagged on it and became ill. For the length of the night, Margaret worried that Dr. Hazzard would discover what she had done. She thanked God the next morning that Dora was fine, and Dr. Hazzard was none the wiser. Even so, there would be no more cream in the broth.

On the rare occasion when Dr. Hazzard was home at meal-time, she would frequently sit with Dora and rave about the quality of her care, her food, her sanitarium in the making. Everything, according to the doctor, was first-rate. It didn't matter that the accommodations were a one-room cabin in the wilderness of Washington, or that her meals were made of heated canned goods. Linda Burfield Hazzard could suggest otherwise.

"Delicious, isn't it? So fresh from the vine."

"Oh yes, it is a most divine broth."

At first when she witnessed such exchanges between doctor and patient, Margaret found it impossible to believe her ears. She could not fathom why Dora, or anyone else for that matter, would agree with such obvious and outrageous lies. It seemed so ludicrous. But Linda Hazzard, it seemed, was the type of woman who could convince anyone about anything. She could bore her eyes into her listener and speak in an unfaltering, assured manner that demanded complete obedience.

Later, Margaret conceded that she, too, had fallen victim to the doctor's considerable powers of persuasion.

"She had such a will that when she placed food of an inferior quality on the table and told me it was the best, it immediately became in my eyes the best. Her great power over people lies in her tremendous will plus mental suggestion."

WHEN THE OPPORTUNITY PRESENTED ITSELF— and she could ask for it in a way that did not arouse suspicions—Margaret Conway moved into the cabin with Dora. The cabin could not have been more Spartan. A couple of beds, a bedstand, and a washbowl. Though summer weather had left the days warm, the evenings in the cabin, however, were still quite cool. Dr. Hazzard and her staff had helped themselves to the blankets and rugs that the Williamsons packed for their global travels.

"One must be fully prepared, particularly if the hotel is in some rustic outpost such as Portland," Claire had said so many months before she had fallen ill.

Margaret slept with the covering of a single sheet. She wound it around her body like a mummy. Her wool blanket was used to cover Dora, who never complained, but who surely needed the warmth more than she. Sometimes at night Margaret would remain awake thinking and listening to the wind as it blew a wake of heavy air from across Puget Sound. As Margaret weighed it, she and Dora, and the handful of other patients, really, were prisoners at the sanitarium. Suffering with weakened ill health, no telephone within five miles, Linda and

Sam and other family members watching always, there seemed no escape.

MARGARET CONWAY HAD TO CATCH HER BREATH. She could not believe it, but there on the top of a stack of papers arranged neatly in a little oak correspondence box on Sam Hazzard's desk was proof. In ordinary circumstances, Margaret was no snoop. But this was a different—a dire—circumstance. She couldn't stop her eyes from wandering where they shouldn't have as she pretended to search for a book to read to Dora. It was by chance, she told herself, that she saw the paper.

Dora, she discovered, had signed a power of attorney to Sam Hazzard. The single-page document had been drafted on May 27, 1911. Margaret put the paper into an apron pocket. With the full intention of getting to the bottom of what surely was a case of out-and-out theft, she went to the cabin.

"Dorie, tell me about this paper you signed," Margaret whispered as she shut the door.

Dora was propped up in bed and failing at her attempts to restring a necklace. Little white shells had sprinkled onto the dark blue blanket like stars at night. She looked up at the document with only the vaguest trace of recollection crossing her face.

"Did you realize what this was?" Margaret inquired, her voice rising to a level of worry that she seldom allowed herself.

Her tone frightened Dora, who set down her thread and sputtered out a response.

"I understood that it was for nothing else but to draw money from the bank in Vancouver."

Dora recalled how Sam Hazzard had told her that she was too ill to draw checks herself and that if he had a power of attorney, he could handle anything she wanted done. The sum in question was $583 drawn on the Canadian Bank of Commerce in Vancouver. It was money from the pension and trust.

"It seemed sensible, Tooddy. I said to Mr. Hazzard I should like to have five hundred dollars sent to Uncle Jose in Toronto. He told me he would see to that, and he promised to give the bank instructions to send it, and then the eighty-three dollars left I said if it was necessary for expenses he could draw it, but if not, I would rather it be left in the bank."

Dora started to cry when a canceled draft was put in front of her.

CANADIAN BANK OF COMMERCE
TRANSFER FIVE HUNDRED AND EIGHTY THREE
DOLLARS TO SAMUEL C. HAZZARD OR ORDER AND
CHARGE MY ACCOUNT.

"I never signed that," she said. "I asked him if he had sent the five hundred dollars to Uncle Jose, and he told me the bank had made a mistake and transferred it to his name in Seattle."

"Yes, a *mistake*," Margaret said. Her voice was rank with sarcasm.

"I asked him to alter it as quickly as he could and send it to Uncle."

She and Margaret wrote to the bank, but never, after two missives, did they receive an answer.

Later, Dora drew Margaret close and whispered how Sam had stalled her.

"Every time I saw him he always put me off. When he came to talk I inquired about everything because he offered to see about my land. He asked me if he could do anything in Vancouver, and he said he would see about my land and look into it. When he came back I wanted to inquire about it, but he always put me off and told me he would see about it later."

Margaret didn't say it, of course, but she thought it. She wondered how someone so educated as Dora could have been so naive about what was happening to her.

"There's no way you could have known," Margaret said. "These people are charlatans of the worst kind."

ELEVEN

FIRST THE BLUE LEATHER WRITING PORT-
folio, and now this. Margaret Conway could hardly contain her
shock. As the doctor sat before her to explain the seriousness of
Dora's mental weakness, she was brazenly attired in Claire's
dressing gown, a pongee kimono she had purchased in Hong
Kong on a previous voyage. If not for the magnitude of what
she was saying, then Margaret might have found it was impossible to comprehend any of it. She could not believe the utter
inappropriateness of such a stunt.

After Dr. Hazzard finished, Margaret went to Dora to ask her
about her sister's clothing. Dora had plenty to tell.

The Monday after Claire's death, Linda Hazzard opened the
dead woman's trunks. In an hour's time, the tiny bed where
Claire had died was spread with gowns and dresses, papers and
other personal effects. Dora could hear noise and laughter coming from the attic room, but was unable to discern what was
going on until Dr. Hazzard appeared.

Later, an outraged Margaret recalled what Dora had told
her.

"Mrs. Hazzard opened her trunks and tried on her evening
dresses and evening cloak, showing herself to Dora in the dead
girl's garments. She evidently appropriated whatever she fancied as only a few trifles were left in the trunks, and Mrs.
Hazzard suggested these be given to Mrs. Burfield, her sister-
in-law, who acted as a washerwoman. Mrs. Burfield got a few
things like shirt waists."

"MISS CONWAY!"
At half past ten one June evening, a harsh voice reverberated

up the stairway. It was the kind of abrupt noise that startles a sleepy person awake and forces them upright in an instant.

"I'm coming up!"

It was Dr. Hazzard.

Over the course of her stay at Olalla, Margaret Conway would experience many such intrusions, though she would never say she became *used* to them. Linda Hazzard made it a point of checking on the old nurse each night. Margaret supposed the doctor thought she would perceive it as being attentive, a gesture of hospitality. After a number of such bedside visits, Margaret began to feel that it was merely an attempt to appear that way. Dr. Hazzard had wished to ingratiate herself. She wanted control of everyone.

It could have been because the fasting specialist considered Margaret Conway a threat. Margaret had caught the doctor in a lie or two and had pressed her for a reconciliation of the truth of several matters. Dr. Hazzard was a woman who did not like to be pushed.

"I am so glad we have become friends, though the inevitable circumstances that brought you here have not been the happiest for you," Linda said during one of her visits.

"Yes, it has been very difficult."

"I have brought you something," she said, surrendering a little red book. Her fingers held open a page headed by the words "My Wishes."

Margaret recognized the volume instantly. It was Claire's personal diary.

"It has Claire's wishes in it. It was written for you, dear."

Trembling a little, Margaret squeezed at the red leather binding of the two-by-four-inch book. She had seen the diary so many times sitting on top of Claire's cluttered dressing table. Curiosity had never gotten the best of Margaret. She had never read any of it. Claire was such a straightforward girl, she doubted there could be any secrets among the book's pages.

"Thank you, Mrs. Hazzard. I am quite weary now."

"Aren't you going to read it?" Dr. Hazzard let her gold-framed readers slide down the bridge of her nose, allowing her to look over the rims. Her eyes were black pits of tar soaking up the yellow wash of the gaslight.

"I rather think I will look it over later," Margaret finally answered.

"Very well, but in the diary she left her most important instructions."

Margaret nodded and managed a slight smile, a reaction she meant to convey appreciation and warmth. Not worry. Not fear.

"It was kind of you to bring it to me," the old nurse said. "Good night."

Alone once more, Margaret flipped through the pages of the little book. She did not know if she was too tired or too distracted to read it. *Or too heartbroken.* Before putting it away, she glanced at an entry dated April 30, 1911.

> *I am improving rapidly and it would be hard not to do so amongst such wonderful love and care as one is surrounded by here, it fills my whole being with a glow of health and warmth and overwhelming love and gratitude.*
>
> *My sister has improved also but today her head has been weak again, however, I am deeply thankful on her account too as Dr. Hazzard says this fast will quite clear her head.*
>
> *We are both fascinated with this really beautiful country and air and look forward to our cabins later on.*
>
> *I am given such beautiful wild flowers by these kind friends here when they know how passionately fond of them I am and spend much of my time in my bedroom drinking in their beauties. The weather is perfect so we are out for hours. No words can express Dr. and Mr. Hazzards' kindness and thoughtfulness in every detail. It certainly is a great privilege to know them.*

"Oh, Claire, what happened?" Margaret said, almost as a prayer to herself. She couldn't look upon the pages any longer. She couldn't bear to glimpse the final days of her beloved Claire. She locked the diary in the small trunk she used as a bedside table and extinguished the light. The room went black.

MARGARET COULD WAIT NO LONGER. SHE SET aside the needlework with which she had occupied her hands, if not her mind, on the voyage on the *Marama*. It was the right time for the question that haunted her. It did not matter that Dora's body and heart were at once broken and weak. Those were physical problems Margaret felt could be temporarily set aside. It was the other concern that sank her heart like a stone. And now, more than anything, she knew after the first week, that Dora was no more insane than she was. And if she had ever been touched by insanity, it had been of the temporary kind, brought on by malnutrition and the loss of her sister. So that night, seven days after she stepped from the *Virginia* to the shores of Olalla, Margaret felt it was time to broach the most difficult subject she could imagine. She needed to know what, if anything at all, Dora knew about the night Claire passed from this world.

Dora broke down and sobbed when her old nurse finally asked.

"I would not ask you if I did not need to know. I loved Claire, as well," Margaret told her.

Dora knew that, of course. Over their many years together Margaret had become far more than a nurse, a governess, or a lady's maid. She was like a mother. Dora swallowed hard and promised to recall what she had tried to erase from her memory.

While Margaret held Dora's hand, she recalled it. All of it.

THOUGH THERE HAD BEEN NO WARNING IN Seattle, or in the first two weeks of their stay in Olalla, Dora had known for about a week before Claire's death that the end was near for her sister. The Sunday before her death, Dora asked Dr. Hazzard if Claire was out of danger. The doctor sadly shook her head. Not yet, she said.

Not yet.

As the days passed, there was little in the way of news on her sister's progress. Dora and Claire barely saw each other, so the only word they had of their health was the reports from the doctor or her nurses. The afternoon before Claire died, Dr. Hazzard came to Dora and asked if she would like to see her sister.

"She is so very ill, my dear."

Dora felt too weak to go, too weak to face the hideousness of the mirror that was her sister's face and body. When she saw Claire, on the few occasions since coming to Olalla, it was a great shock. A glance at her own hands, own face confirmed the very worst. Neither looked presentable.

Though it was the middle of May, and the days were quite warm, both wore gloves all day. Though they were cold and needed the warmth over their thin skin, they also were revolted by the sight of their own flesh.

Dora did not want to venture to the bed where her sister lay. Dr. Hazzard insisted on carrying her up the stairs.

"Your sister wants to see you alone," she said.

"I am afraid."

"It is all right. If just for a moment."

Dora assumed Dr. Hazzard would leave them, but she stayed, lingering in the doorway, watching Dora cradle her sister's head.

"I want to see Dora alone," Claire whispered for a second time, lifting her head slightly from the pillow before letting it fall heavily into the bowl that had formed in the cushion.

The sisters watched as Dr. Hazzard disappeared from view.

Later, the memory returning, Dora recalled what happened next.

"My sister looked at me as if she was going to tell me something. She looked very hard at me as if wondering if she would tell me; she did not tell it to me. I know she was going to tell me something, I know that for a fact because I could see so perfectly well, but she decided not to tell me, she felt I was not in a fit condition. I did not realize she was thinking I was insane at that time or I would have asked her to tell me. I was that stupid with weakness. I did not think of it."

Dora recalled kissing her sister sweetly and gently on her forehead. Claire closed her eyes and appeared to sleep; Dora staggered from her bedside.

IF DORA HAD NOT SEEN WHAT WAS TO COME, others had an unspoken inkling. Sarah Robinson was one of those who could have foretold the events at Olalla. Sarah was one of the dedicated, hardworking women who saw nursing as a profession of distinction. She had wanted nothing in life if not to be a nurse. She trained at the City Hospital four years before she met the Williamson sisters at the Buena Vista. On the evening of April 28, 1911, Sarah took the launch with Dr. Hazzard to Olalla. She had been hired to fill in for Nellie Sherman, who had been occupied with other matters and could no longer stay at the sanitarium.

Dr. Hazzard prepared Sarah for the worst. She said Claire was not expected to live.

"I have done everything I can for the girl. It is only a matter of time. Days really, possibly as long as a week."

Claire had been advised to inform her relatives and attend to her business affairs.

"She suffers from organic troubles with her liver and her stomach which cannot be remedied by the fast or any other treatment."

Dr. Hazzard's prognosis was surprising. The nurse knew Claire was very ill, but from what she had seen at the Buena Vista, she didn't expect her to die. As Sarah saw it, Dora and Claire were faddists who made a hobby of helping themselves to the latest trends of medicine—or the latest treatment concocted by "doctors" like Linda Burfield Hazzard. And though she never said anything, Sarah had personal knowledge that shaded her opinion of the fasting cure. It was a secret she held tightly. As the days passed, it became a personal torture.

The night Claire Williamson died was disarmingly quiet. Air poured through the window, cool, like running water through the cracked hull of a fishing boat. Sarah Robinson reached across the bed and pulled the portal shut. Who was it who kept opening the blessed window? The girl was freezing. Dora heard the nurse call down the stairway for more heated bricks. She was so very thankful for the warmth that radiated off bricks thirty-nine-year-old Frank Lionel Lillie, "Mother" Lillie's son, had procured from Markussen's Practical Horse Shoer and General Blacksmith on the little bay. Inside the great fireplace that ran from the floor to the pitch of the roof, the bricks lay in rows like soldiers sucking in the heat that would give the women upstairs what they needed to make it through one more night. Frank Lillie wrapped the hot bricks in a Tacoma newspaper and brought them to the sisters.

"This should warm your toes, ladies!"

Later that night—the exact time she could never be certain—Dora curled in a ball in the red-painted sitting room downstairs. She waited for her sister to wake up and tell her what was on her mind. Nurse Robinson came for Dora and said something, something so terrible, the exact words would elude her for the rest of her life. For the first time, she understood with perfect clarity. Claire was dying. She lunged for the stairs and collapsed in a dizzy and tearful heap.

Dr. Hazzard appeared from around the corner and carried her up the wooden steps. Claire was moving her tight, dry lips, trying to speak.

"It's me, Dorie," she said, moving to the bed.

As Claire began to speak, a voice, the harsh voice of another cut through the lanternlit room.

It was Dr. Hazzard.

"Dorie, is that a pet name? Oh, what a lovely name. How do you spell it?"

Dora turned from Claire to the doctor.

"D-O-R-I-E."

"I just adore that name. I should like to call you by that name. I do hope that will be all right with you . . ."

The doctor's words became a wall of noise between the two sisters. Dora tried to hear what her sister was saying, but was unable to make out her words. Her ear nearly pressed her sister's lips. She still could not hear anything, for the constant noise coming from the fasting specialist.

Dora began to cry.

Nurse Robinson could see what was happening. She put her hand on Claire's shoulder and asked her to speak more loudly.

"Dear, your sister is here. What is it?"

A faint reply was uttered.

"Say it louder, please," the nurse urged.

"No," Dora said between sobs. "No. I don't wish her to be forced. I would rather lose the message than press her to say it."

Dora Williamson's wishes did not matter. It was too late for that. Claire was far beyond the point of being able to say whatever it had been that she had so longed to tell her sister. She was far too weak.

"Would you like a treatment, Claire?" Dr. Hazzard didn't wait for a response before moving next to the bedside and slipping between the two sisters. She hammered her palm hard against Claire's stomach.

Claire let out a pathetic little cry. The noise sounded like one coming from a small child, not a grown woman. Her eyes rolled in their sockets before lining up in a dazed and bewildered fashion. She went unconscious. Dora kissed her sister tenderly on the forehead and began to wail in agony. A moment later, her wits about her, Dora fought for composure.

"Is it over?"

Linda Hazzard slowly nodded. Nothing passing for compassion crossed her face. Only the blank look of a woman preoccupied with other matters.

"Yes, it is all over," the fasting specialist finally said. "She has gone."

With that, Dr. Hazzard lifted Dora up, placing the young woman's upper torso over her shoulder, like an overgrown babe, and carried her downstairs to the bed she shared with her husband. She told Dora that she and Mr. Hazzard would sleep outside on the porch. A bedroom window opened above the place on the veranda where mattresses had been stacked. Dr. Hazzard swung it slightly ajar.

"For the lovely night air," she announced.

Dora Williamson could not sleep that night, lovely air or not. Her sister was gone and she was alone. *All alone.* There was no one left from her family. Why couldn't she be the one to die? Claire was younger, but in many ways, she was the stronger of the two. She knew what she wanted of life. Claire had only gone through the motions to make life better for her sister. All night, thoughts of childhood kept ricocheting about Dora's aching mind. She thought of Christmases, birthdays, holidays by the sea near Dover, the four wonderful months they had in Paris, the vacations in Switzerland. She thought of dolls, dresses, and baked apples and cream. A lifetime passed through her thoughts. And upstairs, all through the night, Dora could hear the movement of footsteps, the chafing of furniture sliding over uneven fir floors. She could hear the voices of the doctor and Miss Robinson.

Sleep had continued to elude Dora. Around 5 A.M., she felt she could not go on without some air. She needed fresh air.

More lovely night air. That will help.

The window was out of Dora's reach, so she slowly dragged a small bedside table to a place underneath it. How she was able to gather the strength to do it, she would never know. As Dora reached and pushed it fully open, Dr. Hazzard's dour face bobbed up startlingly from her bed below.

Dora let out a scream.

"Dora! What are you doing? I thought you were going to throw yourself out of the window. I am so afraid that you will throw yourself out!"

"I never thought such a thing." Dora caught her breath. She was scared, but even more so, bewildered by the doctor's remark.

"I was so worried, dear. With your mind so weak, you're in such a state, you know."

"I am perfectly clear. I am not in such a state to consider anything of the sort."

After she went back to bed, Dora could hear the doctor sigh as she told her husband that the patient was back in bed.

"She is all right, Sam. She hadn't tried to kill herself."

THE NEXT DAY WAS ENVELOPED IN A FOG. IT WAS the kind of day in which time moves achingly in its slowness. Dora Williamson took her internal bath in the morning, dribbled a couple of teaspoons of asparagus broth down her throat, and lay on a table while Dr. Hazzard worked her over with an osteopathic treatment. Little was said. Little could be said. Claire was gone. In her weakness, the world was spinning out of control. Dora wondered how it could have happened. *Why* it happened. She wished she could flip back the pages of the calendar to that fateful day in Victoria at the Empress Hotel when she and her sister read *Fasting for the Cure of Disease*. If only she hadn't gushed enthusiasm. If only she hadn't pointed out the advertisement.

Alone on the sanitarium porch, Dora watched the light steal away, over the forest that edged the ravine that had no name. It was early evening.

"Dora, I'm worried," Dr. Hazzard said, appearing from the darkness. "I had a patient who tried to throw herself over the gulch to commit suicide. Tell me, dear, you're not thinking the same, are you?"

Dr. Hazzard motioned toward the gulch. It was less than fifty feet away. Was the gaze an invitation or a warning? Dora was too weak from hunger, too wrought with grief, to know with any certitude.

"I don't think it is right for you to bring up such things," the frail woman finally answered. "Considering what I have been through . . . losing my dearie."

The doctor said nothing. It was her silence that provoked Dora's voice to rise.

"I have never had such a tendency to do something like that," she said, with a firmness she had not expected she still possessed. Dora turned her head and stared at the doctor.

"I do not think it is the right thing to mention to a person in my circumstances and in my condition, to mention the subject. I know it would not affect me because I am not given that way, but it does not seem to me the right thing under the circumstance, me lying here helpless and my sister just gone, to mention the subject of suicide to me."

Dr. Hazzard held her ground. She did not flinch at the suggestion. She wore the kind of sweet expression that Dora had seen when she and her sister first came to the doctor's office in Seattle. It was the practiced look of concern.

"Dear, you are insane, an imbecile. You will likely be an imbecile for life. It was Claire's wish that you should remain at Olalla and live here. We shall care for you always."

"I do not wish always to remain at Olalla, I wish to go to Australia—even if it had been Claire's wish that I should remain here. Claire respected the rights of the individual and she would not wish me to remain here against my will."

The doctor lifted Dora from her bed on the porch and held her like a mother holds a toddler, her head held high over her shoulder.

"It is time for a treatment, dear."

"Oh, yes, I suppose it is."

TWELVE

THE MAILBOX WAS LOCKED. IT WAS TRUE that uneasiness cloyed the air, but otherwise there had been little clue that the situation at Olalla had deteriorated to such a state to precipitate such a serious turnabout. Margaret Conway expected such a change would have warranted some notice. But there hadn't been any. And there it was—shining in the sun and alerting the patients at the sanitarium that a little bit of their freedom was gone with the light of day. It came in the form of a large brass lock on the mailbox by the Hazzards' front door. Margaret's face turned red with anger. She was accustomed to being able to access the box in the morning after the carrier left. She waited until Dr. Hazzard returned from Seattle and made an inquiry concerning the subject. It was mid-June.

"The lock is a bit inconvenient," Margaret said as the two women stood on the porch. The sun had passed over the trees. And though the air was warm and light still bathed the stump-studded pasture, there was a chill between the two women. It was the coolness borne of a festering distrust.

Dr. Hazzard fixed her grey eyes at the round little Australian.

"Sorry. An official order has been issued by the postmaster. All boxes in Olalla must be locked to protect the integrity of our mail. No exceptions."

"I see." Margaret assumed the doctor meant that there had been some thievery of the mails of late. She had no choice but to go along with the edict.

Over the course of the next few days and weeks, she waited for Sam or Linda or Rollin, any of the Hazzards, to distribute the mails in the afternoon or evenings. Margaret Conway was told to bring her outgoing letters by in the evening as well.

"I'll see it is sent out tomorrow," Sam promised, puffing a sugary sweet-smelling air from his lungs. *What was that scent?* Samuel Hazzard was such an ingratiating, suave, and mannered gentleman. Still, no matter what he said, almost from the very beginning, Margaret doubted his veracity.

After the lock went on, Margaret Conway's concern began to deepen. Why was it that no mail came for her or Dora? Was their mail getting out at all?

It had gone on for two weeks, maybe longer. In Olalla, time dragged. Quite by accident one day, Margaret Conway arrived at the door to the bungalow, just as the mail carrier stepped from the locked box.

"Anything for Dora or me today?"

"Why, yes. Two letters." He took a key from his pocket, opened the box and handed a surprised Margaret two envelopes.

"What is the reason for the order to lock all the boxes?"

"What order?"

"The official order to keep all mailboxes in Olalla secure, locked."

"There is no such order," he said.

The following morning, while Dora underwent another of those horrid treatments in the bathroom, Dr. Hazzard approached Margaret in the sunroom. As was her custom, she wore her white uniform, head to toe. With the sunlight to her back, Margaret could barely make out her face, the reflecting light was blinding.

In an instant, she knew she didn't have to see her face, to know the expression she wore. The thunderous voice cracked, angry and full of contempt.

"What do you mean by getting the mail? Do you realize that I have full responsibility over the mail to the institute? What would happen should you lose a letter. Do you know that it is my responsibility to see that all patients get their letters!"

The tirade ran its course. Margaret only apologized for worrying the doctor over the mail. It had not been her intent to cause Linda Hazzard concern of any kind.

"I shall not do it again," Margaret said, primly bowing her head as she played the role of the servant woman.

Agreeing with Dr. Hazzard was the only way to defuse her rage. It was elementary to Margaret Conway that Sam Hazzard had learned that technique long ago. He never raised his voice above hers—if such a feat were even possible. Linda Burfield Hazzard was not a woman to cross, ignore, or challenge. To risk any of that, Margaret thought, was to be in danger.

IT WAS AN AMERICAN TRADITION, A CELEBRA-tion marked by picnics and marble games in the dirt. Watermelon and platters of fried chicken would line outdoor tables. And, at night, fireworks brought from the Orient would cap off the festivities. It was the Fourth of July. Margaret had read about the festivities in a Seattle newspaper. She was surprised when Sam Hazzard told her that they would have a fire-works display of their own at Wilderness Heights.

Of course there would be no pies or chicken or games. Food like that and frivolous fun like that were not a part of the treatment. Nevertheless, when Margaret told Dora, the frail woman brightened considerably. The smile crossing her tightly stretched lips was unmistakable. When Margaret humored Dora by fixing her hair, she pretended not to notice the great patches that had fallen out. Margaret simply turned away and pulled clumps of hair from the brush before Dora could see.

"Is my hair growing thicker?" she asked.

"Yes, dear, but it will take some time. You have been through such a fright."

"Yes, in time, I should think I really will be myself once again."

Even in the summertime when the days are long, darkness comes when the sun eclipses the tree line of the hill. Dappled light scattered like confetti on the pasture and over the roof of the Hazzard home. Then, in an instant, the light was gone.

Sam and Linda Hazzard gathered the staff, neighbors, and the institute's very few patients to the clearing west of the house. For almost a half hour sparks fell from the sky and smoke thickened the warm night air. Dora could barely keep her head up to watch the spectacle, and Margaret could not lift her eyes from the faces of two women standing across from them.

The young women were swaying back and forth with eyes so dazed, Margaret doubted that they could see her. They were like Dora; gruesomely thin with hollow features and adorned in clothes that looked so loose they resembled little girls in their mother's garments.

When it was over, as Margaret assisted Dora up to return to the cabin, she felt a slight and tentative tap on her shoulder.

It was one of the emaciated women.

"Please, Miss Conway," she asked, tears oozing from her frightened and cavernous black eyes, "we are prisoners here. Take us when you go. Don't leave us here."

Her response did not come quickly. Margaret did not know what to say. She wanted to help the women, but she didn't see how she could get them out. Her first priority was getting Dora's strength up to the point where she could be removed from Olalla. Though she had great resolve to do so, she sometimes doubted that she would be able to bring her back to health.

She stammered out an answer, "I promise to do all I can."

SARAH ROBINSON RETURNED TO OLALLA ON July 18, 1911. She had not planned on coming back—ever. Yet she felt compelled to when she thought of the circumstances surrounding Claire's death. She had not wanted to attend another Williamson sister funeral. Dora needed the attention of a medical doctor. A real physician. Nurse Robinson knew she was in a delicate predicament. While Linda Burfield Hazzard was an outsider as far as the medical establishment was concerned, she was a powerful outsider. She could make Sarah's life miserable and her career a ruin. Good, private nursing jobs were hard enough to come by. Sarah had seen Dr. Hazzard speak in an utterly convincing manner against Esther Cameron, a hired girl who had worked little more than a week at the sanitarium before being dismissed. Essie, as the girl liked to be called, was only a teenager. More than likely she was too young to cope with such a serious case as the Williamsons'. Sarah didn't know. She doubted, however, the girl would ever be on another case. The fasting specialist had so thoroughly abased her abilities as a nurse, it was unthinkable she could return to work in Olalla, maybe even Seattle.

The nurse knew Dr. Hazzard's reach went far beyond Kitsap County. Miss Cameron had abruptly moved back to Portland, Oregon.

She was as direct as she could be, given her position. Miss Robinson offered to help Margaret Conway pull Turkish towels from the drying line. When Margaret said she could do it on her own, Miss Robinson insisted.

"I need the air," she said, carrying the basket to the line. White squares fluttered like flags in the breeze. The breeze and warm air had dried the towels in nearly an instant.

As the women talked from opposite sides of the line, Sarah lowered her voice.

"It is time for Miss Dora to leave."

Margaret stopped her folding. "Pardon, dear?" she said, the congenial smile melting from her face.

"You must get her out of here. Before it is too late for her, too. There are things about her treatment about which you know nothing."

Sarah Robinson had returned to the sanitarium to offer a warning. The nurse had struggled with her worries since she left Olalla. As the sunlight crinkled her eyes, it was time for her to reveal the secret she had held against her better judgment. She had not divulged such information before—and absolutely *never* to a patient. But she had no choice. The nurse had to make mention of her first brush with Linda Burfield Hazzard and her so-called fasting treatment. Her conscience nagged at her over and over: the stakes were too high.

"Keep folding, and listen to me," the younger nurse said. Her voice was low. She recalled what happened in the spring of 1910. At the eleventh hour, a doctor had summoned her to assist in the care for another Hazzard patient.

"It was the case of a man named Erdman. I never knew him. I only know the gossip and what I read in the papers. He starved to death."

Earl Edward Erdman was a civil engineer who came to Seattle after working on a project on the Columbia River. He had complained of indigestion, and after seeing several doctors and finding no relief, he called on Dr. Hazzard at her office in the Northern Bank and Trust Building. After three weeks of going without food, taking daily enemas, and being massaged by the fasting specialist, the twenty-four-year-old wasted away to a shrunken vessel of a young man. A friend who deplored the treatment ordered an ambulance to take him to the City Hospital. Doctors there determined an emergency blood transfusion was the young man's only prayer.

Sarah Robinson was on the case three days before he died. She would never forget the ravages of the treatment. She had never seen anything like it. His ribs could be counted through the hospital sheets clinging to his sweaty, rail-thin frame. His eyes sunk so deeply into his face, it was necessary to lean over the bed in an attempt to make eye contact. Though he was only a young man, he looked so very old. So very tired and weak. Earl Erdman died on the table before the transfusion could be made.

On March 29, 1910, letters twice the size of the *Seattle Daily Times* nameplate trumpeted the story:

WOMAN "M.D." KILLS ANOTHER PATIENT

Nothing could be done about the case. The county coroner announced that his hands were tied.

"It is one of those cases which come up frequently and points to the need of a more stringent law in regard to so-called doctors."

But in a shocking twist of fate, the next day, the doctor was headline news. But this time she had been vindicated:

DR. HAZZARD GETS LICENSE

Linda Burfield Hazzard had ridden the publicity wave before. Up and down. She had been the subject of court battle after battle. She had been both vilified and adored. As coincidence would have it, the day after the Erdman death made the news, the state board of medical examiners made the announcement that the fasting specialist was entitled to practice her controversial cure. Twenty-eight others were also granted licenses. Beyond the chiropractors and osteopaths, doctors practicing hot air therapy, mechanotherapy, and electrotherapeutics were given the belated stamp of state approval.

Miss Robinson glanced over her shoulder at the house. No one was watching. She passed Margaret a neatly folded copy of an article bearing the headline:

DR. HAZZARD GIVES HER SIDE OF CASE

The nurse had clipped it, she said, because she had cared for the patient, not because she held anything against the doctor.

Margaret Conway put the article in the basket and pretended to straighten the stack of towels. Instead, she read in silence.

> Mr. Erdman came to my office on February 4, 1910, and asked me to consult with him as to his physical condition. He said that he had suffered all his life from aggravated indigestion, that he had been for a long time using a stomach pump in order to relieve distressing pangs that occurred just after eating. He had been under medical treatment for years, and that just at the time that he was led to call upon me, his physician had advised an operation for appendicitis.
>
> Mr. Erdman weighed at the time 115 pounds, which for his height, five feet eleven inches, showed a marked deficiency . . .
>
> After consultation and deliberation he decided to begin treatment, which he did on the succeeding day. By far the great majority of my patients do not fast absolutely, and in Mr. Erdman's case a diet of liquids was ordered at once and gave him marked relief, so that within three days the symptoms that might have indicated appendicitis had entirely disappeared, and on February 14 he was able to climb four flights of stairs to my office.
>
> At no time did Mr. Erdman wholly abstain from food. He was continuously upon the liquid diet, which was omitted only when he himself refused it . . .
>
> When Mr. Erdman came to me I made no promises, and specifically stated to him that I could only do my best first to afford relief, then, if possible, direct a cure . . .
>
> Personally, I am constrained to say that the mercenary

side of the profession is not embodied in the motives that impel me to pursue it, except in so far as the laborer is worthy. But I feel that I have a principle to uphold, and a cause for which I shall die fighting . . .

Something in the final paragraph made Margaret stop her reading for a moment and look up to search her memory. The words seemed so familiar, it haunted her for a second.

. . . upon investigation it was discovered that the man's digestive organs were of infantile size . . .

Infantile size. It hit her. The recollection of that horrible day in Dr. Hazzard's back office. That was were she had heard the phrase *infantile size* for the first time. It was the term Linda Hazzard had used when referring to Claire's organs.

A coldness swept through her.

Sarah Robinson had nothing more to say about it. She had said too much already. She wanted Margaret fully to understand one key point. If Dr. Hazzard's treatments failed, she would not be held accountable. The state of Washington supported the doctor's right to practice the fast cure.

"You need to get Dora out of here before it is too late," she said, ending their clandestine meeting.

Margaret understood. So much had happened that she needed the support of someone she felt she could trust. Sarah Robinson had shown great kindness to Dora when she endured the nightmare of her sister's death.

After the fireworks, after the fiasco with the mail, after seeing Dr. Hazzard wear one of Claire Williamson's favorite hats as if it were her own, Margaret and Dora knew it was time to leave. Dora was stronger. Strong enough, Margaret reasoned, that she could survive the move out of the godforsaken sanitarium that had sucked so much of the life from her, nearly the marrow from her bones. She still looked the picture of a refugee from a plague or famine, but she was feeling better. She was also eating solid foods again.

Dora had written a second letter to a bank in British Columbia concerning her accounts. A reply had been overdue.

Considering the tight rein the Hazzards had over the daily mail, it worried both Margaret and Dora.

After Nurse Robinson left, Margaret Conway escalated the process she had begun after the two women sought her help after the fireworks display: she packed the Williamsons' trunks. Piece by piece, bit by bit, whatever the doctor and her staff hadn't appropriated found its way back to the family who had owned it all before Olalla.

"Dr. Hazzard, I think it would be a good time to collect Miss Claire's belongings in the presence of a third person. We are leaving your sanitarium tomorrow."

Linda Burfield Hazzard's face turned bloodred. Her eyes seethed.

"Dora is not going *anywhere*. It is not in her best interest for her to travel anywhere in the state that she is in."

"We are leaving, doctor."

"No. Dora is not. I have been appointed guardian, and she is not going anywhere. It is her sister's wish that she stay in her cabin!"

Margaret was completely mystified. She sought more information and the raging fasting specialist announced Kitsap County authorities had deemed Dora incompetent, making the fasting doctor in charge of all her personal and business affairs.

"I know nothing of this. I am taking Dora. I am taking Claire's things, and we are going on the next launch."

It was a stalemate. And if Linda Burfield Hazzard had doubted she would ever meet her match, the little Australian woman—a hired family nurse, no less—was up to the challenge.

Dr. Hazzard stomped away, but not without one final declaration.

"I have the laws of the United States of America on my side. We will see about you defying our country's sacred laws!"

Back in the cabin, Dora was equally shocked about the so-called guardianship. She had no clue such a step had been taken—and without her consent. How could it be?

RAIN WASHED THROUGH THE RAVINE BELOW THE house at Wilderness Heights. The weight of the wetness smashed sword ferns to the ground like yard-wide, lime-colored starfish. Droplets had skipped off the cedar-shingled roof of the cabin Margaret Conway and Dora Williamson called home. Sheltered under the narrowest of overhangs, Margaret watched the runoff fall into the gulch and collide at the bottom. Muddy animal tracks ran along the edge before disappearing through the seemingly impervious shield of saber-spiked black-berry vines.

"Dorie, I'm going now."

Dora nodded. The night before both agreed they could not escape the sanitarium without outside help. By the flicker of the stub of a candle, Margaret drafted a cable to be sent to John Herbert in Portland. The missive would implore the uncle to come to Olalla at once. There would be no room for misunder-standing the serious nature of the plea. It was a matter of life and death.

Margaret Conway trembled a bit as she kissed Dora on the forehead and told her to be safe, before slipping away toward the lane that sliced through the evergreens that held up a cloudy, blue-grey lid.

Just as she made her way to the orchard, she heard the Hazzards coming from the house. Rather, she *heard* Mrs. Hazzard. The woman's voice was louder than any man's, any politician's, or an actor's on a stage. The volume and tone of the doctor's voice caused panic to stir within the confines of Margaret's churning stomach. Linda was a good twenty paces ahead of her husband as they argued on their way to the launch. Margaret thought they would surely see her. Then there would be questions. There might even be more threats—or worse.

The frightened woman frantically scanned the roadside for a hiding place. Where to hide? A moss-dipped nurse log with a row of saplings nearly forming a hedge? No, not enough cover. A stump, the remains of a centuries-old red cedar, beckoned her. Inside the dry pleats of the silvery converged roots that formed the remnants of a once-great tree, she waited, heart pounding, until the Hazzards passed down the hillside out of view. She eased up on the root she had gripped to keep her knees from pressing into the wetness of the forest. And she waited until the hands of her timepiece assured her the launch had left Olalla. The Hazzards were gone.

After sending the cable at the store, Margaret hurried back to the cabin. The door was jammed shut. She pressed it with her hands and feet. *Harder*. It refused to budge.

"Dorie? Are you all right?"

No answer.

Margaret pounded as hard as she could without making a spectacle of herself.

"Dorie," she called, "Tooddy is back!"

In a moment, a sliding noise indicated something was being moved. It was a slow scraping on the wood floor.

Margaret Conway pushed her way inside. Dora Williamson, a woman so frightened at the prospect of being alone that she had barricaded the door with a chair, rested by the doorway on her hands and knees.

"I want to go home," she cried.

"We shall. I assure you, dear, help is on the way."

Words like Margaret's had once disappeared in a fog of memory that now was beginning to clear ever so slightly in Dora's mind.

"*. . . help is on the way . . .*"

It was about Claire not long before she died. Dora remembered how Claire had dragged herself to the edge of the stairs leading down from the attic room. Balled up in her hand, she clutched the crumpled remnants of a slip of paper.

"I am going for help, my dear sister," Claire had said. She lurched forward and grabbed for the stairway's handrail. "We must leave! We must go home!"

Dora did not respond as she watched the stranger that was her sister. She could not move to help her. She could only stare.

"I am going," Claire said, nearly in the way a petulant child announces she is running away from home. "I am going this time, I am!"

But Claire did not go then.

She did not go later.

A voice called from the main floor below.

"*What on earth is going on?*"

No answer.

"*Claire, back to bed!*"

Dr. Hazzard was home.

"Back to bed!"

LATER, WHEN MARGARET CONWAY SPOKE OF those grim weeks at Olalla, she did not miss the opportunity to exercise her undeniably advancing flair for the dramatic. No one interupted Miss Conway when she cleared her throat to speak; no one dared to miss a word. Necks stretched forward. Eyes bulged.

"It was all a nightmare," she said, "a period of horror on horror, of starving, emaciated bodies drawing themselves about, an inferno of fear and horror."

THIRTEEN

IT WAS ONE OF THOSE SWELTERING SUM-
mer days when the saffron light of the sun smacks the back of
the neck, causing baby-fine hairs to adhere to the skin and
armpits to rain down, staining the insides of shirtsleeves. On
July 19, 1911, the sky over Puget Sound was a seemingly flawless blue tarp. Its perfection was marred only by the white and
grey of incessantly screaming seagulls. Still clutching the
cabled cry for emergency help from Miss Conway, John
Herbert found his way from the train station to the offices of the
fasting specialist. Not far from Dora's uncle's thoughts were
the memories of their last encounter—the days after Claire's
sudden death.

It was quite apparent fortune had smiled on Linda Burfield
Hazzard. Since Mr. Herbert had seen her last, the fasting specialist had moved her practice to new offices in the same building as her apartment, suite 405, the Waldorf Hotel, Seventh
Avenue and Pike Street, Seattle. The fixtures were elegant, the
rooms more spacious and better lit than the Northern Bank and
Trust accommodations. Carpets thicker than a sable coat covered the expanses of planked flooring. The doctor had been
there so recently, new letterhead had yet to arrive from the
printery. Her secretary—the truth be known, Sam—typed neat
rows of asterisks over the old address.

The uncle announced he had come in response to a telegram
from Miss Conway. He, in fact, agreed with the family nurse
that a change was necessary.

"The best plan is to remove my niece at once," he said.

Linda's face betrayed no anger or surprise, though she surely
had no knowledge that Miss Conway had sent any messages for

anyone. *How could she*? She studied the man seated in front of her. The adversary at Olalla, the old nurse, had been joined by another.

"I see," she said. "You understand, I am Dora's guardian. I was *appointed* guardian because of her mental weakness. You must obtain my consent before anything can be done with regards to taking Dora anywhere."

Inwardly, John Herbert bristled at her words, but he kept his emotions in complete obscurity. The gall of the woman. Though her manner was professional, clinical, Dr. Hazzard had a way of conveying a sense of superiority that he found distasteful.

"I will consult my lawyer on the matter," she added, before excusing herself to administer to some patients.

MARGARET CONWAY WAS NEVER SO GLAD TO see anyone as she was when Dora's uncle arrived at Olalla. Though she had prayed for it, she doubted such quick response to her cables. She wondered and worried that Dr. Hazzard's tentacle reach went as far as the cable office at Nelson's Olalla store. She wasn't sure if the cables had been sent. It was not paranoia. It was, she felt, fully justified. After all, the only mail she and Dora had received came the day the postman opened the box with his key.

"Take us from here!" she pleaded.

John Herbert promised he would. When he asked what Miss Conway or Dora knew about the business of the guardianship, both women had little to offer. They had only barely learned of it themselves.

When nightfall came, it did so quietly, through the cedars and firs and into the windows of a house divided. Margaret and Dora huddled in the sunroom with John Herbert. Plans were whispered. The women were frightened that the doctor would keep them from leaving. John reminded his niece and her nurse that they were not prisoners. They had come to Olalla voluntarily and would be free to leave. When Dr. Hazzard's son, Rollin, lingered at the foot of the stairs, the three upstairs ceased their whispers. No one, no matter how incidental, was to be trusted.

When the doctor returned later, she brought with her an envelope addressed to Mr. Herbert. Linda Hazzard said she had been advised by her lawyer not to allow Dora to leave unless the account was settled—paid in full.

"I am only following his instructions," she said.

Inside the envelope, he found a billing statement. The amount was $2,000, with a balance of more than seven hundred still owed.

Mr. Herbert's face turned red, and his eyes popped.

"Madam, this is exorbitant! This statement shows no detail of expenses whatsoever."

"Listen," Linda fired back with an undisguised indignance, "I am a licensed specialist, and I am entitled to charge whatever I wish for my services. If I wanted, I could charge more. This is not exorbitant. I will have Sam put the details of the expenses and vouchers, and I will show you."

The uncle was not dull-minded. Nor was he inexperienced in the ways of the business world. He held a respectable position at a mill in Portland. Before that he had lived and worked in Honolulu, San Francisco, Los Angeles, and Santa Barbara. It was in Los Angeles that he took the surname of Herbert over D'Almeida. It seemed a better choice for the business world; more accurately, the *American* business world. And as he saw it, sitting there across from the fasting specialist, what Dr. Hazzard was engaging in was extortion, of a kind cruel beyond measure. There was no choice but to pay the fees in order to get Dora out of the sanitarium and into some care that might save her life.

Whiskered sanitarium helper Frank Lillie led Miss Conway and Dora from the house by lantern light, swinging shadows up the path to the cabin. Lillie said nothing; at least, later the two women could not recall if the hired hand, the sometime nurse, had even made small talk. Their minds were fully occupied. They had been admonished by Uncle John to be patient, and all would be worked out. The air was tepid and the night sky was a sable-trimmed hat dusted with diamonds. For the first time in a long while Margaret Conway let a hopeful smile cross her lips.

Back in the house, the negotiations continued. Dr. Hazzard and her husband insisting that the charges were warranted, and

Mr. Herbert fuming that they were extorting money from the vulnerable, the infirm—tantamount to a crime.

Linda tilted her head back and laughed at the idea. She was a doctor, for goodness sake. She had done everything for Dora to ensure that she grew back to healthy womanhood.

"I am a healer," she said.

As the hours passed, the impasse was finally resolved and a settlement was reached. John Herbert left the dining table with a newly typed accounting for Dora's signature. The monies would come from her bank accounts and she alone would have to agree to it. As Mr. Herbert reached for the door, Linda asked if he had seen Miss Claire's diary.

"She wanted me to have it, and I can't find it anywhere."

The comment seemed odd among the litany of things the woman and her husband had said in the dining room, so the uncle passed it on to the women in the cabin.

"She asked me about it today as well. I have it in my trunk," Margaret said.

"Do not give it to her. There must be some reason why she wants it."

"I'm not giving her anything. She's taken so much already."

Dora agreed with the settlement. She would have agreed with anything to leave Olalla.

When John returned to the house he handed the fasting specialist $250 in traveler's checks, a note payable in three months for another $250, added to the amount of $375.90 already credited to the account. It was done. The money bought freedom, and if not too late, a chance for life for Dora. Margaret and Dora could scarcely sleep that night in the cabin; John Herbert lay awake in the attic room. None could wait until daylight, until the morning launch to Tacoma.

The following morning, the subject of Dora's belongings was brought to the dining table. So much had been pilfered by the doctor and her staff that Dora merely wanted to recover her jewels and be done with it. Margaret and Uncle John sought a more inclusive settlement. To their great surprise, Dr. Hazzard agreed.

"All of Dora's things will be gathered for your departure," she promised, handing over an exquisite diamond-and-sapphire broach that had once belonged to Rosolida Williamson, the sisters' mother.

Sam typed up a receipt and Dora signed it.

> *Received from Dr. Linda Burfield Hazzard all personal effects, jewels, household goods, clothing, etc. the same being my property which has been had in storage by Dr. Hazzard or in her care at her home in Olalla, Wash. This constitutes a receipt in full for the above described property and includes the trunks and boxes in which it was packed.*

Margaret Conway did not disguise her disgust and distrust. She told Dora's uncle that she had grown to doubt nearly everything that the fasting specialist told her.

John Herbert continued to have doubts of his own when it came to Claire's body. He did not recognize what the doctor had shown him at the funeral home. It did not look like Claire Williamson at all. Miss Conway told him that she felt the same way.

"Why would the doctor show us a body that was not Claire's?"

Mr. Herbert did not answer. He didn't have to. Both the old nurse and the uncle knew at that moment that something terrible had happened to Claire, and while neither doubted she was dead, both knew the only possible reason for the subterfuge at Butterworth & Sons was to cloak the truth.

"I do believe Miss Claire was murdered by that evil woman," Margaret said tentatively, fixing her eyes on the man from Portland.

"As do I," he said.

Though the note written to Margaret had been considered a codicil to Claire's will, there was another, a more complete and official document. A pair of copies were kept in Sam Hazzard's file drawer, and as Dora and Margaret readied themselves for the trip to the launch from Olalla, the doctor's husband cheerfully presented the women with a copy. It was dated May 17, 1911, and had been witnessed by Sarah Robinson.

In most aspects this codicil was similar to the one hastily

written by Claire before leaving Seattle. It canceled a few annu-
ities—though it doubled a bequest to an old governess from
Wimbledon, England—but left the Hazzard Institute of Natural
Therapeutics the yearly sum of twenty-five pounds.

One thing promptly caught Margaret's attention when she
studied the document. The twenty-five-pound figure was written as a correction over a word that appeared to be "sixty."

It puzzled her for only a moment.

"The Hazzards must have been under the impression folks
might have considered them a bit on the greedy side."

Dora nearly laughed.

"Imagine those two being greedy!"

IF DR. HAZZARD HAD NOT MADE SUCH A TERRI-
ble fuss over it, Margaret might have delayed the reading of the
diary to her passage back to Australia, not the little excursion
across Puget Sound. She hadn't wanted to read it so soon. It
would be as though Claire had whispered from the grave to
remark on the terror of her last days. That, Margaret felt sure,
would be dreadfully painful. Yet it could not be avoided.
Almost instinctively, she turned to the final entry.

It was dated Friday, May 19. It was the day Claire
Williamson had died.

Her fingers trembled so much as she read, she set the book
flat on a table to still its vibrations.

MY WISHES
Doctor Hazzard shall have full charge of my remains
after death. The money I have provided for with her and
the balance shall be hers after all expenses have been
paid. The ashes to be buried in Olalla by my cabin.
My things shall remain with my cabin for life, an exact
list to be taken to be kept by Doctor Hazzard, to do with as
she wishes. I earnestly wish that Margrett will give to
Nellie a jewel for her kindness to me throughout my sick-
ness and to my sister. Also one to Miss Robinson. My dia-
monds shall go to Dr. Hazzard that Claire gave to me and
at my death shall go to Dora, if she is alive. She can never
be repaid for love and tenderness and care. For the peace

and comfort of little home I can never repay. My wish is,
call my cabbin, "Cabbin Claire."

Margaret Conway was somewhat disturbed and bewildered
by what she had read. She didn't quite know what, but something seemed false. Claire had misspelled Margaret's name and
the word cabin. Claire's spelling had always been impeccable.

Perhaps the illness caused Claire's mind to become feeble?

The handwriting was not up to Claire's usual precision, but
Margaret allowed the weakness of her impending death as jus-
tification for that.

Yet something else struck her as curious. The wording in one
sentence suggested that Claire hadn't written the entry at all.

My diamonds shall go to Dr. Hazzard that Claire gave
to me and at my death shall go to Dora, if she is alive.

She took the book to John Herbert.

"This is so peculiar," she said as she held it out for him to
read. "Claire would never have wanted a cremation. Never!
And this rubbish about giving jewels to Dr. Hazzard and her
nurses seems so very strange. It makes me wonder if Dr.
Hazzard or one of her staff wrote this for themselves."

The uncle studied the passage.

"No wonder Mrs. Hazzard should want this so badly. It
seems she forgot herself when she wrote it."

"My diamonds . . . that Claire gave to me . . ."

"It appears she was counting on Dora to die as well."

". . . to Dora, if she is alive."

WITH UNCLE JOHN AND MARGARET BY HER SIDE,
Dora Williamson was carried onto a little steamer the morning
of July 22. It had been fifty-two days since Margaret's arrival at
Olalla, the longest fifty-two days the nurse had known. She
thanked God that the moment had come. For Dora, it had been
a week short of a hundred days at the sanitarium. A short time,
really, when it came to changing so much of her life.

As had been the case in Seattle the morning when Dora and
Claire were loaded on the launch for Olalla, there were onlook-

ers to see them off at the dock. They were country people, a little grimy about the collars, teeth gapped by neglect and hair in the simple and plain style of folks from the hinterlands. They were affable faces nevertheless.

Dora, who still did not comprehend the grotesqueness of her emaciated features, smiled at one of the young boys. Her smile invited comment.

"Ma!" the boy exclaimed, a repulsed and frightened look on his face. "Look how skinny she is!"

"Yes," answered a woman standing near her inquisitive son. "That's one of those English girls from Starvation Heights."

Dora pulled on Margaret's hand. The nurse had heard the phrase, too.

"Starvation Heights? Is that what they call that terrible place?" Dora whispered, her voice crackly and dry from the breeze in the air.

The grim-faced mother looked at her son and whispered, "Yes, dear, it is."

Dora stared blankly as her thoughts took over. Each bit of her memory was like a fog-cloistered island, so fleeting in its isolation. Her mind drifted back to snare recollections that seemed nearly a story told by someone else. She remembered the hot, hot water and steam rising from the washtub by the fireplace at Olalla. Her sister had once told her she had fainted from bathwater so hot, even the nurse had complained about it.

For a second, Dora would allow herself to wish for the sweet comfort of a fitted tub with its smooth, even porcelain surfaces. Then blackness pulled over her as she was set into the water.

The vapor veil thickened the air. Her breathing labored.

And the big hands would hold her, run water down her naked back. A graniteware ladle poured hotness all over her. The hands were rough, fingernails split and dirty. The breath of the nurse was smoky and sour.

Dora wakened to see, but she could not speak.

It was not Miss Sherman. It was Frank Lillie. And his hands were upon her again.

"DORA? DORA!" MARGARET NUDGED THE YOUNG, supine woman as the steamer etched a white line through the choppy blue of Colvos Passage as it headed southward to Commencement Bay and Tacoma. Dora's eyes were open, but they did not have the sharpness, the visage of concentration, that indicated she was looking at anything. The blank gaze scared the nurse.

"Dora! Are you all right?"

"Oh, yes . . . I was only remembering . . . I am fine now."

"Look, dear, look at the snow on the mountain! Imagine, this time of year!"

For a second, Dora lifted her head slightly from the pillow and smiled.

"Yes, Tooddy, I see it."

II

Linda & Samuel

I intend to go right on giving my treatments to these poor, afflicted people that come to me. What else can I do? They all leave, thanking me for bringing them back to health.

—LINDA BURFIELD HAZZARD

I feel fully convinced that nothing but unhappiness can result in anything of a business or personal relation between us ...

—SAMUEL HAZZARD
IN A 1903 LETTER TO LINDA

FOURTEEN

EVEN TO THE EYES OF A WOMAN WHO HAD toured Switzerland and tobogganed the snowy chutes of the Alps, the vision of Mount Tacoma looming over the city was breathtaking in its commanding beauty. Though the mountain's contours were frozen custard-round and smooth—rather than the jagged rocky outcroppings of the Alps—it was nevertheless an extraordinary and supremely powerful presence. Its snow-covered dome stood like a white thumb poking out the entire length of the massive sawtooth of the Cascade Range. Even in her weakness, Dora marveled aloud at the mountain's violet-and-blue grandeur. Of course, she had seen Mount Tacoma from across the little bay at Olalla, but it had never looked so impressive as it did with smoke-sputtering Tacoma nestled at its base. To Dora's eyes, it looked as though the mountain appeared to float above the clouds.

And by 1911, Tacoma, Washington, was as it always would be—the Northwest's favorite bridesmaid when it came to cities. When Seattle, the great rival to the north, captured the railroad terminus it became the favored destination of the region. It was preferred by investors, folks looking for work, even those on holiday. Quite sadly, Tacoma's boosters had started the process of realization that theirs was a second-choice city.

For Dora, however, it was a great sanctuary. It was a city of hope. And, she prayed over and over, a city for vengeance.

CERTAINLY EVERYONE KNEW IT WAS IMPOLITE— even rude—to stare. Yet no one in the lobby of the Tacoma Hotel could quite help themselves from fixing their attention and craning their necks. No one had laid eyes on a woman who

looked like the living remains that passed as Evelyn Dorothea
Williamson. Her dress hung on a frame of bones, leaving her
sleeves looking like loose yardage draped over curtain poles.
Though much of her jewelry had been left behind, a ring with a
dark, heavy stone swiveled around her stoutest finger with
every subtle movement of the five-pronged rake that was her
hand. And Dora's face, of course, was a horror of its own. She
was a stick-necked apple doll with eyes far livelier than they
had a right to be.

Feeling better than she had in weeks, Dora weighed all of
sixty pounds. She, her nurse, and her uncle waited adjacent to a
black iron stand dripping with the green feathers of Boston
ferns. They waited for the man they had been assured would see
justice was done. More than anything, it was a great comfort to
know that in a country of strangers, the man coming to the hotel
was one of them.

AT JUST THIRTY SIX, LUCIAN AGASSIZ CUT AN
imposing figure. Round as a biscuit with a doughy face flagged
by a moustache the size and shape of a boomerang, the British
vice-consul navigated the lobby of the Tacoma Hotel in a manner that was quietly authoritative. He did not have need for an
entourage. He did not see the need to puff up his beefy frame
like a pigeon waging a battle against the cold—as other powerful men in the service of His Majesty. He saw it differently. He
was, after all, in the service of the king of a country far greater
than America. After all, he reasoned, while American presi-
dents come and go in the space of four-year terms, a king is the
axis of a monarchy that has stood proudly for centuries.

Born in Snareston, Leicestershire, England, and a scholar at
St. Edward's College, Oxford University, young Agassiz
entered the consular service just after graduation. His first post
was taken at Tacoma on April 15, 1906. By then, he was married to a lovely woman from a fine, old British Columbia family. Ena Agassiz bore her husband two daughters.

Agassiz's attire was a neat, dark grey suit. That day at the
Tacoma Hotel, it bore no traces of the pet hair that usually
offered observers the telltale clue that the British vice-consul
was a man who adored his orange tabby cat.

Introductions were made, John Herbert identifying himself before tenderly touching Dora's shoulder and introducing her to the vice-consul.

Agassiz smiled, trying to suppress his horror at what he saw. He turned to Margaret Conway and thanked her.

"I understand it is because of your efforts, Miss Conway, that Miss Williamson survived at all. I commend you for your courage."

Margaret acknowledged his kind remark with a warm smile. She had never been in a position like this before. Though she was by far more intelligent than those in the class above her would likely give credit, she had not been one to voice an opinion or to ask a question of a professional man or woman. In her state of shock after Claire's death—and before she figured what had been going on under the guise of "treatment"—she had deferred to Sam and Linda Hazzard. She had bided her time and plotted the escape from Olalla. In doing so, Margaret had tapped a kind of mental strength that had likely been inside her always, but circumstances had never called for it or compelled her to use it. Olalla had changed her. Margaret Conway would defer to no one ever again.

John Herbert had no choice but to let Miss Conway take up the charge. She had seen so much more than he. Dora was also quiet. Her eyelids were heavy, and though she protested that she was quite well, it was plain that she was exhausted.

Agassiz was so aghast he nearly bruised his jaw against the tabletop. He was appalled by the very idea of two of His Majesty's subjects held captive by some charlatan doctor in the dark forests of Kitsap County. Not only that, one of the two had died.

"Murdered," Margaret said loudly enough for others to hear. "I say, Mr. Agassiz, she was *murdered* by Mrs. Hazzard."

And while they had won over the man seated across from them, the nurse and the uncle continued their litany. It was as if they needed to drain the horror of Olalla from their minds. Nothing could be held inside any longer. Dr. Hazzard had imprisoned the sisters. She had stolen their money. She had forged and cashed personal checks. She had swindled them out of their jewels—family heirlooms, at that.

"She is a devious monster," Margaret concluded. "The guardianship is another of her crimes. She managed to gain control of the girls' fortune, and I am certain she did so solely to appropriate their funds."

Margaret related all she could remember. On top of her mind was Dr. Hazzard's tirade on July 18. She recalled the doctor's icy stare when she announced Dora could not leave Olalla.

"She is under my care! She is my ward! She must stay as her sister wished!"

While the threat was at first devastating, it had only served to further strengthen Margaret's resolve to flee Olalla. It was stay and die, or leave and live.

"Mrs. Hazzard declared that she had the law of the United States on her side. She ended her mental tempest with the now significant declaration, 'Well, wherever you take Dora, she won't live long.' "

As Margaret recalled the turning point, she could not forget the others at the sanitarium—the two young women who had begged her to take them as the sparks from the fireworks cascaded over the meadow on the Fourth of July, a middle-aged man from Seattle, a young girl who had come to learn nursing at the sanitarium, the cook, whose child was undergoing Dr. Hazzard's treatment—all who had escaped.

"All fled as they would run from a house of death," Margaret said as she stared unflinchingly at the vice-consul. Who could doubt her grave assessment? Agassiz could not. The grey-haired nurse was a savior of sorts. This simple woman had liberated Starvation Heights.

Agassiz promised to make haste and bring immediate notice to the authorities in Kitsap County.

"After they are notified of this injustice, I imagine they will take swift and immediate action. The doctor will be held accountable for her atrocious crimes!"

The vice-consul left the Tacoma Hotel with writing pad crammed with notes. He knew the first step was to remove Linda Burfield Hazzard's name from Dora's guardianship papers. Then, he would see that she was no longer the executor of Claire's estate. Within an hour of hearing the sordid tale, Agassiz had made his way to a law office in the Perkins

Building, where he enlisted the services of an attorney named Frank Kelley. Immediately the two men were on their way to Seattle to see what could be done in the starvation case.

Frank Kelley was a natural choice for help in such a grave matter. The vice-consul had worked with the young Tacoma attorney a year and a half before. When the Seattle agent for Lloyds of London died, Agassiz was appointed temporary agent for the company. Urgent word came to his attention that another Seattle man had been issuing fraudulent policies.

After a court appearance, Kelley and Agassiz had an injunction against the phony insurance agent. Their swift action made mention in the papers.

AFTER THE TROUBLEMAKERS LEFT HER OLALLA sanitarium, Linda Hazzard could finally release the volcanic anger hidden behind the forced smile of control. She blamed Margaret Conway for all that happened. Though Dr. Hazzard never said so, the truth was that if Miss Conway had not set foot on the shores of Kitsap County, Dora would almost certainly have joined her sister in death. Instead, the fasting specialist focused her ire on the fact that all her work had been cast in an evil light by the woman who sailed on the *Marama* to rescue the sisters.

"That awful servant! Look at the trouble the stupid and meddlesome woman has needlessly stirred up!"

Those who knew her—her husband, her son, her staff—had seen the doctor's stony wall of reserve break down before. They recognized that for all her brilliance, for all of her scientific knowledge, Linda Burfield Hazzard was a woman who could not fully control her anger when confronted with such accusations. Some knew what had happened in her life years before, indeed, some had been on the receiving end of those tempests. Linda Hazzard had underestimated Dora and her old family nurse. She stomped around the bungalow, cursing the trouble that she knew would visit her.

"Certainly, I will rise above this," she announced, once resolve took hold. "I have done so before."

Over the next several days, as Dr. Hazzard learned the depth of the battle lines that had been drawn in Tacoma, she carved her own position in stone. When it became clear that attorney John Arthur was likely a witness, the fasting specialist hired Day Karr, a thirty-two-year-old Kansas-born and -educated lawyer. Karr and his partner, George W. Gregory, had opened their own law offices in a suite at the American Bank Building in Seattle just five years before and had done quite well for themselves. Billings were up, and their reputation was growing. The partners were only too pleased to represent the maligned fasting doctor in what by all indications was surely to be an important case.

Dr. Hazzard also assembled the men and women who had been involved in the care of the Williamsons. All of them could be counted on. All of them were either relations or had experienced the benefits of Linda Hazzard's bank account. Nellie Sherman, Frank Lillie, John Karcher, lawyer John Arthur, and of course, husband Sam and son Rollin gathered at Olalla. The circle of supporters was a fortress. At its center was the woman with all the answers.

Of the money, the jewels, the assets she had collected from the Williamson sisters, Dr. Hazzard began a refrain that would become a kind of mantra. Over and over she would tell those close to her and those who cast doubt upon her story:

"The money? It was a gift. Miss Claire wanted me to have it. She *begged* me to take it!"

As far as Dora's guardianship was concerned, it was Claire who had first seen the ravages of insanity cripple her sister's mind; she suggested repeatedly that Dr. Hazzard take a power of attorney and care for Dora for her remaining days.

Dr. Hazzard had done nothing illegal, nothing wrong.

"Beyond reproach, I am," she said.

THE FINAL DAYS OF JULY WERE CLOSED OUT with a hearing within the walls of the brooding redbrick facade of the Arlington Hotel, at the corner of First Avenue and University, in Seattle. While the jurisdiction issues were sorted out, the hearing over Dora's guardianship was presided over by a visiting judge, Island County's Lester Still. Even as a young man, Judge Still had garnered a well-deserved reputation for fairness. Neither side could be displeased that he would hear the case. But through the days of the guardianship hearing, Judge

Still would see his patience tested by the woman doctor from Kitsap County. Over and over. Again, again. Linda Hazzard confounded the court when she announced she had forgotten her records at home in Olalla. She could not recall if certain figures were reflected in her books or not.

If she hadn't an inkling before she met him on the witness stand, Linda Hazzard was a quick enough study to know the attorney for the Williamson girls would be a formidable opponent.

"Where have you studied medicine?" Frank Kelley asked, fixing a sarcastic gaze upon the woman in the witness chair.

"At two osteopathic institutions, but it would be useless to name them, for they have both ceased to exist."

"Did you prove fatal to both?"

Linda Hazzard offered no verbal response. A toss of her head was her statement.

Whenever a discrepancy was pointed out in the paperwork Dora's attorney had put forth before the court, Dr. Hazzard had a sharp retort.

"My husband wrote that letter. He must have misdated it. He's liable to make mistakes like that."

And while her circle of supporters was strong, over the course of the hearing, one who could no longer be counted on for support was John Arthur. He admitted to the court that he had never been the attorney for the Williamson girls. Further, the lawyer denied he had urged the doctor to take charge of all of Dora's affairs under a guardianship.

Linda Hazzard looked on, appearing confused. Perhaps there had been a great misunderstanding. She shook her head as the witness stepped down.

So sorry about the confusion . . . such a pity.

After it was all said and done, the guardianship was voided and the court ordered Dr. Hazzard to return $973 to Dora Williamson, but allowed the doctor to keep $597 for medical services and expenses. Despite ruling Dr. Hazzard could retain some of her fees, Judge Still left no doubt about who was to blame for the tragedy at Starvation Heights.

"Think of this weak, emaciated young woman lying on her back in the woods of Kitsap County, who, according to Dr.

Hazzard showed signs of insanity, and then think of her doctor sitting by her bedside and telling her tales of that awful gulch close by and suggesting suicide to the mind of the girl. Dr. Hazzard may not have realized what she was doing, but such a person is a dangerous person to administer to women and children."

Agassiz and Kelley had hoped that the door to criminal charges would be opened with the resolution of the guardianship matter. And it was . . . it was swung wide open by the remarks of the presiding judge.

". . . there is something which seems to me 'unholy' about the relations of this woman and her patients. All the money this girl and her sister had was practically in the hands of Dr. Hazzard, and this does not look right to a court of equity."

Dr. Hazzard took the defeat with characteristic aplomb. None of it was her fault. It was a vendetta born of two men and their lust for attention.

She dismissed Agassiz and Kelley as a person would flick an ant off a picnic plate. Quickly. Without even looking in their direction. They were insignificant players in a drama in which she was the star.

"Kelley has discovered a way to become famous. It is the only way he could ever get into the limelight. It is the same way with the British vice-consul. He has never done anything before."

IF LINDA HAZZARD HAD THOUGHT FOR ONE MOment the court defeat and humiliation of having to return such a sum of money was the worst of her impending troubles associated with the Williamson sisters, she could not have been more mistaken. Each day, as Agassiz pressed on with his investigation, Dora grew greater in her strength, greater in her resolve.

"I shall never forgive myself for Claire's death, Tooddy. I should have seen what was happening. I should not have fallen for the doctor's promises," she told Margaret, as the two women sat facing each other across a luncheon table at the hotel. "Sometimes I feel you were sent to me so I could avenge my dear sister's death."

"And so together we shall," Margaret answered.

DUNCAN URQUHART AND HIS FRENCH WAR BRIDE
Cecile Junot had five daughters—not a single son. Duncan and
his girls raised chickens and berries on a gorgeous piece of
acreage in Fragaria first owned by his parents. Born in 1922,
daughter Lucienne and her sisters attended the one-room
Fragaria School, just down the hill from the sanitarium.

Lucienne Urquhart had deep blue eyes that took in everything she saw. Over the years growing up in southern Kitsap
County she would see many things that would never leave her
memory. Dr. Hazzard and her fasting institution would be
among her most vivid recollections.

The patients filed by one by one.

"These people would walk by the school or the house and
they were so thin. Oh, my, they were just ghastly thin. Very sick.
And they always asked for food. They would walk down the hill
to the little Fragaria store. They'd go down there and try to get
food from them. I understand that she used to have them on a
very strict diet, mostly tomatoes and tomato juices. It was
pathetic to watch them. There was one man, I remember. He
walked like he had an ironing board strapped to his back, really
straight for some reason. He was walking to the store. Mama, I
know, fed them. She gave them bread or anything she had. She
felt sorry for them.

"In those days, they had terrible diseases, and people would
come to Mrs. Hazzard as a last resort. I remember one that was
so yellow, so dark. He probably had hepatitis. And a lot had the
last stages of venereal disease. She used to advertise in the
magazines overseas. It was known she did that."

Years later, Lucienne Urquhart would speak for many of the
children who lived in Olalla and Fragaria during the days of
gaunt men and emaciated women. They had heard so many terrible stories about Dr. Hazzard that they feared her more than
any monster projected upon the screen at the Saturday picture
show at the Woodman's Hall on the valley road.

Grown-ups, it seemed, just didn't understand their fears.
Occasionally, they sent their young ones up the hill to
Starvation Heights. They sent them to see Doc Hazzard.

When little Billy Fountain's folks decided the boy could benefit from Dr. Hazzard's treatments, the son of the owner of the

Fragaria store was escorted by Lucienne and her younger sister, Cecile, from school to the sanitarium. The girls were in the third or fourth grade at the time. Each step was punctuated by the quickened pace of a heart choked with terror.

As Lucienne recalled, Billy was about eight.

"Billy had to have some adjustments made on his body somehow or another . . . well, anyway, he was scared to go over there alone. I can remember this beautiful, beautiful sanitarium. It really was. I know I saw these jars sitting on the mantel across there, I heard that was her brother's liver—she pickled it. I saw it there.

"She took Billy off to her room. He just came out of there and he didn't say anything . . . it was kind of personal thing she was doing to him. He had one testicle that was up. She was going to get it down. She would pull on his leg. That's what he said . . . We went up there several times for that. I'll tell you, we were scared to death. So was Billy."

JANETTA NELSON LIVES IN OLALLA'S GRAND OLD house. The white Victorian with the glorious pitched roofline and charming gazebo was built in 1913 and is now listed on the National Historic Register as a particularly fine example of turn-of-the-century craftsmanship using local materials. Built by her in-laws, store owners Charlie and Mary Nelson, it is the only significant remnant of the town that hasn't burned down or been remodeled out of its character.

Janetta has lived alone since her husband Carl's death, presiding over a collection of Olalla memorabilia that proves that the spot in the road has a history. The elder Nelsons were savers, and Janetta was drafted as the keeper of the flame.

"I remember finding a letter among father's old things one afternoon before we moved into the big house. I called for Carl to come and look at it! We couldn't believe it. It was a letter from a sanitarium patient apologizing for stealing food from the store. He felt very badly about it and sent some money, a couple of dollars, I think. The man was starving."

FIFTEEN

LIKE THE INTERMINABLE TICKING OF A timepiece in a gentleman's breast pocket, the reminder was unfailing. Claire was dead, and justice had yet to be served. Vice-consul Lucian Agassiz and attorney Frank Kelley continued with their accumulation of evidence to pressure Kitsap County authorities into issuing a criminal indictment against Linda Burfield Hazzard. Through their investigation, the men had learned Claire Williamson's body had been illegally removed by chartered launch from Finney Creek by an employee of Butterworth & Sons. William Borthwick had told authorities that he had taken the dead woman's tiny body without a removal permit from the health department because there hadn't been time to get one. To Agassiz, the man's story seemed thin and smacked of a conspiracy between the undertaker and the doctor. It was curious that the sisters had been brought into the landing at Finney Creek, and one of their bodies had been removed at the same remote place.

"It seems Linda Hazzard didn't want anyone in Olalla to know the girls were staying there," Agassiz told Kelley.

"I fear we know the answer to that little riddle," the lawyer responded disdainfully.

And while they pieced it all together, there was something they knew they could do to ease the surviving sister's pain. They would try to retrieve the jewelry that had been taken from Claire and Dora at Olalla. Agassiz proposed that he visit the doctor's offices in Seattle under the guise of a patient seeking the fasting treatment. And while it was true that Agassiz's vest buttons tugged against his chest and he could stand to lose a few pounds, Frank Kelley rejected the undercover scheme. Backed into a corner, as she was, who was to say how far Dr. Hazzard might go to halt the investigation? She might kill again.

"It would be too dangerous a ruse, too great a risk," the lawyer said.

"I assure you I would be quite careful."

"Jewels are not worth a human life," Kelley said as he concluded the subject. "Most certainly she knows who you are."

The vice-consul relented. Of course, the so-called doctor knew him. Even so, it nagged at him. There had to be some way to stop her once and for all, a way to make her pay for all she had done. He didn't have to remind himself, but at home were the survivor and the heroine of the Olalla starvation sanitarium. They had sought him out for protection and retribution. He wanted to live up to the desperate faith they had bestowed on him.

AN ENORMOUS TENT, RISING LIKE A GIGANTIC white bumbershoot, was to be the residence of Dora and Miss Conway. The Tacoma Hotel bill was running to a limit beyond their means—much of the Williamson money was tied up until all legal matters were fully settled. A move was an unquestionable necessity. The vice-consul insisted the nurse and the convalescing fasting victim stay in his summer home at Lake Steilacoom, south of Tacoma. He would stay in the city house with his family.

Dora would have none of that.

"I cannot deprive your wife and children of a holiday at the lake. That would be cruel beyond words," she said.

"Nonsense," he replied. He smiled broadly as an idea came to him. "We shall erect a tent house. We should be quite comfortable in it."

"Not for you, Mr. Agassiz, but Tooddy and I will stay in the tent."

Agassiz was skeptical, it was not his intent to have the women stay in the tent. He knew better than anyone that Dora had been at death's door just weeks before. But finally, he acquiesced when Dora invoked the name of her dead sister.

"Claire would have loved the adventure of a quaint tent home. It will help me be close to her."

On an afternoon in the first week in August, Agassiz made a solemn promise to Dora and Miss Conway as they sat in scuffed wicker chairs outside the huge tent put on the sweeping grassy frontage of his lakefront residence. The vice-consul pledged he would do everything in his power to bring back the precious family heirlooms—the jewelry—that had been left at Olalla in the possession of the fasting doctor. Neither Agassiz nor attorney Frank Kelley—now a pair of avengers—knew what they would encounter at the sanitarium that had been the last place on earth Claire Williamson had lived.

Dr. Hazzard had emphatically stated at the guardianship hearing that she had never seen any jewelry other than the watch that belonged to Claire Williamson.

"Mrs. Hazzard is lying," Dora said, now refusing the fasting specialist the courtesy of the title of doctor. It was now *Mrs.* Hazzard who wasted her sister away to a skin-and-bones death.

"She has said that we kept only five hundred dollars worth of jewelry at the Buena Vista. Not true at all. Such a lie! Mother's diamond ring, her diamond-and-sapphire necklace, and a pearl necklace are still missing. Mrs. Hazzard took everything."

Dora estimated the value of missing jewels at $6,000, though the items were family heirlooms and no sum of money could measure their true worth. Dora only hoped nothing had been sold or hidden in the vast, dank forests of Kitsap County.

"Hidden like the sanitarium itself," Margaret Conway said, placing her hand on Dora's shoulder.

And late that day, surprise word came from Dr. Hazzard's lawyer, John Arthur. It seemed a parcel had been received from Olalla at his law offices in Seattle. Nowhere in the manifest suggested, however, that a missing watch had been included in the parcel. Even if it only took a mere telephone call to verify that all was accounted for, Agassiz had already made plans that he would not alter. The vice-consul could not resist the impulse to visit the place where the unspeakable had occurred. He was compelled to visit Starvation Heights.

ON THE MORNING OF AUGUST 4, 1911, LUCIAN Agassiz informed a newspaper reporter of his plan to charter a launch from Seattle to confront Dr. Hazzard in Olalla. He and

Frank Kelley wanted to know where the Williamson heirlooms had gone. They were men in search of answers, and they meant business. The reporter insisted he go along, which, of course, was the very reason Agassiz told him of his intentions in the first place.

For whatever Dr. Hazzard might have said about those who had attacked her personally and professionally, she was absolutely right in one regard. There could be no doubt to anyone who knew Agassiz or Kelley—both immensely enjoyed the spotlight.

"Like crabs that follow the glow of a lantern—that's those two. They want to see their names in the papers," one observer remarked. "No question about that at all."

THE LAUNCH WAS NOT THE *VIRGINIA* OR ANY OF the other steamers seen regularly in the passage. Slung low into the surface of the water, it choked a steel grey plume into the air. Some of the men buzzing wood for cherry boxes and strawberry crates at the Olalla Mill, or red cedar shingles at Lois Shingle and Lumber Company, let their saws slow as they looked up to see who was coming. Sawdust powdered their nostrils. Mud cracked off their boots. And they watched. The shape of Olalla Bay, narrow at its opening and widening to an even, elongated form like a deflated balloon tethered by the steady flow of Olalla Creek, invited the opportunity for everyone to observe strangers when they came. No one could sneak into the bay. Around a small jetty of land where a few muddy kids clammed and crabbed, the steamer swung sharply to the west. In sight was Olalla.

Vice-consul Agassiz studied the shoreline, the dark apron of trees that brushed over the water, the black mud along the bay. It was a gloomy sight even during the balmiest days of a Northwest summer.

"This is a good place to die," he said.

DESPITE THE SMALL SIZE OF THE VILLAGE, secrets could still be kept in Olalla. When it came to the price paid for someone's property, or a woman's decision on a suitor, it was possible to keep it quiet. Privacy, for the most part, was possible. But the case of Dr. Hazzard's Institute of Natural Therapeutics, it was more difficult to sequester rumor and innuendo. Word had seeped through most of Olalla that some British woman had died up on Starvation Heights. Most paid little mind to the revelation—it had happened before and undoubtedly would again. Another death? It was part and parcel of doing business with the ill and infirm.

There were a couple of other reasons little was known about the murder case among the people of Olalla. Though the Seattle and Tacoma newspapers were only a nickel, they were beyond the means of most in the village. In addition, few of the people who lived in the hinterland of Kitsap County spoke English. While their children learned it at school, parents continued to speak Swedish and Norwegian at home. None understood the severity of the charges or the basis of the growing criminal case against their neighbor. They only knew what was talked about on the wharf or in the store. Such gossip brought little alarm, little concern. Few, beyond John Karcher, knew the Hazzards outside of watching them come and go on the launch to Seattle. Sam and Linda were higher folks; a pair with money and fine things. They were educated and accomplished. Their fingernails were clean.

Linda Burfield Hazzard was a doctor! Samuel C. Hazzard was an army officer!

Sam and Linda Hazzard were mysteries of sorts. They weren't chicken ranchers or berry farmers. They didn't fish. The Hazzards weren't even purveyors of goods or merchandise in one of the small buildings stuck on pilings out over the muddy shores of Olalla Bay like bales of hay riding on pitchforks. They owned and operated a business like no other and had been educated far beyond what any of the locals had ever known, could even conceive of. They had other, and some thought, bizarre interests.

Every day, except Sunday, Sam and Linda rode down to the dock on a wagon and boarded the *Virginia*. Since the guardianship hearing in July, they spoke to no one.

THE HAZZARD PROPERTY WENT BY MANY NAMES. Linda liked to call it Wilderness Heights Institute of Natural Therapeutics. Sam called it whatever Linda wanted him to. In

Seattle, some referred to the would-be health center out in southern Kitsap County as Hazzard's Lodge.

Agassiz fished in his pockets for money and paid a man $5 to dump a load of green, summer hay and drive them up the hill to Starvation Heights, the name the locals called it. In a matter of minutes, a handful of men and boys converged around the wagon, talking and laughing as if they were marching in a parade. When the wagon arrived at the base of the steep incline that ran to the top of the hill, most jumped out. A few of the more good-natured even pushed the wagon as it inched its way up the switchbacks. They wanted to make it easier on the horses that dripped sweat and fought for breath in the blaze of the August sun.

When the wagon pulled into the lane leading to the house, the last villagers jumped off. No one wanted to be in the fray of what was certain to become a bombastic row. While few knew Dr. Hazzard personally, all had picked up ideas about her reputation for being a most unusual woman.

"I hear the lady doctor is as sturdy as any man!"

The front door swung open and Samuel Hazzard, tall and well built, stood on the threshold. No introductions were necessary. All had met in court at the Arlington Hotel. Sam was dressed in a dark suit, his glasses sparkled as the gold frames caught the light. His hair was combed back, black oily striations showing the trails left by his comb. For an instant, he seemed the image of a man attired for an outing, but before he could speak, a loud voice bolted from inside the house. It was a woman's voice, though it was the strongest woman's voice either man had likely heard.

"Sam, tell them the things are all gone."

"Yes, yes. The things are all gone."

"Tell them, Sam, that I sent the things to John Arthur in Seattle," the voice came from behind the darkened doorway.

"Yes, we sent the things to John Arthur in Seattle."

The exchange between the woman's voice and the man at the door showed the relationship between the two to be as Miss Conway and Dora Williamson had indicated. Linda Burfield Hazzard wore the pants in the family. It was she who was in charge of Sam.

With that, Agassiz and Kelley turned to walk around the bungalow. Carpenter's tools and the curled shavings of cedar covered the floor of the veranda. The "sunny window" of the room where Claire Williamson had died three months before was closed tight. Agassiz knew that he would never see the inside of the bedroom, the pseudo-apartment where Dora's sister had fought for a few more hours of life. No one would be inviting him inside for tea or anything of the kind.

As they made their way around to the east side of the bungalow, overlooking the gulch, Dr. Hazzard emerged from her house. She was a striking sight. Though she wasn't, of course, she seemed at least as tall as her husband, the six-foot West Pointer. She wore a heavily starched white blouse and a well-chosen khaki skirt that dropped to her calves. Agassiz considered her features not unattractive, though somewhat hard and sharp. Of course, all he knew about her came before that moment. She was a charlatan, a quack. No kind words could be bestowed on her. One look at Dora could confirm the evil done by the woman who purported to pioneer a revolutionary form of drugless, natural healing.

"You did not come for the things?" she impatiently snapped at the visitors. "I promised you that I would take them down to the wharf. But I was afraid to leave them there. I wrote you that I had mailed them to John Arthur. It is not my fault that you did not get the letter."

Frank Kelley stepped forward. "Mrs. Hazzard," he announced, "we would like to have Dorothea Williamson's watch."

The doctor wore a bemused look, then, in an instant, seethed a response.

"I gave it back to her."

The attorney differed. "That was Claire Williamson's watch."

"I know of only *one* watch. That was Dora Williamson's, and I returned it to her."

Around and around it went. The confrontation at Starvation Heights would resolve nothing, and both parties knew it. They had met in court before and undoubtedly would do so again. Dr. Hazzard did nothing to conceal her contempt for the interlopers on her doorstep. Her husband standing mutely behind her, she bid them good-bye with a voice that blasted like a foghorn.

"Get off of my land!"

SURVEYING THE CLEARED PORTION OF THE LAND-
scape, Agassiz noted a barn, a tent, and a few other outbuildings. He also counted five cabins arranged in a semicircle just
past the edge of the woods not far from the main house.

One of the cabins, they knew, was the so-called Cabin Claire.

After a knock on a door, a man who identified himself as
Edward Hickey emerged from inside. He appeared to be in
good health, about twenty-six years old. Agassiz wondered
what ailment could have prompted him to take such a dire
cure?

"There is nothing wrong with me," the Seattle man said. "I
just came over here to fast because I was not feeling right."

Ed Hickey said as far as he knew there was only one other
patient on the premises. The other man lived in the cabin next
door.

"He's a Himalayan monk named Johnson."

The monk could not be found. He did not answer the knocks
upon his door.

"Another victim of the cure?" Agassiz posed, his voice exud-
ing sarcasm.

The patient would have none of that. As far as he knew there
had been no victims of anything.

"Could be out walking," he said.

"Could be dead," Agassiz told the man before turning to
catch up with Kelley. "Seems to happen out here with some
regularity."

LINDA BURFIELD HAZZARD'S EYES STAYED
frozen on the vice-consul and the attorney as she stood in the
doorway of the shingled bungalow that was her weekend
home—the central building of her great sanitarium. She stared
hard, transmitting her ire without words. Sam Hazzard continued to peer from window to window as the intruders walked
along the side of the house. When the visitors were close
enough to speak, Dr. Hazzard barely allowed them to get within
customary, polite range.

"Are you gentleman through on my place?"

Her tone was harsh and loud, more of an implied command than a question.

"Quite through, my dear madam," Kelley said, bowing in a grand, yet obviously false gesture of courtesy. The bow only further incensed the woman in the khaki skirt. The muscles in her neck tightened and her veins rose to the surface like roots on a washed-out hillside. While her husband watched, Linda Burfield Hazzard began to scream.

"Then get off my place at once and mind your own blame business!"

The intruders immediately retreated. Nothing more was said. No threats were made from either side. The war that had been declared the day Margaret Conway embraced Dora on the stoop of the cabin had merely been strengthened. Neither side would give up a speck of ground. Neither side felt they had to.

THE VICE-CONSUL AND THE ATTORNEY CLIMBED into the wagon for the ride down the dusty road to the wharf. At Agassiz's bidding a twenty-nine-year-old hired man named Hans Hansen took a few dollars and made the promise that he would notify the vice-consul at his Tacoma office if Dr. Hazzard caught a boat for Seattle.

By the time the hay wagon made its way along the bay road, the tide had gone out and much of the little bay was a fetid mud-flat. The vice-consul's first impression held true from the beginning to the end of his visit there: More than ever, Olalla seemed a good place to die.

DORA'S EYELIDS WERE STUCK OPEN. WHILE SHE lay awake in the tent, listening to waterfowl splashing in the lake and the rhythm of Margaret's sleeping breath, the memories, real and imagined, would come to haunt her. Dora knew for certain it was her sister who had somehow smuggled the cablegram that sent for their beloved Margaret. She did not, however, know exactly how it was that Claire had managed such a feat. Who had helped her?

Like photographs fanned out on a table, scattered images ran through Dora's foggy memory. In her mind's eye she could see Claire and a faceless boy . . .

. . . The pelting showers had finally stopped and a gust of wind punched a gap in the clouds. The meshed, wet canopy of fir and cedar forced rays to cut through branches like hard-edged knives of light. No matter that he could barely see when he looked along the trail heading east toward the water, the boy had a job to do. He was bound for the store.

The rustling of brush and the snap of a twig cut through the forest. The boy stopped and turned to look for a fox, a deer, maybe a bear.

But none of those were the animal the boy saw. He blinked away the sunlight and looked at the ground a few feet ahead of him.

It was Claire crawling on the path. Her bony hands were muddy and her legs had been scratched to the kind of bloodiness that soaks through a plain woolen dress like a bottle of winy red ink tipped on a blotter.

"Boy!" she weakly cried out. "Please help!" Her tone was undeniable in its urgency. Her eyes were black sinkholes. Her lips stretched tautly over her teeth.

"I have money. I need help. Others need help. Boy, help me!" She held out a dirty slip of paper and some money and pressed it into the boy's hand.

"Please," she begged. "Please send this at once."

The child looked down the flumelike trail unravelling its way down the hill. It wasn't his place to interfere. He had been told it was foolhardy to help someone so ill. Still, there was something in the woman's eyes, a kind of pleading desperation that left him no choice. He took the slip of paper and crunched it in his fist. He did not take her money, and he never looked back.

Ten minutes later, the boy brushed dirt off the seat of his britches as he stepped inside the store.

"Saw one of Doc Hazzard's patients on the hill," he said, as the grimy, wadded paper landed on the counter.

"She gave me this note."

In a nearly indecipherable scrawl, the tattered paper bore the words:

Cable Margaret Conway, Melbourne, Australia. Come SS Marama May 8th, first class.—Claire.

Sometimes the dream varied. A carpenter building the little cabins was the carrier of the rescue message. A nurse, schoolgirl, a farmer's wife . . . all had received the tattered message.

The scenario always played to the same finish. Silent tears would fall from Dora's face to stain her pillowcase. Each morning when Margaret changed the bedding, she could plainly see that Dora had cried herself to sleep. She understood. Claire was gone.

DORA'S FIRST FEW NIGHTS AWAY FROM OLALLA had been permeated by fear. She continued to wake in the middle of the night, her face damp from perspiration, her heart pounding in her concave chest.

Memories that she had hoped would never be retrieved as long as she lived came to her. She remembered hearing Dr. Hazzard's voice rise above others . . . a party . . . a gathering of her spiritualist friends. The talk frightened her.

There was something unearthly about the gathering, though Dora was never in a condition to make inquiry for specifics. She knew something foreboding was going on in the dining room. She began to fear Dr. Hazzard for reasons she could not understand.

One day she cried all day because she knew the doctor would be returning to Olalla that evening. Her sobs couldn't be stifled.

She told Margaret about it:

"When she came she heard me and she rushed into the room and told me to quit. She stared at me hard and grabbed my wrists and I screamed with horror," she said.

"I screamed, I say, I screamed with horror!"

THE PHONE RANG AT THE SEATTLE HOTEL WHERE Frank Kelley and Lucian Agassiz took rooms the night of August 4, 1911. The caller told Agassiz to read an article in the newest edition of the paper. It was about Dr. Hazzard. The fasting specialist was up to something. Agassiz ran to pick up a copy of the morning paper from the front desk in the hotel lobby. He read the article once. To make certain, he read it again. He bolted for Frank Kelley's room.

"The woman is planning to flee. She's going to New York and Hong Kong . . . she's going to teach her methods to the royal family!"

Until that information, no one had considered Linda Hazzard much of a flight risk. It was she, after all, who had drawn the line in the sand and stood firm on her side. She seemed absolutely intent on facing the charges head-on. Dr. Hazzard was playing the role of martyr to a misunderstood method. She complained about the injustice, but there was the consensus among her enemies that it was a role she adored.

Attorney Kelley knew what had to be done. The Kitsap County authorities had moved so slowly and now could afford no more delays. If the warrant was not issued immediately, a very dangerous woman would get away. Early the following morning Kelley took a launch across the Sound to Bremerton, then on to meet with Thomas Stevenson, the prosecuting attorney.

Stevenson was exceedingly polite. He was courteous. But he didn't seem to grasp the seriousness of the information before him. Perhaps it was youth? The man's boyish features were nearly delicate in their form, slightly rounded and small-ish. His brown eyes were lightly lidded, so as to give him an alert appearance—even when he wasn't. The attorney's brown hair was side-parted so high on his head that it barely missed the middle. And while it seemed most who made a living in the courtroom sported bushy walrus moustaches, Thomas Stevenson's face was clean-shaven.

He was either young or stupid.

"Now is the time, or it will be too late," Agassiz urged.

The prosecutor seemed unswayed, but the truth was Stevenson was in a bind. Kitsap County was poor. Very poor. Trying Linda Hazzard on murder charges stemming from a starvation death would be costly and difficult. The county resources were a pittance compared to across-the-Sound King County. Yet, the alleged murder occurred in Olalla, not Seattle, where the doctor had first practiced her treatment on Claire Williamson. Thomas Stevenson ran the scenario round and round. To disregard Claire Williamson's death was to invite an international incident, and he knew it. In preparation for his meeting with Kelley and Agassiz, he had even telephoned the

Olympia offices of the state attorney general. He had to be certain. In the end, however, he really had no choice. But he did have a caveat. Only if the surviving Williamson sister would pay for costs associated with interviews, travel, and hotel expenses for witnesses, would the county do its part. Frank Kelley informed Stevenson that Dora Williamson would be in full agreement.

"If she has to pay to stop her sister's murderer, so be it!"

And so it was agreed. With a great flourish of his pen, Superior Court Judge John Yakey prepared an arrest warrant: Linda Burfield Hazzard would be charged with the willful murder of British heiress Claire Williamson. The British girl had been intentionally starved to death.

SIXTEEN

INSIDE THE BRITISH VICE-CONSUL'S MIND
the image of Dora Williamson flickered again and again.
Sometimes the image brought on a headache of unbearable
intensity. Her eyes were deep and black, her skin protracted so
tight as to crack like the dried-out parchment of a lampshade.
Over and over, he saw her in a mind's eye that could not be
shielded.

Good Lord, the woman was a sight.

And, quite peculiarly, she didn't seem to be aware of it. Dora
Williamson, though sickly and weak as a deer trapped in the
jaws of an iron leg trap, carried on during their first meeting with
the kind of aplomb of the educated and wealthy woman that she
was. Her dress was pinched and pinned to disguise how the
lovely garment nearly swallowed its wearer. Dora didn't seem
aware of it. She seemed unconcerned, so very calm. It was not
afternoon tea in the lobby of the Empress. It was the beginning
of an investigation into a potential murder case. Dora's attitude
continued to reflect her upbringing, not the least bit altered by
the gruesome events that had transpired in the woods on the
Kitsap Peninsula. Her resolve, her calmness were remarkable.

*Had she not been aware how close she had come to joining
her beloved sister in death?*

What Agassiz did not realize was that the diminutive woman
had survived for only a single reason. Not because her life was
so precious, but because her sister's murder had to be avenged.
Justice was only proper. As the steamer charged toward Seattle,
the vice-consul could not set aside the memory of bits and
pieces of his first conversation with Dora Williamson at the
Tacoma Hotel.

"I was quite outraged at the cleanliness of the sanitarium," the half-dead woman confided, as though it were a hotel not up to her expectations.

"Indeed," Margaret Conway chimed in, relishing the game of debasing the doctor, "I doubt that Mrs. Hazzard knows the first things, the most rudimentary things, of nursing. I doubt it highly."

"Extraordinary. Outrageous," Dora muttered, as weakness abruptly sneaked up on her. There had been plenty of excitement for one day. She needed rest.

"Take me to my room, Tooddy. I am so very tired."

Agassiz could not forget how Miss Conway took Dora's spindly arm and wrapped it around her own neck, to support the emaciated woman as she got up to walk the length of the lobby.

Margaret smiled at the vice-consul.

"The dear's gaining, but still light as a feather, I'd say."

IF LUCIAN AGASSIZ HAD GIVEN IT CONCERTED thought, he probably would not have been as stupefied as he was during the initial hours of what he sensed would become the investigation of his career. At first, the vice-consul thought the medical atrocity that took Claire Williamson's life was a bizarre, albeit isolated incident, an aberration of sorts, caused by a strangely powerful and greedy woman. But within hours of hearing the story of Starvation Heights, Agassiz learned otherwise.

Dr. Hazzard, it would seem, was well known by the authorities.

King County Prosecuting Attorney John Murphy, for one, was not unfamiliar with Linda Burfield Hazzard and her methods. He listened carefully and took notes as Agassiz and Kelley told him the story of Claire's death and the missing jewels and stolen bank funds. Since the death had taken place in Kitsap County, he had no jurisdiction over the case, but he knew of others that, in the event a pattern could be proved and witnesses ferreted out, could make it to the criminal courts in Seattle. Murphy asked the two visitors if they would like to discuss some of the past cases contained in her file. They did. He hauled out a beat-up folder from a file drawer and heaved it onto the desk.

The first name was Rader, L.E.

"Lewis Rader?" Kelley asked.

While relative-newcomer-to-the-Northwest Agassiz didn't know the name, Frank Kelley did.

"He died May 11 last year after thirty-seven days of the so-called fasting treatment," Murphy noted, as the men pored over documents and newspaper clippings.

The date grabbed Agassiz like cold fingers to his neck. It was only eight days before Claire Williamson died. The news reports and commentary by the prosecuting attorney told the tale of a man with great potential, cut short.

A member of the Populist party, Lewis Ellsworth Rader settled at Olalla in 1901, a few years after serving a term in the state legislature. No doubt the lure of settling in an outpost near the Home and Burley Colonies of freethinkers was the main draw of the Peninsula. Rader was educated, a man of letters who fashioned himself as the West Coast version of Elbert Hubbard, the controversial leader of the Roycrofters. And while Rader never managed to author anything nearly so well-known as Hubbard's classic "Message to Garcia" he did publish a highly regarded little magazine called *Sound Views*. To many, *Sound Views* was clearly modeled after Hubbard's own *Philistine*. Before his death, Rader's greatest moments undoubtedly were the times when he accompanied Hubbard from Tacoma for speaking engagements in the anarchist colony at Home, Washington.

At forty-six, whatever greatness to which L. E. Rader had aspired would be cut short by treatments from Dr. Linda Burfield Hazzard. It started when the Williamson sisters were wasting away at the Buena Vista. Not far away, Rader was taking treatments at Seattle's Outlook Hotel.

Though he was initially treated at home in Olalla, he was moved to Seattle and into a room at the Outlook, where Dr. Hazzard said she could monitor his progress more carefully. The sanitarium, of course, was not ready.

The vice-consul read from a *Seattle Post-Intelligencer* clipping in which Dr. Hazzard explained the basis of the man's need for the fast.

As the result of an accident in childhood, in which he was internally injured, Mr. Rader's youth and early man-

*hood were filled with a succession of most acute attacks of
painful illness. About fifteen years ago he deserted orthodox means of treatment and turned to what is now known
as the natural, or drugless, method, with the result that he
experienced the first relief he had ever known . . .*

As far as Agassiz and Kelley could discern the fasting specialist's words were more of her typical, self-aggrandizing,
self-serving blather. What interested the men was not what Dr.
Hazzard had to say, but the *facts* of the case.

And the discovery of a potential pattern.

THE SECOND WEEK OF MAY 1911 BROUGHT A TIP
to Seattle authorities that had a maddeningly familiar ring.

*"There's a man starving to death at the Outlook. Dr.
Hazzard is looking after him."*

Officials at the health department had heard it before, but felt
helpless to intercede. Linda Burfield Hazzard had a license to
practice her form of treatment—no matter how dangerous most
viewed it. Those who willingly sought her expertise could not
be protected from their own foolishness.

"I told my inspectors to watch Dr. Hazzard and to report to
me if she treated any infants and they died under her care. All
the cases we were able to find were those of adults who had put
themselves voluntarily under her treatment," Dr. J. E. Crichton,
head of the health department, later said.

And though Lewis Rader's was certainly such a case—and
the patient was a most intelligent and accomplished man—
Crichton's men still investigated.

Acting on a tip received from the Seattle Mayor Hiram C.
Gill that a man was reported to be near death from a quack starvation treatment, health department inspectors found Rader and
proceeded to interview him. Instead of being grateful for their
concern, he insisted he was being treated according to his
wishes and admonished them to leave him be. Since they considered him to be out of his mind with weakness, the inspectors,
both doctors, sought to remove him from the hotel to a physician of their choosing. The former state legislator, they said,
could be saved. All he needed was nourishment.

When Dr. Hazzard learned how health department doctors had seen her patient she was outraged. And at the mayor's bidding!

When would the persecution stop?

As she had been for most of her life, Linda Burfield Hazzard was a woman of action. She quickly decided she would have no more of it. No more intrusions. No more questions of her patient. She hoisted Rader up from his bed and carried him to the bath. She would have no more of it. She locked the door and climbed out a window and walked through a narrow courtyard to another room where she could call for legal help. No one had the authority to interfere with her methods. The stress was undoubtedly hastening his demise.

"Until the coming of these officers, Mr. Rader was able to walk from his room to the bath, but since that time he continually begged to be protected from outsiders and permitted to die, if need be, in peace," Linda Hazzard explained later.

That night, she moved her frail patient to a location she refused to divulge to anyone.

Lewis Rader died at noon on May 11, 1911. He was survived by his wife Emma, and four sons, Lewis, Jr., Wendell, Thoreau, and Gladstone. The 5' 11" man weighed less than a hundred pounds.

It was Linda Hazzard who performed the autopsy. Among the vague causes of death noted was "prolapsis" of the stomach. Butterworth & Sons received the body. Cremation followed—though there was a slight delay as the coroner sought to reexamine the corpse. Nothing came of the investigation, however.

There were no laws on the books to stop the woman. It would take an act of the legislature to do anything about the fasting treatment.

"I am helpless in this matter," the coroner said.

TO AGASSIZ, THE SIMILARITIES BETWEEN THE Rader and Williamson cases were profound. The man had been spirited away in the night—as had the sisters. Rader had been isolated from others. Dr. Hazzard performed the autopsy, and Butterworth handled the cremation. But there was something else, something that was not contained in any of the paperwork.

Before the men moved on to other names on the list, the King County prosecutor recalled how he had heard a rumor that some of the property Linda and Sam Hazzard held in Olalla had been owned by Rader. He thought the name of the tract was Wilderness Heights. Now, of course, it was known by another name.

Among the papers, the "Hazzard complaints," as Murphy called them, were other names and other deaths. Edward Erdman, the civil engineer who died March 29, 1911; Frank Southard, who died May 30, 1911, after a prolonged fast; Mrs. Maude Whitney, who died on July 20, 1910, after fasting under Dr. Hazzard's supervision; Mrs. Blanche B. Tindall, who died on June 18, 1909, after twenty-eight days of fasting; Mrs. Viola Heaton, who died on March 24, 1909, after a Dr. Hazzard fast; Mrs. Daisey Maud Haglund, who died on her birthday, February 8, 1908, after abstaining from food for fifty days; and Mrs. Ida Wilcox, who fasted for forty-seven days and died September 26, 1908.

Another prominent name on the list of dead was C. A. Harrison, the publisher of the *Alaska-Yukon* magazine.

In the cases of Tindall, Erdman, and Heaton, death certificates were issued by medical doctors—not Linda Hazzard—deeming the cause of death as "starvation." In the Whitney case, however, the death certificate was signed by Linda Burfield Hazzard. According to her autopsy findings, chief among the causes was "chronic pancreatis [sic]."

Frank Southard was another among the notables in the Hazzard case file. He was a highly regarded partner in the Seattle law firm of Morris, Southard, and Shipley. He weighed in at 230 pounds, but over the course of the fast cure was reduced to 153 pounds. After resuming eating again, he suffered kidney trouble. Again, he put himself under the doctor's care, and a few days before his death he took an unexpected trip to the Cascades. At a camp near the Skykomish River, he suffered paralysis. An emergency trip to the hospital failed to save him.

A notation in the Southard file seemed somewhat revealing. While the doctor who signed the death certificate indicated the victim died of nephritis, he wrote *"patient was under my care only two days."*

And yet, while King County's pages of information on the other patients was of interest in the event a pattern could be proved, and thus assist criminal prosecution in the Williamson case, two deaths quickened Agassiz's heartbeat. Two of the names belonged to subjects of the British crown. Just like Miss Claire.

LUCIAN AGASSIZ HAD NO IDEA WHO THE ANONY-mous caller had been talking about when she referred to the "Wakelin matter" as it related to Dr. Hazzard. Since the fasting specialist's arrest, he had been the recipient of numerous tips. Some panned out, some were the bitter ruminations of loved ones who had watched a family member waste away under the guise of treatment. Most names were familiar to Agassiz. Wakelin, however, was not.

The caller spoke in a hushed voice.

"Some two years ago, Mr. Wakelin was a patient of Dr. Hazzard's. He came from New Zealand to take the fast cure . . . and he shot himself. Though I doubt it quite a bit. You see, they didn't find the decomposed body for three weeks after his death, yet Dr. Hazzard was supposedly treating him daily."

The woman's voice was somewhat familiar to the vice-consul, but she refused to say who she was.

"Butterworth's involved in that one as well."

Then the line went dead. Agassiz fiddled the receiver's hook and asked for the operator to get the woman back on the line. But that was impossible. She was gone, and the line was deadly quiet.

A nurse? An enemy? The wife of one of Dr. Hazzard's patients? He had no idea who she was.

The case of Eugene Stanley Wakelin would be a great mystery, at least in regard to the true circumstances of his death. What happened after the twenty-six-year-old died, however, was without a shred of doubt, unabashedly criminal. Agassiz went to the newspapers, to the coroner, to the funeral home—anywhere he could think of to piece together any small detail. He hit pay dirt when he came across the probate records for the dead New Zealander. Once again Linda Hazzard had appointed herself administratrix of a dead patient's estate. Unbelievable as it was, it got worse. Valued at $223, the estate had been exhausted of all funds. The funeral bill from Butterworth & Sons was a ridiculously high $155. That detail affirmed to Agassiz further proof of a nefarious connection between Dr. Hazzard and the funeral parlor handling most of her business.

Agassiz learned Wakelin had come to America after reading Dr. Hazzard's book *Fasting for the Cure of Disease.* Though papers found on the dead man's body indicated he was the son of an English lord, it was discovered young Wakelin had obtained funds for passage and Dr. Hazzard's fasting treatment by borrowing on a reversionary interest. Perhaps he had been ostracized from his aristocratic family for one reason or another? Maybe he was a black sheep because of his belief in nature cures? Agassiz recalled how Dora and Claire hadn't wanted their relations to know of their involvement with Dr. Hazzard. They didn't want to be gossiped about as frivolous faddists.

The vice-consul was dumbfounded by his discoveries. At first Agassiz believed the man's death had gone unnoticed by the authorities, but after further discussion with King County authorities officials it was certain that they were not only aware of it, they had chosen to look the other way.

The reason, he felt, could only be sinister in nature.

Later, he wrote about it:

> *My contention is that the County Coroner's Office, or at least the Deputy County Coroner of King County, has been working for some years past hand in hand with Dr. Hazzard. It is very hard to get all the real facts.*

Agassiz cabled New Zealand at once. He wanted information from Wakelin's survivors and his lawyers.

The other name that seized Agassiz's attention was John "Ivan" Flux of Gloucester, England. Flux had come to America with plans to buy a ranch in the summer of 1910. He began Dr. Hazzard's fasting cure on December 19 that same year and died on February 10, 1911.

Agassiz took down what little information he could drum up on the Flux and Wakelin cases and made a mental plan to follow up everything with a serious investigation of his own when he returned to his offices in Tacoma. Concern could not be stricken from his face. The fact that in less than six months three British subjects had succumbed under treatment of a seemingly obscure American doctor was startling. How could it be? What were the odds of such an occurrence?

THE VICE-CONSUL KNEW THAT WHEN THE WORD got out about Linda Burfield Hazzard's troubles, it would incite others to add fuel to what he hoped would be a bonfire. He needed people to come forward to tell him whatever fact or gossip they knew about Dr. Hazzard and her treatment. He wanted her enemies to know that the investigation into the goings-on at Starvation Heights was of importance to the authorities beyond the weak and poor jurisdiction of little Olalla and Kitsap County. It was a matter in the hands of King County prosecutors as well. The power and wealth of Seattle was involved.

"We have obtained many damaging facts already," he announced to reporters, "and it is not unlikely that other criminal informations will be filed against Dr. Hazzard by Prosecuting Attorney John F. Murphy of King County."

ONCE THE BRITISH VICE-CONSUL ISSUED SUCH statements and word spread about his purpose, many, as he predicted, stood in line to debase the doctor and her treatment.

Most who derided Dr. Hazzard were men. As had been the case throughout her life, few of the male gender defended her honor and methods. One notable exception, however, was Frank Southard's law partner, Will Morris.

Morris issued a statement to the local dailies. It would be the only time someone other than the doctor's family would rebuke the charges against her.

Mr. Southard was a man of not only extraordinary intelligence and learning, but one who was well acquainted with his own case and knew just with what he was suffering. He began a course of treatment with Dr. Hazzard about two years ago and greatly reduced his weight. Then he stopped the treatment and for the first time in many years was able to sleep well and eat his food with enjoyment. By treatment I do not mean starvation, for Mr. Southard never starved himself. At the most he merely abstained from solid foods for a time and consulted with Dr. Hazzard about the kind of liquid foods most beneficial for his case. He also took massage treatments from her and frequently commented on her remarkable strength. He had completely ceased the treatment when he went on the trip with the mountaineers carrying a heavy pack on that occasion and suffering no inconvenience. After his return the old trouble began to come back and later on he resumed the dieting again. But he did not starve himself. Why, on that last trip to the mountains he ate a hearty dinner on the way out.

The doctor informed me that the immediate cause of his death was drinking two cups of strong black coffee in camp. He was suffering with a kidney affliction, with the result that the coffee caused uremic poisoning. I am convinced that the treatment he received from Dr. Hazzard really prolonged his life.

Following his death, Mrs. Hazzard came to me and wanted me to write and sign a certificate of what I thought about the matter for publication. I told her that I did not want any publicity in the matter, regardless of what I thought of the treatment. Mr. Southard had paid for the treatment, and we felt under no obligation to do anything of the sort.

A LETTER WAS SLID UNDER AGASSIZ'S DOOR late one hot August night. Florid handwriting addressed the envelope to the attention of the British vice-consul. It was written by a woman, a former patient of Linda Hazzard's. She wrote how she had been rescued from the sanitarium barely in time to save her life.

The writer did not give her name. She was still afraid of Dr. Hazzard and what the "fast fiend" might do to her.

IT WAS SO VERY CLEAR. THOUGH AGASSIZ KNEW he didn't have all the facts, he was certain that whatever could be unearthed would only solidify his position that the sanitar-

ium operator was an evil opportunist who killed for profit.
Word from Frank Kelley, however, showed him that not
everyone understood the danger of allowing a woman like
Linda Burfield Hazzard to go unpunished. Thomas Stevenson,
the Kitsap County prosecutor, was decidedly cool about the
whole affair. Agassiz was outraged by the man's seeming
indifference.

Could it be he was afraid of her and her reputed powers?

Could it be that he felt there was not enough evidence?

*Perhaps he feared that the county was no match for a woman
of seemingly vast resources?*

*Or was it simply the fact that the victim in primary question
was seen as some foolish British faddist; someone who had
availed herself a treatment and suffered the consequences of
her poor choice?*

Frank Kelley felt it was a question of resources. Kitsap
County had few, and could not well afford an expensive legal
proceeding against a woman who could hire a topflight lawyer
to defend her against any charges they could levy. As things
stood, she might be the better endowed financially. The
Williamson estate was hopelessly tied up, and Dora and
Margaret had but a small stipend to live on. The money would
have to come from somewhere other than their coffers.

It was at that suggestion that Lucian Agassiz crossed the line
into territory onto which he had never trod. He told his lawyer
friend that His Majesty would foot the bill.

Kelley blinked in surprise. "King George?"

"Yes."

"But this is an American matter, not a concern of the king of
England."

Agassiz shook his head. He saw it differently. The woman
who died was one of three Britishers who had perished undergoing treatment at the hands of an unscrupulous quack. Claire's
was not an isolated case.

The attorney was skeptical.

"What if your King refuses to join this little battle?"

"Then I shall pay out of my own pocket."

"What if Stevenson refuses to indict the woman?"

"Then I will do as I see fit."

The lawyer didn't pressure for details. At that particular juncture, none were necessary. He knew that once his friend made up his mind, the stout little man with the refined British accent would do everything in his power to see it to the end. He could charm and cajole. He was dogged. He was determined. Lucian Agassiz had already made provisions for the possibility that Stevenson would ignore his pleas—*Claire Williamson's* pleas—for justice.

Agassiz met with his immediate superior, the British consul at Seattle, Bernard Pelly. The discussion was lengthy, and to Agassiz's utter joy, quite fruitful. When the two men drafted a cable for the British ambassador in Washington, D.C., they spared no words. They suggested British Ambassador James Bryce arrange for a meeting with U.S. President William Howard Taft to seek his aid in forcing Washington State Governor Marion Hay to apply pressure on Kitsap County in order to avoid international repercussions.

SEVENTEEN

LONG BEFORE THE FIRST SETTLERS CAME to the Pacific Northwest, an audacious mix of spiky-needled evergreens and lush, deciduous foliage sparred for dominion of both sides of mile-wide, beach-deprived Colvos Passage. By the turn of the century on the west side of the passage, however, it seemed clear that another victor was emerging. Stumps burned amber into the wee hours and smoke wove itself into the layers of salty mist rising off Puget Sound. Slowly at first, then more quickly, progress was forced upon the fertile soil heaped atop Vashon Island. The alteration of the landscape was brutal, a pilfering of a forest covering for the sake of fruit trees and their promise of income and prosperity. For the settlers on the island rising in the dark waters between the mainland and the Kitsap Peninsula, it became so. Not long after orchardists cleared great sections of land, apple tree limbs sagged under a ripening crop. Yet on the Kitsap side of the waterway—the western shore—it was a different tale. A mat of greenery extended its dark, light-choking sprawl. Little had sliced into the density; at least little could be seen by passengers against the handrails of steamers from Seattle or Tacoma. Only one spot on the west side of Colvos Passage suggested a future of any kind. It was the place where a tributary fed a little bay; the only point on a nine-mile stretch where wagons could be driven inland.

It was at the place called Olalla.

John Karcher ranched a good-sized spread not forty rods from the Hazzard place on the hill above the Olalla Bay. In time, proximity and circumstance led him to know Linda and Samuel far better than nearly any of the Scandinavian immigrant neighbors who made homes in the area. In fact, Mr. Karcher became so involved, so very enthralled with the Hazzards and their plan for a new kind of healing, he invested funds out of his own pocket for the sanitarium. He had done so, not because he saw a great deal of money pouring from the heavens to fill the coffers of the sanitarium and the bank accounts of its investors. Not really. Like most who swarmed the space around the woman doctor, John Karcher was a believer in her fasting cure.

The rancher with hands as worn and large as his broken heart had seen his youngest son, Waldo, endure the ravages of inflammatory rheumatism. His bank account bled as well; an astonishing $2,000 was handed over to various doctors for treatments that, in the end, offered no relief. Then he heard of Linda Burfield Hazzard.

... I took a great interest in her methods of treatment. She cured a child of inflammatory rheumatism. My child suffered untold agonies for three years and is a cripple.

If only. The feeble phrase uttered by so many of the desperate and disillusioned fit Mr. Karcher and his plight better than most. If only Dr. Hazzard and her treatment had been available when his boy needed it, John Karcher knew he would have been a much happier man, and certainly a less anguished father. Each herky-jerky step Waldo Karcher struggled to take—be it to walk to the outhouse or make his way to gather eggs in the forty-five-foot-long chicken house—was a reminder that conventional doctors who had treated the boy for three years did not have all the answers. They did not, Mr. Karcher said, know how to save his son from a lifetime of pain. They had outright failed. Linda Burfield Hazzard had succeeded with similar cases. He needed no other recommendation. All he wanted was hope.

After the Williamson girl died and the trouble was stirred up by the British vice-consul, it was not difficult for John Karcher to cement his loyalties. Dr. Hazzard was a misunderstood woman with a mind of untold scientific brilliance and possessing unquestionable moral character. Those against her were jealous fools. It was that simple.

"I am right here to meet the doctors to the last ditch," she told a listener as her enemies circled around her. "This is merely a case of persecution. Really, I am glad of it. When you praise anything, you never help it. When you knock it, you improve it."

IT WAS NOT UNEXPECTED. LINDA AND SAM KNEW men with badges would be calling at Wilderness Heights sooner or later. Linda prepared the staff, telling them if she was arrested, it would be merely for show, an act to break her spirit and concede that the fasting cure was ineffective. She told them she'd be out on bond until the charges were dismissed. Life and work would go on. An arrest would not stop her.

"I shall go to New York to demonstrate fasting to the world, and I shall go to Hong Kong to fast the Chinese royalties at $100 a day. My husband and my son will continue the building of my great institution at Olalla."

It was about 3 P.M., Saturday, August 5, 1911, when Deputy Sheriff George Posse arrived by chartered launch with Judge John Yakey's arrest warrant for Linda Burfield Hazzard. John Karcher recognized the uniformed intruder right away. Since Dr. Hazzard had forewarned Mr. Karcher that the law would be coming for her, the rancher knew the reason for Deputy Posse's visit to Olalla. He pulled his wagon alongside the deputy, who had decided to walk the dusty road in the direction of the sanitarium. He offered him a ride. The deputy accepted.

"On the way up," the rancher wrote four years after the day of the doctor's arrest, "he told me his business, and he also told me what a wonderful criminal she was and they would get rid of her now."

John Karcher was appalled by the outrageousness of what he heard. He nearly spit at the deputy. Yet, he knew there was no sense in that. Instead, he ordered Posse out of the wagon and returned home to put up his team before heading for the sanitarium and the woman who had acknowledged her sacrifices were for the good of humanity.

"So no one's child will suffer as yours has, my good friend."

DESPITE YEARS OF INCREASING BOOSTERISM, and a growing population, Kitsap was still too poor a county to build a new jail of its own. Those prisoners unable to come up with bond money were incarcerated in jails in Seattle or Tacoma pending release or trial. Linda Burfield Hazzard, of course, knew that. She knew that she would not spend a single night in a jail cell.

Instead, after booking, her destination would be a room in a modest Port Orchard home off the Sidney road. Mrs. W.O. Breed was a deputized officer of the Kitsap County Court who, when need be, took female prisoners under her charge.

Since no one expected she would be a laconic prisoner, few were disappointed when Linda Hazzard did not go quietly from her Olalla home. She talked nonstop. About the five years of persecution she had suffered since arriving in the Pacific Northwest. About the medical men who were against her. She berated Deputy Posse for taking her away from a blind boy she had fasted for three weeks.

"His eyesight," she said curtly, "would have been restored any day now."

The fact that a boy was blind was on the hands of the county.

Throughout his wife's ordeal, Sam Hazzard offered little in the way of conversation. As he did when Agassiz inquired of the Williamson sisters' belongings, he merely repeated his wife's remarks. Whenever she said something to George Posse Sam matched her words.

"The medical board is in back of the whole thing," she said firmly.

"Yes, it's the medical board," her husband echoed.

And as she spoke Linda Hazzard peppered her commentary with the unlikely combination of self-aggrandizing and thinly veiled threats.

If her son Rollin was by her side, he might commit a desperate crime to free his mother.

"What sort of crime?"

"I cannot say."

She proclaimed her unparalleled success was the envy of the medical world.

"I have only lost twelve patients out of a thousand."

She was "cheerful martyr" to a great cause.

"The great thing about my persecution is that it will bring this cause before the world. I will have more patients than I can take care of. For every truth there is a martyr in the pathway. Now, isn't that pretty? It isn't me they are after. It is my method."

And while she had prepared her staff and friends that an arrest was likely coming, she played the surprised captive when the time came.

"Why I had no idea that they were really going to bring such a charge against me. I thought they talked just for the press. After all these years I did not imagine for one minute that they would get up the courage."

BACK IN SEATTLE, AND TOO LATE IN THE DAY TO make the trip south to Tacoma, Lucian Agassiz made his way for a telephone to relay a message to Dora and Margaret. Even with the arrest, it was not all good news. The value of the goods Dr. Hazzard had sent to John Arthur's law office came to no more than $500—substantially less than the $6,000 figure ascribed to the worth of the missing jewels.

He told a house servant to pass the good bit along, though he wished he could be there himself to convey it personally.

"Linda Burfield Hazzard has been arrested for the murder of Miss Claire," he announced, his voice rising with the combination of fervor and urgency. "Tell the ladies at once!"

EVEN AS SHE SPOKE IN HER DEFENSE, THE CASE against Linda Hazzard gained considerable, and seemingly, unshakable ground.

Frank Kelley was quick to tell his thoughts of the doctor's guilt, so convinced was he that she was a killer.

"Claire Williamson died at the hands of Dr. Linda Burfield Hazzard," he announced to members of the press. "Criminal intention upon the part of Dr. Hazzard is shown by misappropriation of funds, the hasty execution of the first codicil, and the execution of the second codicil."

A few days before the indictment, Agassiz dropped off a letter from Dr. Hazzard and Claire's red leather diary at the

Tacoma offices of Charles Bedford. Bedford was known among law enforcement as an expert at photographic reproduction. On the page opposite "Claire's Wishes" ten lines had been erased to such a degree that nothing could be discerned with the naked eye. Bedford was asked to look at the page under a microscope. He was also instructed to enlarge the letter forms of known samples of Claire Williamson's and Linda Hazzard's handwriting and compare each with the diary entry.

"I want to know who wrote the so-called passage 'Claire's Wishes,' " Agassiz said.

A few days later, the answer came when he was invited to return to Bedford's office.

"There is no doubt," the man said as he passed the originals over his desk to the vice-consul's outstretched hands. "The letters on the section you wished analyzed is an attempt to copy Claire's handwriting."

"Could you say who wrote it down?"

"The letters resemble Dr. Hazzard's samples. I'd say she did it."

"Swear to it?"

"Yes, I would."

"What of the erased matter?"

"I can't make out a single word. Whoever eradicated it, meant for it to be gone forever."

CLIFF HURD AND HIS WIFE, FLORENCE, WERE young parents when they moved to Olalla from Port Orchard in 1943 to rent an old two-story house above the bay for $25 a month. Later, they bought the place and owned a couple of successful businesses—first, a "brush picking" operation for the floral industry, and later a rubber stamp company that still bears their name: Florenclif Stamp Company. And though, years later, Cliff figured it took them twenty years to break into the somewhat clannish Olalla community, it was worth it. More than fifty years later, the Hurds feel no place could measure up to their home above the bay.

Some of Cliff Hurd's earliest memories of his adopted home featured an old man he saw nearly every day. He was an immaculately dressed gentleman in his early seventies, an old fellow who never went anywhere without a beautifully buffed leather briefcase and a perfectly pressed business suit.

"I would see him almost every day walking from the place where he lived up there on the hill, down to Nelson's store. Finally after seeing him many days I became curious. Who is this man? Why is he always walking? One day I felt the urge to ask seventy-five-year-old Charlie Nelson about this man.

"'This gentleman that comes down every morning with his brief case . . . 'Charlie, tell me why does he darry that brief case?'

"He says, 'You know who it is, don't you?'

"'Well I think he lives up at Starvation Heights up there some place.'

"He says, 'Yeah, he lives up on the place there. That's Sam Hazzard. It was he and his wife that used to own the place.'

"Well, why does he always carry that brief case when he comes down here? Is he selling something or what?'

"Charlie laughed. 'No', he said. 'I don't know as I should tell you this. Truth is Sam's got a bad habit. He doesn't want people to know what he buys down here. He comes down and gets high alcohol content extracts. Each day he brings that case down here and puts the bottles of ectracts in his brief case and carries it home with him.'

"I said, 'That's all right, but that is kind of a bad habit.'

"He says, 'Yeah, but you can't tell Sam that.'"

BORN IN 1924, CAMMIE STEWART WAS JUST BEGIN-*ning her life as Samuel Hazzard continued the slow wind down of his own. The daughter of logger Edward James "Pops" and cook Ina Stewart, Cammie first lived in the valley and later, in the old hotel. By then it was a "rickety, old, tumble-down" house on the beach. Olalla kids came to the Stewart place to change clothes or just hang out before swimming in the bay. Folks up and down the valley depended on Pops to keep an eye out for their children in the water. What they didn't know: Pops couldn't swin a stroke.*

Cammie was barely in her twenties when she took a job checking out groceries and dry goods at the Olalla Trading Company, a mercantile on pilings south of the bay bridge. While

Cammie would see many customers, none would hold a spot in her memory more concrete than old man Hazzard.

"Sam was a customer of Andy Fagerud, the store owner, because the product being traded was vanilla for Sam's consumption and he went to Andy to preserve the illusion that nobody knew. But everybody knew who was downwind.

"I would walk to work and he'd gone into the store early to do business with the boss so I would meet him as he was coming back down the road—sometimes with a bottle to his lips. He'd buy a case of these little bottles, five, six inches high. Regular vanilla extract like you'd use in your cookies. I thought it was strange. It was my first encounter with a vanilla imbiber."

EIGHTEEN

LIKE MANY PEOPLE, LINDA HAZZARD HAD two faces. She wore one for the world and one only those closest to her could see—her husband, Sam, and son, Rollin. The sheriff's launch taking her into custody proceeded north through Colvos Passage, then west, around Point Southworth and into the glass-still waters of Yukon Harbor, before sliding through the narrow channel at Rich Passage and into Sinclair Inlet at Port Orchard. Linda Hazzard appeared in good spirits, her familiar voice, stalwart and clear, carrying itself through the cool marine air. And all along the way she laughed out loud at the preposterous charges leveled against her. She was a doctor, for goodness sake. A common criminal? Hardly. She was, as she often repeated, a martyr for a great cause. The medical profession had been desperate to ruin her, and this was their latest stunt toward that end. Everything that happened had been calculated by the men who feared her methods were superior to their own. The fasting specialist even wondered if Dora and Claire had been sent to her as a part of the plot. Even the date of her arrest was part of the scheme. By taking her into custody late in the afternoon on Saturday, officials knew that it would be highly unlikely, if not impossible, for her to secure bond—the amount having been set at $10,000. She would be forced to spend Saturday and Sunday incarcerated. It was a purposeful act of humiliation.

Of course, that was the side she wanted the world to see. Inside, deep inside, Linda Burfield Hazzard was a little uneasy, worried even. Things had never reached this point before, and she was concerned, a little afraid. A night under guard was inevitable. She knew her detractors would gloat. They always did.

When told she must go inside Mrs. Breed's residence jail, the fasting specialist offered her last words to a small group of reporters that in time would thicken like flies on a dog's bone. Her smile stayed tight, forced against her teeth as if the very pressure, and not facial muscles that control the reflex, kept it in place.

"Dr. Hazzard," a newsman posed, "is it true you are having difficulty in securing bond?"

The fasting specialist stepped back. Her face went red.

"Pooh! Trouble getting bail! I would not take $30,000 right now for my property, and I started back in Minnesota with $15 in my side pocket and two babies. My husband had died, and I had not married Mr. Hazzard. I have practiced fifteen years, ten in Minneapolis and five here. I had no trouble in Minneapolis of any kind. The medical men there are different from the medical men in Seattle.

"I am not worried in the least. I know that I will get bail. They purposely kept the thing off until the offices were closed. But I am not worrying here," she said, motioning toward Mrs. Breed's neatly painted little house.

"I have a nice clean bed, and I can sleep with a clear conscience."

When a reporter asked her what she was going to do now that her career was on hold, Linda Hazzard let out a loud laugh.

"I can assure you, this arrest and trial will not interfere in the least with my plans."

WHENEVER SOMEONE BROACHED THE SUBJECT of the alleged facts of the case, Linda Hazzard proved she was the kind of woman always primed with a quick retort. It was *she* who was the victim. It was *she* who had endured the false accusations.

About the control of the sisters and their estates, she snapped:

I asked to be appointed administrator that I might carry out Claire's wishes. I had myself appointed guardian of Dorothea for the same reason. Claire wished to keep

Dorothea from her relatives, who, Claire knew, would be antagonistic to the new belief.

About suggesting suicide to Dora, she volleyed back a lively commentary:

> *They lie foully when they say that I put Dorothea to sit on the porch and talked to her of committing suicide by jumping into the gulch. Think of me talking to a patient like that! It is a lie of that Kelley. He made it out of the whole cloth. He imagines all sorts of things.*

And, as she would throughout her martyrdom, Linda Hazzard blamed Margaret Conway for stirring up a stinking kettle of innuendo, false claims, and outright lies.

> *Dorothea was in full sympathy with my methods until the arrival of Miss Conway, the nurse who has unreasonable contempt for any but orthodox methods. It was she that swayed the tractable mind of Dorothea against me and brought about, through the British vice-consul and his clever attorney, this trumped-up charge of murder.*

THE NEXT MORNING BROUGHT SUCH A HARSH, mean-spirited assessment, it made the prisoner flinch. Linda saw it as a personal attack, and as such it stung like a flame red andiron through her taut bosom. While impertinent Nurse Conway and Dora Williamson were undoubtedly gleefully reading the accounts of her arrest, the incarcerated fasting specialist seethed while studying the Sunday edition of the *Seattle Times*. Dominating the top of the page was an unflattering sketch, the supposed likeness of herself, drawn by a newspaper staff artist. It was a three-quarter view of her face to just below her waist. Sleeves puffed outrageously and a high collar choked her neck. Dr. Hazzard's eyes were drawn heavy and dark; her mouth was a deep, straight line. The headline labeled the story:

STARVATION SPECIALIST
WHO FACES MURDER CHARGE

It was not the illustration that antagonized Dr. Hazzard, nor was it most of the content of the collection of articles that accompanied the artwork. It was the reporter's assessment of her age. While newsmen had frequently derided her and her treatment, this, this was too cruel a smear even for them.

"Dr. Hazzard appears about 50—her husband looks 42..."

At forty-three, Linda was proud of her looks. It was not because she considered herself an exquisite beauty. It was because her appearance stood in incontrovertible testimony to her medical ideals. She was her own best example. Her body was firm without the numbing bolstering of tight undergarments. Her eyes were clear and sharp. But more than her appearance, the doctor's determination was of the sort that took admirers back and earned the scorn of critics. She was the kind of woman who told the world that her gender did not limit her in any of her ambitions. What was it about the women that made up the majority of her contemporaries? Why was it that they found so little need to press their own point of view? Linda had often wondered why it was that she had so many views and most of the women she had come to know were without a worry except for the chance to marry.

Marriage, she knew, had only brought her trouble.

"Thank you for the newspaper, Sam. It was thoughtful of you to bring it to me," she said, staring hard at the smudged, inky sheets and refusing a glance in the direction of her husband. Sam Hazzard said nothing.

She need not look up to know he was still hovering over her. The air wafted a sweet vanilla scent. It was the kind of scent that some mistook for cologne. Linda sighed. She knew better.

She figured Samuel C. Hazzard ought to know better, too.

The rest of Sunday, August 6, 1911, brought more news, bravado, and disappointment to the quasi jail at Mrs. Breed's. Bond money had yet to materialize. John Karcher had stepped forward with the offer to put up a portion of his assets and set about procuring the rest of the $10,000. Dr. Hazzard posed for Seattle newspaper photographers outside the home of Sheriff

Harry Howe while her attorneys, Day Karr and George
Gregory, met with officials inside. And while she had sent word
to Prosecuting Attorney Stevenson that she wanted to meet him
and a stenographer at the Breed home for the purpose of making a sworn statement, that appointment was abruptly canceled.
She had been admonished by her attorneys to say nothing. She
had said too much already.

Rollin Burfield made the trip to Port Orchard to help Mr.
Karcher secure bond and, of course, support his mother. Rollin
also had another reason to jump into the fray. His mother was at
the center of a brewing storm of publicity. Reporters would
surely linger for any scraps of information they could turn up.
And while his mother had the starring role, Rollin Burfield,
actor, figured he'd carve a nice little part out of the whole affair
for himself. The fact that his mother had been silenced was all
for the better. He'd have all the lines.

He told reporters it was a lie that the Williamson sisters had
been separated at Olalla.

> *Dorothea would often go into Claire's room, lie in bed
> with her, read to her frequently and brought flowers for
> her room. When my mother brought the two Williamson
> girls with her from Seattle my father and I did not particu-
> larly approve of her action as it has not been our custom
> to take patients into our own home because there are cab-
> ins especially constructed for patients. As no cabins were
> available at that time they first came—they were building
> them nearby. Before the cabins were finished, Claire died.
> Both girls were cheerful and happy and so agreeable that
> they overcame my objections and those of my father to
> their presence in our home. Claire, who was the sicker of
> the two, said she had ruined her health in taking care of
> and worrying about her sister Dorothea. Even to the day
> she left the sanitarium Miss Dorothea expressed great
> belief in the fasting cure and was well satisfied with the
> treatment.*

Like the stage hog that he was, twenty-three-year-old Rollin
Burfield went too far. Youth and inexperience and the hope that

press attention would bring him greater roles in Seattle theater were part of his motivation. He bragged to reporters that his mother's treatment had garnered worldwide attention. Testament to that, he said, was the mysterious Himalayan monk taking the treatment at Olalla. According to Rollin, Charles Johnson, a monk of Scandinavian blood, was a man of great intelligence and training—he had studied for "eleven years under the great Swami."

The monk, however, had disappeared.

SOUTH OF TACOMA ON THE SHORES OF THE little lake, relief brought by the news of the fasting specialist's arrest was short-lived. New emotions took over Dora and Margaret. The surge of bitterness, of course, had everything to do with Linda Burfield Hazzard. Dora and Margaret were at once astonished, amazed, and angry. There seemed no limit to Dr. Hazzard's falsehoods. They reviewed the content of one of the interviews the doctor had given to a newspaperman on the eve of her arrest.

> *The Williamson sisters did not hear of me through reading my book, Fasting for the Cure of Disease. They heard of me through a friend of theirs. It is true that they corresponded with me a year before they came to Seattle. Claire did not allow Dora to write because she knew she was incompetent.*

"Through a friend? What friend?" an incredulous Dora asked, ignoring the doctor's harsh words about her mental state. "Another of her outrageous lies!"

"Everything that comes from her mouth is a lie," Margaret said.

In the course of the next few days, there would be many opportunities for the women to tell their side of the story. While the vice-consul had given the press secondhand accounts of what had taken place at Starvation Heights, none would be more effective, more sought-after by the reading public, than the tale spun by the ladies who had escaped.

Nervousness would abate after the first interviews, and Miss Dora and Miss Margaret would become accustomed to telling the story, posing for photographs, and, by doing so, saving the lives of others. The press cast Margaret Conway as the plucky heroine and Dora the forlorn wealthy spinster who barely escaped the wilds of Olalla with her life.

"I was afraid of Dr. Hazzard from the first," Dora told reporters while she sat, pillows supporting her frail frame, on the front porch of Agassiz's home. A shawl covered her thin shoulders.

"I had a kind of instinctive fear of her. She knew I did not like her. But she won me over—it seems to me now it must have been her psychological methods. Soon I did not protest at anything she wanted me to do. It seemed to me that she acted afraid of me most of the time. It was funny. She would glare at me so sometimes with those terrible eyes of hers."

Dora seemed so calm. She looked so much the part of a frail woman on the mend. A tray next to her chair was loaded with beverages, a bowl of nut meats and raisins. Margaret had told her to eat as often as she could, and it appeared to be working. She had gained back pound after pound. Her sunkenness was plumping.

She even laughed a little, before allowing her earnest tale to carry on.

"Dr. Hazzard's actions all the time were so funny that I believe she must have a strain of lunacy. Really, I think she is insane. She was always making such awful suggestions about comitting suicide and telling how her patients had. She was afraid of the dark, too. It was so extraordinary."

Not only did Dora and Margaret soak up the attention, they saw a greater purpose to talking with reporters. Both felt that by fanning the flames of publicity the chances for a criminal conviction would increase. Neither Agassiz nor Kelley offered advice to the contrary. They hoped news coverage would lead to more information. And, in fact, it was Agassiz who set the tone for the press coverage.

COMPARISONS WERE PROBABLY INEVITABLE. They were also immediate. When Lucian Agassiz reviewed the ever-expanding list of Linda Hazzard's patients and the circumstances surrounding their untimely deaths he thought of a

La Porte, Indiana woman. Three years before, Belle Gunness had quite literally carved her horrific place in the annals of American crime.

In her middle years, widow Belle Gunness was not a raving beauty, but whatever charms the Norwegian immigrant had, she apparently put to profitable use. Starting in late 1906 advertisements appeared in matrimonial columns of several Midwestern dailies promising wealthy suitors a rich and comely wife. All they needed to do was to bring proof of their assets and make a personal visit. *"Triflers need not apply."*

As the men prepared to meet Mrs. Gunness, many stopped at the bank for land deeds and money. One by one they came to the Gunness farm. One by one, like fog in the late-morning sun, they disappeared.

In the spring of 1908, the brother of one of Belle's would-be paramours became convinced his brother had met with foul play. He refused to believe his brother left to visit relatives in Norway as Mrs. Gunness had insisted. The brother's nosing around panicked Belle into setting up a scheme that would eventually force discoveries that would shock the world.

The turn of events started with a fire on April 28, 1908. It was on that night that the Gunness farm burned to the ground. Amid the rubble, four bodies were found under the grand piano, which had fallen through the burned-out flooring to the cellar. They were the remains of three small children and the headless body of a woman. Belle's false teeth were found nearby. Though the corpses were charred to a ghoulish blackness, it had not been to the point of complete obliteration. The children were identified as Belle's adopted daughters and son. While the clothing on the headless woman most certainly came from Belle's wardrobe, the body was far too small, too thin to be Belle's. Authorities announced that the cadaver was an impostor. Mrs. Gunness had disappeared.

The farm was turned inside out and the dismembered bodies of more than forty men and other small children were unearthed, most in the area inside the hog pen.

Belle Gunness had murdered dozens, faked her own death, and fled with more than $250,000. She became the kind of mur-

derous female that inspired skipping rope rhymes like Lizzie
Borden who took an ax and gave her parents forty whacks.

> *Belle Gunness lived in In-di-an;*
> *She always, always had a man;*
> *Ten, at least, went in her door—*
> *And were never, never seen no more.*

While there were many differences—the similarities in the
two cases were undeniable to Agassiz. Belle Gunness killed
suitors for their assets and Dr. Hazzard murdered Claire
Williamson and certainly others for their assets. Both women
were domineering, possessing incredibly strong will over those
around them. *What else could account for such evil schemes to
go undetected for any length of time?* Both women published
advertisements in newspapers to drum up business. Both
women were physically strong—the farmer's wife dragged the
bodies to the hog pen; the fasting specialist carried Claire about
the house; Lewis Rader from the hotel to a hideaway. Finally,
the Gunness and Hazzard residences were hidden in rural areas
where encounters with anyone other than the invited would be
rare.

Like La Porte, Indiana, Olalla, Washington, was a good place
to die.

"In the Gunness affair they dug up bodies from all over her
farm," Agassiz told reporters. "In connection with Dr. Hazzard,
we have the records and friends of many patients who died
while under her care."

And while the Tacoma Chamber of Commerce was buzzing
with the prospect that President Taft would pay the city a visit
and become the first president to tour Mount Tacoma, the real
news that had the man on the street talking was about the starvation doctor from Kitsap County.

The *Tacoma Daily News* ran a banner headline on August 7,
1911, that if Lucian Agassiz had devised it on his own it would
not have brought him greater pleasure.

OFFICIALS EXPECT TO EXPOSE STARVATION
ATROCITIES. DR. HAZZARD PICTURED AS FIEND

British vice-consul says revelations will surpass Gunness case before investigations end.

THE PRESS LOVED LINDA HAZZARD for the reason that she provided them with endless opportunities for sensational copy. They never supported her, but took every opportunity to sully her reputation. The establishment despised her, and masses who read the papers were not of the means to use a foolish treatment as she practiced. Fasting, or the starvation treatment, was a rich person's folly.

Whenever the opportunity to insinuate evil was offered, reporters seized it.

Concerning L. E. Rader, the *Times* carried a quote from a Seattle doctor, W.C. Woodward, followed by a sinister comment from the reporter.

"Rader, from all we could ascertain, died of starvation. We found that he had trouble with his wife."

"Rader's widow now lives near Dr. Hazzard's place and is on friendly terms with the starvationist."

The implication caused a stir in Olalla among the few who heard about it. Some wondered if it could be true Dr. Hazzard and Mrs. Rader had plotted to murder Rader. Adding credence to the gossip was the fact that the sanitarium was built on land that had been transferred from Rader to the Hazzards.

THE HOURS PASSED FAR TOO QUICKLY AS LINDA Hazzard's attorneys and supporters scrambled for the bond that would release the doctor from custody. John Karcher was unable to put together the necessary funds and collateral, and Sam Hazzard, as usual, was "temporarily short of funds." Linda had characterized her stay with Mrs. Breed as a lovely "visit." But she naturally wanted nothing more than to go to her Olalla home—not to a jail cell in King County. Finally, after considerable coordination between her lawyers, county officials, and representatives of the Seattle offices of Pacific Coast Casualty Company, a $10,000 bond was approved and Linda Burfield Hazzard, charged with first-degree murder, was free pending trial.

At 1:30 P.M., August 8, 1911, Dr. Hazzard stepped from Pacific Coast's office on the second floor of Colman Dock with her own agenda. Against the advice of her attorneys, she had made the decision that she was going to talk. It was time to tell her story. From the beginning.

NINETEEN

A HOT BREEZE ALWAYS BRUSHED OVER Star Lake in the summers of Linda Burfield's memory. The two-story farmhouse with soot black shutters, the outbuildings that pockmarked the flatland, the sawmill where her father put in eleven hours a day, all came to her mind when she allowed it to seep back to her days in Ottertail County, Minnesota. She remembered the rope swing and how the fringe coming from its knotted end suggested the tail of an unkempt draft horse. She could smell the rankness of the mud clinging to her ankles when she emerged from a swim in the lake. She could feel the subtle dips and rises in the terrain of a trail she and her brothers had cut from the house to the water—their own secret path. She could recall milk cows, their dangling udders pointed to the gleaming bottom of a pail.

Even though she sometimes smiled at the thought of it, so very glad was she that those were such distant memories. A life in Ottertail County would have left her with nothing to show for her years. She would have lived and died in the hot breeze over the lake. She would never have achieved her heart's desire.

Born in Carver County, Minnesota, in 1868, Linda or Lana, as she was also known as a child, was the oldest of seven. Her mother was Susan Neal Burfield, a Canadian woman whose first husband drowned when a Union boat sunk in the rage of a river during the Civil War. Susan married Montgomery Burfield in 1869. Born in Bellefonte, Pennsylvania, in 1828, Montgomery had been a corporal in the Ninth Minnesota Infantry during the Civil War. The family went west and home-steaded in Star Lake Township, Ottertail County, in 1878.

Linda was an outgoing ten-year-old girl then, more interested in tree climbing than dolls.

Montgomery and Susan shared similar views on diet and exercise that would clearly shape their eldest daughter's life. The Burfields set a mostly vegetarian table. Occasionally small amounts of meat were offered, but Susan never forced her children to partake of it.

And no matter how Linda regarded what might have been if she had been inclined—or forced—to stay in Minnesota, she owed her interest in natural therapy to those days, and she knew it.

Linda traced the beginnings of her search for a better way to the medical doctor who called yearly on the Burfield children. Montgomery, foolishly, Linda would later say, had decided his children needed the care of a doctor. No one was sick, but he had bought the idea that the medical men of the day could ward off potential problems with their black bag of tricks. Montgomery did it out of love, out of the idea that it was a prudent measure. The father adored his children, especially Linda.

The doctor convinced the Burfields that their children were silent, uncomplaining victims of potentially fatal intestinal parasites. "Blue mass" pills were prescribed as treatment for the malady that had not appeared evident in the slightest. The cure brought horrific results—frequent bouts of vomiting and diarrhea. Over and over, through the course of several years, the treatment was tried.

Linda wrote of it many years later:

> I now know, what of course I could not then suspect, that this powerful poison did irreparable injury to my intestines, retarding and preventing their development and growth to such a degree that even to this day I am compelled to resort to the enema daily.

FROM THAT TIME TO HER MARRIAGE TO ERWIN A. Perry at eighteen, Linda had been in a constant state of ill health. Her delicate and damaged stomach could hold little in the way of nourishment. Linda would attribute the loss of many of her upper teeth to the purgative calomel administered by doctors tending to her stomach trouble. She was thin and tired, and in a constant search for the "cure." Erwin was fourteen years older, the son of a well-to-do pioneer. Linda had been a somewhat reluctant bride. She had pledged undying love, but, as she later suggested, she didn't really have the heart for it. She was searching for something else. Something greater.

In March of 1896, less than a month after her marriage to Erwin Perry, tragic news reached Linda. Her father had died. Montgomery Burfield had been taking logs to his mill when the reach broke, upsetting the load. Sixty-year-old Montgomery never had a chance. The rolling logs pulled him under and, in an instant, crushed his skull. His body was taken to the town hall at Perham, but an inquest was deemed unnecessary. With Linda, his oldest, and his other children in attendance, the man was buried in the family plot at Star Lake.

Linda would grieve for the loss of her father for the remainder of her life. He was, she thought, the only completely honorable man she ever knew. Not her husbands, not her son. No one had been as true to another as Montgomery had been to Susan Burfield.

Linda and Erwin settled in Fergus Falls and had two children. Rollin was born in August 1889, a daughter named Nina Floy was born two years later, in March 1891. While Rollin would be the source of repeated and public humiliation in later years, Floy would be an apparition. Only a few Olallans ever heard of the fasting specialist's only daughter.

AS FAR AS MOST OLALLANS WERE CONCERNED, NINA Floy Perry was nonexistent. No one had ever seen her and, years later, only one out of all the old-timers could recall Dr. Hazzard talking about a daughter. Perhaps because her father was such a close friend to the fasting specialist, Helen Buchanan was around the sanitarium enough to pick up bits and pieces about the mysterious daughter.

"Her name was Floy. What a strange name? I always thought. Oh, she did talk about her. Many, many times. Whenever she asked for a new dress, Dr. Hazzard would always give her money for material—but never buy her a new

dress. She gave her money for material to make herself a dress. I heard the story about the dress business umpteen times!

"To my knowledge she never came to see Dr. Hazzard. She was always a mystery. The only thing I thought was, 'How sad.' It didn't seem like a normal mother-daughter relationship. It seemed harsh.

"And yet, one thing we all wondered about was her affection for Rollin. He was, as far as I was concerned, worthless. He just ran around in puttees all the time."

YEARS LATER, NO ONE COULD BE SURE WHAT happened between the Perrys. It was likely some dark family secret, some speculated, that was never meant for the light of day. Linda had claimed in court papers filed in Hennepin County, Minnesota, that her husband had abandoned her and her children on April 5, 1898. She had been left with no support. No word of his whereabouts. The divorce became final in the fall of 1902, and the court decreed Linda could resume her maiden name—and if she desired, her children could also be known by the Burfield surname.

Her son and daughter were shipped off to live with their grandmother Susan Burfield in Star Lake. Linda's ambitions for a career as a fasting specialist had usurped her desire for motherhood. She simply couldn't be bothered by it. She rationalized her decision. As a man would put his ambitions ahead of his family for "the good of the whole," she would do the same. She would become a healing authority such as the world had never known.

"I am a divorced woman," she said years later as she slammed the book shut on her first marriage, "but I am not ashamed of that. There are some men a woman can't live with."

And so she left her son and daughter behind in the process of her quest for the cure that had eluded her as a child. While the son would later return to her, the daughter would hold a grudge against her mother for the rest of her life. The two would never reconcile. Many years later, in her last will and testament, Linda would bequeath Nina Floy the slap-in-the-face sum of $1.

THOSE WHO KNEW THE DOCTOR ALWAYS FELT her story of the abandonment by Erwin Perry had a falseness to it. Linda always made a point of telling the faithful that she had "come to the fast" by way of treating herself in 1898—the same year Erwin had supposedly deserted her. Even those who admired the fasting specialist reckoned from what they knew of her character, Linda had been the one who had done the leaving. It left a few to wonder: What woman who loved her husband, had just been left by him with two small children, is going to have her children raised by her mother?

For Linda, the answer was, always, a woman with a greater purpose sets aside convention. And so she did.

She had first studied osteopathy with designs on a position as a nurse. Then she came across a copy of *The Gospel of Health*, written by Dr. Edward Hooker Dewey. The book changed her life. In it, Dr. Dewey promoted the therapeutic benefits of the fast.

Dr. Dewey had seen the light in 1877, when he assumed charge of a typhoid-fever case. Regular treatment failed the patient, so Dr. Dewey "let nature take her course" and employed the fast. Thirty-four days later, the patient recovered from what had been an illness that would most certainly have killed him.

Dewey wrote his other famous treatise on health and diet, *The No-Breakfast Plan*. It, too, was embraced by the long-suffering woman from Ottertail County. She made contact with the doctor and, in time, convinced him that she was the one to carry on his teachings.

The student and the great teacher, however, did not always agree. She, who was dependent on the internal bath, insisted that it was the best course.

"A necessary hygienic accessory of the fast," she insisted.

Dr. Dewey, however, felt the bowels should be allowed to function "naturally." Despite their disagreements on the subject, the two remained close until Dr. Dewey's death. By then, the pupil had become the protégé.

Linda Perry opened an office in downtown Minneapolis, and, in time, her practice thrived.

"Cases pronounced incurable by medical physicians recovered under the regimen I imposed, and the symptoms presented ranged from chronic constipation, diabetes, Bright's disease and syphilis to paralysis."

It, of course, was only the beginning. It was before Sam Hazzard. Before the wealthy English spinsters would call in her office at the Northern Bank and Trust Building. *Before* Starvation Heights.

TWENTY

THERE WAS NO GETTING AWAY FROM IT. The woman with the unblinking eyes and booming voice had made an indelible impression. Lucian Agassiz could almost hear her saying the words, though he had only read them printed in the newspaper.

I had no trouble in Minneapolis of any kind. The medical men there are different from the medical men in Seattle.

The vice-consul weighed the veracity of the statement made by Dr. Hazzard shortly after her arrest. *No trouble in Minneapolis?* Agassiz doubted that. There had to be something. Just had to be. And yet, no matter how loudly he proclaimed to the world that he sought information about Dr. Hazzard and her methods, no one from the Midwest hurried forward to tell of suspicious deaths linked to the woman. Agassiz didn't give up. In his impatience, he called a newspaper in Minneapolis. It paid off.

"Young was her name," came the voice crackling on the line. "Gertrude Young. Case made a stir here."

Agassiz's heart thumped in his chest. He could hardly contain his excitement as he listened to the story. Gertrude Young was so very important. The late Mrs. Young had been the very first on a roll call of the dead that would in time number more than twenty.

THE TIMING HAD BEEN UNBELIEVABLE. *THAT* letter on *that* day. Among the drifts of paperwork piled on the desk of Minneapolis mayor D.P. Jones, was an envelope from a world away. The neatly scripted return address was 45 Drury Lane, Dumfermline, Scotland. Addressed to the mayor, it had been sent by a man named George Downie.

The date: November 1902.

I shall be much indebted to you if you can give me any information as to Mrs. Gertrude Young of Minneapolis, U.S.A. I would have written to her, but I don't know her full address. I saw in one of our papers that she is promised a certain cure for paralysis by a doctor who claims to cure by a system of fasting twenty days at a time. I am paralyzed in the lower limbs and would do anything for a cure. Kindly let me know if there is any truth in the claim of the doctor.

Picking through his papers, Mayor Jones bellowed for his secretary to handle his daily correspondence. Chief and most easily disposed of seemed to be the letter seeking information about fasting specialist Linda Burfield.

Pity the poor paralyzed man! All the way from Scotland he had heard of the fasting cure? Who would have imagined it? And on that particular day, no less!

The mayor spread out the morning paper and advised the secretary.

"Send him today's news accounts."

IT WAS OBVIOUS TO THOSE WHO KNEW HER AND few had quarrel with her sad mental state. It was very unfair. For the past two years, Gertrude Young's forty-one-year-old body had been contorted by the ravages of a stroke that had left one foot and arm slack and nearly useless. She could barely dress herself, and putting her own hair up was out of the question. So many things, she came to learn, required two hands. Doctors offered treatment to ease the pain, but they offered no hope for recovery. The rest of her days would be unremitting torture.

In desperation, Mrs. Young undertook a course of treatment she almost certainly saw as a last hope. With the fasting cure, she was told she might be able to walk without assistance. She longed to smile without the sorry droop that accented the corner of her mouth.

In mid-October 1902, she called Dr. Linda Burfield to her apartment at 711 Third Avenue S. It was three weeks after that meeting that the trouble began.

On November 12, Mrs. Young woke to violent fits of vomiting of a dark, acrid-smelling gruel. Hope had turned to horror. The rapid spasms of retching left her a damp, wilted figure slumped against a row of stained pillows in a darkened bedroom. Despite the frigid winter temperature, windows were opened wide to refresh the room's thick air. The cold only worsened Gertrude's condition. Late that day, a nurse telephoned a physician of the regular school who had treated Mrs. Young in the past and asked him to hurry over.

Immediately upon arrival, U.G. Williams, an M.D. who also held the position of Hennepin County coroner, recommended Mrs. Young break the fast immediately. No matter how plain it was that she was desperately ill, the patient and the friends who had gathered around her bedside disagreed. Gertrude Young, they all insisted, must stay the course of the treatment as prescribed by Dr. Burfield. The fast was to be broken on the fortieth day—not an hour sooner.

Dr. Williams was at once both worried and bitter. He felt the fasting treatment would certainly end in death, and there was nothing he could do about it. *God, the woman needed nourishment.* Her body was sunken beyond any measure, her skin, the pasty yellow of decomposing eggshells.

Gertrude Young died on November 18—the thirty-ninth day of her fast. Dr. Burfield said the cause of death was "paralysis."

Not everyone agreed. Coroner Williams was sufficiently outraged to announce an inquest would be held forthwith. He moved to stop the shipment of Mrs. Young's body to the place of her birth in Wisconsin. A day later, a postmortem exam was conducted at the University of Minnesota. Scientists at the university ruled that the dead woman, who weighed just 105 pounds, had died of starvation. Among the strangest of their findings was noted in the report: *The body contained practically no blood.*

The crippled woman, Dr. Williams concluded, was a victim of cruel and unnecessary quackery. Hennepin County Attorney F.H. Boardman was apprised of the matter and a criminal case against Dr. Burfield was seriously considered.

The *Minneapolis Daily Times* bannered the story across the front page on November 20, 1902:

CORONER IN CRUSADE AGAINST STARVATION CURISTS URGES PROSECUTION AS SEQUEL TO WOMAN'S DEATH

Among the mysteries faced by the dead woman's family was the whereabouts of Gertrude Young's jewelry. Costly rings that had been on her fingers until her death were among several missing valuables. Dr. Burfield scoffed at detractors who dared to suggest she would have stolen from a patient. The jewelry, she said, had been given by the deceased to one of the nurses.

The nurse, however, was never to be found.

OF COURSE THERE HAD BEEN A GREAT DIVIDE between regular physicians and the handful who practiced fasting or any of a number of unorthodox, natural remedies. Linda Burfield had known that throughout her training. She saw the purveyors of drugs and costly hospital stays as frightened men, weak and desperate to guard fiercely their corner.

Others had stepped forward of their own accord or had been forced into the public eye by circumstances, but they were men. She was the first woman; a bona fide martyr in an important, revolutionary cause.

When she invited a reporter to her office at the Globe Building, Linda Lana Burfield boldly stepped into the unforgiving glare of the flashbulb and spotlight.

"I have a great cause, you see."

The scribe nodded. That was all very fine, indeed. But what he wanted to know was whether she had a medical degree or license.

The doctor leaned back in her chair and let out a forceful laugh.

"Thank God, I have no license to kill!"

And while melting snow dripped from the reporter's boots, forming a tiny pool on the floorboards, Dr. Burfield announced the true cause of Gertrude Young's death was, in fact, as far removed from her hands as could possibly be. Barely stopping to take in a breath, Linda Burfield continued her litany while the reporter did his earnest best to keep up his note-taking. As others would find out many years later, keeping up with that particular woman was not easy.

"I undertook to cure her of paralysis and during the latter part of the treatment her condition was so much improved that she had free use of her right leg and arm, but her improvement was not satisfactory to me on the whole, and I questioned her more closely.

"She would not allow me to make the usual examination which is my custom.

"As her case seemed to grow worse and worse, I finally insisted that she tell me all, and she at last admitted that she was suffering from an incurable disease which had been checked by her former physician. She also admitted that she had not faithfully obeyed the instructions which I had given."

Before she finished her dissertation, Dr. Burfield laid the patient's ultimate fate at the feet of her chief critic—the coroner.

"Mrs. Young was given up two years ago as incurable by two of her former physicians, one of which was Dr. Williams."

As the interview concluded, the fasting specialist invoked for the first time what would become an oft-repeated theme when physicians of the regular school attacked her.

"All of this talk about 'getting after the starvation curists' indulged in by certain members of the medical profession doesn't alarm me in the least. Any new remedy which is effective where pills and powders fail is bound to stir up the ire of the regular medics."

She would tough it out. And in time, she was certain, she would prevail.

The coroner puffed up with anger against "that woman and her dangerous cure" and her slanderous comments met with bitter disappointment. No criminal charges would be levied against the fasting specialist. No laws prohibited her methods. Dr. Burfield was free of any liability.

Only one more time did Dr. Hazzard ever publicly comment on the Young case. The occasion was more than a decade later, when fingers had once again sharply pointed at her treatment as the cause of the death of one of her patients.

"The first trouble I ever had of any kind in regard to fasting was in Minneapolis," she stated, "when a woman named Young died while under my care. The medical officer there, who was a friend of the woman, made some trouble and the newspapers took it up, but it was proved that I had not starved her to death."

TWENTY-ONE

LINDA BURFIELD HAZZARD SPOTTED IT
the instant she took a seat for an interview in Seattle three days
after her arrest for Claire Williamson's murder.

A strand of silken thread strayed from the doctor's hemline
when it had brushed the rough, splintered surfaces of the hand-
hewn timbers that served as the gangplank of the steamer *H.B.
Kennedy*. Back and forth her skirt had swished until a slight
tug, like a fish on a line, made known the presence of an unraveling of her seams. Linda knew the edges of her garment were
failing, and she was sure her visitor had noticed it as well. She
was not a woman who enjoyed the scrutiny of a critical eye.
She didn't tolerate flaws of any kind. The doctor fixed her eyes
on the reporter and, with a quick, fluid movement of her right
foot, caught the thread and tucked it under her dress, out of
view.

Yet it was more than her hemline that was disintegrating.
Linda knew the man sitting across from her had come to the
interview armed with as much information as he had planned to
glean from his visit with her. She saw it in his face. He knew
something about her past. It was something no one in Seattle
knew.

An uncommonly sordid dispatch had arrived from
Minneapolis on the desk of a gleeful *Times* editor the night
before.

"Doctor," the reporter began, "be so kind as to tell me about
your husband's prison sentence."

Prison sentence. It was so revolting, so incongruent that a
man of Samuel's character had to bear the indignant tarnish of
such words.

Linda's eyes flashed, and she pursed her lips. A spot of anger gave way to the faded brave smile of a memory. To her way of thinking it was a love story, so great in its depth that she sometimes had felt it was imagined. It had been both a dream and a nightmare. She knew the whole story—not because she had read about it in the daily newspapers that served the booming Midwestern city—but because she had been in the very center of its sensational swell. She also knew that she had been seen as the cause of the whole affair.

Linda motioned for more tea and cleared her throat.

"No sugar," she told the reporter as she put the cup to her lips. "That business in Minneapolis was merely the work of a jealous and vindictive woman."

It was long ago.

CLEAN-SHAVEN AND WITH GOLDEN EYEGLASS frame gleaming, Samuel Hargrave was a gorgeous man. His head of dark, wavy hair was surely the envy of any woman. So thick. So shiny. His penetrating eyes promised both danger and devotion. Men without the blessing of such allure could never fathom the effect such a man could have on women. Samuel stood tall and erect. By any accounts, a military bearing could not have been in doubt when he walked or spoke. It was a woman of potential wealth that drew this deliberate man's attentions one Chicago evening.

Viva Estelle Fitchpatrick, the daughter of an Iowa state senator who was also president of the First National Bank of Nevada, Iowa, was considered by her family to be a bit of a flibbertigibbet. Twice divorced, Viva had told her mother and father that she had come to Chicago to learn the seamstress trade. She had, in fact, studied the craft a bit, although with no serious intent. But her true reason—her "calling," as her family gossiped among themselves—was to seek the affections of yet another suitor. Viva was legendary for the folly of making one poor choice after another. She was a woman who never learned or at least never *seemed* to learn.

In the early part of an unseasonably warm spell in October 1902, Viva made her way to a streetcar as the clouds began to leak like water through a colander. From the shadows on the corner of State and Monroe, a man offered a smile and an umbrella. His name, he said, was Sam Hargrave. He was an insurance salesman for the Chicago office of the New York-headquartered American Credit Indemnity Company.

Viva had caught his eye.

"I would very much like to call on you," he said, sheltering her from the downpour.

And though there was no hesitation in her answer, the woman would later wonder if she had made a fateful mistake. God knew that this, more than any other, was one time when Viva Fitchpatrick should have said no.

Over the next several months, as she kept company with the handsome and hardworking Sam Hargrave, she said yes. Again and again. But as 1903 approached, Viva had given up any pretense of sewing for a living. The very idea of it seemed absurd. Her place, she told her parents, was beside Sam as his wife. The Fitchpatricks were relieved that their daughter had not turned into some kind of consort, a woman of ill repute.

In February, Sam Hargrave agreed to take an assignment in the Minneapolis office of American Credit. Viva would join him as soon as he was financially set, but money was scarce. Sam told Viva that her patience would be rewarded with a wedding and a lifetime of happiness.

On March 2, 1903, Sam sent a note to his intended.

My Own Viva:

Your letters have just come and I do need you and want you, sweetheart, we certainly can get along all right, dear, and I believe you can arrange it to come this week, can't you? How I'd like to take you in my arms and hold you close to me, my own girlie.

Good night, and God love you, dear.

Samuel was a charmer. His words lived atop the pages of his letters. The promise in his love letters brought a quiver of excitement through the reader's body. Each day, Viva Fitchpatrick made a point never to stray from the area below the transom when it came near mail delivery time. Most days she was not disappointed. And never would Sam feel as though she did not feel the same love for him. She flooded his Minneapolis hotel with letters.

On March 3, 1902, he typed a letter on company letterhead and mailed it to Viva in Chicago.

> *My Own Dear Girlie:*
> *... Can you come to me, dear, on Saturday? Let me know about it, so I may make arrangements at once, I am only waiting for you, sweetheart ...*
>
> *I wish I could send you the cash to come with. But come soon, and know my arms are open for you and my heart and love are all your own.*

It was not to be the white gown and coat and tail wedding that she had dreamed about—that she had once before. This time, Viva didn't really care. When she arrived at the train station in St. Paul on March 7, 1903, Viva Fitchpatrick only cared that she would be marrying the man she loved. She didn't think it odd that when Samuel—who had told his boss that he wanted the day off to meet some friends across the river in St. Paul— came to take her to the court commissioner's office he was rushed and a bit out of sorts.

"Make it short, old man," Sam Hargrave told the commissioner as he swept into his office. "We are in a hurry."

The bride was also in a hurry. It had been far too long since she and her man had been together.

The next day, on March 8, 1903, when Viva wrote to her mother telling her of the wedding, her new husband added the following postscript:

> *Dear Mrs. Fitchpatrick:*
> *Viva has told you all there is to be told and I am only adding this postscript to assure you of my earnest desire to be all that you can ask in your son-in-law. We shall try hard to get along comfortably and I want you to feel that this first letter brings both you and Mr. Fitchpatrick the knowledge that I shall care for her and love her all through my life.*
> *Faithful always, Sam*

Over the next few months, at least as the new Mrs. Hargrave was concerned, their life at 1098 Thirteenth Street South, in apartments owned by Frank and Kate Strong, was as happy as any new couple's. The apartments were furnished with dining table and chairs, full bedroom, and a small sitting room. Mrs. Strong was delighted to have rented the rooms to people of such obvious refinement as the Hargraves. It would mean less work for herself, and that was a relief. Her husband Frank had taken ill and was being treated by a doctor, a fasting specialist named Linda Burfield.

And though the doctor made frequent visits to the Strongs', neither Mr. or Mrs. Hargrave had the occasion to see her. At least neither said so. They were far too involved with their new life together. When away on business at Fairbault, Minnesota, that June, Sam wrote to his bride.

I shall be so lonely without you dear, and I want you every minute of the day. Tomorrow is my birthday—34— so you see the grey hairs are justified. This is a pretty little town and I hope I may get something out of it. Love me, dearie girl, as I love you, and know that I will always be your very own loving husband, Sam

He followed it with another brief note, dated the next day:

. . . Be my good girlie and Saturday will see me back. I do so long to creep into your arms and hold you close to my heart for every day I love you more and more and you are always my own dear wife.

VIVA HARGRAVE, FLIBBERTIGIBBET AS SHE WAS, was not totally lacking in sense. She began to suspect something was amiss in her latest marriage.

Suspicions were kindled when William Tanner, the indemnity company's general manager, visited the Hargrave apartment to check on Samuel, who had been ill. It was Tanner who suggested Sam take some time off from his duties at the insurance company in order to break the grip of a stubborn cold. It was after Sam didn't return to work after several days that Tanner came calling. A strange woman answered the door.

The woman led him to a bedroom in the back of the second story apartment.

Sam wore a surprised look on his pallid face and made a startling and abrupt introduction.

"Allow me to introduce you to my wife, Mrs. Hargrave."

Tanner dropped his jaw like a curtain and a surprised Viva spoke up.

"Why, Sam, doesn't Mr. Tanner know of our marriage?"

"No," he answered, lifting his head from his pillow. "I wanted to keep this quiet. I have some matters in the East I wanted to arrange and fix up before I made it public; furthermore, I thought the general agent from Chicago would think I was a fool to get married at this time upon the small salary that I am getting."

Viva turned to her husband's employer and smiled. "Why, we were married last March. March 7," she said.

Later, William Tanner found the encounter was strange enough that he would not forget it. It seemed a little peculiar that a man he worked with side by side would not have confided a marriage. Tracing the lines of his memory, Tanner would also later recall that date in March and how Sam Hargrave had told him he wanted to meet some friends who were passing through St. Paul from Chicago. It was March 7. Sam hadn't said he was going to get married, and that was very odd. Tanner tried to put it out of his mind. It wasn't really his business.

Still, something Sam had said in the apartment kept coming back to his thoughts. Tanner was left wondering what sort of matters Sam Hargrave had need of straightening out in the East?

MONTHS PASSED AND THE CHANGE IN VIVA'S husband became more evident. Linda Burfield, the woman doctor who considered herself a pioneer in the fasting treatment, showed up everywhere Sam Hargrave went. Or at least it seemed so. Dr. Burfield kept offices on the fourth floor of the Globe Building in downtown Minneapolis and Sam Hargrave was also seen frequently in her offices. He told Viva he planned on going into business with the doctor. Viva Hargrave was supportive of her husband's plans at first. She had occasion to meet

Dr. Burfield when Sam introduced the two women in mid-October of 1903.

Viva was introduced as his wife, Mrs. Hargrave.

The next morning, Sunday, October 17, 1903, Viva complained of anonymous letters full of vile innuendo sent to her. Someone had typed messages emphatically stating that Sam was in love with Dr. Burfield and that his marriage to Viva was a lie. The words stabbed at her—as they had been meant to do.

When Viva confronted her husband, Sam dismissed the content of the notes. It was rubbish, plain and simple. He didn't have any idea who was the source of such hateful allegations.

"There is nothing more than a business relationship between Dr. Burfield and me. I assure you."

"Sam," Viva tearfully pleaded, "you mustn't see her again. I know you are true to me. I know it in my heart. I don't believe a word of these letters. But promise me you won't see her, work with her, talk with her?"

Sam put his arms around his crying wife and agreed. On the night of October 18, as if to to cement his vow to Viva, he tapped out a letter to the fasting specialist.

Dear Linda:

After thinking matters over thoroughly, I have come to the definite conclusion that it is better to let things stand as they are. In other words, my first duty, no matter which way it comes, belongs to my wife. Therefore I shall stand by my first decision, and will attend strictly to the business I am now doing. I am very sorry to occasion you an inconvenience or any displeasure, but I have talked it all over with a disinterested party, and I have heard from my father-in-law, who also advises me in this way.

Yesterday another of those disreputable letters reached my wife, and I at once took steps to prevent their recurrence. They can be productive of nothing but harm to all concerned, and they have only succeeded in putting my duty more strongly before me. The latter consists in attending to the work I am now engaged in doing the right thing for her who bears my name. This should appeal to you, and I believe that after what has occurred you will someday realize that I have risen to a proper conception of right living. I feel fully convinced that nothing but unhappiness can result in anything of a business or personal relation between us . . .

Linda Burfield disregarded Sam's letter. He was foolish. He was weak. Even so, she had made up her mind that she would have him and no woman would stand in her way. Not even his bride.

NOT FAR FROM OLALLA, HOME COLONY ON THE KEY Peninsula, was an anarchist enclave that celebrated personal freedoms other Americans had lost sight of, or worked overtime to squelch. Linda Burfield Hazzard and her fasting theory had always been welcomed at Home.

In 1945, long after the colony had been abandoned by its dreamers, former boyhood colonist Radium LeVene wrote about the fasting cure as it related to the colony.

"I recall the time when Dr. Hazzard came over from Olalla to lecture to us on the benefits of fasting after which the grocery stores were almost compelled to close their doors. My mother fasted for 21 days following (Hazzard's) lecture and benefitted greatly. Kingsmill Commander fasted for two or three weeks and everything went well until he broke his fast, then his hunger became so great that Mrs. Brewster had to lock up the food to keep him from gorging himself to death. He would get up in the middle of the night and break into the pantry.

"Then came the time when Joe Rosenberg decided to go to Tacoma to break his fast with a bowl of tomato broth—but instead of stopping there, the broth tasted so good he ordered another one, after which he decided to eat a full course dinner. By this time he was actually intoxicated with food. He felt like a million dollars and wanted to tell everybody how wonderful fasting made you feel. He recalled that Mike Rubenstein had a ladies' tailor shop in the Fidelity Bldg. on the 9th floor, so off Joe ran to the Fidelity Bldg. But there were no elevators ready to go up when he arrived, so up the nine floors Joe ran. Joe had a relapse which almost killed him after the experience, but he pulled thru."

TWENTY-TWO

NOVEMBER 11, 1903, WAS A DAY LINDA
Burfield would never forget. Neither would her rival.

Viva and Sam shared a midday meal at Ben Hang's Chinese
restaurant on Fifth Street, downtown Minneapolis. What was
said between the two of them would forever remain clouded.
Witnesses later observed how Viva had reached across the table
and soundly slapped her husband on the cheek. What had provoked it? Had Sam told her that he was unable to break off his
relationship with Dr. Burfield? Or was it something else?

"I didn't call him any names," Viva later said. "I don't think
we had a particular quarrel, but I did strike him at the table . . .
he didn't raise a finger at me."

It is doubtful any woman could forget her wedding day. It is
even more unlikely when she is marrying another's husband.
Linda Burfield and Samuel C. Hazzard—not Hargrave—were
married by a minister in the office of her fasting practice. Clay
Gilbert, a friend and music teacher, witnessed the wedding.

Linda Burfield Hazzard's wedding night was memorable for
a reason few brides could lay claim to. The groom was nowhere
to be found. Linda slept alone at her apartment, and her husband, Samuel, went home to his other wife.

And while Sam saw Linda during the course of the next few
days, he stayed each of the next four nights with Viva.

On the morning of November 14, Samuel Hargrave kissed
Viva and asked her to meet him at his office at 4 P.M. When
she arrived at the appointed hour, her husband was nowhere to
be found. While she waited, she discovered a note on his desk.
It was directed to her, written in Sam's beautiful script. He
indicated another business engagement had come up and he

would be detained. He assured her he would see her later that day.

He did not keep his promise.

In fact, Sam did not return to their apartment, and Viva spent a restless night. She was unable to sleep. Worry consumed her. Where was Sam? Was he hurt? She prayed for him to return safely.

When morning light flushed over the streets of Minneapolis and sent sunshine through her window, her all-night prayers were answered. Or so she thought. Relief and confusion swept through her when Viva found her father and her husband entering the apartment. Her father? Why, he was in Iowa with no immediate plans to head north to Minneapolis, as far as she knew. She felt something terrible must have happened. Both men were grim in their demeanor. Their facial expressions were fixed in the stony, tormented and grieving way worn by those who suffer an inexplicable death in the family. In a sense, it was.

Sam spoke first. He offered no apology for his absence. He offered no explanation.

"You are not my wife," he told her. Viva was stunned. Though by no means a thin wisp of a woman, for an instant she looked frail and weak. She reached behind her for a chair.

"You are my common-law wife," Sam continued, his tone uncharacteristically cold and matter-of-fact. "There is no record of any marriage in St. Paul."

"What are you talking about? There is some terrible mistake," she muttered, as shock was supplanted by a flood of tears.

"Sam, am I your wife or not?"

"Viva, you are not."

Senator Fitchpatrick tugged at his little beard and reached a hand out for his daughter. "It is true, I'm afraid."

Sam continued hurling spikes at Viva's heart.

"I am married to Dr. Burfield now."

"I do not believe this. If I am not your wife, am I your mistress?"

"You are my common-law wife."

She turned to her father and saw the cold look on his face.

"Does my daughter believe that she has entered into a marriage with you?"

"Yes. But she is not my wife."

"Sam, but I *am* your wife."

"No, you are *not*."

Senator Fitchpatrick was angry and befuddled. He knew his son-in-law was a man of great promise, and though he tired his brains in an effort to make sense of the man, he could not. He recalled how earlier in the marriage he had sent Sam $200 to set up a household, but instead Sam had spent the money on himself. Careless, yes. Even selfish. But not a harbinger of a proclivity toward criminal activity.

Samuel C. Hargrave or Hazzard—or whatever his name was—held such promise.

"If he had come to Iowa and been a straight man, he would very soon have led his district and perhaps the state in politics and affairs. I can't understand such a peculiar makeup as he has," the senator later said.

The day after the confrontation with his wife and father-in-law, Sam quit his job at the indemnity company. He offered no notice, no apology. He was moving on to better things. *Bigger things*. A health and treatment center would make him and his new wife rich and famous, the toast of Minneapolis.

Samuel was extremely intelligent, capable in all areas of business. But when it came to affairs of the heart, no matter that he could write a love letter to cause a girl to swoon, Samuel C. Hazzard was a poor risk for any reasonable girl. And though he could woo and bed any woman he wanted, and had done so with the regularity of a tomcat, he underestimated the tenacity of a woman scorned.

Viva Estelle Hargrave would not fade quietly into the background. If Linda Burfield Hazzard thought the Iowa woman could be brushed aside like so much rubbish, she was sadly mistaken as well. Mrs. Hargrave would fight for her husband with all she possessed. If that meant the fasting doctor was a casualty of the little war of the heart, then so much the better. If it meant Sam had to suffer along the way, then that was the price he paid for being so foolishly misled.

Viva Hargrave responded to a friend's inquiry into the matter on November 25, 1903:

Dear Mrs. Smith:
... There is nothing I can say; it is all too dreadful. But in the sight of the Lord and in my own heart Sam is my husband, nothing can change that and some day I am sure he will realize what he has done. I shall never cease loving him and shall try earnestly to forgive all who have caused him to do wrong. I can not wait any more now. I feel I cannot endure this.

Viva did not have to wait long. With her father driving the point and using all his political pull, the Hennepin County Attorney's Office filed bigamy charges against Samuel C. Hargrave, aka Hazzard, just after Thanksgiving. It was the beginning of a sensational case—a spectacle to which hundreds flocked.

ALL OF MINNEAPOLIS HAD WAITED FOR THE trial. It was no wonder that they should. It was a shocking and twisted affair. Two women fighting over the affections of one man. Each woman claimed she was the only true wife. From the beginning, it was clear that it was the cast of players that brought the attention as much as the sordid nature of the circumstances: a handsome West Pointer, the daughter of an Iowa state senator, the woman doctor who led the crusade for the defendant.

Linda Burfield Hazzard had done more than act as a supporting player. She had gone to St. Paul to review records and interview people associated with the county commissioner's office regarding the wedding ceremony performed on March 7. After she returned from her mission, she and Sam announced to the press that she had proof that there had been no wedding. The state's case, she said, had been "deprived of its spinal column."

But merely winning the case would not be enough. Dr. Hazzard wanted Viva indicted for perjury.

"She fabricated the marriage—and I have proof," the doctor announced. "I doubt she'll testify against Sam."

Defense attorney George Leonard, satisfied that Linda's evidence would vindicate Sam, vilified Viva Fitchpatrick as a woman of dubious moral character.

"She came up here to live in illicit relations with Mr. Hazzard. It was a scheme in which both the defendant and the prosecuting witness were guilty of deceiving the young woman's parents."

Viva's family fumed at the defense's proclamations of ill-reputed behavior. They saw Linda Burfield as the true instigator of all the trouble. She had known from the beginning that Sam belonged with Viva. Though she had met Viva as Sam's wife, she apparently didn't care. They cited proof found in the phone directory just before Sam's arrest. Dr. Linda Burfield and Mr. S. C. Hazzard were listed with the offices in the Globe Building *together*. There could be no doubt Linda Burfield knew full well that Sam Hazzard was married to Viva Hargrave—and that he went home to her each night.

The Fitchpatricks and the prosecutors felt that if they could not prove a wedding, it was because the commissioner had deleted the records. Perhaps Linda Burfield was more powerful than they could know? They knew that Dr. Burfield was using all her influence to ruin Viva, and thus validate her own marriage to Sam. The doctor's reach was far. A woman from New York purporting to be Samuel's first wife dispatched letters to the Fitchpatricks stating that she had received telegrams threatening her not to come to Minneapolis to testify against Sam.

It seemed, the woman wrote, that *her* divorce to Sam Hazzard had not been final at the time of the Fitchpatrick/Hargrave nuptials.

ON FEBRUARY 4, 1904, SAMUEL HARGRAVE/HAZzard wedged his commanding frame through a gap between the spectators overflowing Judge F.C. Brooks's Hennepin County Superior courtroom. And though he seemed nervous, even surprised, at the number of people studying his every move, Sam still had the debonair manner that the ladies had come to expect. With the flourish of a gentleman of great breeding, he offered a seat to Linda Burfield before taking his own at the defense table.

Linda had never looked more lovely. She wore a form-fitting autumn brown suit and hat. Over the course of the trial she would not let a moment go without registering her approval or disapproval at any of the witnesses. She would not let an opportunity pass in which she could offer advice or words of support to the man she loved.

Viva Fitchpatrick, however, was somber and somewhat sullen in the plain shirtwaist suit that she had donned for the trial. She sat quietly, nearly blending into the spectators who had lined the walls of the courtroom. Though she said nothing, her feelings were noticed by one of the newsmen covering the case.

The young woman's glances in the direction of her former lover and the present object of his affections were anything but kindly.

As the days passed, there was a weakening division among the spectators when it came to "Wife No. 2" Viva or "Wife No. 3" Linda. At first, some shook their heads in disbelief when Viva, dressed in a black coat and hat, gave her teary-eyed testimony. Still others shot hard, frosty glares at the woman doctor who had broken up such a happy home. When Viva walked out of the courtroom after testifying, a mob of fashionably dressed women besieged her with congratulations for a job well-done.

Women of all walks of life crowded into the courtroom. One newspaper even did a kind of inventory of the ladies there to watch:

. . . the woman who wears a black velvet hat over her left ear and who is a devotee to the gum chewing habit . . . the frivolous young thing with an exaggerated pompadour and the grey eyed stern-visaged woman who greases her head to prevent any possible curl, are both there, but the young girls with flowing veils and chromo hats lead them all in point of numbers.

One woman who had positioned herself in the front row brought a camera. She set it on the railing and snapped an image of the defendant when he turned to survey his admirers. The lady photographer was admonished by a deputy to cease the snapping, and she did so. She had only wanted a souvenir.

A woman leaving the courtroom summed up the reason most had come to watch.

"Honestly, it is as good as a play, and you don't have to pay for it, either."

Throughout the trial, Linda Burfield Hazzard scribbled notes and kept her lips next to her husband's ear. She had advice to impart—advice she was certain would catch the other woman in a lie.

But it was the introduction of the nineteen letters written by Sam and Viva that convinced so many that some harm had been done and the marriage to Linda Burfield was more than a mistake. It was, in fact, a crime against Viva. Headlines in the *Times* and *Journal* trumpeted the mood of the courtroom.

JURORS LISTEN TO BURNING NOTES IN BIGAMY TRIAL SPINNING WEB ABOUT HAZZARD

Four days after the prosecution started, it rested its case. The defense for Samuel Hazzard offered only three witnesses. None were of consequence. None helped in the least. It seemed to observers that there was no defense for what the two-timer had done.

As he brought the case to a close, the prosecutor reminded the jury of the letters, loving as they were. They had indicated a happy home, a viable marriage. He laid the blame for all that happened at the feet of the other woman—Dr. Linda Burfield.

"Some one was interfering with this home. The Garden of Eden was a perfect home until a serpent crept into it. These apartments at 1098 Thirteenth Street South were a perfect home until something or somebody crept into it and with a virus that is perfectly damnable, destroyed the peace and happiness."

Linda stared straight ahead. She made no notes. She offered no reaction. The insults and insinuations would make no difference. In the end, Sam would be free and her marriage would be sound.

Or so she hoped.

IT TOOK THE JURY FIVE HOURS OF DELIBERATION
to issue a verdict in the Hazzard/Hargrave bigamy case.

"*Guilty!*" was called out into the courtroom at nine o'clock
the evening of February 9.

Linda and Sam seemed stoic and composed. An appeal
would be filed. The trial was a sham! Viva Hargrave was a liar
who should not have been believed.

"There had been no wedding on March 7!" Linda called out.
"Samuel was free to marry me! I am his wife!"

By virtue of the verdict, she was not. She was once again Dr.
Burfield.

Sam remained dignified while Linda railed on and on. By the
time they arrived at the jail office, her tirade had turned to tears.
The jury was unsympathetic and unreliable. She was the victim
of the Iowa woman. She continued to mutter about injustice and
the woman who had caused the terrible trouble.

"*Liar!*"

Viva, on the other hand, seemed to be in the throes of a
change of heart. Her parents were mystified. Viva now felt
sorry for Sam. She still loved him. She sent word for a reporter
to come to her apartment for an interview.

"Oh, I feel sorry for my poor boy," she explained. "I wish I
could serve the time for him. Isn't there some way they can let
him off?"

She still had feelings for Sam, she said. While he was respon-
sible for what he had done, he had been misled and manipulated
by an evil woman.

"Don't you honestly think that woman knew I was married to
Hargrave when she married him? I thoroughly believe that she
knew it all the time, and I think she is the more guilty. She has
threatened that she would take him right from under my nose."

And as she finished her litany against Dr. Burfield she
dropped a bombshell that would make headlines the next day.

Mrs. Hargrave had just received a telegram that an uncle in
Fresno, California, had left her a sizable inheritance. Details
were not known, though the reporter pressed for them.

"I don't know how much I'll get, but he was rich," she said.

AS EARLY AS FEBRUARY 10, LINDA BURFIELD could feel her man slipping away from her and back to Viva. She visited the jail in the early morning, but left with tears in her eyes and no comment for the press.

Viva kept visits, too. But she was the winner now, first in the eyes of the jury, and, she felt, in the eyes of Samuel.

"I shall never get a divorce from him," she said that afternoon, hinting that reconciliation might be forthcoming. "I have had enough of both marriage and divorce, and from this day on [sic] I shall live quietly with my parents."

The *Minneapolis Times* ran a West Point photograph of Sam Hazzard that same day. He was dashing. His hair was parted in the center, and his moustache was as dark and big as a blackbird on landing.

The next day the *Journal* broke Linda Burfield's heart.

FORTUNE SMILES ON S.C. HAZZARD

The paper reported that now-wealthy Viva, accompanied by her mother, had paid another secret visit to the Hennepin County Jail. When Viva emerged from the hour-long visit, her eyes were red from crying.

"But she wore an unmistakable smile of hope," the paper reported.

Later, the article revealed, Viva was seen talking on the telephone with Sam. A reconciliation appeared imminent. Dr. Burfield was most certainly no longer the object of Sam's affections. Viva spoke about the woman who had stolen her husband and thereby caused the whole courtroom debacle.

"I do not wish any harm to come to her," she said later. "I have tried to keep from being vindictive, and she suffers enough now. I know what it is to love and be denied the one I love, and she has the same agony now."

"Would you pursue charges against her for knowingly being a consort of a bigamist?" a reporter asked.

Viva pondered the question for a moment. "No, I would not testify against her if I could help it."

Dr. Burfield wouldn't let it die and insisted on calling Sam "my husband." She refused to believe he truly wanted to stay with Viva Fitchpatrick. After all Viva had done to him, Sam should hate her. But it was Viva who had prevailed. As with the doctor, she made frequent visits to see Sam in jail.

The *Journal* noted the continuing love triangle in an article on February 12, 1904:

NEITHER WILL GIVE UP HAZZARD

... Meanwhile Hazzard is in a dilemma which, to any sensitive man, would be more embarrassing than a criminal trial itself.

When the judge handed down a two-year sentence at the state penitentiary, Sam faced it alone. Neither wife was there. He apologized to the court for what he had done and conceded that he was addicted to drinking. Though he held out for a successful appeal, the basis of which would be that the state had failed to prove that he and Viva had a valid marriage, the hope was dimmed on March 16, 1904.

The court ruled that there would be no new trial for Sam Hazzard.

THE FIRST DAY OF SPRING WAS COLD AND HEARTLESS. Viva was unable to procure the funds needed for the $5,000 appeal bond. The papers trumpeted the fact that Sam would have to wait in prison. The inheritance money was months away from being transferred to Viva, and her father, while certainly able to wield some influence, refused to help.

"I am going to try to get Papa to help us, but, although he says he will help to get Mr. Hazzard pardoned when he is in the penitentiary, he seems to want him to go there first."

And While she continued to do all that she could to save her husband from prison, she had only one request of him. She insisted he must tell Dr. Burfield that she was not a welcome visitor at the Hennepin County Jail, where he awaited the transfer to the prison.

Sam agreed to his wife's demand.

"We didn't want a scene," he explained a little later. "I have made up my mind, in fact, I made it up some time ago as to where my duty and my love lie, and it might as well be thoroughly understood for now and all time."

A JEALOUS WOMAN ALWAYS HAS SECRETS. Some memories were too dark and Linda Hazzard refused to tell the *Seattle Times* reporter long after the Minneapolis scandal might have faded from memory. Not anyone. She would leave the reporter believing she and Sam were devoted to each other right through the trial to his release from the prison at Stillwater. The truth was far from that. She had been betrayed and humiliated in a way no woman would wish to relive. Linda could try, but she would never succeed at eliminating the embarrassing memories associated with a Saturday afternoon in mid-March 1904.

As she had done during the days after Sam's conviction, Linda came calling at the jail. The jailers knew her, and because of her authoritative personality, they allowed her special freedoms within the cellblock. She was, after all, a doctor. When she arrived, they waved her inside. Linda usually found Sam in the midst of an array of legal tomes in the jail's library researching his appeal to the state supreme court, but that was not the case that particular day. He was nowhere to be found. Linda decided to organize papers and clear away the clutter that seemed to threaten the process.

Among the papers was a stack of letters addressed to S. C. Hazzard.

Linda picked them up and noticed the postmark.

"*Nevada, Iowa.*"

The letters were from Viva. They were not letters of hate or requests for Sam to admit the error of his ways. Each of the string-tied bundle was clearly a missive of love.

Linda's heart stopped beating for a second. Her legs buckled. And as the walls caved in, the room went black.

The next day, the doctor was told that her visits to the jail were no longer desired. Sam was in love with Viva.

Dr. Burfield was not a woman given to tremble, but she could not stop as she read her statement to some of the Minneapolis newspaper reporters who had covered the bigamy trial. Her voice, usually quite strong and authoritative, was choked with emotion. Tears pulled at her eyelids as they slipped down her smooth cheeks.

> *"I married Mr. Hazzard because I loved him and after he had sworn to me that he was not legally married to any other woman. If the law has declared our marriage illegal, it is my misfortune and nothing I could foresee. If Mr. Hazzard has chosen to state that he would marry the Iowa girl when released from prison, I have at least done what I could to fulfill my marriage vows to "love, honor and cherish." I have done no more than any loyal woman would do for the man she loved. If I am to be left alone, I can bear it; but the distress and the affliction are enough to bear, without having my every natural action the cause of unsympathetic comment in the public prints."*

The next day, March 24, 1904, the pages of the *Minneapolis Journal* told the city of Dr. Burfield's sad realization. It was, Linda hoped, the last humiliation she would face in connection with Samuel C. Hazzard.

AT LAST BELIEVES HAZZARD IS FALSE

The following day, Sam Hazzard made his only public statement concerning his misdeeds and plans for the future. Convict #2586 spoke as guards led him toward the gates of the penitentiary at Stillwater.

"If only I had left women alone, I would have been all right," he said sheepishly.

"As it is I feel that I have only myself to blame. I played the fool and now I am going to take the consequences with as good a grace that I can. As for the future, I am going to try and live up to the poet's advice: 'Build upon resolve and not upon regret the structure of the future.'"

Exhausted from lack of sleep and worry for Sam, Viva pulled herself together for the transfer to Stillwater.

"Oh, why didn't you have this change of heart a few months

ago? Why couldn't you see that it would all lead to nothing but trouble?" she cried.

Sam told her to stifle her sobs.

"It's bad enough as it is without you rubbing it in," he said.

And so she quietly wept, vowing to wait for her Sam.

Seeing the case to its end, the reporters were elated to note that "shorn of his raven locks, clad in baggy grey striped clothes, the 'military Beau Brummel' was hardly a sight calculated to charm the fair ones who have heretofore been his abject slaves."

"YOU SEE," LINDA BURFIELD HAZZARD TOLD THE news reporter nearly a decade after the bigamy trial, "there was *no* marriage. This woman—this Viva Fitchpatrick—was never, ever married to my husband. She never had his name.

"I stood by my husband in that case and spent $10,000 in his defense. You will find the people of Minneapolis know me, and they won't say anything against me.

"I tell you, I have nothing to hide."

TWENTY-THREE

THE COMBINATION OF A HANDSOME FACE,
mental brilliance, and a prison sentence likely wasn't enough to
give Samuel Hazzard pause to consider the error of his ways. It
was true the stellar prisoner had lost weight, read all of the clas-
sics shelved in the prison library, and even taught French to a
few of the most hardened inmates. He had, as expected, fared
exceedingly well at Stillwater. Rested and in high spirits from
the quickened pace of earned good time, he was discharged on
October 30, 1905.

Humiliation, indignation and the scorn of Viva Hazzard had
not been enough to lead Linda Burfield to the realization that
the man who had hurt her so badly, so publicly, was such bad
news. Though Linda announced to the world their love affair
was over and she never wanted to see the scoundrel again, no
other man shared her bed while Sam Hazzard was away. She
always held out hope.

Her friends called her foolish, but she didn't listen to any of
them. Dr. Burfield could only hear her heart.

After prison, Sam was expected to return to Minneapolis to
Viva's waiting arms. Viva came back from Iowa and took a
room at Mrs. Strong's when her husband's release date
loomed. The Iowa state senator's daughter had stood by her
man throughout his imprisonment. She had written the warden letter after letter inquiring about what she could do to
make her husband's sentence endurable. She sent money and
magazines. When he required a tooth extracted, it was Viva
who paid the bill for the gold tooth that filled the vacant
space.

His wrong has been done more through weakness than wickedness and I feel that I want to do anything I can to make him more comfortable.

The woman whose complaint put him behind bars had become the wife of any prisoner's dreams.

And to a waiting Viva, Samuel was as dashing and charming as he had been the day they met. Sam told her his big plans for the future. He was in a hurry. He boasted how he'd prove all his doubters and enemies wrong. He had spent a year and a half in prison, and he was not about to waste a moment's time.

Samuel C. Hazzard was everything he had always been. He was not a changed man.

When he got out of prison, it was not to Mrs. Strong's boardinghouse that he went knocking. Instead, he made his way to the Globe Building and the apartments and offices of Linda Burfield.

The doctor was in.

GREAT AMBITION CALLED FOR A PARTNER. LINDA Burfield understood that from nearly the beginning of her journey from the obscurity of Ottertail County to the city streets of Minneapolis. She was going to found a great sanitarium and teach the fasting cure to a legion of devotees. Sam was the man to help her realize her exalted aspirations.

The doctor's office had been as busy as she could manage on her own. With Sam back, the two of them could resume where they had left off. Before the Viva Fitchpatrick incident ruined everything.

In 1906, the listing in the Minneapolis telephone directory read:

Burfield, Linda,
Specialist of Fasting, Physical Culture and Health Home.
Hazzard, Samuel C.,
Mgr. Linda Burfield's Health Home.

The following listing, in the 1907 directory, carried no mention of Dr. Burfield. But the notation for Samuel Hazzard indicated he had *"moved to Seattle, Wash."*

What happened in the year between Minneapolis and Seattle would remain unclear. Neither Sam nor Linda would ever say much about it. Most assumed they had arrived together. Sam following Linda after she was "called to the Pacific Coast," where some of her family lived.

The fasting specialist opened Seattle offices in the spring of 1906.

Years later, she wrote:

> Soon after this I began to encounter organized persecution from medical sources, aided by newspapers controlled by the profession. Such deaths as occurred under my care received the widest publicity, and the accounts written concerning them were distorted and filled with implication, innuendo, and threat.

And while business thrived, the relationship between Sam and Linda suffered from Sam's infidelity. Though Linda had a lovely figure—her body reflected her livelihood, her proof that even for the sickly good health was attainable—Sam could not keep his pants buttoned when it came to beautiful girls. It didn't matter how fetching Linda could make herself. In his mid-thirties with row after row of wild oats sown, Samuel could feel his charms fading. As if drinking the energy of a young girl would somehow bolster his own waning youth, Sam Hazzard made the rounds. He would flirt, bed, drink, and beg for forgiveness. Linda would cry, slap, and yell. And give in to him if that was what it took.

As she had proven before, Linda would not let him go.

AN ATTORNEY FROM THE OFFICES OF THE STATE penitentiary at Deer Lodge, Montana, wrote the warden of the Minneapolis prison inquiring about Sam Hazzard at the beginning of February 1907. He wrote how a young woman at Deer Lodge had become "interested" in Sam and sought information about his incarceration for bigamy in Minneapolis.

The warden immediately fired back a single-page letter which gave a stunningly direct account of his once-star prisoner's character:

Hazzard is a dangerous man with the female sex, as his past career will prove and he has had lots of experience. He is a bright, intelligent, well-educated Lothario, and he knows just how to use his talents. If you are well enough acquainted with the young lady to give her some good, plain advice, I think you will do her a lasting favor by telling her that if she wants any future peace of mind she better cut him out, and all remembrance of him.

On March 2, 1907, the Deer Lodge lawyer wrote back to the warden, thanking him for the warning, which, as it had turned out, was heeded by the infatuated girl.

Do not know this party. He is now residing in Seattle. There is a widow lady from this town, accompanied by her daughter, went to Seattle to take medical treatment and, as near as I can understand her daughter became very much attached to this man Hazzard. Hazzard's wife is carrying on some kind of fake medical business there.

MAYBE IT WAS THE PLEASURE OF TWO BODIES under the sheets that kept them together? Maybe it was that one had designs on a future that could only be realized with the assistance of the other? Maybe it was even love, though in later years few would see the remnants of great affection between the doctor and her husband.

Few could recall seeing the faintest trace of anything of the kind.

TWENTY-FOUR

FROM THE FIRST TIME SHE LAID EYES ON him, Linda Burfield knew she had to have Samuel Christman Hazzard. He siphoned every bit of her good sense with his good looks and kept her enthralled with his wit and charm. If a darker side was only hinted at when Linda first met Sam, it only furthered her interest in him. If Sam had any troubles before Viva Fitchpatrick shared his bed and ruined his life, he made no mention of it.

No one could have imagined a man with greater promise than Samuel Hazzard. Quick-minded, clear-eyed, and tall, with the perfect posture of a man of assurance—he had all the hallmarks of a hero. School classmates in Pottsville, Pennsylvania, where he grew up, bet their nickels that Charles H. Hazzard's boy—one who always claimed a spot in the front row—would go far. He was a natural born leader. He was the kind of man that inspired confidence and jealousy in others. He could lead men into battle in the morning, and dance with a new widow in the evening. He could do both, it seemed, equally well.

He set his sights.

The United States Military Academy at West Point, New York, was the gilded pinnacle for young men with potential. Three days before his twentieth birthday, on June 15, 1889, Sam Hazzard entered the Academy. He was the pride of Pottsville, fulfilling a great destiny.

Sam was, as expected, an extraordinary student. He graduated fourteenth in a class of fifty-one on June 12, 1893. He excelled in all studies, though he could have finished with a higher class ranking if only he had worked a little harder. But because things came so easily, Sam Hazzard did not find it necessary to consider the benefits of hard work. He never had to. Just after graduation he accepted appointment as additional second lieutenant of the artillery.

Three months later, he took what would be the first of three wives. Agnes Hedley Hazzard was a beautiful young bride, the daughter of a boardinghouse keeper. In many ways, she was a perfect match for the man with great ambition. She was vivacious and intelligent. She saw nothing but wonderful things when she studied the dark eyes of the man she had married. The future, she thought, belonged to them.

Agnes was also of modest means, and in the end, that would be her downfall.

Over the next couple of years Sam progressed quite nicely in his career. He was lauded by superiors for his command of languages. He was a reader and a speaker, fluent in French, Spanish, German, and Latin. He was appointed as the Academy's instructor of Modern Languages in 1896. Continuing in that capacity for almost two years, he finally accepted a promotion to the post of military adjutant. It was a plum. The appointment involved many social duties and all who knew him saw him as a man who loved his work—especially the social aspects of the position.

In a performance review in 1899 Col. A.C. Mills, the superintendent of the Academy, wrote:

> . . . *He is a very efficient officer and can be relied on to give an excellent account of himself in any position or duty to which he may be called.*

Sam had carved out a powerful niche at West Point, one that gave him social standing and power. He was having fun. He was eating and drinking as well as the richest of New York. He also kept a secret, the inevitable legacy of a good-looking man who could have his pick of any woman. Unbeknownst to Agnes, Sam had taken a mistress. The money. The power. The illicit thrill of it all was as intoxicating as the whiskey he used to slake his thirst and ease whatever conscience he possessed.

When the army recommended Sam for a promotion to first lieutenant of artillery in April 1899, he did his best to stall the transition. He applied for a three-month leave. He wrote how he had not had a leave since the summer of 1897. He also reminded his superiors he had done more than double duty by adding to his language instruction responsibilities the role of assistant professor of French while adjutant of the post.

The request, however, was denied. Officers in the First Artillery were scarce. No delay could be allowed. Sam, claiming he had not received word, asked a second time. His request was denied once more.

In August, he tried a new approach: lying.

I ask this because of the serious physical condition of my father who has just been stricken with total blindness.

The delay was granted. How could it not be?

AND, AS A FIRST AUTUMN LEAF FALLS TO START the mass that cloaks the Academy's impressive grounds, misdeed after misdeed came to be known. One at a time. Sam Hazzard left New York, his wife, and his perfect military record behind. In time all would be sullied and shamed by his actions. And though none knew what he had been doing at the time, none would be shocked. Sam Hazzard was many wonderful things.

And Sam Hazzard was something else, as well.

A drift of unpaid bills had been left behind in New York. Sam immediately claimed none were his responsibility. From Fort San Jacinto, Texas, he wrote that the bills were an apparent misunderstanding. He had closed out his brother-in-law's affairs and some outstanding invoices were to have been paid by the estate. There was no problem. It would be handled.

Big misunderstanding.

The War Department received letter after letter concerning outstanding debts that had been ignored by Hazzard. On February 12, 1890, Adams and Company, New York, a beef and poultry wholesaler was owed $68.81. A tailoring bill was also delinquent—and had been for more than a year.

Sam dashed off a quick response to the War Department.

Linda Burfield Hazzard

An advertisement appearing in Olalla's short-lived newspaper, the *West Pass Record*.

Wilderness Heights Sanitarium

OLALLA   **WASHINGTON**

Under the Direction of

Dr. Linda Burfield Hazzard

A contemporary view of the Empress Hotel, Victoria, British Columbia, Canada, where the Williamson sisters received their copy of *Fasting for the Cure of Disease.* (Courtesy of Claudia Olsen)

Linda Burfield Hazzard at the time of her trial for the murder of British heiress Claire Williamson. (Courtesy Tacoma Public Library collection)

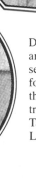

Nurse Margaret "Toody" Conway took a steamer from Australia to rescue Claire and Dora from Olalla. Dora Williamson (seated) weighed scarcely fifty pounds after her rescue.

Dora—recovered and determined to see justice—poses for pictures during the 1912 murder trial. (Courtesy Tacoma Public Library collection)

Dora (l.), Claire and unknown woman pose for the camera during happier times—before Olalla. (Courtesy Tacoma Public Library collection)

British vice consul Lucien Agassiz—as depicted in a *Seattle Times Daily* illustration—orchestrated the prosecution of the American doctor.

The Kitsap County Courthouse where the trial played to its stunning conclusion. (Courtesy Sidney Museum and Arts Association collection)

The front steps of the bungalow at Starvation Heights, 1911. Among the group is nurse Nellie Sherman and handyman Frank Lillie. Standing in the center is Rollie Burfield, Linda's son. Linda is in the back obscured by the man in front. (Courtesy Sidney Museum and Arts Association collection)

A view from the bluff over-looking Olalla Bay, circa 1911. (Courtesy Janetta Nelson collection)

The weakened sisters were carried from Seattle to Finney Creek (just north of Olalla) on a special launch arranged with the captain of the Virginia. (Courtesy Janetta Nelson collection)

L.E. Rader, publisher and state legislator, was among the two dozen-some victims of Linda Hazzard's fasting regimen. (Courtesy of Sound Views)

Linda Burfield Hazzard sat for this portrait in Minneapolis. It was mistakenly published as Claire Williamson in one of the Seattle dailies during the trial.

Samuel Hazzard was a rising West Point officer when he succumbed to "wine, women and song." He served a prison sentence in Minnesota for bigamy. Linda was his third wife. (Courtesy Minnesota Historical Society, Stillwater Prison collection)

After her release from prison, Linda Hazzard took her fasting cure to New Zealand where she practiced as an osteopath for several years. She lived in this house near Auckland. (Courtesy Beverly Simpson)

A relentless self-promoter, Dr. Hazzard ran ads like this in various New Zealand directories.

WILDERNESS HEIGHTS
SANITARIUM
DR. LINDA BURFIELD HAZZARD, Supt.
OLALLA, WASHINGTON

Dear Charlie-
Please swear to signature
and mail the Washington letter
Also- please send to
Caity tomorrow
30 - 2¢ stamps
5 - 3¢ "
Am at the bills-
Sam A.X-

3 C M letter

The only known
photograph of Olalla's
greatest building is on
the doctor's letterhead.

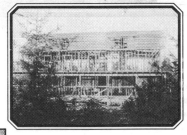

After five years in the South
Pacific, Dr. Hazzard returned
to Olalla and built her great
sanitarium. (Courtesy of
Verna Fagerud)

After Linda's death, Sam
Hazzard moved his things back
into their bedroom and slept
there for the first time
in years. (Courtesy Janetta
Nelson collection)

A 1964 photograph shows Cabin Claire in its final ravages of decay. Today, only the foundation of the sanitarium still stands in the forest. (Courtesy Warren B. Anderson)

A panel of a 1937 cartoon inspired by the Olalla murder case: "The Tragic Case of the Living Skeletons" by Robert Wathen. (Courtesy Bernice Crouse collection)

This latter bill had been contracted by a young man at that time staying at my house.

It was not his fault.

Brooks Bros., New York, submitted a bill for $56.05. Three pairs of pajamas, six collars, six pairs of cuffs, coat and vest, three pairs of trousers, a vest, a scarf had been delivered to Lieutenant Hazzard, but the account had never been settled.

Even the bicycle repairman in Highland Falls, New York, was owed money—$1.30—for repairs to Agnes Hazzard's bicycle.

The account was not his, Sam informed his superiors. It was the mysterious young man's fault again.

The bicycle repairman wrote back, that beyond a shadow of a doubt, it was Samuel C. Hazzard who made the order for work.

The amount is very small, but I am poor and I need it.

The blacksmith in Highland Falls retained an attorney for $9.00 left unpaid by Hazzard. A harness maker claimed a $31 unpaid bill.

While the charges piled up, it revealed a man living well beyond his means, trapped in a desperate desire for the good things that money could buy. And while it was embarrassing to the army, all would have been forgiven if two things hadn't happened. The first was Sam's constant denial of his responsibility.

Secondly, Sam starting biting down hard on the hand that fed him. The first complaint surfaced on February 9, 1900. Samuel had not made good on a debt of $72.56 at the West Point Post Exchange.

Then, a day later, at his command in Key West, Florida, Samuel received a leave of absence for one week. He would be given the time to get his affairs in order, to straighten out the compounding mess that he had gotten himself into. On February 17, he telegrammed his superiors from the St. James Hotel in Jacksonville.

Am ill at Jacksonville. Will join as soon as possible. Request an extension of leave.

The extension was granted.

On Feb 28, 1900, Sam Hazzard chose not to face up to what he had done. He telegrammed a resignation request to army headquarters.

Certain obligations which I shall be unable to fulfil in the service impel me to forward this application . . .

In the days and weeks that followed the reasons for his actions became increasingly clear. The sum of the missing dollars grew. The Post Exchange was out $229 when Sam forged checks to himself.

On March 8, a telegram that the Pickwick Club in New Orleans had been stiffed with a bad check reached Hazzard's superiors. The captain of the First Artillery had introduced Sam and the manager cashed a check on his word. It left the club $150 short and the captain with a red face.

And there was more. Forgeries. Lies. And then the sad realization of the men who served under him, and those who had taken him under their tutelage. Sam Hazzard was a cad and a crook.

Rumors of Sam's continual womanizing and habitual dishonesty fueled the escalating complaints. On March 16, 1900, a friend of Hazzard's late brother-in-law wrote a letter to Secretary of War Elihu Root, in Washington, D.C. He informed the secretary that Sam had borrowed $500 for the purpose of assisting a relative. The money, of course, was never returned.

I have since learned that no part of the money was used for that purpose, but was used for his own personal use, and I am led to believe that the purpose for which it was used, were it known, would reflect great discredit on him. I think the life he is leading would not bear close investigation . . .

On March 22, Second Lieutenant John E. Stephens, 7th U. S. Artillery, wrote to the adjutant general of the U.S. Army. He had given Sam a note for $250, so he could get change for collecting bills due the Post Exchange. Sam Hazzard took the money and ran. The next day, the army learned how another check written to S.C. Hazzard had been cashed for $75.00. The check, like the others, was no good.

The end of the following month, Andrew Alexander Company submitted a bill to the army for $106.75 for boots, shoes, and slippers Sam Hazzard had seen fit to buy. Everything, of course, was the best.

SAM'S WIFE AGNES HAD CRIED UNTIL THERE were no more tears. It seemed nearly every day there was a knock on her door or a letter in the postbox. Everyone wanted to know where Sam had gone. She responded to the inquiries with several letters of her own. She could never quite put into words what she knew to be the true reasons behind Sam's desertion. When the Hazzards last saw each other in a Florida hotel room it was the most unpleasant of circumstances. Agnes never knew the other woman's name, but she knew her husband held deep interest in another. She also heard Sam had borrowed money, as much as $5,000 from the lady, and the two of them were bonded by love and money.

It was not pretty.

Agnes Hazzard, who had been the joy in her mother's life when she married the handsome young officer, was now the scorned woman.

She wrote the army in the spring of 1900. She was alone in New York and she fully expected she would never see her husband again. She was preparing to support herself. She had been left for another woman, a woman of means.

I am much distressed and ashamed to make this acknowledgement . . .

On April 29, 1900, the *New York Times* carried an item about Sam Hazzard.

LIEUT. HAZZARD'S DOWNFALL ORDER IS OUT FOR ARREST OF A POPULAR ARMY OFFICER
. . . Social attention and the effort to maintain the position he had attained has resulted in the downfall of a popular young army officer.

A little more than a month later, the *Times* carried a second mention of the sullied pride of Pottsville.

LIEUT. HAZZARD A DESERTER
DROPPED FROM THE ARMY ROLLS—LEAVES
BEHIND A WIFE AND FAMILY IN NEW YORK

YEARS LATER, WHEN THE BIGAMY CHARGES would bring his name to the forefront again ("He is said to be one of the most brilliant graduates of {West Point} in purely scholastic attainments . . ."), those looking for Sam Hazzard found him in a Minneapolis jail. Agnes Hazzard, as the very first Mrs. Hazzard, was one. By then she held no more feelings for the man that had hurt her so terribly. She wrote to an army financial agent who had kept in touch with her over the years with the hopes that she would tell him the whereabouts of her estranged husband.

The missing money, she suggested in her letter, might be recovered through the assets of a "rich woman" he had married.

The rich woman's father, of course, was none too happy with his two-timing son-in-law. When he learned there were skeletons in Hazzard's military closet, J.A. Fitchpatrick sent a letter to Elihu Root, secretary of war. If Hazzard was wanted for crimes committed prior to his desertion, Viva Fitchpatrick's father wanted to be certain the army knew where to pick him up.

Since leaving the army, he has been a regular guerrilla in his warfare upon society, devastating homes and causing ruin to innocent women, and, owing to his natural shrewdness, does his work in a way that so far he has escaped prosecution . . .

Under the belief that there was the possibility of an acquittal in the bigamy case, United States officers of the Secret Service were sent to Minneapolis to arrest Hazzard for forgery and cashing government vouchers—the charges which had been hanging over him since he left their ranks in Florida. It was assumed by many that Hazzard had used the name Hargrave to thwart the detection of army investigators who tailed him.

Of course, the agents were not needed. Sam was sent to Stillwater for other crimes—crimes of the heart.

When his past caught up with him once more, after Linda's arrest for Claire Williamson's murder, Sam feigned surprise and indignation about the scandalous charges.

"Well, I would be perfectly willing to face any accusation of that kind," he said. "It is the first time I ever heard of such a thing but in the event of its being true any claims of this kind are outlawed long before this."

Nobody in Olalla ever knew of Sam's criminal past. To the locals, he was always Sam Hazzard, the West Pointer. Impressive. Honorable. Intelligent.

As he had been in Pottsville.

LINDA HAZZARD THREW HER HEAD BACK AND let out a forced fit of laughter.

How wrong could her enemies be?

She reached out for her husband's hand and drew him closer and smiled as they stood on the dock for the boat to Seattle, so many years later.

"And yet they say I have hypnotized him!" Her voice was drenched in merry sarcasm. "Why, one look at him ought to convince anyone of the falsity of that statement. Besides it surely would be a most difficult thing to influence a man who has had twelve years of the severest army training."

As if to mock the charges, Sam held his eyes frozen from any blinking before he chortled at the ridiculousness of the rumors about his wife's supposed mental powers.

Linda smiled broadly and laughed.

"I shall have to study to see if I do have hypnotic power."

TWENTY-FIVE

IN THE DAYS JUST BEFORE AND JUST AFTER her arrest for Miss Claire's murder, Dr. Hazzard got reacquainted with a number of the surviving relatives of her patients. Many felt that it was high time the woman was prosecuted for what they were certain was a mixture of evil and quackery—though none were sure what the proportions were. Many of her critics were aghast that it had taken so very long for the fasting proponent to be stopped at all. They wondered what kind of power she held? How was it that she had been allowed to get away with repeated murder? There was talk of the doctor's interest in Theosophy, even the occult. Some gossiped that perhaps she had put a spell on the factions against her.

One of the first who came forward was Oscar Heaton. He supported Dora's contention that the fasting doctor did, in fact, practice some kind of powerful hypnotism or mind control over her patients. He saw it for himself. He pleaded with his wife Viola to seek the services of a medical doctor—not a fasting quack.

Mr. Heaton believed Viola had succumbed to the tremendous will of the doctor.

"When Mrs. Hazzard was giving my wife the 'starvation treatment' I must say that I felt this influence," he told reporters. "I did not want Mrs. Hazzard to take it up at any time, but through other women she was treating she prevailed on my wife to take it up. She has a way of surrounding her patients with adherents of the starvation theory, and sending others who are converts to the theory and are also fasting to talk with sufferers, so that it is almost impossible to get to them. When I finally did order her out and insisted on a regular physician, it was too late."

IT WAS ABOUT CONTROL OF THE WILLIAMSON money. As Lucian Agassiz saw it, the so-called doctor and her husband had hatched a plan to murder Claire, which would pass the inheritance on to Dora, who, in turn, would remain a life-time prisoner at Olalla. The Hazzards would be able to appro-priate and plunder the fortune as they saw fit. Agassiz allowed Mrs. Hazzard that it was, in fact, a diabolically clever plan. But he also knew that in haste, the greedy always make mistakes.

By unraveling the fiscal transactions that took place while the sisters were under the care of the fasting specialist, the vice-consul was certain he could strengthen his theory, which would strengthen the criminal case.

Early one August morning, Agassiz started for the offices of the Northern Bank and Trust Building, Fourth and Pike Street. The appointment at the Seattle bank followed an investigative excursion made to similar financial institutions in Vancouver and Victoria. The stop at the Bank of Montreal in Victoria had brought a lingering smile of irony to Agassiz's lips. With walls five feet thick, it advertised itself as the most secure bank in the world.

Not safe enough from the likes of the Hazzards, he thought.

As expected, the money trail had led back to Seattle, nearly to the front door of Dr. Hazzard's old office. Out of curiosity, the vice-consul passed by her window. Still painted on the glass in black letters:

> 424-423-422
> *Dr. Linda B. Hazzard*
> *Fasting*
> *-And-*
> *Natural Methods*
> *Osteopathy.*
> *Walk In.*

Said the spider to the fly, Agassiz thought as he moved on to the Northern Bank and Trust office. Inside, he asked for the cashier.

Slightly stoop-shouldered William Collier, was the cashier—one of the principals—of the firm whose letterhead boasted

"Capital and Surplus of $115,000." Collier, not surprisingly, knew the Hazzards quite well. Not only did Linda and Sam run their personal and sanitarium accounts through Northern Bank and Trust, they also conducted business there relating to their fledgling Hazzard Publishing Company.

Fasting for the Cure of Disease had been the company's first title.

To Agassiz's great relief, Collier was very accommodating. From the onset of their meeting it was clear that he held no particular regard for the Hazzards. It took only to ask to persuade him to check his records.

As he leafed through the papers and laid them out on his ratty, stained desk blotter, the cashier recounted how Sam Hazzard had come to see him with an order signed by Claire Williamson on April 22, 1911. It was drawn upon her account at the Bank of Montreal at Victoria in the amount of $1,005.00. It was payable to Linda Burfield Hazzard.

A little later, a letter written to the London & Westminster County Bank of London concerning funds in another account was brought to Collier's attention by attorney John Arthur and Linda Hazzard. The fasting doctor and her attorney apprised Collier that the bank had disregarded the intent of an original letter. The funds had been sent to Claire—not directly to the doctor's account, as had been specified.

On May 26, Sam Hazzard burst into the office and demanded to know the source of the delay of Miss Williamson's money. He had need of the cash right away. Since it hadn't come, Collier could do little more than to offer to make further inquiry. He wrote a letter that same afternoon.

"I have that letter somewhere around here," he said, calling for the secretary to help him find it.

After another moment's search, a copy was retrieved and shown to the vice-consul.

On April 22nd Miss Claire Williamson left a letter addressed to your bank with the wire to be forwarded after noting the instructions contained therein. All monies held or received by you in the future for her account were to be remitted to Dr. Linda Burfield Hazzard at the address

given or possibly in care of this bank. One remittance has
arrived made payable to Miss Williamson, who desires us
not to have you follow out instructions so that she will not
be bothered when the money arrives.

Dumbfounded to such a degree that Agassiz could not conceal his feelings, he blurted out a question that carried the firm conviction of a statement.

"Did you not know Miss Claire had died on May 18?"

Collier hadn't heard anything of the sort. "No one said a word about her death."

"Did Mr. Hazzard lead you to believe she was alive? Did Mr. Arthur?"

"I tell you, sir, as far as I knew, Miss Williamson was alive at Olalla."

The cashier pulled up a bit more information, this time concerning Dora's affairs. More than $110 had been received from Dora's pension money and put into Linda Hazzard's account on April 17. And, on June 4, with the power of attorney in hand, Sam Hazzard helped himself to $539.10 of Dora's savings.

Ignited by the discovery at Northern Bank and Trust, Agassiz hurried to Tacoma that evening and made additional calls on a pair of schoolteachers who had taken the fast cure at Olalla. He wanted statements, but the ladies who had once implored Margaret Conway to take them from Starvation Heights had been reluctant. He pleaded with them once more. He didn't care if they thought he was a pest. Lucian Agassiz wanted everything he could get his hands on.

His great day ended with disappointment. The teachers would not cooperate. They were too afraid.

IT WAS A WONDER THAT THE HOT TYPE EVER cooled enough to print the article, so outrageously inflammatory was it. When she saw the *Patriarch*, Linda laughed it off as another brazen—yet blatantly transparent—attempt by the establishment to crush her with words molded by fear. Negative as it was, she rather liked the attention. It put her name in the company of William Jennings Bryan, Elbert Hubbard, and L.E. Rader, all forward thinkers of varying notoriety.

The spotlight was hers to take, as it had been for other mar-
tyrs throughout history.

Linda even liked the title of the article.

> *HERE IS ANOTHER "SUPERWOMAN"*
> *Mrs. Dr. Hazzard of Olalla, Kitsap County. What's in a*
> *name?—"Hazzard." Linda Burfield Hazzard "tortures*
> *her victims to death." Let us see; is this not the same*
> *"Hazzardous" outfit that got away with "L. E. Rader" by*
> *the "starving process" some few months since? This*
> *"Olalla gang" of "Superwomen" and their "Hazzardous"*
> *subordinates with a beard, fraternize with Elbert*
> *Hubbard. This degenerate of East Aurora, N. Y., when he*
> *comes to Seattle to spread his disease and "secure the*
> *stuff" a la W. J. Bryan, he always visits Olalla, then in the*
> *next issue of the "Philistine" will be found a "write up"*
> *for his scientific peers of Olalla. This is so! And it is very*
> *corroborative too of the old moral that "birds of a feather*
> *flock together." To think that "systematic murder" can be*
> *conducted right under our very nose by a notorious cold-*
> *blooded woman with a "doctor's diploma," is not only a*
> *blast upon our morality but it is a challenge of our sanity.*
> *This "Hazzardous" murderous systematic "Lucretia*
> *Borgia" is fortunate that she is not in the country from*
> *whence "her victims came," or she would in less than four*
> *weeks be lying side by side with the late "Dr. Crippen"*
> *instead of being subjected to a bond of a paltry $10,000.*
> *The whole country hunted for a full quarter of a century for*
> *"Kate Bender" and found her not. We have got this wicked*
> *"Superwoman" with a "doctor's diploma" in our grasp.*
> *Shall we do her justice? Or shall we do ourselves an injus-*
> *tice and make a "heroine" of her? The "prohibitionists"*
> *should place her upon a pinnacle of fame for she is a rigid*
> *abstainer.*

The day after the outrageous article in the *Patriarch*
appeared, Dr. Hazzard's troubles worsened considerably. A
man tapped her shoulder on the steamer leaving Seattle for
Olalla. Linda spun around, confirmed her identity, and was

served with a summons in a civil suit filed jointly against her and E. R. Butterworth & Sons.

Dora Williamson sought $25,000 in damages for the anguish and suffering caused by the desecration of Claire's body.

> *The defendant Hazzard, a resident of Kitsap County, maintains at Olalla an institute for the pretended treatment of disease and holds herself out to the public as a physician duly licensed to practice medicine under the law . . .*
>
> *On May 20, 1991, defendant E. R. Butterworth & Sons permitted defendant Hazzard to have access to said body and to desecrate the same by cutting open the body and mutilating it and removing from it many of its internal organs and taking the same away and converting the same to her own use . . .*

As expected by anyone who either hated or admired her, Linda Hazzard never missed an opportunity to channel her anger when people mucked up her path in life.

She loathed Agassiz and his "little puppet" Kelley.

"Kelley has raked up all the rubbish that he could find. I think that he has now about reached the end of his rope. He will get enough and more before he is through with me."

Old man Butterworth also made a statement upon the filing of the civil suit. The founder of the undertaking establishment attempted to distance the firm from the controversial Dr. Hazzard.

"We had no connection with Dr. Hazzard any more than that we were sent for to get the body and did it just as we have done it in many other out-of-town cases. Dr. Hazzard performed a postmortem here as other doctors do. Our instructions from the authorities are to let doctors perform postmortems when they say they have the consent of the relatives."

THE EDITORS OF SEATTLE AND TACOMA'S MULTI-tude of newspapers could not have been more overjoyed with the turn of events in Olalla. It seemed every minute of the day the papers were embroiled in the race to show readers which of them reigned supreme. If Linda Burfield Hazzard was the woman of the hour for her purported evil, Dora Williamson was cast as the trampled rosebud, a victim, and it was Lucian Agassiz who was the unlikely hero. On August 8, 1911, photographs of the cabins and the Hazzard home ran in the *Seattle Times* under a top-of-the-page headline touting:

SCENES AT "STARVATION HEIGHTS," NEAR OLALLA

A full color cartoon of Agassiz occupied a quarter of the front page.

BRITISH OFFICIAL PLAYED BIG PART IN HAZZARD CASE
C. E. Lucian Agassiz, vice-consul at Tacoma, Man who did as much as anyone to cause woman's arrest

AGASSIZ WONDERED IF HE HAD HEARD CORRECtly. He was somewhat surprised when British vice-consul Bernard Pelly made the disclosure that he had in fact received inquiries from the father of one of the British victims. Ivan Flux's father wrote from Gloucester, only to learn from the vice-consul that his son had died in a home on Seattle's Lakeview Avenue while under the care of Dr. Hazzard. The father wrote back, stunned and in grief. Why hadn't anyone contacted him? Why hadn't the doctor in charge of his son's case made notification? He also inquired about his son's personal effects and his assets. Flux had several hundred dollars when he left for the U.S., where he planned to scour the great forested regions of the Pacific Northwest for property. A ranch was the young man's American Dream.

The money, the man's father learned, was gone. Dr. Linda Hazzard, who appointed herself administratrix of the estate, claimed that the deceased had less than $70 when he died.

"The man's father indicated his son had significant holdings in Canada as well," the fifty-two-year-old Pelly told Agassiz.

Agassiz continued reading, his heart pounding inside his chest as he took in each word, scrutinizing the small bundle of paperwork for the cause of death. It was pneumonia, and the signature of the doctor who had made the autopsy findings was *L. B. Hazzard*. He didn't need to see any more, though there wasn't much else. The vice-consul knew the circumstances surrounding the Flux and Williamson cases were too striking in their similarities to be ignored.

To charge the so-called fasting specialist with one murder, merely set the stage for the other.

WHEN FORCED INTO IT BY THE WORD OF SUSpicion coming from the vice-consul's office Dr. Hazzard finally contacted the late Flux's father. She wrote it was his son's roommate—a former patient she identified as Gallagher—who had sent the young man to her for treatment. In her letter, she enclosed a letter written by J.F. Gallagher, apparently included to back up her claims. Gallagher described Flux's suffering and his desire to have Dr. Hazzard treat his case. He further stated that he was a witness to the young Englishman's final hours. He had been in the next apartment when Flux died on February 10, 1911.

If Linda Hazzard had expected the two letters to ease the suspicions around the Flux case by satisfying the dead man's family, she was correct, but only for a while. When Agassiz picked up the case from Pelly he intended to do a thorough check. He especially wanted to talk with Mr. Gallagher. One problem. As far as the vice-consul could determine, no one knew one iota about the mystery man.

"Then who wrote the letter to young Flux's parents?" Frank Kelley asked, while they mulled over the investigation.

"I suspect it was the doctor, or possibly her husband."

"We need the letter for analysis right away."

Agassiz smiled. He was a step ahead of his friend. He already had the note . . . and when the time was right, would leak it to the press. In the meantime, he made inquiries as he followed Flux's path in Seattle. Doors were knocked on. Telephone calls were made. And though nothing was turned up, it was clear that everyone associated with Dr. Hazzard—nurses, included—knew just what the relentless little man was after.

Dr. Hazzard did, too.

An unsigned, typed letter arrived at the vice-consul's Tacoma office the morning of August 21, 1911. The writer informed him that mystery man Gallagher had left America for British Columbia. A Seattle telephone number was included to aid Agassiz if he sought additional information. The number, however, proved bogus.

Agassiz, miffed at what he considered an overt attempt to make him the fool, considered the time was right for the newspaper leak. The *Tacoma Daily News* ran a story on the front page of their August 21 edition, under the headline:

DID DR. HAZZARD INVENT GALLAGHER?

Agassiz knew the answer, of course. He was certain the letter had been written to call off the hunt for any true witness to Ivan Flux's death. Such an evil ruse! Agassiz announced a handwriting expert had been summoned to determine if the "Gallagher letter" matched known samples of the fasting doctor's handwriting.

The *Daily News* reporter even offered the implicated Linda Hazzard a backhanded compliment.

If Gallagher does not exist this letter is a work of art in its way.

Later, Agassiz wrote his understanding of the Flux matter:

It appears that Dr. Hazzard paid no attention to Mr. Flux after she had placed him in an isolated house outside of the city of Seattle, and that he died without Dr. Hazzard having seen him for over two weeks. She wrote to the father in England, however, stating that she had seen him every day up to the day before he died, and that she had done everything that a mother could do for him. She stated further that the son had practically no funds, no effects, no property, the truth being, however, that he had several hundred dollars in cash and a number of equities in property, all of which as I understand it, she has apparently converted to her own use . . .

TRANSPIRING ABOUT ONE HUNDRED DAYS APART, the Flux and Williamson cases, it seemed, were malevolently identical. The Wakelin "suicide," however, was vastly different, though no less disturbing. In fact, as Agassiz learned more of it, he began to wonder if it was not the most horrific of the three deaths involving British subjects.

Wakelin was reported to have committed suicide with a .38 caliber revolver to his head on November 7, 1909. Linda Hazzard held power of attorney over the New Zealand man's estate and appointed H.G. Sutton as administrator. Sutton's lawyers—not coincidentally, were also Dr. Hazzard's attorneys.

Agassiz cabled the dead man's Wellington-based attorneys for more information. A day later, he learned Dr. Hazzard had complained to the New Zealanders that there had been barely enough money in the man's estate to defray funeral costs. She wanted to know where the rest of Wakelin's money was, but was told there weren't any additional funds. Agassiz wondered if the young man had been killed out of rage because it was discovered that he did not have the means expected of the son of an English lord? The suicide story, nagged at the vice-consul. It didn't seem to ring true.

The vice-consul-turned-detective uncovered more. He learned that on July 24, 1911, just as Miss Conway and Miss Williamson had disclosed the horror of Starvation Heights, Mr. Sutton hastily finished his obligations to the Wakelin estate and was dismissed by a King County judge as administrator. The timing loomed as a huge red banner. It suggested to Agassiz that Sutton had been warned that someone was going to be making a complaint about what had been going on at that little death camp in the woods.

Dr. Hazzard was a little nervous. Good.

The way the vice-consul perceived it, Linda Burfield Hazzard had targeted wealthy and vulnerable subjects of the British Empire. It was her practice to have herself appointed administrator of their estates, and once accomplishing that, she and husband Samuel were in the position to submit enormous bills to the dead patients' estate and extract large sums of money. Everything had been for greed. For the love of money.

ULYSSES GRANT SMITH HAD SUFFERED a terrible bout of pneumonia that left him weak and poor, but did not abate his reserve of determination. Down on his luck, Smith moved his family from Seattle into an old farmhouse on the Hazzard property, only a stone's throw north of the site of what the woman doctor announced would be her great sanitarium. Ulysses's son, John, born in 1915, spent his early years in Olalla forging an unshakable opinion that Dr. Hazzard was a pushy, demanding woman who didn't treat his father with any semblance of respect. Linda paid Ulysses very little and insisted he take care of every chore at a moment's notice, be it chopping wood, clearing land, hauling building materials.

"It will be done, now!"

After a time the Smiths moved into the old Rader place across the road from Starvation Heights. The family was glad to be away from the doctor's easy reach, and even more so, away from the things they saw at her fasting institute. Of course, they never got away from the woman herself. That, they had come to learn, was impossible. Linda Burfield Hazzard turned up in the most unexpected of places.

Seared forever in John Smith's memory was a discovery he and some other boys made in a little outbuilding that had once been where Lewis Rader published his beloved copies of Sound Views.

"They used to have an old hand press there ... had a little old newspaper there at one time. They weren't turning out the paper when we lived there. They used to make tickets for strawberry picking. You know, little jobs like that. I remember us here looking around—we were kids—we were looking around and we found a picture of Mrs. Hazzard nude. She was posed like a muscle man, arms up. It was kind of a tintype picture it was so old. She had a fantastic figure, an athlete type. They were showing it around there. She was a real physical culturist. I can still remember that. She sure was the talk of the town."

TWENTY-SIX

NEARLY EVERY DAY SINCE NEWSBOYS from Seattle to Tacoma waved the Starvation Heights story like little black-and-white flags, the British vice-consul's correspondence box was inundated with letters and telephone messages from local and far-flung British expatriates urging retribution for the murder of Claire Williamson. Each scrap of paper, each telephone call, amplified Lucian Agassiz's conviction of the worthiness of the case. He promised supporters he would press on and prevail.

Still, deep down, Agassiz had the sinking feeling in his substantial stomach that with the least bit of provocation, the authorities in Kitsap County would let the case fall by the wayside. County prosecutor Thomas Stevenson had been reluctant to make a stand against the fasting doctor in the first place, and whenever leads failed to materialize, he freely expressed skepticism the case could be won in front of a Port Orchard jury.

The men who settled the county were farmers, fishermen, lumberjacks. The idea that some rich—*foreign*—spinster wasted her money on a foolish treatment likely would not sit well with men of their ilk. The soggy outposts of Puget Sound had been settled by the curious blend of free and forward thinkers like those in Burley and Home, and those men and women who scarcely gave *anything* a thought at all. By the beginning of September, it was clear to Agassiz that if he and Frank Kelley didn't continue to force the prosecution, the matter would fail.

With Miss Dora and Miss Margaret camped out day and night on the grounds behind his home, they had become more than refugees from an ordeal. In some very real way they had become friends. Agassiz vowed he would be damned before he would disappoint the ladies who lived on his lawn. He would do everything within his personal power to secure justice. He wasted little time. With the terrible facts outlined before him, Lucian Agassiz drafted a detailed letter and dispatched it to His Majesty's Consul James Laidlaw in Portland, Oregon. It was September 12, 1911. Agassiz was direct and specific.

After Dr. Hazzard had gone into the financial standing of these girls very carefully, ascertaining exactly where their money was and the amount of money they had, she suggested that the girls should be taken to what she called her 'Institute,' which is a matter of fact a piece of acreage at Olalla, Washington, a most isolated spot in Kitsap County . . . She put them upon a total fast, the result of which was the death of Miss Claire Williamson . . . and would have resulted in the death of Miss Dorothea had it not been for the timely arrival of an old nurse of the family, Miss Conway, who reached Olalla just in time to save Miss Dorothea . . .

The vice-consul also gave a description of the Ivan Flux case, informing the consulate that the young man had died "under the most appalling of circumstances."

Agassiz closed with the reason for the letter. He had taken care of investigation expenses out of his own pocket, but in order to secure a trial, particularly in the Flux case, he needed additional funds. He suggested a sum of $500 American money would be adequate in securing a decent attorney who could act in an advisory capacity to the British government and, of course, to the survivors of the victims.

Three days later, came the answer from HMC Laidlaw. It was not the kind of response Agassiz had sought. Laidlaw left little doubt that monetary help from the British government would be difficult, if not impossible, to procure. Agassiz's face turned red. He had felt so certain His Majesty would foot the bill. The dead woman's father, uncles, grandfather had served their country in the Indian service. The fact Claire Williamson had been hoodwinked by an American charlatan had been proven beyond any doubt, but for her death to have meaning, and to stop others from a similar fate, the murderer had to be convicted of all charges.

It was on his honor that he assured Miss Williamson and Miss Conway that the government would come to their aid.

"You are not alone in your outrage and grief," he told them.

And now Laidlaw's response left the whole of it in American hands. It was the Americans, who as far as Agassiz could see, had allowed the numerous deaths of Dr. Hazzard's patients to go unchallenged in the first place. Their record was appallingly poor. Agassiz had tallied more than a dozen names in a roster kept in his office. It was likely there were others. How many other patients, he asked, had been stripped of their assets and left to die unattended in isolated cabins, strange houses, or apartments?

In his response, Laidlaw correctly reminded Agassiz that with the exception of the state's attorney general, it was the duty of the county attorneys to prosecute an alleged criminal. It was not within the province of the consul's office. The only instance that would cause him to seek the employ of an attorney on behalf of Mr. Flux or Miss Williamson would be if the county prosecutors had demonstrated no interest in the case.

The consul indicated that Agassiz and Pelly should take up the Flux matter with King County's prosecuting attorney.

> *It is his business and not that of H.M.'s Government to prosecute a criminal, and it must not be presumed that he is not able to do so in this case.*

James Laidlaw ended the one-page directive with a bottom-line concern and the vague assurance that the matter was not completely dead. He considered the figure named for retaining an attorney to be "pretty high" for merely advisory counsel.

> *Please advise me if Governor Hay is still absent from Olympia and ascertain when he is expected to return.*

When Frank Kelley, Margaret Conway, and Dorothea Williamson asked about the consul's response, Agassiz put on a brave face. He told them that James Laidlaw was considering the matter and was planning on taking it up with Washington's governor as well.

NO TIME COULD BE SPARED. SO MUCH SEEMED AT stake. While Dora's strength and resolve grew and Miss Conway found respite from the worry that Dora would not make a full recovery, Lucian Agassiz wore a smile as fake as a carnival doll. The man could not savor the relief and joy that the two women obviously shared. He worried about Dr. Hazzard day and night. Agassiz drafted an answer to his superior on September 16. Perhaps he had not stated things as clearly as he had thought? Perhaps he had not imbued his prose with the unequivocal urgency which he had intended?

> *Mr. Flux is absolutely without means and cannot himself employ any counsel, and it is my opinion that the King County Authorities will not prosecute Dr. Hazzard without all the facts being laid before them in the form of statements and affidavits, which can only be prepared by some regular attorney.*

Agassiz stated further that unless an attorney was brought in on behalf of the senior Flux, the case would most certainly be lost. He doubted a vigorous, fair, and impartial prosecution was possible.

Finally, he readdressed his request for funds. He indicated that after more discussion with Bernard Pelly, the two vice-consuls concurred that no decent Seattle lawyer could be engaged for much, if any, less than the $500 he sought in the previous letter.

> *It is needless to say, however, that I should bind any attorney down to the lowest possible figure that I could get a good, and thoroughly competent man to perform the service for.*

WHILE LUCIAN AGASSIZ AND THE REST OF THE bastion of British interlopers sent correspondence bearing her name halfway around the word, Linda Burfield Hazzard busied herself with her own writings. The world had whispered in her ear that she had been chosen for a great cause. People cared deeply about her views. And so she wrote in longhand on the launch to and from Olalla. After a time, when much scribbling and editing had been accomplished, she turned a sheaf of papers over to Sam.

"Type this section by morning," she instructed her husband, as if he were a clerk and she the leader of all modern-thinking women.

Sam did as he was told, softening his personal indignation with a swig from a flask he kept wrapped in a "dust cloth" beside his typewriter.

His wife's newest tome was called *The Perfect Man*. It tackled the elements both physical and mental that made up the ideal specimen. Sam polished the language, though Linda never seemed to notice.

"The perfect body is everything," she wrote. "And today it means more to the development of the human race than it ever did."

A STARTLED ESSIE CAMERON NEARLY DROPPED A porcelain figure with a crooked painted smile onto the floor. When she swung the door open she found James Watson Webb waiting on the stoop of the Portland home where she had taken employment as a nursemaid. The twenty-three-year-old man stood with the light brushing against his back, illuminating the reddish tones in his dark hair and making him look almost ethereal.

Essie knew he was nothing of the sort. Wattie was, in her estimation, a shady man. A man of questionable motives. He was firmly entrenched on Dr. Hazzard's side, a deep believer in her dangerous, maybe even *homicidal* treatment. Though she didn't know how, it was clear that he had his hand in the death of Miss Claire. He had been at the Hazzards' place several times during the week of the girl's death at Olalla. From what Essie Cameron knew, Mr. Webb had been at the Buena Vista as well.

"Miss Cameron," the visitor began, smoothly, as if the pair were old friends, "I have come to see you about an important matter." What he didn't tell her was how he found her. It was

Dr. Hazzard who had learned her whereabouts when she spied the girl's name and address on the list of witnesses to be subpoenaed by the prosecution. She gave the address and an edict to Watson Webb.

"*Find her and see that she is on our side.*"

"*If she is not?*"

"*See that she is.*"

The young woman had seen more than meant for her eyes at Starvation Heights. The meddlesome Brit Agassiz had already sought the girl and they needed to get her on their side. They needed to ensure that when it came to a trial, Essie Cameron was aligned with the defense.

Essie quite stupidly let the man inside the house. She later doubted she would have done so without the presence of Mr. and Mrs. Babcock, both home that day. She felt it would be all right to hear what the man had to say.

"It would be a good thing if you came up to Seattle to work this out."

"I do not want to be a party to any of this."

"You may be subpoenaed by the prosecution. Is that what you want, Miss Cameron?"

"I want nothing to do with this case."

"Dr. Hazzard's attorneys are framing her case now. Now is when we need you. For the truth, you know."

Watson Webb did not care to take "no" for an answer. He kept at the young woman, who began to cry at the pressure of it all, until Mr. Babcock emerged from the next room. His face was scarlet and his manner agitated.

He turned to Essie and pulled at her elbow.

"Don't you go up. You don't have to go to Seattle and if they want you, do not go!"

The soft-around-the-middle and shiny-pated Mr. Babcock pivoted toward Webb and began to shout at the top of his lungs.

"Sir, leave now!" he yelled. "Leave the girl alone. Never come back, young man. I say, never!"

"There is nothing wrong with what we want to do!" Webb called over his shoulder as he disappeared down the steps. Essie watched until Mr. Babcock, still stomping his feet and outraged, slammed the door with nearly enough force to tear its hinges.

TWENTY-SEVEN

AN ARC OF FLUSH-CHEEKED AND CRUSTY-nosed children from a lakeside bungalow gathered shoulder to shoulder to witness the workers collapse the great tent that had been Dora and Margaret's residence for what the surviving sister called "my summer of despair and convalescence" on Lake Steilacoom. Dora Williamson had adored the adventure of living under the droopy roof of the grey canvas structure. *Out in the country!* She could hear mallards and Canada geese smack against the water's smooth veneer as they landed for feeding. One night a raccoon even made his way just inside the tent opening and delighted the two ladies with his glinting black eyes, and paws so much like human hands in appearance it looked as though he could sign his name.

Sadly, the very idea of living so close to nature made Dora think of her sister and how she had longed for a holiday in the woods.

"Claire would have loved the splendor of the lake," she told Margaret, as the two walked along the water's mossy edge after the excitement of the tent removal.

"Indeed, she would have, Dorie."

And though it had been half a year since Claire died, the tears came as easily as if it had been the day before. Dora remembered more, not less, as time went on. It was as if as she gained strength and perspective, the shadows on her memory would lift and disappear.

In late September, the temperatures had dropped too low at night for comfort, and Agassiz insisted the women move into the main house. Dora wanted to pay for the lodging, but her money was still in the grip of the legal mess started in

Olalla. When she brought it up, Agassiz had a hurt look on his face.

"I do not wish to hear of any such thing. My dear woman, you are a guest here, not a boarder."

And while under ordinary circumstances Agassiz would have moved back to Tacoma for the winter—it truly was a great deal more convenient—he felt it would leave him too removed from Miss Margaret, and especially Miss Dora. He would stay at the lake cottage.

As had been the case throughout the investigation, Agassiz had spent little time at the lake anyway. He had been seized, his time stolen, by the relentless drive that possessed him to prove the starvationist was a killer. He still sought the help of His Majesty's consul in Portland.

"If the Americans refuse to stop the woman who preys on Britishers, then we must step in," he said.

British Consul James Laidlaw asked his vice-consul why he was so concerned that the prosecution would fail in its duty in Kitsap County? What evidence did he have that Linda Hazzard would face a prosecution of inordinate weakness? After all, Frank Kelley's reputation and role as special prosecutor would certainly bolster the side of justice.

In the end, Agassiz admitted, it came down to money.

Prosecutor Stevenson claimed there was no money in Kitsap's coffers to fight a woman of Dr. Hazzard's means and influence. When Stevenson sought additional funds—$200— for out-of-town witnesses, he was denied the cash.

According to the prosecutor, all expenses must be paid by relatives or the estate of the dead Williamson sister.

"Can you imagine," Agassiz later declared to Laidlaw, "the murdered girl must literally pay the price for justice!"

The consul was not surprised. But then, more than ever, he knew things were handled so differently in America. Justice was slow and peculiar.

"In England," Laidlaw acknowledged, "the woman would be in prison by this time."

SOME TWO HUNDRED MILES SOUTH, JAMES LAID-law was holding up his end of the bargain. Though the consul considered official British assistance somewhat dubious from the start, he was sufficiently outraged enough to pull whatever strings he could manage. On October 4, 1911, he drafted a letter to Washington State's Attorney General W.P. Tanner.

> *Mr. Agassiz fears that the County authorities are not fully alive to the dangerous and criminal character of this woman's business and that the prosecution is not as energetic as it should be.*

Laidlaw also noted the Ivan Flux case and how Dr. Hazzard had likely murdered him, stolen his money and property, and made false statements to his parents to cover her crime.

> *I beg to request that you will look closely into these cases, and take such steps as may be practical to see that this dangerous woman may be prosecuted to the fullest extent of the law.*

LUCIAN AGASSIZ WAS NOTHING IF NOT PERSIStent. While he continued to follow up the slightest detail that came over the transom, he also bombarded Laidlaw with inquiries as to the state government's response. He made inquiries in Olympia on his own. No answers were forthcoming. He began to wonder if the state was lax on the woman for some unknown reason. Maybe she had more clout than he imagined. He recalled how she had gotten out of scrapes with the law before when accused of starving patients to death. She had fought her way to the state supreme court and won back her license. She was a menace to society, and yet she was untouchable.

Would she escape prosecution if it had been a wealthy American who had died?

A week and a half after his letter, Laidlaw finally received an answer from Olympia. The attorney general was away and the letter had been signed by an assistant. The state was tied up in civil matters and could not offer any assistance in any criminal case pending against Linda Burfield Hazzard.

Later, when he would see the letter, Agassiz would laugh out loud at the last two lines.

> *... the Prosecuting Attorney of Kitsap County has*
> *called to his assistance an able lawyer, Mr. Frank Kelley,*
> *of Tacoma. We think that you may feel certain that the*
> *prosecution of this case will be vigorous and to the full*
> *extent of the law.*

British Consul Laidlaw was offended by the dismissal of the matter. The information relayed to him by Kitsap County's Thomas Stevenson was an out-and-out lie. What was it going to take for the men in Olympia to see that their intervention was needed? It was true that Kitsap County was the hinterlands of the state, but the alleged murderess was luring the unsuspecting, the desperate, the rich, from more populated, more powerful cities and towns.

He called in his secretary and dictated the following to the attorney general on October 16, 1911:

> *I may point out to you that no credit is due the State or*
> *County Authorities for the assistance that may be ren-*
> *dered by Mr. Kelley, who is being paid by the relatives of*
> *the deceased Miss Claire Williamson ... I cannot feel at*
> *all certain that the State of Washington is doing its duty in*
> *the premises and that this is a case in which, under the law*
> *of Washington, the Attorney General's office should take*
> *an active and not a merely passive interest in the prosecu-*
> *tion of this woman ...*

Again, the Flux death was brought up. The circumstances were so strikingly similar that it was only reasonable to consider that Claire Williamson and John Ivan Flux suffered the same dastardly fate. Though some time had passed since his death, the Flux case languished because his relatives were unable to foot the bill for the prosecutors in King County.

Laidlaw implored Attorney General Tanner to intervene to ensure that King County authorities fully investigated, and if the facts bore it out, prosecute the fasting expert.

Two days later, the mail brought acknowledgment from the attorney general's assistant that he had received the letter.

Tanner was still away, but the assistant felt the second plea for help would receive the same response.

> *... he will find it impossible to take any active part in this prosecution.*

THOUGH SHE WAS LOATH TO ADMIT IT, WHEN THE Bremerton and Port Orchard papers hit the stands on October 18, 1911, Linda Hazzard could breathe a little easier. She was not the top of the news. Instead, President Taft's visit to Kitsap County's expanding navy interests in Bremerton pushed Dr. Hazzard to the bottom of the front page.

The *Bremerton Searchlight* trumpeted the news in its October 18, 1911 edition:

> *With the guns of the navy yard booming a noisy welcome, President W. H. Taft stepped ashore at the navy yard, Tuesday afternoon, and spoke for a few minutes to about 3,500 people assembled on the bluff over looking the new dry dock . . .*

The report that the fasting specialist had finally entered her plea—almost six weeks after her arrest—was buried.

> *NOT GUILTY IS HAZZARD PLEA*
> *... In no uncertain manner and with eyes flashing indignation, the woman charged with the fiendish crime, stepped close to the judge and snapped "Not guilty!"*

JAMES LAIDLAW WAS AS APPALLED AS AGASSIZ. If he hadn't felt that way, he hardly would have endeavored so vigorously to have the state's authorities intervene. A consul is only effective when he has curried favor, not antagonized governments of foreign lands. If Laidlaw hadn't seen the seriousness of the crimes that could go unpunished, he would never have moved forward with Agassiz's cause.

Yet there were concerns that had bubbled to the surface. Laidlaw was hearing from others that Agassiz was overzealous and out-of-bounds with his investigation into Starvation

Heights. Some of the comments were the result of jealousy—
Agassiz could not walk the streets of Tacoma or Seattle without
some newspaperman charming a quote from the man. Other
comments were out of concern. The vice-consul was too deeply
involved for his own good.

Laidlaw had to admit to himself that he had seen it coming.
He could see that the vice-consul was expending all his time, all
his energy, on the Williamson and Flux affairs. The man looked
haggard, but he kept going. He was a train that had no depot.

In mid-October 1911, Laidlaw sent a letter marked "personal" to Agassiz at the Tacoma office. He chose his words
carefully. His mission was to temper the man's unbridled enthusiasm, and refocus his attention to his true duties as vice-consul.

> *My dear Agassiz,*
> *. . . In this whole matter your official and private actions*
> *are more or less mixed up. As an official you were only*
> *bound to make such representations as you could to the*
> *Washington Authorities, but you are not permitted to*
> *administrate as a vice-consul though you are required to*
> *conserve as far as possible all property belonging to the*
> *deceased . . .*

The Flux matter, having taken place in Seattle, was clearly
out of his jurisdiction. It was the responsibility of Bernard Pelly
to pursue King County authorities into fully reviewing Dr.
Hazzard's involvement in the Englishman's death. Who better
than Pelly, who had been in the position in Seattle since 1899,
to handle such affairs?

Laidlaw did not think Agassiz should have accepted the
power of attorney from the Flux estate. At best, it was foolish
and inappropriate. He was not expected, nor authorized, to get
so involved in such matters. As a consul he was bound to protect the assets of the British subjects—and power of attorney
was not required for that endeavor.

He wrote that he would await a response from Attorney
General Tanner, then, if need be, he would query Governor Hay
before putting the matter before the British government through
its embassy in Washington, D.C.

With all that stated, Laidlaw was pessimistic about the Embassy's support in the matter of Linda Burfield Hazzard.

I do not believe that they will authorize any expense in the matter, for it is only in the most unusual cases that they will take part in a prosecution.

James Laidlaw had no doubts Agassiz was an earnest man, a loyal aide to His Majesty. But Laidlaw could see that the vice-consul was treading dangerous waters out of a sense of justice for the wronged British subjects. The consul wanted to help, but he knew it must be handled in accordance with the treaty with the United States. As far as he understood, the crimes of malpractice and negligence were handled by civil, rather than criminal, courts. And over the course of late-night hours at his office, the consul's tired, red rimmed eyes came up short as they ran the endless lines of the statute books. Justice for the murders of the British subjects was out of his hands.

WHENEVER DORA THOUGHT OF MARGARET AND her arrival at Olalla, tears came to her eyes. Even though she was grateful for being saved, she struggled with an awful conflict over what had transpired. Claire had starved to death, and she was so thankful that she had been spared. Dora's heart was torn.

How could she be happy, in any way, when Claire had perished?

Dora never doubted that if not for Margaret's timely arrival and tireless devotion at Olalla, she would have died as well.

Her voice broke when she spoke of it later.

"(Tooddy) tried to make me as warm as she could. I suffered very much with the cold. I used to wear my big coat, she got my hot water bottle and bags and rugs . . . and did everything she could to restore me to health, but she could only just give me a very little food . . ."

TWENTY-EIGHT

IT WAS UNMISTAKABLE AND, FOR MOST, invigorating. The Puget Sound area had a newness to it that was not lost on the men and women who chased dreams of gold strikes in the Klondike, fortunes born of felling timber and, of course, the great prize for lonely hearts ladies from the East—husbands. Like a big old green-and-blue pillow, the softness of its vast landforms seemed barely marred by the small bumps and tatters of civilization. From a ship coming through the straits connecting the Pacific Ocean to the calmer inland waters, there were scant clues to what was taking place. It was true that burgeoning Seattle and Tacoma spouted steam and smoke as did any of the number of tiny mill settlements sawyering lumber for frame houses that, in time, would cover the thick, green hillsides. But that was like the top of an emerald iceberg. Beyond the smoke and the hilltops, there were others. More and more, every day.

The influx of people was so rapid that necessary services in outlying areas could not keep pace. Kitsap County, the tax-poor relation on the west side of the Sound, was a perfect case in point. With services limited and the judicial case load stretched to the breaking point, often times Kitsap cases were tried in King County venues—it saved Kitsap money.

And so, the Arlington Hotel in Seattle became one of a number of buildings that did double duty. The hotel's meeting room served as a makeshift courtroom for Kitsap County. On Saturday, October 21, 1911, many of the principals in the Hazzard-Williamson case would face off once again in a civil hearing over the fees that Dr. Hazzard had charged for alleged services rendered to Miss Claire and Miss Dora.

In the end, Judge Lester Still once again sided with the plaintiff. Dr. Hazzard was ordered to return $973 to the Williamsons. The judge found the fasting specialist's professional fees had been outrageous and unreasonable. The court, however, withheld $250 from the judgment—until it was determined if Miss Claire's mind was sharp and had given the "gift" of her own free will.

Or if she had given it under duress as Lucian Agassiz insisted to reporters and courtroom observers.

After another defeat was handed them, Linda and Sam Hazzard left for their Olalla home in spasms of anger. Sam, as usual, said little but for the echoes he offered in his support of every word uttered by his wife.

Dr. Hazzard had kept her mouth shut longer than her enemies considered possible. She had taken the advice of her attorneys to heart, bitten her tongue, and tried to maintain the composure of the woman that she was. At Olalla, there was a steady procession of supporters, each of whom was able to hear her side of the saga.

There were a few newsmen whom she also trusted to print the truth.

Just after Judge Still's decision was announced, Dr. Hazzard told a Bremerton reporter that Dora's healthy physical appearance was incontrovertible proof that her fasting cure had been a complete success.

"See how well she looks!" she exclaimed. "Note the rosy cheeks and the health-sparkling eyes of Dora Williamson. She owes her present good health to the efficacy of my fasting cure.

"Dorothea herself admitted on the stand that she was a physical wreck when she came under my treatment. She had sought aid from specialists in many lands, but they had given her up as hopeless. Her fasting removed the cause and the rest and proper living has destroyed the effect."

Once Linda gave movement to her bitterly clenched jaws, it seemed she could not stop herself from speaking her mind. A slight tug from Samuel only brought a brief, but dismissive, glare. As had been the case since the last week in July, her ire was shot like a pistol at Lucian Agassiz. Along with Margaret Conway, it was Agassiz she blamed for sullying her name and treatment in the courts. When the legal affair was over, she would be the victor and the vice-consul would be out of a job.

"I'll make that Britisher, Agassiz, think he has taken hold of a hot potato before he gets through with me," she vowed.

HOT POTATO OR NOT, LUCIAN AGASSIZ WAS NOT inclined to worry about any of the overt or veiled threats made by Linda Hazzard. He had greater concerns, the chief being his relationship with Consul Laidlaw. The "personal" letter he received was kind enough in its tone, but Agassiz felt bad that Laidlaw considered him a loose cannon. Though he knew that he had expended a great deal of time on the Williamson and Flux cases, he felt it was time well spent. It was only for the good of British subjects who could not speak for themselves. He had not sought to supplant American justice, only to ensure that the proper prosecutorial authorities would have enough evidence to do their jobs.

His power of attorney status in the Williamson case was given to him on a personal, not professional, basis.

He wrote:

> *I regard, therefore, all my actions in this case and the many trips I have had to make to British Columbia, Seattle, Port Orchard, Centralia and to Portland as all purely unofficial, and have taxed the expense of the same to the Williamsons, who have, as I state, assumed and agreed to pay all my expenses in the matter.*

It was during his "unofficial" investigation of the Williamson case that he discovered Dr. Hazzard's alleged murder of Ivan Flux. After finding that Seattle-based Vice-consul Pelly was aware of the case, but had more or less washed his hands of it, Agassiz took up the cause. It was the dead man's father who assigned him power of attorney. Again, the authorization was made to the vice-consul *personally*, not as an agent for the British government.

> *. . . it appears to me to be more and more apparent that this woman had a distinct object in procuring this man's death. I have discussed the matter a number of times with*

Mr. Pelly, and whilst he appears to be thoroughly in sympathy with everything that I am doing, he has not offered to take any decided action with me in the matter . . .

He stated further that for HMC Laidlaw to seek information from Pelly would be a waste of time. Any contact with the King County prosecuting attorney would also prove futile.

Agassiz was the one who amassed the information and knew Linda Burfield Hazzard's dealings better than anyone.

IF LUCIAN AGASSIZ HAD THOUGHT FOR EVEN THE slightest moment that James Laidlaw regarded the Williamson and Flux deaths as merely tragic and inconsequential mishaps, he was greatly mistaken. British Consul Laidlaw had read the case files and had seen the photographs of Dora Williamson after her rescue from Olalla. Her uncle John Herbert had been to the Portland office to make a personal plea for retribution for Claire's murder. No one was forgetting what happened at Starvation Heights. James Laidlaw wore the look of frustration and dismay that certainly must have mirrored the vice-consul's face some two hundred miles to the north. He wondered what it was about the people of this country and their willingness to look the other way when it came to Linda Burfield Hazzard.

So many deaths, and no prosecution. Laidlaw's mind wandered back to something Agassiz had told him near the start of the case after he and Frank Kelley had been out to the Hazzard sanitarium.

"Probably more than a dozen killed. Maybe many more . . . who knows how many are at the bottom of that gulch?"

The woman from Olalla, Laidlaw thought, was making a jolly good business of murder.

The lack of support from the state attorney general boggled his mind. The request for help had been made in all sincerity. It had not been demanded, only asked for. Yet the request fell repeatedly on deaf ears.

It was an assistant, for God's sake, who answered the queries from the British consulate!

On October 24, 1911, Laidlaw could take no more. Following a chain of command procedure that had done nothing but show that the attorney general in Olympia did not think enough of the British government's concerns to respond directly, he went to the top.

> *My dear Governor,*
> *... I beg to bring before you the case of a certain Mrs. Hazzard, of Olalla, against whom an indictment is pending in Kitsap Co., for causing the death of a British subject named Claire Williamson, with the apparent object of robbing her estate ... The Kitsap authorities appear to have thrown the burden of the prosecution and attendant expenses upon the relatives of the deceased. A similar condition appears to have surrounded the death of another British subject, Mr. John Ivan Flux ... I have had some correspondence with the Attorney-General's office on these matters, and would ask you to examine these letters and consider the advisability of calling special attention to the energetic prosecution of these cases and directing the officials to use their best endeavors to bring this dangerous woman to justice for her misdeeds ...*

More than a week later, a three-sentence reply was sent to Laidlaw in Portland. It was from Governor Hay and it promised nothing, only that he would seek information from Kitsap County's prosecuting attorney regarding the status of the Hazzard case.

Nothing more.

FOR A BRIEF TIME LINDA HAZZARD COULD NOT care less what the meddlesome British were up to. When a telegram arrived from California, she could scarcely contain her joy. A torrent of satisfaction and pride washed over her. Clutching a Western Union cable, she spun around the kitchen of her Olalla bungalow with an excitement and vigor few had seen since the Williamson sisters came to the sanitarium the spring before. Linda's face beamed and a smile broke the straightedge that had been her expressionless mouth. The doctor's eyes showed a kind of verve that had seemed drained from them for so many months.

"Dr. Tanner is coming to be our guest! He will stand by me in support of the fast."

A local girl who helped with household chores on weekend afternoons looked on blankly, somewhat stunned by the woman she considered as cold as a foot stuck deep in a mudflat. The girl quickly smiled, an obvious reflexlike expression which immediately betrayed her lack of understanding of the importance of a visit by this doctor named Tanner.

"The great Henry Tanner," Linda repeated, after pausing only long enough to discern the girl scrubbing down the floorboards did not have the foggiest notion who it was she was talking about. "He is the father of fast cure, and he's coming here to see me."

HENRY TANNER WAS AN OLD MAN WITH LOFTY ambition and hope for the complete acceptance of the "fast cure" that he claimed had been his own invention since 1880. At eighty-three, he was round-shouldered and balding, with a white fringe banding the side of his crown. His mind was as sharp as it had always been.

When he stepped off the launch at Olalla, arm in arm with Linda Hazzard, he did so with the aid of a cane. He had come from San Diego with the single purpose of investigating his maligned follower's methods. He came to assure the world that the fast cure was as sound as it had always been. A few steps behind the two doctors, Sam Hazzard walked, smoking a pipe and trying to stay out of the way of the two. Having someone else around to listen to his wife's constant raving was a much-welcomed relief. A friend for Linda was a diversion Sam needed as much as his wife did.

Over the course of the weeks they would spend together, the two doctors would give numerous speeches as they tried to bolster the contention that fasting was a proven method.

Wherever they went, the curious and the followers encircled them to catch each word. It was a good blending of the old and the new. Linda Hazzard had cast herself as a Joan of Arc of health and Dr. Tanner as her greatest, most trusted, supporter.

Despite his age, or because of it, whenever he spoke listeners fell silent.

"In the spring of 1880 I was abandoned by seven M.D.s as hopelessly beyond professional aid. I concurred with the unanimous verdict. Life to me was not worth living and having been taught in the schools of medicine that ten days was the limit of human endurance under total abstinence of food I resolved to take a shortcut to inferno by the starvation route, but found to my surprise that I was on the wrong road to the desired end. Starvation proved my savior."

One night over dinner, while Sam cleared the dishes, the pair of fasting specialists continued a lively rail about the perpetual persecution both endured at the hands of the practitioners entrenched in the regular school of medicine.

Linda raised her voice as though it were a gesture of courtesy to her husband who had lingered in the kitchen. When Sam returned, a look of studied interest was on his face. He had, of course, heard it all before.

"Every time a patient's family went to the newspapers, there were attempts to revoke my license. Pity, pity those who cannot accept it, but I am a licensed physician whether they like it or not. My enemies are great in number, but I have certainly showed them all and I will again," she said.

Dr. Tanner pushed his chair back and smiled at Linda. The old man liked the spirited personality of his host.

"And, my dear, you have many friends as well," he said as he recalled an encounter with a newspaperman at a train station in Southern California. The reporter had learned that the elderly fasting specialist was destined for the Olalla sanitarium. He had but a single comment.

"You will find, doctor, that Mrs. Hazzard has not a friend in the country."

"Strange," Dr. Tanner replied in such a manner as to suggest a magician pulling a rabbit out of a top hat, "that a woman so despised could readily secure bail for $10,000!"

TWENTY-NINE

COURT DELAYS WON BY DR. HAZZARD only served to give the prosecution more time to tamp the rough edges of the criminal case against her. Witnesses were located, depositions taken, and evidence collected from all points of the Northwest. Frank Kelley had a law practice of his own to manage, so it was Agassiz who gladly did most of the footwork. He was away for days at a time. When other British subjects sought the help of the vice-consul at Tacoma, all they had to be told was that he was away working on cases involving the infamous Starvation Heights crimes and they patiently set aside their own needs. Nothing was more dreadful than what the American doctor had done to the English spinster. Nothing was so important that it couldn't wait. Justice had to be served.

By the time the windy weather of November stripped all the remaining leaves from trees that shed them, press accounts throughout the British Empire had made all the principals well-known worldwide. As early as November, when the trial was first scheduled, there were reporters from across the world queuing up for their coverage of the case. Dorothea's relatives from California and Australia took up residence in the Tacoma Hotel to await the court proceedings.

And nearly every person who had come in contact with Claire and Dora while on American soil were interviewed. Nurses and doctors made up the bulk of the witness list. Each time Agassiz heard a little more, he could envision the headlines the testimony was sure to make. Essie Cameron, the young maid at the sanitarium, Mary Fields and the other ladies of the Buena Vista, and of course, Margaret Conway. So many would stun the world with their revelations.

Linda Burfield Hazzard had complained about what had been batted about in the newspapers back in July. To Agassiz's way of thinking, the woman with the answer for everything had seen nothing yet.

THE BRITS HAD PUSHED A BIT TOO HARD. THOMAS Stevenson seethed in his office when his aide brought him the letter from Governor Marion Hay. Imagine, the audacity of writing to the governor to incite him to pressure the prosecutor? *Who did they think they were*? Their citizens were guests of America. They didn't own the damn country anymore, and hadn't for 135 years! Troublemaker Lucian Agassiz had transformed the case into a worldwide spectacle and had dared to raise a fuss with Governor Hay. Reluctant prosecutor Stevenson hadn't wanted to file charges in the first place. He had been bullied and shamed into it. And now, the governor was making inquiry on behalf of those interfering English.

It was, he thought, beyond belief.

For his response, the Kitsap County prosecutor carefully trod the line between providing a clear response and slinging a little mud.

> *Both Mr. Agassiz and Mr. Kelley were insistent upon filing the information charging Mrs. Hazzard with murder in the first degree. I hesitated about the filing of this information, realizing the difficulty in obtaining a conviction . . . I told them I realized that a case of this kind would, in order to handle it properly, necessitate the expenditure of considerable money for detective service etc. Mr. Agassiz advised me that Dorothea Williamson was a wealthy spinster and that he would personally guarantee that funds would be forthcoming . . . to assist in the securing of evidence and in the prosecution of the case.*
>
> *It is an exceedingly difficult and unusual case, and it is very doubtful as to whether a conviction can be had, especially so if no assistance can be had in the securing of evidence.*
>
> *Agassiz has apparently acted in good faith in the matter. If Mr. Kelley should decline to be further connected*

with the case, it would become necessary for me to request the Attorney-General's office for assistance.

ON NOVEMBER 9, DORA AND MARGARET SUR-praised Agassiz with an icebox-chilled chocolate layer cake— "four velvety layers, Tooddy, it must be at least four layers"—to celebrate his thirty-seventh birthday. And though Frank Kelley and several other Williamson friends and relatives gathered for the little party, for Miss Dora there seemed no one in the room save for her benefactor, whom she now called by his Christian name, Lucian. Margaret noticed how Dora studied the vice-consul's every move as if she wished to capture the image forever. If there was a pronounced, more obvious, attraction that evening, it had been brewing beneath the surface for some time. After a light dinner, Agassiz and Dora bundled up in sweaters and overcoats and walked along the shore of the lake, the vapors from their warm breath puffing like steamers across the Sound.

For most of it, Margaret bit her tongue and said nothing to Dora about what she saw happening. She knew it wasn't her place, though she thought it was outrageous. If Dora was to find happiness with a man, she could think of no man more gener-ous, more able, more deeply concerned than the vice-consul who had made them a home. And who had endeavored like no other to bring an evil woman to justice. But there was a major problem: Lucian was married to Ena.

JAMES LAIDLAW COULD DO NOTHING IF NOT read between the lines. If the consul based in Portland could discern one iota from the letter written by Thomas Stevenson and forwarded on by Washington's governor, it was that the prosecution considered the whole Williamson affair a waste of time. It was a case they couldn't afford; a case they considered unwinnable. The only reason the case had gone as far as it had was the fact that interlopers Agassiz and Kelley had handed the evidence over on a gleaming silver platter.

And allowed Kitsap County to keep the damn platter as well.

If it was possible that any prosecutor could be more lax than Kitsap's, it was the authorities in King County. After repeated assurances that if the evidence was there, County Attorney John Murphy would file charges in the Flux case, they were still at an odd impasse.

Murphy told Agassiz that King County would pay keen attention to the results of the Kitsap trial.

"If there is a conviction there, we will take another serious look at Flux," he said.

Agassiz had the distinct feeling that Murphy didn't think a conviction was a possibility; therefore, there was no bandwagon on which to jump. No one, it seemed, wanted to battle the woman doctor. Though they loathed her methods, it was only behind her back that the majority of detractors would voice disparaging opinions.

"It seems they are afraid of Mrs. Hazzard," Agassiz told Laidlaw and others.

Consul Laidlaw was perplexed. What was Dr. Hazzard's hold on so many? Why the pervasive trepidation?

"I don't know why," he finally agreed, "but certainly they seem to be frightened."

On the evening of November 18, James Laidlaw put the finishing touches on the package he had promised Agassiz he would send when the time was right. After he saw an item in the newspaper that Washington's Governor Hay was in contact with the British Embassy concerning the Hazzard murder charges, he knew it was time.

It was addressed:

His Excellency
The Right Honourable
James Bryce, O. M.,
British Embassy.

Inside the deep, grey envelope was a copy of all of the correspondence from the case: letters from the vice-consul, the governor, the governor's secretary, the attorney general, the attorney general's assistant, the Kitsap County Prosecutor's Office. It was a neatly organized package of dead ends.

Laidlaw's cover letter briefly highlighted the vital points of the Williamson and Flux cases.

In both instances this Mrs. Hazzard appears to have got possession of the property of the deceased, and, but for the efforts made by Mr. Agassiz, might have succeeded in her designs.

In utter frankness, he wrote the British ambassador that Washington State's attorney general had absolutely refused to take an active part in the prosecution of the cases.

... and if H. M. Government could see its way to granting Mr. Agassiz's request, a vigorous prosecution would result.

A few days later, the consul's secretary burst into James Laidlaw's office with a telegram sent from Washington, D.C.

Ambassador Bryce requested three answers. First, the probable date of the Williamson trial; second, the address of the Williamsons' home in England; and finally, if the Williamson case fails, what were the prospects of the Flux case succeeding?

As far as the request for money went, the ambassador indicated he was "disposed to give reasonable assistance." It would be up to Laidlaw to fix an amount.

The consul approached Vice-consul Agassiz immediately for recommendations. Laidlaw had felt all along that the figures first mentioned had been excessive. Since he felt comfortable with the work done thus far by Frank Kelley, and the fact that Kelley was already engaged by the Williamsons in seeking the recovery of their property, Laidlaw felt he would probably be willing to accept a reasonable fee for acting as "special counsel on behalf of the Government" in the murder trial. In the event of a trial on the Flux case, he would be the best man for the job.

Agassiz was instructed to name separate amounts for each case and telegraph a response immediately.

And so he did his best, though he came up short:

Kelley already assisted prosecution in Williamson murder trial, paid by Williamson, trial January 10th; authority from Government would greatly assist. Flux case represents many peculiarities, also Wakelin case. Impossible to

explain by wire or letter. Shall I come to Portland tonight
with all files? Williamson resided in London, sometimes
Australia. Impossible quote definite figures without inter-
view.

If he had been there in person, James Laidlaw would have
told Agassiz to take a deep breath and relax. There was no reason to bob about like an apple pitched into a pond. No need to
come to Portland. *Relax.* He telegraphed back that he needed
the Williamsons' address and a figure for the "reasonable fees"
to bolster the prosecution's efforts against the "so-called physician."

That night when Agassiz returned to Lake Steilacoom, Dora
was waiting up for him. She sat primly next to the fire, sipping
warm tea with milk and sugar as she had when she and Claire
were young women—before the great quest for perfect health
had overtaken, then ruined, their lives.

She smiled a small, but lovely, smile when she saw him.

Lucian Agassiz shared the news from Washington D.C., and
Dora drank in every word.

"You were correct all along, Lucian," she said. "Even though
we were so far from England, we were not alone."

"And I am here, always," was all he said.

From that moment he no longer saw the living human skeleton he had first seen at the Tacoma Hotel. Gone were the weep-
ing recessed eyes, the lips that had been stretched over teeth
like a taut rubber strip. Gone was the vague acrid odor.

He saw a lovely woman.

CODE MESSAGES AND LETTER-GRAMS PITCHED
back and forth from Portland, Oregon to Washington, D.C., like
rifle shots across the continent. Fire one, then two. James
Bryce, the British ambassador, and James Laidlaw, the consul,
were doing most of the dispatching. If the epistles reached
President Taft or the British minister, it was never disclosed
within the text of stacks of confidential communiqués. Linda
Burfield Hazzard, quite naturally, had no idea that she was the
subject of messages to and from the British Embassy. If she had
known, it would have fueled her belief that those who ran the

world were against her. She stood alone on the front lines, the seeping trench of a new world. It was a position she readily embraced. And she would not let go.

The maligned fasting specialist referred to her mission as the "new gospel" of good health.

The British government considered the woman and her ideas pure rubbish. Yet as Laidlaw, and later Agassiz, would learn, the government saw no need to hire an attorney to handle the Flux case. The government concluded that the Williamson estate had assured a forceful prosecution. What was the point of risking untold sums of money? If Dr. Hazzard couldn't be convicted in an American court for what she had done to Claire Williamson, what would make anyone believe she would be punished for the far weaker Ivan Flux case?

The tide was turning somewhat, and Laidlaw knew it. Even so, he stuck his neck out. By then he had met Dorothea Williamson and Margaret Conway and had heard firsthand the heinous crimes of the American starvationist.

He cabled back a request for $300 for expenses and reimbursement to Agassiz for the Flux matter.

On December 4, 1911, James Bryce sent a confidential dispatch to Sir Edward Grey, Bart., MP, in London, concerning the request for funds.

> Should His Majesty's Government agree that the circumstances of these cases and the sensation they appear to be causing on the Pacific coast justify such an outlay, I would suggest that any communication to that effect be made by telegraph as the date of the trial is set for the 10th prox . . .

AT OLALLA, HIGH ON THE HILL, LINDA HAZZARD chatted with friends as if she hadn't a worry in the world. They talked of Theosophy and Spiritualism. The world beyond fascinated Linda. Nellie Sherman and Frank Lillie were there, as was James Watson Webb. Nellie had seen a new psychic reader who lived on Queen Anne Hill in Seattle. The reading had foretold great things for Nellie—as they always did.

As the evening worked toward its sleepy end, Linda scolded

Sam for his negligence in chopping a scant amount of kindling for the woodstove. She intended to take a hot bath later that night and "soak away" her cares.

The subject of the court case and how it all started came up in conversation, as it tended to whenever the five gathered.

"Oh, those Williamson sisters! I should have known they were more trouble than they were worth," Linda said, as usual, commanding the absolute attention of her devotees and her husband.

"I had never wanted to take them in," she went on. "Not at all. They were so desperate to have treatment. Claire opened up the correspondence with me, writing from Victoria. Claire did not allow Dora to write because she knew Dora was incompetent.

"She wrote to me and pleaded with me to take her into my institution at Olalla. She begged me. She did."

IN TACOMA, DORA WAS INCENSED AT THE LATEST lies coming from the woman who would have been her guardian—*her captor*—for the rest of her life.

"How she sleeps at night with all her lies is beyond my understanding," she told Agassiz.

A grin broke across his face.

"Maybe that's why she needs a lamp on?"

THIRTY

SOMETIMES MEN AND WOMEN DON THE mask to conceal what they are; sometimes they do so in order to hide what they once were. Linda and Sam Hazzard were experts at the manner of pretense. It was an ability derived of necessity and years of practice. Linda had done it magnificently during the humiliating Minneapolis bigamy trial—at least until she finally reached her breaking point when Sam was led from the courtroom to a cellblock in Stillwater. Sam, of course, had mastered the role of the stoic. Nothing fazed him in the least. While his wife's ups and down were seen by those close to her on a daily basis, Sam was nearly always on an even keel, his ruddy, handsome face calm, his big feet planted firmly on the ground.

He always managed the appearance of control with the much-needed help of a drink.

And yet as the weeks moved from a warm, damp autumn to an even rainier and chilly Northwest winter, Sam showed the strain of the impending criminal proceedings. While he was grateful for the legal maneuvering that delayed the case from November to December to a date in January, he worried Linda would be sent to prison. He told confidants that if the worst came true and she did suffer a conviction, it would be partly his fault.

"She would be imprisoned falsely, for mistakes that I made."

Sam Hazzard stepped boldly forward and offered to take the witness stand to explain how it was that he had typed Claire's new will, how it was that he had gone to the banks in Canada to extract cash, how all of his deeds had been grossly misrepresented by the roly-poly vice-consul at Tacoma.

"Everything I did was according to Miss Dora and Miss Claire's wishes," he said. "I'll swear to it."

Attorney Day Karr told Sam he would have to sit with the spectators. The fact that he was married to the woman on trial notwithstanding, there was another reason why he would not be called by the defense.

"Your past reputation might harm your wife."

And so, as the days grew shorter, Samuel Hazzard would settle in his chair and ponder how his life had gone. He would lean back, glasses pulled low on his nose, and drink. Never so much that he was impaired. Good Lord, no. If Linda saw that he was drunk, she would castigate him in front of staff or friends alike.

"Sam! You are a disgrace! A terrible disgrace! A drunkard is what you are . . . and it will be the death of you!"

Sam would only agree and promise to stop. In turn, Linda would stomp out of the room, yelling at him as she disappeared. Her voice always staying behind, ringing in his ears.

It was an odd relationship in a difficult time. But despite the cold words she so easily flung like snapped-off icicles, she, in fact, did love him. She also needed him.

In turn, Sam protected her.

He refused to tell Linda the truth that the two of them were running out of money. Civil suits, the criminal case, and the cost overrides on the sanitarium had drained their financial reserves to a mere trickle. Though Linda's fasting practice picked up handsomely from all the notoriety, it was not enough to make up the difference in the money drain. Still, the books Sam kept showed more red than black. Others could see it, though Linda did not.

Lucian Agassiz, for one, relished the idea of the Hazzards running their bank accounts dry. Greed took them to the spot where they now stood. He hoped, he prayed, that King County would do what was right and indict her for Ivan Flux's murder before the Williamson case made it to a courtroom in Port Orchard. He wanted the woman to suffer and felt certain that if she were arrested, a lack of resources would force her to wait it out in jail.

"I am satisfied she had impounded everything she has to secure her $10,000 bail, on which she has procured her liberty."

IN LONDON, THE BRITISH POWERS THAT BE WERE divided by the Williamson and Flux cases. At issue was not whether the case against the American woman was extraordinary enough to warrant involvement—Agassiz and Laidlaw were never admonished to cease their pressure upon the prosecuting authorities in King and Kitsap Counties. The crux of the matter was whether the British government should make further funds available for the retention of special counsel. No one worried about the Williamson case; all understood that Claire's estate held sufficient funds to bankroll the prosecution. It was the Flux matter that hung in the balance.

On January 1, 1912, it finally tipped in favor of Dr. Hazzard, when the British treasurer issued his edict.

We have the opinion of the Prosecuting Attorney of Kitsap County that he does not believe in the possibility of securing a conviction in this case. The value of that opinion is discounted by the fact that he wishes to get out of prosecuting, but as he is the legal advisor of the U.S. authorities whose duty it is to prosecute if a prosecution is necessary, I do not see why we should go behind his opinion.

Yet, while the treasurer did not agree that a special lawyer should be hired to represent His Majesty's Government, he did concur that Vice-consul Lucian Agassiz should be reimbursed for out-of-pocket expenses—up to $300.

The chief clerk approved the expenditure. In addition, the clerk mulled it over and came to the conclusion that if the British government retained a special counsel outright, it would imply that U. S. authorities were not up to the job of prosecuting their own criminals. No one desired a ruffling of such feathers.

Linda Burfield Hazzard's fate would ride on the Williamson prosecution alone.

As her enemies saw it, Ivan Flux and Stanley Wakelin—the Englishman and the New Zealander—would be forgotten footnotes to the American woman's unpunished crimes of greed and murder.

THE KITSAP COUNTY COURTHOUSE COMMANDED attention like a grand pinnacle on a stubbly, logged-out hillside high above Sinclair Inlet. Its foundation was sunk into land donated by civic boosters as an incentive when Port Orchard won the county seat designation from Port Madison in an election twenty years earlier. Painted chalk white, the two-story structure was a vivid beacon from the Bremerton shoreline.

As her January trial date rapidly approached, it was a good place for the fasting specialist to contemplate her future.

The wind grabbed at her hat and cut an icy chill through her skirt. Linda Hazzard stood on the courthouse steps and announced the doors at her Olalla sanitarium would remain closed until after her unfortunate legal mess was cleaned up. She understood that her trial would last a couple of weeks—naturally an acquittal would result—then she would be free to reopen on February 15, 1912.

From the worn jaws of a black leather doctor's bag, she produced a stockpile of letters and telegrams. After pushing up her slipping readers, Linda cleared her throat to speak.

"I have heard from all over the country from people asking me to reopen, and I am going to. I have spent a lifetime in my work, and do you think I am going to give it up now? No, never! I am going right back to it harder than ever."

LUCIAN AGASSIZ TOOK THE TRAIN TO PORTLAND to interview Essie Cameron for a second time. While Miss Cameron had been supportive of the prosecution, her reluctance to tell the full story had been evident. She was one of the witnesses Agassiz kept insisting should not be overlooked.

"We must talk with Miss Cameron!" he had said again and again, very near the point of annoyance.

Essie Cameron was the hired girl who worked for Dr. Hazzard from the beginning of May to a few days before Claire Williamson died. Her duties were to assist Nellie Sherman with the cooking, and cleaning as needed.

It seemed so long ago.

Back in her hometown, the vice-consul found her working for a well-to-do family, assisting with the care of a little girl. She did not want trouble. The job was a good one, and the pay was more than she made at Olalla. She had already been hassled by Watson Webb.

She stoked the fire in the kitchen stove and ushered the vice-consul into a little parlor off the kitchen.

"I don't want the little one to hear any of this," she whispered as the door closed.

"Sir, I always knew you would find me. I have worried about that since the day I learned Miss Claire had died."

Essie Cameron's expressive brown eyes had seen so much, yet on the afternoon Agassiz met her, she seemed childlike and naive. Decidedly so. She looked no older than a schoolgirl. Clearly intimidated by the vice consul with the black shoes that shone like cracked coal, the eighteen-year-old had little to say beyond few-word answers.

"Yes, sir."

"No, sir."

"If you please, sir. I am not certain."

"No, not at all."

As she grew more comfortable and could see that Agassiz was only there to listen to her—not put words in her mouth—she finally released from her heavy heart the terrible memories she held of those two weeks at Olalla. Nothing any of the others would say would match her story. Nothing anyone could imagine could match the horror.

She recalled how the girls cried during their "manipulation" treatments. From the kitchen, she could hear Dr. Hazzard slapping their bodies with such force the sound would carry down the stairs. She observed how at bath time, the tub was filled with water so hot that she could not touch it, yet Claire and Dora were submersed in it.

She confirmed Dr. Hazzard had purposely kept the sisters apart. She did not want them to have access to their belongings.

"Do not get anything out of their trunks, no matter how they beg!"

The sisters had been led to believe the source of the broth— the tomatoes—were fresh.

"Do not tell them that they are canned tomatoes!"

When Essie inquired if the sisters could eat something to ease their terrible hunger, Dr. Hazzard flew into a rage. Her voice was loud enough that Dora heard it from the upstairs bedroom.

"They must not have solid food for it would kill them!"

And then there was the greatest horror of all. Essie Cameron saw Claire Williamson's body. The picture of it had been seared like a nightmare into her mind. She remembered how Louise Burfield, Dr. Hazzard's sister-in-law, who occasionally helped out at the sanitarium, had asked her if she wanted to see the body.

The bathroom was washed in a murky darkness when Essie stepped inside the little room with a kerosene lantern.

"Go on, Miss Cameron, in there."

The body sprawled on an ironing board lifted off the floor by the height of the washtub. The swinging lantern wiped light over the dead woman's face and naked body. Her abdomen was so concave and hard-looking, Essie imagined it could hold a gallon of water. Miss Claire's eyes popped from their sockets. The young woman held her hand over her mouth to stifle the reflex that would have her vomit on the spot.

Every bone could be counted. The corpse was so emaciated it almost looked like a skeleton that had been dipped in some kind of paint.

As the lantern swung again as she spun around to leave, Essie noticed that a jar of tiny-tipped steel knives had been placed next to Miss Claire's head.

UNDER THE CLOCK TOWER AT COLMAN DOCK, Lucian Agassiz stood before a crowd of onlookers and newspapermen. It was just minutes before the call to board the launch to Port Orchard where he would meet with Kitsap authorities. Like a politician on the stump, he waved the crowd closer. If Linda Hazzard was going to make bold statements, so was he. The veins in his neck found their way to the surface of his skin as he shouted above the din of a steamer's throbbing boilers.

A witness, he exclaimed, had been found that would "add fifty percent to the probability of conviction!"

"The witness's description of the scene at the sanitarium is almost awesome. It certainly shows the horror of the treatment. None can convince me it was not criminal, even if there was no ulterior motive. Of course, I feel certain from the circumstances there was an ulterior motive.

"Dr. Hazzard, our witness tells us, walked over to the bed where Miss Williamson lay in a comatose or dazed condition apparently unaware of the doctor's entrance. Miss Dorothea Williamson lay on another bed babbling incoherently. Our witness will testify that Dr. Hazzard rolled Miss Williamson over on her side, threw off the bedclothes and began a vigorous slapping of the young woman's body with her bare hands. The slaps were laid on with considerable severity—enough so that a perfectly well person would probably wince with pain. As she slapped the prostrate form she repeated over and over the single word, *Eliminate! Eliminate! Eliminate!*

"She also tells us that while Dr. Hazzard was in the room slapping the body of the young Englishwoman, she looked over her shoulder toward a nurse who was with our witness and remarked that a young Englishman had died that morning. Dr. Hazzard then said, our witness states, that she had cut up the remains, remarking: 'The kettle I have was not large enough to hold him, I'll have to get another one.'

Agassiz never identified the witness by name, but of course it was Clara Corrigan, the young woman who lived at the Buena Vista and helped Nurse Sherman care for the sisters when they began their slide toward death.

Miss Corrigan had sent a message to Agassiz when she read the criminal trial was approaching.

She promised she would help any way she could.

III
Murderess or Martyr?

During the time we were fasting I wanted food oh so much, but she kept on saying just wait a little bit. Finally I got into such a condition I did not care for food and really believed against my will that I did not need any.

—Dora Williamson

Even if all that has been said of Dr. Hazzard were true, she has still done more for suffering humanity than any other living doctor.

—Fast Cure Supporter in a letter to Lloyd Jones, New Zealand

THIRTY-ONE

JANUARY BROUGHT ONLY WASHTUBS OF precipitation. Linda Hazzard had hoped for snow: a good snow, an Ottertail County snow, not the gauzy, clear white of what frequently passed for a flurry in the warm breath of Puget Sound. A good dusting would conceal the deep scars on the soil that were the disheartening and constant reminder that the doctor's plans for the sanitarium had lain fallow for months. Nothing seemed to be progressing as she had designed. Her cheeks turned scarlet, and the veins in her neck pulsated from the surface of her skin. The thought of the humiliation of her situation made her angry.

John Kellogg and the breakfast bunch must be reveling in a chortle over everything they read and heard out of Olalla.

The sanitarium's wild huckleberry bushes had not been trimmed into topiaries depicting the glories of nature; only one of a dozen stumps had been fashioned into a resting chair, and only a handful of cabins had been roughed in among the cedars and firs that crowned the hillside.

Snow would hide all of it, she knew. Snow would provide an excuse as well as a covering.

Instead, rain and wind had only left her with an empty feeling. But as she had done for most of her life, Linda Burfield Hazzard did her best to hide her desperation deep inside. Sheltered by the broad eaves over her porch, she studied muddy animal tracks that passed by the gulch and disappeared into the woods by the cabin that would have been Claire Williamson's home, her tribute.

"When this is over," she told her husband, "I shall still call the place 'Cabin Claire.' The poor girl did nothing but believe in the fast. She will live on here at Olalla. She is deserving of a tribute fitting to her beliefs in the cure."

Sam Hazzard agreed, partly because he seldom dared to disagree. It was also because the day was too important to battle the woman he alternately loved and tolerated.

It was January 15, 1912, the first day of Linda's murder trial.

Earlier that morning, before daylight seeped through the gash in the forest of the Hazzard property, the doctor had dressed for the occasion. She did not wear the perfectly pressed and starched medical whites that had been her uniform of late, though she did weigh the benefits of looking the part. Her attorneys advised her to dress as though she were going on an outing with pleasant company. Linda Hazzard gave herself a once-over in the full-length looking glass that occupied the corner of her bedroom. Even without face coloring of any kind, she looked quite becoming in her brown velvet gown. Ostrich feathers tinted a matching shade sprang from a hat she pinned to her hair. The plumes moved like underwater sea grasses whenever she walked across the room.

While Sam went outside to hitch the horses for the long, bumpy buggy ride through the valley and along the edge of Long Lake to Port Orchard, Linda made a tight fist and pounded the surface of her black oak dining table. She let out a quick wail of disgust followed by a nearly inaudible sigh of resignation. She had counted on a jury of men *and* women. Women, she was certain, would see beyond Dorothea's "false act" and not get drawn into the affected emotions of a poor little rich girl. In addition, she felt ordinary women could recognize the value of fasting and, she hoped, would support her activities.

"And my success as a physician, a *woman* doctor," she said.

Linda would have gladly taken her chances before a jury of women. She embraced the very idea of it. Women bore children, nursed and nurtured them. Women could accept fasting, whether they would employ the treatment or not, as an option for the very ill. Fasting provided, at its very least, a last stand for hope. Giving life was a woman's sacred trust. Preserving it was her duty. Hope was part of womanhood.

Such a jury would not be called in Kitsap County. Though females could serve as jurors by 1912, prospective jurors' names in the Hazzard case had been pulled from voters' records. No women had been among the voters' rolls in Kitsap's most recent election.

Men, Dr. Hazzard railed time and again, resented her and wished to see her imprisoned because of her gender alone.

Besides, her best patients were always female.

DORA WILLIAMSON COULD STILL FEEL THE TOUCH of Lucian Agassiz's hand as he patted hers with assurance the end of the ordeal was nigh. Margaret did not approve of Dora's fondness for the vice-consul, though she understood a need for gratitude. Because of the special closeness with her sister, the attention of a man had been a rare occurrence. It had been missing from Dora's life. In Margaret's estimation, now was not the time, nor the proper place, for such feelings.

The Sunday night before jury selection, Agassiz checked the two women, along with their uncle John Herbert, and cousin, Dr. Arthur Langley of Melbourne, into rooms at Port Orchard's "most modern hostelry," the forty-five-room Navy View Hotel. The hotel had just reopened, and it sparkled with newness. Two years before, a flash flood had made the integrity of its foundation dubious. To remedy the problem, the building owner moved the three-story structure—turrets, verandas and all—two blocks north with the aid of log rollers and a donkey steam engine. The doors reopened in time for the Hazzard trial.

The rooms overlooking Sinclair Inlet and the navy's dry dock had been applied for in mid-December. Rooms were scarce even then. The interest in the starvation murder case had filled every available room in Port Orchard and many across the water in Bremerton and Charleston. The Navy View had set aside all its rooms for the jury and the one hundred witnesses expected to testify.

Dora and Margaret were told to occupy themselves until called before the court. Margaret took up her needlework, and Dora picked through the pages of a book. But as the hours dissolved, neither woman could keep her mind fixed on her task. If only the trial would begin, so that in time it would be over.

Monday passed into Tuesday, Tuesday into Wednesday . . . and still no jury.

Friends in London and Melbourne had been aghast at the delays following the starvationist's arrest. With word that the jury was finally about to be seated, many shook their heads in disbelief and wonderment. What happened to the supposed concept of swift justice? None could get used to the laggard pace of American courts.

WITHOUT QUESTION IT WAS A TRIAL MADE FOR newspapers. It was a case with more scandal than a novelist could conjure—hypnotism, strange mental powers, forgery, the desecration of a body, the pressure brought by the British in a prosecution on American soil, and of course, a hideously cruel murder of a beloved sister.

Considering such a scandalous recipe, most estimated that securing a fair jury for the Hazzard trial would be exceedingly difficult. None, however, expected that four special venires would be needed to fill the twelve seats in the jury box. Kitsap County Superior Court Judge John Yakey—just back from his honeymoon the day before the start of the proceedings—declared the jury would be comprised of "intelligent" men, unbiased by the international interest and press coverage of the starvation case.

The examination of jurors was so spirited that Judge Yakey admonished observers to stifle unruly outbursts. He slammed his gavel with the decided force of a man who often used the instrument.

"This courtroom is not a place for amusement," he warned more than once.

Something peculiar seemed to be at work. For attorneys and others in the courtroom, finding a qualified juror to take the twelfth chair became a bizarre amusement in its own right. Court watchers called the twelfth chair the "Hoo Doo chair," because for some mysterious reason no one sitting on it seemed to be able to pass the examinations of the attorneys. One potential twelfth juror from Olalla had his mind made up about the doctor, one couldn't write or read English, another considered a person charged with a crime already guilty, and so on.

Even a local dignitary was excused from service. Bremerton

mayor Paul Mehner's father had been a patient at the Olalla sanitarium—and was on the list of witnesses for the defense.

"Excused!"

Throughout the long mornings and afternoons, the Hazzards were magnets for all eyes. At times, an aloof and seemingly unconcerned Linda stared out the window, playing with the fringe of her dress. Sam chewed a piece of gum. Occasionally he appeared oblivious to his wife—until she snapped him on the shoulder with a sharp finger and mouthed his name.

Only when the potential jurors were questioned about the death penalty did the proceedings rivet the fasting specialist's attention.

A reporter on the coveted Hazzard beat wrote about those rare flashes of concern:

> *Then a peculiar look, seemingly half of fear and half of defiance came in to her eyes to vanish in an instant as she would quickly look up and perhaps let her gaze wander over the courtroom.*

On Wednesday, January 17, 1912, the lead story of the *Tacoma Daily Ledger* blared:

MRS. HAZZARD DOMINATES ALL
SAYS SHE IS STRONGER THAN ORDINARY MAN

The reporter asked the defendant what she would do if she lost her case?

"There is no such thing as 'if,' " she fired back. "Besides, don't you know there is a whole lot in being right with yourself? If one is right that way, then nothing else matters. And I have not lost a moment's sleep nor shed a tear thus far and don't expect to."

At 11:40 the next morning, the jury was finally seated with the acceptance of a navy worker named Jerry Ahearn. More than half of the all-married jury were naturalized Americans, born in Scandinavian countries. None were of British extraction. The defense had wisely seen to that. No loyalties would be put into play in that courtroom. Most jurors worked in the navy yard, a few were farmers. None were peers of Dr. Hazzard's.

"None among those men can fully understand my mission," she loudly whispered to her husband.

The opening statement by the prosecution was swift and pointed as the state's case was detailed. The defense offered no statement; they would reserve such remarks for the opening of their case—if the case went that far. More than a hundred witnesses were to be called. Four doctors by the defense, eleven by the prosecution. It was a case, both sides agreed, built upon lies. Dora was a liar. Linda was a liar. Whom to believe? But it was also a case that went beyond mere finger-pointing. As Linda Hazzard had often said, it was to be a battle between factions in the medical world—the drug and hospital purveyors and the proponents of the nature cures.

Before the first witnesses were called, before the story of Starvation Heights would unfold, Dr. Hazzard took a moment to smile for photographers. She was confident that with her husband and lawyers by her side, she would be cleared of all charges.

"It is strange," she said, "but this is the first time I have had to lean on anyone. I find it hard to get used to it."

MARGARET AND DORA NEARLY LAUGHED OUT loud when Agassiz read in the paper what their nemesis had said.

"*Lean* on someone? That woman leans on no one except for her stony self. She trusts no one!" Margaret declared with a harshness her words seldom carried.

Dora nodded, surprised once more by Margaret's passion and outspokenness. *How Margaret had changed.* While she was a servant, and never would be more than that in her entire life, she was also a woman who stood as firm in her convictions as anyone of greater means and education. Olalla and the whole dismal experience of it had transformed Margaret Conway. It had made her stronger.

"Mrs. Hazzard is begging for sympathy, but she'll find none here," Dora said as her thoughts of the conversation returned to her.

"Indeed not!" Margaret agreed sharply.

Like the mother who runs into a flaming nursery to save her baby and emerges without the slightest burn, Margaret Conway had found some kind of inner strength no one knew—including herself—that she possessed. She had been pushed to the edge of battle and kept her wits about her. In Margaret's mind she knew that if she and Dr. Hazzard faced off in a contest of wills, the doctor would lose. The greying Aussie would not give an inch. She had lost Claire through sheer ignorance. She had saved Dora through perseverance and courage. She was not the type of woman who would make the same mistake twice.

THIRTY-TWO

COURTROOM WATCHERS HAD SPECULATED who would stand for the prosecution when the moment came for the taking of testimony. Some speculated that Thomas Stevenson, the Kitsap County prosecutor, would make a show of questioning the first witnesses—those who only laid the time line for the tragic events at Olalla. It would be a way for the prosecutor to grandstand a bit, to show the world that this was, in fact, *his* case after all. It was not justice bought and paid for by the British government, as had been gossiped throughout the county and beyond.

"That Frank Kelley is being paid by the English! They are running the whole case!"

It was, however, Frank Kelley who stood to call the first witness.

Linda Hazzard shot a quick glance in Sam's direction. How the two of them had ridiculed the county and spineless Stevenson! Out loud they had wondered if the county prosecutor would claim even a small role in the courtroom. Sam's eyes met Linda's. They had been right all along. Satisfaction, however, was fleeting. Even though the two had been the source of much of the innuendo about the prosecution, vindication was not so sweet.

Unfortunately for Linda Burfield Hazzard, Frank Kelley was the superior lawyer.

Rasmus Van Deerling, the pastor of the Episcopal Church, Los Angeles, California, who had seen Claire and Dora just before they left for the Northwest, was the first to sit in the witness box. The pastor testified that he considered the sisters in good health, with Claire weighing a robust 115 or 120. He had last seen Claire and Dora in February 1911. He recalled how the sisters had confided they were going to take some treatment in Seattle.

During a break, a noise came from the defense table. It was laughter, loud and jarringly inappropriate. Mouths nearly rested in laps while the defendant with her life on the line exhibited an oddly jovial take on the proceedings that had done all but swallow her with a torrent of paperwork and suspicion. Leaning her head to her husband's shoulder, Linda whispered something and laughed again.

"Tell us, what is so tickling, Mrs. Hazzard?" a newsman up front inquired when he finally seized the defendant's attention.

"Do you know I can't feel serious about this trial as I suppose I ought? I really feel almost as if I were at a play," she replied.

"But Mrs. Hazzard—"

The reporter was halted in mid-sentence. The smile had dissolved from the defendant's face. Her eyes projected a stern and annoyed look.

"—I have told you time and again. It is *Dr.* Hazzard! *Mrs.* Hazzard is my mother-in-law."

Court was adjourned early while the attorneys hotly debated the admissibility of evidence concerning Dora's treatment at Olalla. The defense asserted that the state's proof was confined solely to Claire's treatment—not the treatment of others. Both sides had much riding on that point. Kelley considered it key, Day Karr considered it a sham of justice. Judge Yakey decided in favor of the prosecution.

There would be no more secrets.

BY THE END OF THE FIRST DAY OF THE TRIAL, vague rumors of witness tampering and attempted bribery reached Dora and Margaret at the hotel. Officers of the court had heard from a prosecution witness that someone associated with the defense had offered money and a job to silence damaging testimony. While the name of the perpetrator had not been revealed, Lucian Agassiz had heard who the witness had been.

"Who is it?" Dora pleaded.

Agassiz didn't like to pass along misinformation, but he could not resist Dora's appeal for every detail she could glean.

"It was Essie. Miss Cameron is the one," he said.

ESTHER CAMERON WAS AFRAID TO GO TO THE trial in the first place. She had a sense of foreboding about the starvation case and worried that if she crossed Dr. Hazzard, there would be a great price to pay. She was unsure what would come of her testimony.

She came up from Portland to the Navy View Hotel with a girlfriend, Mae Midgley. It was the nicest, grandest, place the two young women had ever stayed.

Shortly after checking in, a sharp knock sounded on their door.

"*Porter, Miss!*"

In the split second it took Essie to turn the knob, Watson Webb stuck his foot into the doorjamb.

"Remember me?" he said with a broad smile, as though trying to charm her.

The color siphoned from the young woman's pretty face. She was chalk.

"I do. Please *go*," Essie answered quickly as she tried to shut the door without breaking the intruder's foot.

"I have come to talk with you," he said. "It is important, and I promise to be done in short order. I will only take a minute. Dr. Hazzard sent me."

With Mae Midgley there for protection, she agreed.

"You know very well I did not offer you any money in Portland, that I simply said Dr. Hazzard would get a place for you, a job," he said.

Essie shook her head.

"That is not true! You know full well what you said!"

Webb started to speak, but the young woman cut him off as his mouth began to move.

"Mr. Babcock consulted his lawyer and his lawyer told him it was a plain case of bribery," she snapped.

Webb bristled at her retort.

"You may call it such," he said before leaving in a blur of haste.

THIRTY-THREE

THE HILLSIDE ROAD TO WILDERNESS heights was slick and muddier than a log flume. Such conditions were inevitable. Along with steady rainfall, there had been increased comings and goings since the starvation murder trial lurched to a start. Locals considered a pair of considerable wagon wheel ruts too deep, so teams of horses, thick with winter fur, were diverted to the opposite side to run a new pair of tracks. The horses hardly needed such coats—the temperature had risen to almost fifty degrees.

The turn into the lane that cut to the Hazzard bungalow was dumped with a layering of hay from the barn and wind-snapped fir branches. Somebody, it was obvious, had been thinking. A barrier between wheels and mud was always greatly appreciated in a community in which roads were primitive, famously rutted, and, after a heavy rain, veritable rivers in their own right.

Visitors had come to the Hazzard place to show their endorsement of the lady doctor, if not her methods. Some brought bread and cakes packed in baskets. None considered it odd that they brought food to a place dubbed Starvation Heights. They did it to be neighborly. Many figured Linda Hazzard wouldn't have time to cook a proper meal with the trial in Port Orchard consuming her every waking minute. Most didn't know that she seldom cooked anyway, preferring to direct the process while hovering over a hired girl.

Only one clue might have indicated to neighbors that the home belonged to the maligned fasting specialist. In a corner near the kitchen door, a length of damp tubing had been coiled like a rattler inside an enema can. It had the look and smell of a bucket of fishing bait. It was silent proof that despite all against her, her beliefs—*her treatment*—prevailed.

John Karcher, Nellie Sherman, Watson Webb, and Frank Lillie visited with Linda and Sam nearly every night. They were among the faithful aides-de-camp of the greatest woman healer the world had ever known. For Dr. Hazzard, the diversion of such company was pleasant and welcome. Linda had never been one to silence a compliment. But more so than ever, kind words were especially appreciated during her trial.

All who came were on the witness list. All, she was sure, would tell her side.

Before going to bed, Samuel set out a clean shirt and a new collar to wear with his favorite black suit. Linda fussed about her wardrobe before settling on her courtroom attire. She chose a form-fitting black silk gown that flattered her figure like a woman barely thirty. For the first time in five days of court-room appearances, Linda would not wear a hat. She twisted and fastened her hair to her head. It was a stylish coiffure. Even if she had not been the defendant, Linda Burfield Hazzard undoubtedly would have been noticed.

Rollin Burfield, who now occupied the upstairs room where Claire had died, was more concerned about his courtroom pres-ence than his mother. The doctor's insolent son tried on two suits before settling on a natty grey one he had worn only once before.

It had been at the occasion of Claire Williamson's memorial at Butterworth & Sons.

FIRST THE STAGE IN SEATTLE, NOW THE COURT-room. Rollie had always longed to be the center of attention. Even years later, when he ended up running local movie houses on Vashon Island and in Gig Harbor, he did so with a kind of overinflated style that suggested great importance. He was not the director, after all. He was merely the projec-tionist. And as lazy as he was about most endeavors, he put great effort into looking and acting the part of a person of fame. Whenever it presented itself, Rollin was only too happy to capture the reflection off the blaze of his mother's notoriety.

Hugh Buchanan recalled Dr. Hazzard's son as old-time Olallans knew him:

"He was a very flamboyant character. I remember when he was heading for the theater, and Rollie was about to step into his car—he always tried to have an open type of car—it was flashy, the color and everything. I don't know if he wore goggles; I don't know that he went that far—but he had his leather jacket, his puttees. He would step into the car with a flourish, and off he went in a cloud of dust. And everyone in the community could tell it was Rollie coming from the cloud of dust and the speed of the car."

In later years, Rollin Burfield continued to wreak havoc on his mother's life. John Smith and other old-timers recall the scandal that drove the Olalla school principal from town. The principal's wife—also a schoolteacher—had polio and was being treated by Dr. Hazzard. While the missus took treatment, the family, including a teenage daughter, stayed at the sanitarium. The couple most likely regretted their decision.

Rollin Burfield, ever the charmer, got their daughter pregnant.

"You know, in those days it was a terrible thing to happen," Smith observed years later. *"It just broke her mother's and father's heart, and they suddenly moved away. I don't know where that family ever went. I also heard—you know he had a movie place on Vashon Island—I heard he got a gal over there pregnant, too."*

Smith felt sorry for the fasting specialist.

"She was probably getting him out of trouble all the time, bailing him out. Kind of a worthless son living off of his mother."

ON THE MORNING OF JANUARY 19, 1912, MARGARET Conway kissed Dora softly on the cheek and clasped her gloved hand so tightly the younger woman blinked. If the gesture was meant to communicate a fondness without words, it did so. Margaret smiled at the grown woman who had once been the child she had adored. Tiny Dora Williamson looked lovely. She wore a plum-colored suit trimmed with a black velvet neckline, cuffs and half-dollar-sized covered buttons. Her hemline was charminly out of step. It nearly grazed the floor. A wide-brimmed black-and-dark green hat garnished with a green plume, deep-hued peonies and cabbage roses and a big, somewhat dowdy, old-fashioned handbag completed her ensemble.

Evelyn Dorothea Williamson was no longer the apple-head on a stick doll that she had been the summer she was saved. At about one hundred pounds, she was very much an attractive lady. There was, at last, more joy than sadness in her eyes.

Lucian Agassiz gladly took the duty of escorting his star witness from the Navy View Hotel to the courtroom. He soothed her worries with promises that by the end of the day, the worst would be over.

"The worst was losing Claire," she said sadly, as photographers spotted them and moved quickly to catch up.

Agassiz nodded. "I know. And that, my Dora, will never be completely over."

A camera's flash bounced off her smiling face as she stopped in front of the hotel. Then it was time to leave.

Dora joked that she had a "doctor's appointment."

And so she did. It was Friday, January 19, 1912, the morning of the great face-off. Linda Hazzard and Dora Williamson, the doctor and patient, the torturer and victim, were to meet again in Judge Yakey's courtroom. It was not lost on anyone that much of the case was dependent on who would be seen as the victim of such a confrontation. Like some kind of a bizarre seating arrangement akin to a wedding, proponents of Dr. Hazzard sat behind her, Dora's supporters rallied in a cluster on the opposite side. Most, including scads of society women from Bremerton and Seattle, however, were forced to stand. Amid those who managed to secure a much-coveted spectator's seat were the elegantly accoutered wives of the attorneys, the judge's new bride, and Capt. C.F. Pond, commander of the U.S.S. *Pennsylvania*.

ALTHOUGH JUDGE YAKEY INDICATED THE REA-son for convening court an hour earlier than customary was in the interest of saving time, it really had to do with money. Kitsap County had been on a cash basis the year before, the several thousand dollars in its coffers now would almost certainly be drained by the Hazzard trial.

Court was called into session at 9 A.M. Friday morning and predictions by the defense held true: Judge Yakey considered Dora's fasting and osteopathic treatments and her recollections of them admissible.

The gavel whacked.

JOHN HERBERT WAS SUPREMELY CONFIDENT when he strode to the witness stand. Maybe more so than his niece, Dora, he had a score to settle and was well prepared for the task. He felt he had been conned by Linda and Samuel Hazzard that day when he left Dora in their charge after Claire had died. He had been duped by their reassurances that his niece was in good hands. Embarrassment and bitterness fueled an anger that begat an all-consuming need for retribution. He stared unflinchingly at the defense table.

He wanted Dr. Hazzard to know she could not talk her way out of this. Not this time. The uncle from Portland wanted her to know he hadn't forgotten anything.

Linda Hazzard barely returned his gaze.

Under direct examination, the girl's uncle described family relationships, his nieces' health, their plans for the future, and their trip up north to Seattle the winter before. He told of his utter shock when learning of Claire's death by telegram sent by Dr. Hazzard on May 22. He recalled how Dr. Hazzard had displayed what she purported to be Claire's internal organs.

"Where were they?" Frank Kelley asked.

"Wrapped up in a cloth; she brought them from a part of the room."

"Wrapped up in a cloth?" the lawyer repeated, his tone incredulous.

The witness nodded.

"She brought them from the room."

A few spectators squirmed in their seats. The very idea was so disgusting, so revolting.

In an unblinking manner the uncle told the court what Dora had been reduced to under the fasting cure. She was emaciated beyond recognition.

As Frank Kelley probed for more details, spectators leaned forward and turned their attention to Linda Hazzard who seemed barely to give the witness a cursory glance. Instead, she whispered to her attorneys and her husband.

"*Lies!*"

The uncle's descriptive words stung, as he had meant them to.

"A living skeleton . . . just bone showing through the skin . . . skin and bone . . ."

"What appeared to be her mental condition?"

"Perfectly sound and competent, she recognized me and spoke to me."

"What appeared to be her attitude of mind toward the defendant?"

"She complained of being nervous."

Defense lawyer George Gregory sprang from his seat as if someone had poked him in the rear. *Objection!* If Dr. Hazzard had not been there when the alleged conversation took place, it was improper direct testimony.

Judge Yakey agreed.

Kelley tried another approach, but it gained him little and he moved on to the conversations the witness had with Dr. Hazzard about Claire's death. The uncle told the court the defendant knew for some time that Claire was going to die.

"How long?"

"A week before, Mrs. Hazzard knew Claire was going to die, and she told me she had told Claire that she was going to die and she could not save her."

"Did Mrs. Hazzard say when she told Claire?"

"When she knew it herself, and had told Claire to prepare for it, to make arrangements, and she had done so. Claire had made all necessary arrangements, that all her expenses even to her funeral expenses were all arranged for by Claire herself. Claire had given an order on the bank to pay the doctor a certain sum of money. What that sum of money was—she did not know what the amount was—but had agreed to accept that as full settlement for all her claims against Claire."

Next, the special prosecutor led John Herbert through statements Mrs. Hazzard had made about Dora's alleged insanity. According to the witness, the defendant pronounced Dora a mentally spent woman with very little time left.

"She told me in her experience such cases grew worse and the patient grew worse and generally became hopelessly insane. She also gave me her opinion as a doctor that she would not live much longer. She said she was in a very precarious condition and would not answer for the results."

The uncle recalled seeing a dead woman's body, lying in a white casket like a small, lifeless bundle of kindling. He did not recognize the body as Claire's.

"The color of the hair and eyes were different to anything I had seen before, the length of the face was different, the condition of the face, cheeks, and hands was not in accordance with the condition told to me by Mrs. Hazzard."

The body was not as thin as he had expected. He did not believe it was Claire Williamson at all.

Mr. Herbert concluded his direct testimony with a description of the financial demands Linda and Sam Hazzard had levied at the sanitarium in July 1911. The Hazzards asked for $2,000 to settle the Williamson account—before Dora could leave Olalla.

Even more disturbing: Dr. Hazzard had appointed herself Dora's guardian. The doctor was in full and complete charge of everything.

Cross-examination by Day Karr was thorough, if not particularly enlightening. How could it be? Mr. Herbert was a well-prepared witness and had been told what to expect when it came time for the other side to try to force him to back down on his testimony.

The defense lawyer tried to get the uncle to admit Claire had been predisposed to serious illness from an early age. The uncle balked.

"Did you ever hear about her being sick?"

"Nothing more than childhood ailments."

"Did you ever hear about her not being sick?"

"If she was sick, I would hear about it."

"What was the condition of her health?"

"Good."

"Are you sure it was good?"

"Yes, sure as I can be."

During the line of questioning, an exasperated Karr turned to address the judge.

"We believe the witness is evading the question."

Judge Yakey did not agree.

And so the testimony of Dora and Claire's uncle continued, the defense coming up short each time they posed their theory in the form of a question. All the Portland man would concede was that if either girl had an illness that he had not been told about, it was *possible* they had been ill. *Period*. Their health was good in February 1911.

John Herbert bristled with each question concerning Dora's mental competency as the defense attempted to convince the jury Dora had been insane all her life.

"Was there any period during the few years prior to Claire's death that Dora had mild spells of insanity?"

"I said, no."

"Do you know she did not have such spells?"

"I tell you," Mr. Herbert said, his voice rising, "I do not know of any occasion when she had them."

The area that brought the greatest attention from the gallery of spectators concerned the corpse at Butterworth's. Nothing Day Karr could pose could mitigate the impact. His questions only increased the suspicions.

"Do you mean to say now there is a doubt existing in your mind whether or not the body shown you was Claire's?"

"Yes. There is a doubt in my mind."

Four hours after he took the stand, John Herbert stepped down and walked past Linda Hazzard and her supporters. By all accounts he had been an unshakable witness. He had done right by his sister's daughters.

HER VOICE WAS SO TINY, IT SEEMED TO REGISTER barely above a whisper. Evelyn Dorothea Williamson was sworn in as the day nearly came to a close. Frank Kelley could have asked the court to recess for the day, but he knew Dora would welcome the chance to take the stand if only to get it started. While Linda Hazzard wasn't a large woman, she was strong and sure of herself. She had a commanding presence. Dora was more tentative, her steps small, her stride to the witness box slow enough for observers to compare the two women. Back and forth, back and forth. Eyes measured the two.

Dora's charming accent also gave her a kind of daintiness that reinforced the perception she was a somewhat fragile lady. One reporter called her a delicate "English rosebud," another wrote she had captured the hearts of everyone in the courtroom. Under Kelley's direct, she recounted her childhood, her closeness with her sister, their financial affairs, their belief in alternative medicine, and how it was the two had come to call on Dr. Hazzard. She showed the jury how the fasting specialist performed her osteopathic treatments—in a manner and with such force she had never known before.

"Like that, she hammered with her fists." Dora's eyes winced in pain as she pounded the air.

"Backs, heads, and foreheads . . ."

The memory brought tears and the day's testimony halted. It was a good place to stop. Dora would get into the principal of the case the next day. Frank Kelley had left the jurors right where he wanted them. They would go back to their hotel rooms wanting to know more. They could ponder how it was that these two women, witness and defendant, would end up in court. One, the sister of the victim, the other, the alleged murderess. Two women brought together because of the death of a third.

As they walked outside, darkness enveloping the soggy landscape, the two women brushed past each other. Nothing was said. There was no need for the bitter words of disagreement or angry confrontation. Both ladies knew what had really happened in the woods of Olalla. They would always know.

CONCERNING THE BODY IN THE COFFIN AT Butterworth & Sons, Lucian Agassiz had no real answer as to who it was. As he sat up late at night preparing for the next day in court, he wrestled with the most curious aspect of the case. He didn't believe for one second that the body was Claire Williamson's. He speculated on the possibility Linda Hazzard shared more with infamous Indiana murderess Belle Gunness than a rural abode and a proclivity for murdering for money.

It was supposedly Belle's headless body that had been found in the seared ruins of her burned-down farmhouse. Yet, the corpse did not match Belle's physical description. The remains belonged to a woman, small in frame, even dainty—words never ascribed to formidable Mrs. Gunness. It was believed by some that Belle had murdered a stranger, a charwoman from Chicago, dressed her in her own clothes, and used her as a prop to throw the authorities off her tracks.

It was conceivable Linda Hazzard had gone that far, too. To cover up Claire's hideously skeletal appearance, the fasting specialist easily could have substituted the body of another patient—or borrowed one from her friends at the morgue. The meatier cadaver was only a prop to trick Claire's emotionally ravaged survivors into believing that their beloved died of some malady or condition unrelated to the withholding of food.

Suspicion about it was on everyone's lips in Port Orchard: *"If it wasn't Claire Williamson in that coffin, who was it?"*

THIRTY-FOUR

AT 10:40 A.M. SATURDAY, JANUARY 20, DORA resumed the stand. She wore the same plum-colored suit as she had the day before, perhaps providing the only clue that her wealth, while great, was not nearly as liquid as people believed. She also wore it because it made sense to do so. After all, she had been in the witness box less than an hour. The garment was in impeccable condition, certainly clean and crisp enough for another day. No matter. It was not a fashion show, and, no matter what the tiny, British woman wore, she had most observers on her side. The *Tacoma Times* lauded Dora with the ultimate compliment: "She is an engaging woman who looks more like 23 than 38."

She appeared stronger, less tentative as she told the court of her days at the Buena Vista subsisting on thin vegetable broths made from boiling tomatoes or asparagus sprigs. She and her sister had two such meals a day.

"Did the course prescribed for you include any other kind of food or any additional food except vegetable broth?" Frank Kelley asked.

"No, we never tasted any other food except fruit juice."

Testimony about the enemas was a little uncomfortable for Dora. She blushed a little when she talked about the indelicate procedure. She preferred to call the treatment "water injections." The procedure, she said, became more and more taxing as the weeks went on. She fainted when the quantity and length of time to inject the water increased.

Kelley asked Dora to describe her sister's condition at the Buena Vista.

"She looked weak and did not seem to have any strength,

but she was still able to go about and we both struggled out as it was represented to us it was better for us to keep going all the time as that would help us to eliminate the poison in our systems."

"What was said to you about the poison in your systems?"

"Dr. Hazzard told us we had a great deal and it was better to have it worked out and the more we walked about however bad we felt, it was better to walk and struggle against it and we went out at first mornings and afternoons for a week."

"Did Dr. Hazzard say anything about what the result would be when this elimination of poison was accomplished?"

"Yes, that our bodies would be clean and in perfect health."

And it would come swiftly.

EVEN MORE SO THAN THE DAY BEFORE, PORT orchard had swollen to near capacity. Restaurants were jammed. Hotels completely full. Society women—some dragging along husbands—were the most noticeable contingent among the observers. Many had risen early and come from Seattle to linger all day near the courthouse. Gossip and truth stewed in the stockpot of public opinion. Most thought the fasting specialist was guilty, though they doubted she'd be convicted.

"The lady has too much influence with officials," one man said. "Look, her patient is the mayor's father. What do you think?"

And as the grey-skied morning moved toward the afternoon, word would leak from the courtroom to reveal bits of testimony to the scores of unlucky who could not get inside for a personal inspection of the proceedings. Dora Williamson was acknowledged to be the "finest witness" in the history of the county, and the story she had to tell was the most shocking of all time. It was a story on everybody's lips.

"*. . . Dr. Hazzard told Dora her brain was affected. She was insane. And she believed the woman!*"

"*. . . The starvation doctor kept asking about the girl's fortune and who was in charge of it!*"

"*. . . She took their money. She took everything she could put her hands on!*"

DORA'S GLOVED HAND HELD A LACE-TRIMMED handkerchief to dab at tears before they would roll down her warm cheeks. She alternated her gaze between Kelley, Dr. Hazzard, and the jurors. Two jurors held handkerchiefs of their own. One in the front row bit his lip as if to keep it from trembling.

Linda Hazzard sat only fifteen feet away, her face white as she fixed her attention on Dora, only occasionally leaning over to her lawyers or husband to whisper. It was not her finest hour, and she knew it.

Frank Kelley directed Dora to the matters of money. The witness told the jury how she had signed a pension voucher of $110.33, but never saw the funds. Traveler's checks were brought to her for signatures, but she never saw that money either. She had also given Dr. Hazzard more than $100 in cash—but no accounting was made.

The Canadian Bank of Commerce draft exhibit was shown to the jury.

> *Transfer five hundred and eighty three dollars to Samuel C. Hazzard or order and charge my account.*

Dora Williamson emphatically shook her head when asked if she had recalled signing that draft.

"I *never* signed that."

And she never got the money.

At 2:15 P.M., court was adjourned over a defense objection about the admissibility of testimony of what Dr. Hazzard had allegedly told the sisters about the course of their treatment. The defense argued the fasting specialist's directions did not fit within the state's charge of first-degree murder through the withholding of food. Judge Yakey indicated he would make a ruling on Monday, but was none too pleased with the delay. Night sessions the following week were a distinct possibility.

When observers gathered at the dock to catch the launch for their homes on the other side of the Sound, Lucian Agassiz listened intently to their remarks. He could see that it was one bit of testimony that stood alone at the forefront of their minds. It suggested a darker, more evil characterization of Dr. Hazzard.

Nothing, it seemed, had riveted their attention greater than the
story of the gulch.

" *'Dora, what are you doing? Oh, I was so frightened. I
thought you were going to throw yourself out the window . . .'* "

While Agassiz had no doubts about what the self-proclaimed
fasting specialist was capable of, he was soon to find her reach
was greater than he imagined.

SPLINTERS OF BROKEN GLASS SHIMMERED LIKE
frost on the dark wood of the kitchen floor of the lake bungalow. It was both pretty and disturbing at the same time, like the
sinister shimmer of a spiderweb, all beaded with dew. It took
only a second for Lucian Agassiz to make sense of what he saw
when he stepped into his home. A pane in the French doors
leading from the kitchen to the veranda had been broken from
the outside, which clearly meant that someone had smashed it
to get inside. With the Port Orchard trial consuming every waking minute of his day, coming home to a burglary was beyond
aggravation.

The vice-consul's eyes raced over the household valuables.
Paintings, silver plate, crystal, a set of cherished gold pocket
watches . . . all were quickly accounted for in an inventory of
things he would take from his home if the roles were reversed
and he had been a thief in search of goods to sell or pawn. It was
so curious. Nothing was missing. Everything seemed fine.
Beyond the broken glass, no open drawers, no disheveled furniture indicated anything had been disturbed downstairs.

It was late Saturday, January 20, 1912.

In the corner of a bedroom, he saw what the thief had done.
Claire Williamson's trunk—one clearly labeled in block letters
with her first and last name—had been pillaged. The intruder
had smashed the lock, breaking it in two. Another labeled with
only the Williamson surname had been rifled as well. The contents of both had been disturbed in the abrupt manner of a thief
who was looking for something.

What was the burglar looking for?

Lucian Agassiz had no idea who had come into his house, but
he had no doubt that somehow the perpetrator was associated
with the Hazzard camp.

Other trunks that were not marked with names had been left untouched. The intruder had to move heavy crates and trunks to get to Miss Claire's things. Whoever had been there, was in search of something specific.

But what? The diary? Some letters?

Late that night, Agassiz made a statement to reporters. He tempered his outrage and measured his words carefully. He theorized that the "burglary had been committed by someone in the employ of Dr. Hazzard, who is now on trial for the murder of Miss Williamson, and thought possibly Dr. Hazzard had wished to secure some of the property of the deceased girl. Nothing else had been touched in the entire house, and circumstances certainly pointed to the theory that the thief had been in the employ of the alleged murderess."

Dora cried when she learned that her sister's belongings had been disturbed by the dark hand of a stranger. She also felt Starvation Heights was connected to the plundering of Claire's trunks.

"It was Mrs. Hazzard who put the burglar up to it. I don't care that she was here in Port Orchard or back in Olalla. The woman has an awesome power over people to do her bidding," she said tearfully.

"Let's just hope," Agassiz said, "they didn't find whatever it was they had so desperately sought."

The violation of her sister's personal effects both sickened and outraged Dora for days afterward. Her stomach felt as though someone had stretched it to the point of snapping, then let it loose to bounce around her insides. She thought she might vomit. It was so cruel, so upsetting.

NEARLY EVERY DAY AT LAKE STEILACOOM, LETters arrived from strangers who had read of Dora Williamson's perilous ordeal at Starvation Heights. Men suggested marriage, women commiserated at the horror of losing a sister to the evil scheme of another woman. Dora, who had grown stronger by the day, became as eager for the mail delivery as she had for her first meals after the fasting treatment. She had Miss Conway slice the envelope tops open and stack the letters into separate piles. One for the men she was "considering yet," and another for those who would not be suitable.

"You aren't serious, dearie, are you?" Margaret asked when she discovered a stack under Dora's pillow while turning down the bed sheets.

Dora laughed.

"Don't be silly, Tooddy. I just want Lucian to see the interest in my plight. There's the chance that such devotion, such interest, could help the case against Mrs. Hazzard," she answered as she flitted about the room.

Margaret bit her tongue. She refused any further commentary. She suspected Dora's motives held a deeper resonance. She wondered if Dora had set out to make their benefactor a little jealous.

Later, when the subject came up over dinner with Lucian and his wife, Ena, Dora giggled about the horde of missives she kept at her bedside.

"It is so ridiculous," she said, blush warming her cheeks. "To think of absolute strangers proposing to me!"

NATURALLY, THE NEWSPAPERS CAPITALIZED ON the sensational aspects of the case. Papers across the world picked up on the reports of Dorothea Williamson's testimony. The United Press International wire service transmitted the story from Seattle to Vancouver to New York. From New York it was dispatched to England, Australia, and New Zealand. Newspapers of all sizes and reputations made space for the Linda Burfield Hazzard Starvation Heights saga. Even the little *Fergus Falls Weekly* in Ottertail County, Minnesota, picked up the story. The prodigal daughter was in deep trouble—again.

THIRTY-FIVE

MONDAY MORNING'S FLAT WINTER LIGHT skated over the cold waters of Sinclair Inlet to the windows of the Navy View. Dora Williamson woke that morning to find herself barely ready for battle. A day of rest had been sorely needed, but a nervous stomach kept her awake several of the past few nights. Dora tried to put her physical weariness aside. She was ready to finish what she had started when she vowed to avenge her sister's murder.

The day was an important one. Lucian Agassiz had arranged a small surprise for the starvation doctor and her attorneys that morning. From the beginning, there had been a great dispute over the source of the entries in Claire's diary bequeathing diamonds to Dr. Hazzard and her staff.

Dr. Hazzard had steadfastly maintained Claire had written the entries as a final act of kindness for her sister and Miss Margaret.

"So they would not have to worry about such things at such a sad time."

The surprise Agassiz had arranged came in the guise of a compact gentleman with two oversize placards. Enlargements of words photographed from the little red diary were pasted to the cards. Charles Bedford sat in the back ready to place his hand on the Bible and testify that in his expert opinion, the author of the diary entry in question was not Claire Williamson. It was his expert opinion Dr. Linda Burfield Hazzard had done the writings.

Frank Kelley told the court Mr. Bedford would be called to testify that they were forgeries—and if they were forced to go that route unnecessary delay and needless further argument would ensue. In the end, Kelley insisted, the prosecution would prevail.

Linda Hazzard could see that even without the evidence before the jury, the court of public opinion was swinging wide and far from her. Women shook their heads disapprovingly. Eyes stared at her telegraphing the message that she had done the unthinkable.

"For diamonds, she did this," a lady told a companion.

After much conferring with his client, attorney George Gregory conceded Linda Hazzard had written the excerpts in question, but the jury should not infer any relevancy to the testimony about the entries. Murmurs of surprise swelled from the observers. Many had assumed Linda Hazzard would fight validity of the diary writings with an expert of her own. Her attorneys, after all, had sparred with the prosecution at every turn. It seemed that to allay the pressure now would only mean certain defeat. Linda Hazzard was a woman who hated to back down.

The diary was quickly admitted into evidence.

A GORGEOUS SABLE STOLE WRAPPED AROUND her neck and shoulders, and a hot water bottle placed beneath her tiny feet, Dora took her seat at the front of the courtroom. She had been chilled the past days on the stand. A cold was coming on, and her tiny voice was husky from it and the strain of talking. Direct examination was concluded with a series of questions concerning whether any other nurse had been engaged in Seattle or Olalla. Dora mentioned Watson Webb. He had nursed the Williamsons at the Buena Vista and later, he visited and helped out at Olalla. He was a friend of Dr. Hazzard's.

"Did she say anything about the boy?"

"Yes, she said he was a good, nice, pure-minded boy."

It was Webb's duties and Frank Lillie's that shocked the courtroom and brought a reporter to his feet to search for a telephone.

"I thought he was just going to come and help carry water, but I found afterwards he helped to give me a bath, I was very ill and used to become unconscious when in the bathtub, but I knew he gave—helped Miss Sherman give me a bath."

During a break in testimony, Dora reached in her handbag and retrieved a photograph wrapped in a couple of thicknesses of cream-colored card stock. She had debated it within her own mind and had finally come to the conclusion that her sister deserved to be known for what she had been *before* Dr. Hazzard's hideous starvation treatment. She unfolded the covering. Inside was a picture of Claire. It was the only photograph Dora had of her sister.

"It is recent," she explained, handing it to a reporter she had grown to trust. "We were photographed in Riverside before we came to Olalla."

The reporter promised to return it after it was printed in the *Ledger*.

"She was quite beautiful, don't you agree?"

"Yes," he said, "very."

IF THE DEFENSE STRATEGY WAS TO PORTRAY Claire and Dora as faddists for cures, wealthy and fickle women, they knew they must tread very gently. Day Karr and George Gregory had conferred numerous times since Dora took the stand the Friday before. They could see clearly that the jury liked the diminutive English lady. They knew the public was on her side. To press too hard would make them—as extensions of Dr. Hazzard—look the part of the bully. Dora's sister was dead, and that was the reason they were there. No one could doubt her sincerity, that she believed Dr. Hazzard's fasting treatment was the cause of it. They just wanted to prove otherwise.

As effective as she had been in direct, Dora was even greater in her battle with the defense attorney. George Gregory could not shake her. When he asked her to tell about childhood illnesses that incapacitated her sister, the little witness balked.

"On the whole she was well and used to run about and play all sorts of games. We used to play hockey with my cousin and play about the garden and climb trees. She was quite a tomboy."

Many observers were enthralled by testimony brought forth during cross-examination. It was like a good story of wealth, houses in the English countryside, seaside vacations, trips to the

Continent, fashionable parties. It was far, far removed from the grimy, stinky shores of Kitsap County.

According to her sister, the only physical ailment of concern struck Claire in adulthood. It happened after returning from an extended winter holiday.

". . . for the wintertime we went to Switzerland for the winter sports like most Englishwomen do and did skiing and tobogganing and skating all day long, and after that, my sister got this trouble, she overdid it."

Later, she testified, Claire had in fact gone to a sanitarium in Hampshire called Broadlands. It was a nature cure center.

"It was fruit and vegetarian food; she had no meat, and then she would be out in the open air and slept three weeks out of doors. She had baths, cold baths, and then I think they used to have clay compresses put on at night."

"Where did they put these clay compresses, what were they for?"

"Some had them on their heads, and some had them on their arms or backs and stomach."

"Where did Claire have them?"

"She had hers where her trouble was, over the abdomen."

Dora identified letters her sister had written praising Dr. Hazzard and her treatment. They were admitted as defense exhibits.

Some questions posed by the defense about Claire's weakening condition at the Buena Vista backfired.

"Was there any time during that time she did not know what she was doing that you know of?"

"She gave in to Dr. Hazzard in a way she would not have done when she was well."

THE "HOO DOO" CHAIR STRUCK AGAIN. THAT afternoon Jerry Ahearn, the juror who took the mysteriously cursed twelfth seat, fell ill. The Bremerton man grabbed ahold of his stomach and caterwauled that he could not sit in the jury box any longer—he was suffering from the effects of lead poisoning from working at the navy yard. Though he had taken medicine for his stomach, it was not enough to ease his pain. The man simply could not continue. Court was adjourned for the day.

Linda Hazzard told her husband that the juror should come out to see her at the sanitarium after the trial.

"I can fix him," she said.

HALFWAY ACROSS THE WORLD, THE *MELBOURNE Argus* rolled its presses with the story of the strange American murder case in its edition that Monday, January 22. By then, thousands were following the saga.

> *STARVED TO DEATH*
> *WEALTHY AUSTRALIAN GIRL*
> *FOUL PLAY ALLEGED*

Though the headline writer and copy editors were confused about who was on trial, the rival Melbourne paper, the *Age* also covered the case.

> *A RICH GIRL'S DEATH*
> *STARVED IN A SANITORIUM*
> *DOCTOR AND HIS WIFE ON TRIAL*

IT WAS WORLD WAR II WHEN KARL BECK, STATIONED on a ship at the Bremerton navy yard, took his young wife of twenty-two to visit his uncle and aunt Ted and Lydia Ensminger on their small farm in Olalla. Those were happy times for Becky Beck. Eventually the farm would become their home, too. The years would lapse, children would be born, and, in time, Becky would mark the spot where Carl succumbed to a fatal heart attack, with the planting of a monkey puzzle tree. There would be so many memories of Olalla.

Naturally, there would always be the first ones. The ones about Sam Hazzard and Starvation Heights.

Uncle Ted and Aunt Lydia had made the acquaintance of a nice old widower who lived at the place locals called Starvation Heights. He, of course, was Samuel C. Hazzard.

"He was a lonely old man living there by himself across the road. So he would come and visit them. He had meals there occasionally. Very intelligent man, a West Point graduate. He used to bring Aunt Lydia little things. I have one little thing still,

a little silver sugar bowl. He used to bring those things in hopes that Aunt Lydia would give him a glass of homemade beer. He was an alcoholic, and she only gave him one. He was tickled to death to get that.

"The story goes that while she had the sanitarium so that he wasn't aware what was going on, she kept him drunk all the time. Dr. Hazzard would get people who didn't have dependents and she would get them to sign over their insurance or any assets they had and she would keep them at the sanitarium and slowly starve them to death. I know that Aunt Lydia and Uncle Ted thought she was guilty. They were very unhappy about what she did to Sam, you know, keeping him drunk all the time."

THIRTY-SIX

No ONE IN OLALLA COULD CONCEIVE OF such notoriety. Few read newspapers from Seattle or Tacoma, let alone papers from all over the world. In fact, few read at all. And though the Hazzard case was mentioned around the counter at Nelson's Store or as the day's catch was sorted, no one took any firm position on what had really happened to the unfortunate English girl. Wasn't that interesting. Didn't put food on the table. Didn't amount to anything at all. The truth was, however, that the world away from Olalla was riveted to the drama of the Starvation Heights trial.

On January 23, 1912, the *Sydney Morning Herald* in Australia joined the fray and picked up a story cabled from an obscure and faraway place in America:

STARVATION CURE
THE WILLIAMSON CASE

... The Misses Williamson, who had independent means, were known in Melbourne about 20 years ago. They were always ready to give ear to the newest cure for any disease, real or imaginary. For a time they were keen enthusiasts of the protein diet. The news, therefore, that they were experimenting with the starvation 'cure' did not cause their friends great surprise ...

THOUGH DORA TOOK THE STAND FOR THE fourth day, January 23, it was really only a matter of finishing up loose ends for the prosecution. She had done her job and was off in less than an hour. The headlines that day and the days beyond would belong to other players in the drama. Agassiz told Dora as she exited the courtroom that Margaret would almost certainly testify in the afternoon session.

Thomas Stevenson stood for the direct examination of the next witness, Mary Fields of the Buena Vista Apartments. Under his direct, Mrs. Fields testified about the Williamson sisters' weight and apparent health while they lived in the apartment adjacent to her own.

The most revealing aspect of her testimony came after Stevenson had her acknowledge that she had met Dr. Hazzard once before—at the home of S.E. Harrison in Seattle.

"Mrs. Fields, did you ever see anyone die of starvation?"

"No sir," she said, "not of starvation. I have seen them waste away from not eating."

"Who was that?"

"I saw Mr. Harrison."

Attorney Gregory jumped to his feet to object, but Judge Yakey allowed the testimony to continue.

"Was the appearance of Claire Williamson similar or dissimilar to the person that you saw die from lack of food?"

Again another objection. Again, overruled.

"Yes sir, it was quite similar."

Mary Fields was followed to the stand by her Buena Vista neighbor, Clara Corrigan. Miss Corrigan testified about the severity of Dr. Hazzard's osteopathic treatments—the pummeling of Claire Williamson.

"That seems a severe treatment."

"No, that does her good, that promotes circulation."

She told the jury Dr. Hazzard's remark about the disposal of a patient's remains at Olalla.

"She said, 'I must bring home a larger kettle today.' "

A squeal shot from the gallery. Enough so, that the prosecuting attorney turned to see where the noise had come from. It was a gasp of horror. Stevenson's eyes floated over the jury box. The idea of a kettle of body parts had visibly shaken them as well.

ALONG WITH DORA AND MARGARET, ESSIE Cameron was easily one of the more eagerly awaited prosecution witnesses. The teenage nursemaid from Oregon became the focus of interest when the rumors of witness tampering began to leak. Though she never commented to reporters who besieged her for details, word somehow reached the gossip wire of trial watchers.

When she took the stand on January 23, she was the picture of youth and beauty. Her skin was clear and lovely. Her thick, curly hair was unencumbered by a hat.

Because she was critical to the case, Essie Cameron was Kelley's witness for direct examination. Thomas Stevenson was back at his seat at the prosecution table.

In hushed tones, Kelley asked her to describe what she had seen during her "two weeks and one day" at Olalla.

"Miss Claire was terribly thin, and she had a sore on the lower part of her spine . . . it was ulcerated and red and quite large, about the size of a dollar or larger."

He asked her to elaborate.

"The skin was drawn over her cheekbones so as to give her almost a skeleton-like appearance. Her upper lip did not come over her teeth, and she had some difficulty in talking because she could not close her lips."

"How about her eyes?"

"Her eyes bulged some."

The images played in Essie's mind. And as she spoke, her descriptions clearly moved the jury and the spectators. Two ladies knitting in the front row all but dropped their skeins of yarn. People scarcely breathed so as not to miss a word.

"Claire's body had purple mottled spots on it . . . you could feel her backbone by putting your hand on her stomach . . . Miss Sherman showed me . . . I noticed a fetid odor about her . . ."

When she told the Court about the twelve-gallon enemas that lasted hours, a woman nearly fainted from the thought of such an ordeal.

"Who gave her these enemas?"

"Sometimes Mr. Lillie and sometimes the nurse."

Again, another gasp from the spectators.

"Could you, and did you, observe the effects of these enemas?"

"While they were giving her the enemas she seemed to be in great pain, and she often clinched her fists and groaned."

Nearly every bit of testimony from the young witness unnerved spectators throughout the courtroom. Linda Hazzard fixed a hateful gaze and shook her head very slightly.

Essie told the jury how she had left on Tuesday, May 16, and returned after Claire died that Friday, May 19. She had come to pay a visit to Mrs. Burfield, one of Dr. Hazzard's sisters-in-law. While at the sanitarium, Mrs. Burfield inquired if she wanted to see Claire's body.

". . . and she took me to the bathroom and it was on the ironing board across the bathtub."

Kelley paused a long time. He wanted everyone in the courtroom to draw their own hideous mental picture before he sought the horrific details.

"What was the condition?"

"The eyes were half-closed."

"Do you know whether the body was in such a condition that the eyes could have been closed over the eyeballs?"

Essie shook her head.

"I don't think they could have been."

"What was the condition of the body so far as emaciation was concerned?"

"It looked like a skeleton, there was no flesh on the body whatsoever. The skin was drawn over the face."

"Did Dr. Hazzard say anything to you at that time relative to the death of Claire?"

Essie stared hard at the defendant.

"Yes, she told me not to mention it to anyone."

Dr. Hazzard had told Essie previously that doctors in Seattle were "against" her. They tried to get dead bodies away from her before she could perform a postmortem. Essie didn't ask the doctor, but she assumed that the body was stretched over the tub for the exam. She figured Dr. Hazzard planned to perform her examination before the authorities were notified Claire had died.

George Gregory could do little for the defense when it came his turn. Essie had come across as a believable witness, and she had done considerable damage. The defense lawyer's final questions were aimed at chipping away at her credibility, suggesting she was lying because she had been fired from a job she had wanted to keep.

"What was the cause of your leaving?"

"I was ill, and Mrs. Hazzard was angry because I was ill and said she would get someone else."

"You were discharged?"

"Yes, sir."

OUTSIDE THE COURTROOM ESSIE CAMERON FELT a thud, not a tap, just below her shoulder. It had been driven with such force that she felt certain it was meant to hurt her. She turned around and was immediately confronted by a woman dressed in an ankle-length black coat, a slit in the front revealed the top of a white nurse's uniform. Her handbag swung again, this time grazing Essie's side.

The woman was Nellie Sherman.

"Miss Cameron, you think you are so smart, don't you?"

Essie took a couple of steps back. The woman scared her.

"I don't know what you are talking about, Miss Sherman," she answered in a soft voice.

"Oh, yes you do. What you don't know is that I sat in the judge's chambers and I heard every word of your testimony."

The young woman turned away as quickly as she could. She would not respond to such tactics. Not anymore.

"This is not over, my dear . . ." the nurse called. "*Liar!*"

THOUGH NO ONE SAW WHAT HAD HAPPENED between the two women on the streets of Port Orchard, what happened in the courtroom was a much-needed respite from the testimony. A lighter moment. Jurors had been overloaded with horrific detail.

The twelve had pooled some hard-earned dollars to purchase bailiff Jack Coburn a new pair of shoes. He had joked to them earlier how his old pair were scuffed beyond the remedy of any polishing. Working for Kitsap County, he said, didn't earn him enough salary to replace the pair.

A little later, after an extended break in the testimony, a broadly smiling Coburn appeared in the jury room bearing a sturdy cloth bag filled with a dozen hacksaw blades.

"May come in handy if you're ever in jail," he told the men with a deep, good-natured laugh.

MARGARET CONWAY'S STORY HAD BEEN WELL reported. There would be little new told before the jury in Kitsap County Superior Court, yet when the silver-haired family nursemaid with the plain vocabulary and the less-than-refined British accent began her story, the room fell very quiet. She told of the emergency cable from Claire, the primitive conditions at Starvation Heights, the surprise of the doctor's guardianship over Dora. And as she struggled to answer Frank Kelley's questions over the defense attorney's numerous objections, much of her testimony was wrapped in tears.

She testified about the trip to Butterworth & Sons with Dr. Hazzard.

"Did you see the body?"

"I saw *a* body," she answered, emphasizing the "a."

"Was the coffin opened for you?"

"Yes, part of it. It seemed part of it was glass, and the lid was raised up. Perhaps it wasn't glass and that the lid was raised."

"Did you recognize the body as that of Claire's?"

"Not in the least."

"What was the appearance of the head and neck so far as it was seen, with regard to emaciation?" Kelley asked.

"It was not at all emaciated."

The day ended with Margaret on the stand and defense attorney Karr doing his best to run the list of illnesses Miss Claire and Miss Dora supposedly suffered. No one paid much mind to it—the testimony of Essie Cameron juxtaposed with Margaret's description of the body was the topic of the day.

Agassiz was at the forefront of the rumors. Though he cautioned the press that he could say very little, private investigators had been engaged to get to the bottom of the gruesome mystery.

"Coffins may be exhumed, before this is all done," he said.

United Press Leased Wire led its dispatch out of Port Orchard that evening with a series of questions:

> *Did Mrs. Hazzard hold autopsies over, dissect and cremate all the patients who died at her establishment?*
> *If she did, what became of the corpses? Did she cremate the remains to cover up the cases? What was in the coffins buried, supposedly containing bodies of her patients?*

THIRTY-SEVEN

HE WOULD NOT BE ON THE STAND LONG and there would be little the defense could throw at him to discredit his testimony. It was through William Collier's direct examination that Frank Kelley intended to provide the jury the motive for the unthinkable. The money trail from Olalla to Canada and England had, in fact, converged within the walls of Mr. Collier's office.

The bespectacled cashier from Northern Bank and Trust was sworn in first thing Wednesday morning, January 24. Mr. Collier recalled how he had received the April 1911 letter from the Hazzard's attorney, John Arthur, to be submitted to Williamson's bank in London requesting Claire's funds be transferred to the Hazzards' account. According to Collier, the Hazzards were eager to get their hands on the money—more than $1,000. The witness further testified that the defendant and her husband came in to inquire why Claire had been given the money directly, instead of following the wishes of the letter.

(Frank Kelley and Agassiz had wrestled frequently over the question of Sam Hazzard's involvement in the crimes against Miss Dora and Miss Claire. Agassiz thought Sam Hazzard should be charged alongside his wife.

Kelley did not agree.

"It is not because I believe him innocent of involvement. On the contrary, he had his dirty hands all over the money. We have to go after the one we can convict—the one who has done the greatest harm."

If Samuel, however, could be used to cast the defendant in a sinister light, that was certainly fine with the special prosecutor. In fact, that was the plan.)

In a voice that boomed across the gallery, a voice not yet heard, a voice meant to garner full attention, Frank Kelley asked if Sam Hazzard had informed the cashier that Claire had died on May 19 when he returned to the bank on May 26 to demand all monies from her London account?

"In accordance with Miss Claire's wishes, sir."

William Collier shook his head.

"I never knew of a death at all. I was never advised of it."

Samuel Hazzard shifted uncomfortably in the seat as he felt all eyes target him. He had been that route before. *Caught.* In Minneapolis the letters he wrote to Viva and to Linda were incontrovertible proof of his guilt. He was a man who laid his own traps. He leaned over and rested his hand on Linda's shoulder and pretended to say something to her. In reality he had nothing to say. And as the people watched him, he had nowhere to hide.

LINDA HAZZARD'S FORMER LAWYER JOHN ARTHUR was sworn in. At sixty-one, he was an exceedingly pleasant-looking fellow, with a receding hairline that still revealed his hair had been wavy and black. He was a man who carried himself with integrity and certainty. As an attorney, the man was in a precarious position. The prosecution wanted to use Arthur to convict his own client, a woman he had successfully represented when she had battled for the return of her medical license. The defense would use all it could to press the issue of attorney-client privilege into every bit of his testimony.

Frank Kelley had decided to tread lightly. He wanted to get as much as he could out of the lawyer who would never reveal everything. To tell the full truth, Kelley thought, would be for Arthur to admit he had been a party to the murder of Miss Claire. Kelley knew that the man on the stand came with the armor of a sterling reputation. He had been the first president of the Washington State Bar Association.

Attorney Arthur testified that on the evening of April 21, 1911, he was notified of the Williamson sisters' planned departure to Olalla. Dr. Hazzard had related that Claire had wanted him to prepare some documents. They arranged to meet at Colman Dock the following morning.

The witness repeated that he did not remember what Dr. Hazzard had said insofar as instructions about the codicil to Claire's will.

"Was there any reference made to any orders for drawing money?"

"Not that I remember."

Frank Kelley pulled out a copy of the order on the London & Westminster County Bank signed by Claire.

"In whose handwriting is the body of this communication in?"

"My handwriting."

"I call your attention to these words: *This order is intended to cover all monies or credits for me which you now have or may hereafter have.* I ask you if those words are in your handwriting?"

Karr realized where this was going and stood up with an objection, but Judge Yakey overruled it.

John Arthur's confidence was shaken. His cheeks went pink.

"They are," he said.

"I ask you further if those words were there before the signature of Claire?"

"I think that after she signed she recalled that she wanted that addition, and I told her there was room enough to write it before her signature."

Arthur was adamant Dr. Hazzard knew nothing of the bank order, yet it was she who later inquired if he had sent it directly to London or if he had handled it through Northern Bank and Trust.

Next, Frank Kelley asked the lawyer to identify the $1,005 order on the Bank of Montreal.

It was also written on the dock by John Arthur. The witness, however, could not say what he did with the paperwork.

"Now to refresh your memory, don't you know you gave that to Mrs. Hazzard?"

"Maybe I did, I don't recollect."

"That you gave it to her on the dock that morning?"

His face now two shades nearer the color of a holly berry, John Arthur finally agreed.

"That is possible."

And so John Arthur's testimony went. Denial, confusion, admission. He said he had never seen Dora Williamson's order on the Canadian Bank of Commerce in Vancouver. Linda Hazzard was no party to the letter to Margaret, the codicil. It was Sam Hazzard, the witness insisted, who later came to his office with a memorandum stating additional changes to Claire's will.

"In whose handwriting was it?"

After a long pause, the witness finally gave breath to an answer.

"I don't remember," he said, stepping down.

JOHN ARTHUR NEVER SAID MUCH ABOUT THE trial, at least not to the newspapermen who had linked him somewhat to the money motive of the Williamson case. His reputation had been impugned by the disclosure of the hastily written codicil and the trips with Samuel to see the cashier at the bank. Still, no matter that his connection to the fasting specialist had harmed him in the eyes of many, he continued to back Dr. Hazzard years after the case went to the jury. He later wrote in her support:

> *I know all about her relations with Claire Williamson, for Miss Williamson, privately to me, directed that a certain bequest be made in her will to the Hazzard Institute at Olalla. Miss Williamson was a physical wreck when she put herself under Dr. Hazzard's treatment, and she realized that was the last resort. She became a sincere convert to the treatment and had the utmost faith in Dr. Hazzard's methods.*

Linda Hazzard was not a common criminal, the lawyer asserted. She was a woman with a greater cause.

> *(Dr. Hazzard) is a strong woman who believes she has a mission in the world and that mission is to save the people from the injurious effect of drugs and to heal their troubles by cleansing of their systems and the administration of light foods.*

RAIN HAD FALLEN FROM MORNING THROUGH THE afternoon, turning the streets of Port Orchard into a soupy, muddy brown mess. The inside fabric on Margaret's and Dora's skirts was sprayed with mud tipping off the end of their shoes as they walked to the Navy View. Agassiz had gone home, seizing the chance when court was halted early so the defense could prepare for the testimony of a witness. More than anyone Dora hated the delays. She also hated the continuing downpour. She longed for the summer of Australia, still taking place half a world away. She longed for the orange groves of Riverside.

Dora remembered Claire's joy at the waxy green leaves and the fruit-laden branches of their aunt's citrus trees.

"Oranges from your own tree! Auntie, that is so very marvelous."

THE WOMAN STANDING IN AUGUSTA BREWER'S doorway at Hadden Hall had once been a friend, a very good friend, indeed. Only circumstances and Linda Burfield Hazzard had changed that.

"Please, can I come in?" Nellie Sherman asked. Her face was tired and plaintive.

Dr. Augusta Brewer, the osteopath who had seen Nellie when she agonized over the sisters' health, motioned her inside.

"Augusta, these are difficult times."

"This is certainly true."

"Please, I need your help. Please, do not be a witness against me at the trial. We are friends."

The doctor looked down. She did not want her eyes to connect with Nellie's.

"Nellie, I am not against you. I am for the truth of the matter."

"Please," the nurse tried again, her eyes moist with emotion, maybe even fear. "They sent me here to ask you."

The osteopath said she felt she could not change her statements to the prosecution, but she would think on it. Their friendship meant a great deal to her. She did not want to hurt her.

As she left, the doctor saw that Nellie's hands were trembling.

The next day, Dr. Brewer left a message for Nellie.

Come over on 8:20 boat. Stay the night. We must talk.

Nellie Sherman never showed up.

THIRTY-EIGHT

THE RUMOR THAT THE STARVATION heights jury was in trouble abated Thursday morning. For days since his illness was obvious to all in the courtroom, Jerry Ahearn had been the object of much discussion. The poor fellow's clammy skin took on a chalky, yellow pallor, nearly the color of the moon. Some wondered if the lead-poisoned juryman would remain well enough to complete his task. The Hoo Doo had almost done it.

With the exception of Linda Hazzard, Judge Yakey was likely more concerned than anyone about the possibility of a mistrial. He knew Kitsap County could not afford to start the process over. To lose Juror #12 from a bout with lead poisoning was beyond his control, yet he could feel his neck was stretched out, taut on the line. County commissioners made it clear: *Finish the case if Jerry Ahearn has to be propped up with a stick. Finish it fast!*

A stick was not necessary. The navy worker spent Thursday evening drinking and eating and was looking dramatically better when Friday morning came. He had not submitted to Linda Hazzard's starvation treatment. And he felt fine.

While the end of the prosecution's case was near—only the doctors would testify—the defense had a list of nearly seventy witnesses. Judge Yakey told the lawyers to prepare for night sessions for the following week.

"I want this in the jury's hands a week from today."

WHEN COURT CONVENED AT ONE O'CLOCK, LINDA Hazzard had made good on her prediction. She had told her followers the case would eventually strike a battle between her

methods of healing and the regular school of medicine, the purveyors of drugs and surgery. The doctors who would testify
against her were the enemy. Not only the enemy of the fasting
cure, but the enemy of lifelong good health. Doctors of the regular school were greedy and closed-minded. And most, she
pointed out, were men.

"The doctors of the regular school prefer women to dress in
whites and polish hospitalware," Dr. Hazzard told a friend
while she waited out the end of the prosecution's case.

Frank Kelley's plan was to simplify the medical questions
put before the jury when it came to Claire Williamson's death
by starvation. He planned a lengthy hypothetical question for
each of the physicians called. The question would encompass
Claire's known health problems, her weight, and the result to
her body under the fasting and osteopathic treatments as
described by the other witnesses.

Dr. T.J. Baldwin, a Port Orchard physician, who was more
acquainted with Dr. Hazzard than most, took the stand as the
state's first medical expert. He told the jury that in his opinion
Claire Williamson's death was the inevitable result of Dr.
Hazzard's fast cure. Over repeated objections from the defense
table, Dr. Baldwin agreed with the special prosecutor that Dr.
Hazzard's treatment was a "gross ignorance of the healing art"
and a "gross disregard on the part of the defendant of ordinary
and usual care and knowledge of the human body . . ."

Dr. Baldwin's mouth was straightedged as Frank Kelley
went over the litany of hideous symptoms—the backbone pro-
truding through the stomach, the foul odor of her body, the
bluish spots on the skin, eyeballs popping from the sockets . . .
The doctor's face never betrayed his emotions behind his testimony. He never sneered. He never even looked down his nose
at the defendant. In fact, he didn't look at her at all.

"She did not get the right amount of food, either quality or
quantity," he said.

"And death was caused by what?"

"Starvation."

More hypothetical questions followed concerning the mental
control Dr. Hazzard might have had on Claire as she grew
weaker and weaker under the fasting treatment.

Dr. Baldwin was of the opinion that the weaker Claire became, the greater her hope Dr. Hazzard would cure her. The greater her misguided faith grew.

The doctor testified Claire and Dora's diet as prescribed by Linda Hazzard, was less than one-fifth of the amount of food needed to sustain life.

Attorney Karr, seemingly somewhat bored by the long-winded answers—or playacting in a manner as to suggest Dr. Baldwin didn't know what he was talking about—began cross-examination. First, he attacked the witness's understanding of various schools of medical thought.

The doctor admitted he knew little or nothing about homeopathic, chiropractic, eclectic, or osteopathic schools.

"Then all you do know is what the regular school knows?"

"The regular school includes all other schools."

"Well you know something about them, don't you?"

"I have answered your question."

"From your answer I take it you do not know anything about the regular school, is that true?"

"You are privileged to understand my answer as you take it."

"All of these schools treat diseases and practice the art of healing, do they not?"

"They *claim* to."

Bremerton surgeon John Munns followed Dr. Baldwin to the stand. Dr. Munns was asked similar hypothetical questions concerning the health and treatment of Claire Williamson.

He agreed with Dr. Baldwin. Linda Hazzard had not exhibited usual care and understanding of the human body and the treatment of its ailments. The defendant's health regimen put Claire in "a great deal of danger."

Based on everything stated by Kelley in the form of his hypothetical questions, Dr. Munns emphatically believed Claire Williamson had died from starvation.

And yet on cross-examination, it was Dr. Munns who gave up a little of the prosecution's ground.

Defense lawyer Karr had hypothetical questions of his own. He asked the witness to consider the possibility that the dead woman had suffered from peritonitis—a condition in which the abdominal lining or the peritoneum is inflamed and irritated by excessive stomach acid. He suggested Claire Williamson suffered from constriction and blockage of the bowels caused by peritonitis.

It was a condition that could not be fully remedied. Sufferers frequently only grew weaker and weaker.

"When a patient has had peritonitis and the bowels become matted together, as a result, digestion is very much impaired?"

Dr. Munns conceded such could be the case.

"It might be for all time, might it not?" Karr asked, his voice rising as he felt his momentum surge.

"Possibly. These are questions that a man cannot answer definitely, medicine not being an exact science, you can ask questions no man can answer."

"Then a doctor is never sure of the diagnosis of a case, is he?"

"Yes."

"Then medicine is an exact science?" Karr asked, turning his attention to the jury.

Dr. Munns pondered his response for a moment.

"Now there is the question."

FRIDAY BROUGHT THE END OF THE PROSECUtion's case. The state rested after a third physician, Charles A. Smith, testified much as his two predecessors had. Smith had the most sterling of credentials. He was a Yale and Columbia University graduate. He had practiced two years at New York's Bellevue Hospital prior to coming to Seattle in the spring of 1899. He believed Claire Williamson had been denied enough food to sustain her life.

On cross-examination, however, he was forced to admit that it was possible Claire died because of some organic disease—if she, in fact, had suffered some disease.

"Ordinarily assuming you have two persons in the same condition of health, one fat and the other less, and assuming further that you put them both on a starvation diet, which one would die first?"

"Your best authorities on that say that you cannot predict because an apparently well person may die first. This is often seen in cases of famine, the apparent robust often die first and the thin ones live longest.

"In a case where the fleshy one dies first it is generally assumed that death is attributed to some other cause than starvation?"

"Oftentimes, yes."

Moments after Dr. Smith stepped down, the jury filed out of the room. George Gregory asked the judge to accept his motion for the jury to be instructed to bring a verdict of not guilty. He claimed the prosecution had not introduced enough evidence to warrant a guilty verdict.

"*Motion denied.*"

The case would go to the jury, but not without a startling interruption. Frank Kelley had absolute proof that a "person connected with the defense approached one of the state's witnesses with offers of 'any price you may name' not to tell her story."

Judge Yakey halted the trial until the following morning.

THAT AFTERNOON, WHILE AGASSIZ HOLED UP IN a room at the Navy View Hotel, Dora and Margaret boarded an early launch for Tacoma. The women had quite enough of mudsoaked Port Orchard and its legion of smug-faced supporters of Dr. Hazzard. Since the likelihood loomed that both could be recalled during the rebuttal phase of the prosecution's case, neither Dora nor Margaret was allowed a spectator's seat in the courtroom. The women guessed it was just as well. They had had their fill of Linda and Sam Hazzard.

Dora could not help notice, nor help herself from declaring to Margaret, that in exactly one month from that day, she would mark the anniversary of meeting Dr. Hazzard. So much had changed in the eleven months since she and her sister had first stepped into Dr. Hazzard's office in Seattle.

"Claire trusted her. Claire fancied her as a great healer. The only licensed fasting specialist in the world!" Dora said, as though she couldn't understand how Claire had believed any of it.

"And now she sits there and acts as though she did nothing wrong. Her defiance is nearly as detestable as her crimes."

THIRTY-NINE

LINDA HAZZARD TOOK THE FLIMSY LITTLE newspaper, rolled it into a tube, and shoved it at her husband's belly. It was Saturday morning, the first day of her defense and the tenuous *Town Crier* had made her blood nearly seethe to a boil. Sam also made her furious. She had done so much for his relations with the newspapers during the little matter in Minneapolis. She had gone to reporters to tell his side against the charges of that conniving Viva Fitchpatrick. And what was he doing to help her? Nothing. He had once worked for a newspaper, for goodness sake. He knew how those little information scavengers went about their business. They could be led for the promise of a good interview. Sam, she knew, could get them to believe anything. He could talk a ravenous dog off the back end of a meat wagon.

And why didn't he help her out? The *Town Crier* was the last straw.

It had ruined her morning.

"Sam! Look at this! Why aren't you stopping this kind of attack? Sam, are you paying attention?"

"Yes, Linda," he said, opening the paper a fasting supporter had brought over on the launch. He studied the front page.

"At least it is indicated to be 'editorial comment'."

PUT AN END TO IT

Regardless of the outcome of Dr. Linda Burfield Hazzard's trial for murder by starvation, means must be found to prevent her, and others like her, if any there be, from continuing such practices as resulted in the death of Claire Williamson . . .

. . . life cannot be sustained without adequate nourishment and the rigid course of fasting which this fanatical woman imposes upon those who credulously submit to her treatment has already resulted in the death of a number of well known persons. None may know how many others of lesser prominence she has hastened on their way to the hereafter . . .

First thing that morning, Dr. Hazzard's attorneys went before the court to put a stop to the planned night sessions. The defendant, they pleaded, was under a great deal of strain and was not feeling well enough to take such long days.

Judge Yakey reluctantly agreed.

THE DEFENSE HAD MADE IT RESOUNDINGLY clear during the weeks before trial that most certainly the jurors knew its strategy for garnering an acquittal. The plan was to make a brief statement and immediately proceed with the calling of witnesses. Linda Hazzard was no criminal, to be sure. She was a healer—licensed by the state to perform fasting as a cure for disease.

The problem rested solely with Claire Williamson. She had been ill from the time of her birth. She was destined to die young.

George Gregory spoke for the defense.

"We believe the evidence will show that the illness was in some way directly connected with an apparent ailment, it probably might have been peritonitis and affected the stomach as cirrhosis. We believe the evidence will show at that time Claire began to fail rapidly and she was treated all over the country with all the schools and doctors she believed in for that disease, and just prior to the time she came to Seattle she was beginning to go down more rapidly and at that time she came to see Dr. Hazzard as a last resort . . ."

The sisters were not deprived of food. On the contrary, they were able to have all they could eat. Claire's digestive system, however, was in such terrible shape she could not assimilate food of any kind. Dr. Hazzard had tried to prolong her life.

"We believe the evidence will show that probably to encourage both of these girls she tried to make them believe that there was some hope. We believe she was justified in doing so in hope that such hope would tend to build up their physical condition . . ."

"We believe the evidence will show that during the time these girls were under Dr. Hazzard's treatment they received care such as the tenderest mother would give her child."

THE FIRST DEFENSE WITNESS WAS A FOLLOWER. Seattle man Johan Ivar Haglund told the jury he had known the defendant for four years, most recently having taken his son three times a week for treatments at her office. It was during those occasions that he saw Claire and Dora Williamson.

As early as the beginning of March he considered Claire to be suffering from illness.

"What was the color of her face?" Gregory asked.

"It is difficult thing to describe the color." The witness slowly searched for words. "But as near as I can come to it, if I see myself in the looking glass I would say her appearance would be the same to me."

After cross, Mr. Haglund stepped down, dignity intact, belief in his healer unshaken.

What no one among the jury and the observers in the courtroom knew—what Frank Kelley had not been permitted to ask—was how it had been that Mr. Haglund had first come to know Dr. Hazzard. It was through Dr. Hazzard's connection with his late wife. She had been a patient of the fasting specialist. In fact, Daisey Haglund had met her maker in February of 1908 after fasting for fifty days under Dr. Hazzard's direction.

WILLIAM BORTHWICK, BUTTERWORTH & SONS undertaker and chief deputy with the Coroner's Office of King County, was sworn in next. With bombastic flair he told how he had been summoned by the defendant on May 19, 1911, to retrieve Claire Williamson's body. The defendant had directed the witness to land a launch at Finney Creek—not Olalla.

"The road is better to Dr. Hazzard's home than from Olalla to her place," he explained.

Borthwick saw Dr. Hazzard again on May 22 at Butterworth's when he joined the fasting specialist and Dr. Stephen Olmstead at the autopsy. In fact, he testified, it was he who had done the postmortem examination. He was certain the organs and entrails taken from Miss Claire's body were examined and returned to the body cavity. There was no opportunity for Dr. Hazzard to keep anything. No chance that she put Claire Williamson's stomach in a dirty little bag.

"I replaced the organs myself," Borthwick announced.

He emphatically insisted Miss Conway and Mr. Herbert had seen the same body he had brought from Finney Creek to Seattle.

Mr. Kelley's loathing for the witness remained barely in check, just under the surface. Those who knew the Tacoma lawyer well could see it. Others, such as members of the jury, could not—unless they were astute observers. The special prosecutor considered Borthwick and the "Butterworth Boys" conspirators in the cover-up of the murder.

"You say you performed the autopsy yourself?"

"Yes, sir."

"Are you a surgeon?"

"No, sir."

"Are you a medical man?"

"No, sir."

Point made, the incompetence issue was dropped. Kelley's next queries focused on the possibility that Dr. Hazzard had gained access to the body between the autopsy and the viewing in the Blue Room.

"Do you know anything about Mrs. Hazzard or anybody representing her visiting Butterworth's establishment between the time of the autopsy and the time of the funeral?"

"They did not."

"How do you know?"

"I would in all probability know it."

"Are you there all the time?"

"No, sir."

"If Mrs. Hazzard came there and wanted to see that body, would she have been permitted to do so?"

"She probably would."

THE GASOLINE ENGINEER FOR THE STEAMER *VIR-*
ginia was called before the jury. W.H. Anstead testified that he
had taken the sisters from Seattle to Finney Creek on April 22,
1911. The schedule was tight, he said, so there had been no time
to go the extra distance to Olalla. The witness carried Miss
Claire off the *Virginia* and estimated her weight to be between
ninety and ninety-five pounds.

Frank Kelley cross examined him on the figure.

"How did you happen to make an estimate of her weight, did
you do it at that time or are you doing it now?"

"I just made it at that time; it was quite a little effort to carry
her."

Among the spectators there that day was Nels Christensen,
the owner and operator of the West Pass Transportation
Company. He came to Port Orchard with employee Anstead as
a show of support for the doctor accused of an unthinkable
crime. Christensen was certain Dr. Hazzard was nothing like a
murderer. And later, when he felt it would do some good, he
made note of a meeting he claimed that took place while he
waited for Anstead to take the stand.

> *I was talking with the girl that lived when I was over to
> the trial at Port Orchard and she told me that her and her
> sister had been traveling all over the world in search of
> Health. She told me that they had been in Denmark, my
> native state, and she had also said they had spent thou-
> sands of dollars and carried private nurses with them
> wherever they went, and when they got to Seattle they
> heard of Mrs. Hazzard. And Mrs. Hazzard demurred at
> taking their case as they were nearly dead when they got
> to Seattle. But they entreated of her to take them over to
> her sanitarium at Olalla. She finally consented to take
> them over there and done all any living being could do for
> them under the same conditions. We must take in consid-
> eration that the girls had been traveling for days and days
> and were nearly completely worn out when they went
> under Mrs. Hazzard's care. And that these girls had been
> from one Doctor to another and could find no relief for
> many months . . .*

THE FINAL DEFENSE WITNESS OF THE MORNING was Dr. E.W. Young. Dr. Young was called to testify that as past president and current member of the State Board of Medical Examiners, Linda Hazzard was, in fact, authorized by the state to practice osteopathy and fasting. Certificates were identified and admitted into evidence.

Under cross, Dr. Young was all too pleased to testify that the defendant's license had been issued because the Washington Supreme Court had ordered it so. Linda Hazzard had met the required number of years of practice—two years prior to the medical act of 1909. She did not have a college medical degree. She had not passed the required examination.

None of that was required, he said.

THE SMALL LADY IN NURSE WHITES WAS THE great hope. She would offer much to contradict Dora and other state witnesses. She was, of course, Nellie Sherman. Dr. Hazzard had put much of her defense in the small hands of the woman she considered as close as a sister. If ever there was an enthusiastic witness for the defense it was Miss Sherman. Breathless. Eager. *Willing.* Whatever Dora had said, whatever Miss Cameron—or even Mrs. Fields from the Buena Vista had claimed—Nellie Sherman's testimony was in complete contrast. According to her, everything at the Buena Vista and Olalla had been entirely beyond reproach.

Linda Hazzard had never restricted Miss Claire from eating—in fact, she said, the sisters were fed every few hours. It was Claire and Dora that restricted themselves from food. The enemas were never more than two quarts of warm water, never lasted longer than three-quarters of an hour.

The sisters were fussy. They were flighty.

The osteopathic treatments were not harsh and brutal slappings.

". . . manipulate the neck very gently . . . then vibrated gently . . ."

She saw plenty to eat at the Buena Vista.

"I found health bread and butter and eggs, rice and cornflakes and even cherries, nuts and raisins and then Claire told me I could phone to the grocery and I went down to the Public

Market myself nearly every day and brought supplies and went over to the grocery on the corner of Pike."

Still, she said, no matter what she served at the table, it was not to Claire's liking. Everything made her sick to her stomach.

"She would often say, 'Miss Sherman, that soup you gave me last distressed me,' and I would have to prepare something different."

While Dora was delirious much of the time, Claire was brilliant, according to the nurse.

"She had a very fine mind. She was a student and had a very fine mind. She was very much interested in anatomy in England. She had taken a course in first aid to the injured. She was very much interested in those things and had also taken a course in botany and of course dietetics. That was a favorite thing with her and she told me a great deal about the nature cure at Broadlands and how interested she was in everything along that line."

"While you were preparing the food at the Buena Vista apartments how often did you prepare asparagus water?" the defense lawyer posed.

"Any of those waters, either tomato water or asparagus water they used as a hot drink. I didn't consider it a food. They liked a hot drink in between and we gave them that. Dora sometimes had hot milk, though she wouldn't always finish it."

"What was her reason for not taking it?"

"She just didn't want it. She didn't like it. If anything did not happen to strike her fancy, she would always make an excuse."

The defense shifted the witness to the day the sisters were taken to Olalla.

"What was Dora's mental condition during the time of transferring them from the dock at Seattle to the home at Olalla?"

"She had mental aberrations, was flighty and was talking constantly. After they were put in the wagon Claire asked her several times to be quiet. It annoyed her very much."

As she spoke, Miss Sherman's head bobbed up and down with great emphasis and conviction. She also turned her head from the defense table to the jurymen with such a regularity it seemed almost the steady movement of a metronome. And, at times, she accelerated her answers as if speed would assure her everything she wanted to say would get into the record.

At Olalla, the witness insisted, Claire could have anything she wanted.

"We didn't limit her. I oftentimes carried her more than she wanted to take. I remember one day Dr. Hazzard urging her very much to have some chicken broth. They had nice fat chickens of their own and we killed one and made broth of it and when we took it to her she said, 'I don't want any of that horrid cockerel.' The vegetarianism was such a principle with her that she could not overcome it and would not take the chicken broth, but Dora took some of the broth and some of the chicken."

Lawyer Gregory feigned surprise.

"Are you sure about her having some of the chicken?"

"Yes."

The witness dismissed Miss Cameron as a hired girl, who had nothing to do with the care of the sisters. She only cooked a little, hauled water from the well, and occasionally carried hot bricks up the stairs.

She denied Watson Webb and Frank Lillie ever bathed the sisters.

"I bathed them alone," Nellie said sharply. "I had assistance in carrying water and bringing implements. Claire had sponge baths. I remember giving Dora one or two tub baths. She teased for them so I took the tub near the big fireplace in the living room."

"Were the girls clothed when Mr. Lillie was there?"

"I always had them covered. They had on bathrobes. He sometimes helped me lift them on the couch."

"Did Frank Lillie assist you in the giving of enemas?"

"No sir, he never did anything but carry the water."

"What was Dr. Hazzard's attitude toward Claire during this time?"

"One of the utmost kindness and friendship, and Miss Claire seemed to have a feeling of real friendship and regard for Dr. Hazzard."

George Gregory held up the red leather diary, his large hands nearly swallowing the little volume, and asked Nellie Sherman to identify it.

The witness had seen the book many times sitting on the stand next to Claire's bedside.

"I will ask you, if you were present when Dr. Hazzard was writing in that book, and if so, I would like to have you tell the jury what the circumstances were and what was going on at that time?"

"As near as I can remember about that last day, or next to the last day at Olalla before I left, I was passing back and forth and saw the doctor sitting by the bedside of Claire who seemed to be dictating something to her. She was writing in this book or in a book just like it."

"Did you hear any of the dictation?"

"Not continuous because I was passing back and forth. I heard just a word or two."

Nellie also identified the typewritten statement Miss Claire had supposedly dictated to Sam Hazzard.

"I was in the room at the time she was dictating it and it lay on the stand there for a day or two after, and I remember reading small scraps of it."

"Was Dr. Hazzard present?"

"Dr. Hazzard was in the city at the time."

Her last words to the jury were a description of how Dr. Hazzard had treated the Williamson sisters.

"Great love, kindness, tenderness, and friendship."

AS THE AFTERNOON CONCLUDED, IT WAS LOST ON no one that Linda Hazzard's health and confidence had surged with Nellie's testimony. Linda, who had been so bitter about the *Town Crier*'s nasty assessment of her that morning, was in a friendly mood when she chatted with reporters on the way to the launch.

"I intend to get on the stand and show up that bunch. They've been playing checkers, but it's my move. I'll show them a thing or two when I get on the stand," she said.

"Then you are going to take the witness stand, are you?" a reporter for a Seattle paper asked incredulously. It had been rampant around Port Orchard for days that the doctor's counsel had advised against her doing so.

The woman can't hold her tongue and they know it. Kelley

and Agassiz want her to take the stand. They'd be gleeful for it.

"Yes," Dr. Hazzard quickly answered the reporter, as she smiled broadly as the flash from cameras winked across her triumphant face. "Bet your life I'm going to."

That night a reporter closing in on the deadline for the Sunday paper typed:

> *Owing to the unevenness of temper attributed to Mrs. Hazzard, perhaps at the time when the guardianship proceedings were heard, when she took the witness stand and talked so fast that the court stenographer threw up his hands in despair and didn't get a word of what she said, considerable interest has been displayed and speculation has been rife as to whether or not she would be a witness in the first degree murder case . . .*

FORTY

THERE WAS NO DOUBT AMONG HIS COL-
leagues and the ever-growing throng of Williamson supporters
that Frank Kelley held a certain level of contempt for the
woman he would cross-examine first thing Monday morning.
Yet even though he despised Nellie Sherman for her role in the
sordid affair, Kelley was a man with a little room for pity. Who
was to say how much control Dr. Hazzard really had over Miss
Sherman? Was the nurse blind to the truth or just stupid?
Victim or villain? The lawyer half hoped the nurse had enjoyed
her Sunday away from the Port Orchard courtroom and savored
the little victory to which she likely felt entitled.

Or what Linda Hazzard had allowed her to feel.

January 29, 1912, would be brutal for Miss Sherman. Kelley
had conferenced with Dora and Margaret at Agassiz's home the
night before. Everything the nurse had said had been a lie. Now
she would be made to answer for all of it.

Kelley promised Dora it would be the worst day of Nellie
Sherman's life.

If anything, the Tacoma lawyer was a man of his word.

THE AIR WAS CHILLED. THE STOVE HAD NOT BEEN
stoked by the bailiff until just before court was called to order.
A spectator, who had brought a lunch bucket and set it on the
stove to heat, would have a hot lunch by the noon recess. The
fire burned hot and quickly.

Nellie Sherman wore her tired, little white uniform again.
She pulled her faintly frayed coat against her body as if to brace
herself from the air and the man representing the state of
Washington.

Frank Kelley wasted little time. He rattled off question after question. At first, the witness held her own. She said her interest in Spiritualism was slight, and she had no fascination for Theosophy. She disavowed any connection with Frank Lillie. Nellie denied a close connection with Dr. Hazzard, saying that she had only been to the Hazzard home professionally, though maybe once or twice as a social call.

She insisted the Buena Vista—the apartment she said she stayed at for thirty-eight days—was well stocked with fruits, vegetables, pine nuts, raisins, milk, cream, a carton of corn-flakes, puffed rice. They consumed nearly two quarts of milk a day, purchased from Keck's grocery.

"Now Miss Sherman, isn't it a fact that the use of milk so far as these two girls were concerned, was confined to the very few days before they went to Olalla?"

"No, I couldn't say that, Mr. Kelley."

"Can you say that it was not so?"

"I remember distinctly giving it to Dora a good many times." And around they went.

After numerous objections from the defense, Nellie Sherman was finally asked if she had told a friend that the girls had no milk? She denied that also. She had spoken to Dr. Augusta Brewer about the sisters' diets, but never mentioned a lack of milk. She only sought advice.

"I asked her to. help me think of something that would be helpful."

When Kelley reached the matter of under whose control the patients were insofar as what they ate, the nurse insisted Claire ate only what she wanted. No one—not even Dr. Hazzard— could force her to eat more than she desired.

"Your instructions, as you now testify, came from Claire?"

"I stated that from day to day after we tried one thing, it was left to Claire, and she would think of something else which would not give her distress."

"Then the question I asked you as to what Claire had to eat was left to you and to Claire, you now answer in the affirmative?"

"I had all the advice and help I could get."

"From whom?"

Nellie moved her lips and spoke begrudgingly.

"From Dr. Hazzard."

"Then you did talk over with Dr. Hazzard and did so report to her and she did superintend and direct the diet? Did she not?"

"You will make me contradict myself. It was left to Miss Claire from day to day what she could take and what would give her less distress."

"I believe you said you had no connection with Dr. Hazzard at all prior to the time you went on this case?"

"I think I said I had a case one day."

Day Karr objected to the relevancy of the line of questioning. Judge Yakey overruled him.

"What case was that?"

"A case like one—"

Again Karr jumped to interrupt and object. Again, overruled.

"Mr. Webb's brother?"

The witness sat mute.

"Watson Webb's brother?" Kelley asked again, his voice nearly to a yell to try to shake a response loose from her lips.

"Yes," Nellie answered, with great and obvious reluctance.

"You were with them how long?"

"One day."

"Where is his brother now?"

Another objection, overruled by the bench. Nellie Sherman was told to answer.

"He is dead."

WHEN THE SPECIAL PROSECUTOR PRESSED MISS Sherman on the point that Dr. Hazzard—not Claire, not Dora, not even herself—was the one in full charge of the treatment, Nellie Sherman talked in circles. She seemed unable to answer the query fully.

"I think the witness ought to be instructed to answer the question," Kelley snapped loudly over the continued rantings about the beauties of Dr. Hazzard's treatments.

Judge Yakey turned quickly toward the witness chair. His red face betraying his anger, his voice rising to a shout, "I will instruct you to answer the question and not argue—"

"I am trying to—"
"Madam, will you shut up until I get through talking?"

FRANK KELLEY CALLED FOR A RECESS. HE HAD
made a startling observation and wanted to bring it before the
judge—out of the presence of the jurors.

The twelve men filed out of the room, their faces no longer
showing traces of skepticism at the state's case. Nellie Sherman
had been so effective on Saturday, but Monday, that had all
changed.

"Mrs. Hazzard has been seen signaling to the witness in an
effort to direct her testimony," Kelley announced.

Linda Hazzard looked doubtfully at her attorneys and her
husband.

"That's not true!" she said.

The judge had not seen anything, but he put Miss Sherman
and the defendant on notice: There would be nothing of the sort
in his courtroom. He told the affable bailiff with the new shoes
to keep watch on the defendant at all times.

NELLIE SHERMAN, FLUSTERED BEYOND REPAIR,
returned to the witness box and the meeting with Dr. Brewer
was brought before the jurors once more.

"My question was, did you not, in reply, state the girls would
not take any food unless Mrs. Hazzard told them to?"

"I did not say that."

"What did you say?"

"They would not take the kinds of food I would like to have
them take."

"Did you not state they would not take the kinds of food
unless Mrs. Hazzard told them to?"

"I did."

"Did you not go on further to say the girls were absolutely
under Dr. Hazzard's dominion and would not take any additional food unless Dr. Hazzard ordered it?"

"I did not say under her dominion, in perfect accord and har-
mony in treatment. Anything I could say had no force upon
them, and I wanted them to take meat and chicken broths."

The witness continued wrapping her denials in a cloak of

uncertainty. If she had thought by being unsure, she would stave off having to say anything that would cast Linda Hazzard in a bad light, she was wrong. She appeared evasive. She seemed unforthcoming.

Nellie denied telling Mrs. Keck of Acme Grocery that the girls were hypnotized. She could not recall what she said to Miss Corrigan at the Buena Vista concerning the Williamson case.

"*I could not say positively.*"

"*I do not think so.*"

"*I did not say that.*"

ONE OF THE AMBULANCE DRIVERS WHO PICKED up the sisters from the Buena Vista was sworn in after Miss Sherman. Andrew Hill had signed the codicil as a witness for Miss Claire. Under Gregory's direct, he told the jury how John Arthur had a broken fountain pen and asked to borrow one to take Claire's dictation.

"... I gave him mine and he asked me if I could stay there where I was and I said yes, and I stayed there while she dictated this codicil."

She also signed several traveler's checks.

"Did she say anything at that time about a gift of one thousand dollars or thereabouts, if you remember?"

The witness nodded.

"That was to go to the Hazzard Institute to complete the cabins."

Frank Kelley used his cross-examination to show the jury that Hill was either lying or ignorant of what was really going on in the ambulance.

"Whose ambulances were they?"

"E. R. Butterworth & Sons."

"You are connected with Butterworth?"

"Yes sir."

"In what capacity?"

"My capacity as funeral director and embalmer."

"What are the business relations between Butterworth & Sons and this defendant?"

Karr objected as irrelevant, but the judge allowed the line of questioning to continue.

"Through Mrs. Hazzard, Butterworth & Sons within the last two years have had a considerable amount of business, have they not?"

"No sir, we have not got a big amount of business from her."

"About how many cases came into your hands within the last three years through Dr. Hazzard?"

Andrew Hill took his time to answer. The best he could come up with by way of an estimate was between four and six.

Frank Kelley narrowed his brow and tipped his head.

"Do you know an Englishman named John Ivan Flux?"

The witness did. The man was buried by Butterworth.

Then, amid a shower of objections, the special prosecutor engaged in a roll call of dead patients, each one acknowledged by the ambulance driver as one that had been buried or cremated by Butterworth.

Wakelin, Rader, Webb, Tindall, Whitney . . .

AFTER THE DAMAGING TESTIMONY, LUCIAN Agassiz joined the special prosecutor for an impromptu meeting with the soggy pack of newsmen who by then had become familiar and, at least to their side, very friendly faces. All joked and laughed about how Kelley had "bulldozed" Nellie Sherman with his relentless cross-examination.

"Yes, I'd say so," he said so in response to a reporter who said he had destroyed the defense witness.

"Imagine that—Miss Sherman turned into one of *our* best witnesses," he added.

JAMES WATSON WEBB WAS A PUFFED-UP YOUNG man. He bore the kind of self-satisfaction and transparent smugness that seemed inconceivable for a man still in the bottom end of his twenties. Was it confidence in Dr. Hazzard's case or egotism of his own that caused his insufferable cockiness? As he raised his hand to be sworn in, he smiled at the parties lined up behind the defense table. Linda Hazzard clasped her hands and nodded. Samuel Hazzard reached for his fountain pen as if to ready himself for note-taking.

For the prosecution, Wattie's eyes signaled no animosity or bitterness. There was no need for direct defiance. He made his allegiance known by never looking in their direction. Not once during Gregory's direct examination did he look at Kelley or Stevenson.

Webb told how he had been invited by Dr. Hazzard to get acquainted with Claire and Dora in mid-March 1911. After the course of many, many visits—nearly every day—he became quite friendly with the sisters, visiting and walking about the Buena Vista. He judged Claire's weight to be about seventy-eight pounds. Dora was lighter, somewhere in the sixty-pound range.

"They told me when I first visited them they had no visitors before that and were pleased to have someone call on them and were eager that I call again. They seemed so eager and earnest about it, so I did."

He read to them, brought milk, picked up copies of the *London Times* and ran other errands at their bidding. When Nellie Sherman needed time away, it was Webb who took over.

"Mr. Webb, what was the longest time you ever remained?"

"I have stayed there all night. I slept in the apartments there and once or twice I slept across the hall in another apartment."

He said he slept on a couch pulled out into the hallway.

"*With* your clothes on?"

Webb's eyes popped and he drew back in great indignation.

"*Yes, sir!*" he huffed.

The defendant studied the jury. One by one, she reviewed each man, looking for clues as to their reception of what was being said by the "pure-minded boy." If Nellie Sherman had been such a disaster, then Linda Hazzard could ill afford another witness to be cast in such a bad light. Watson Webb was critical. To believe him, however, was to understand that Dora Williamson was more than mistaken. She had to be viewed as a vengeful liar.

According to Webb, Dr. Hazzard had told him of the sisters' health "a day or so" after they came to Seattle.

"She said two English girls had arrived and seemed to be in a very poor condition, their breath smelled foul, and there seemed to be an odor from them—general ill health. They came to her for treatment, but she would only take them on the condition she would give them advice regarding her diet and could take them under her full control. They were not able to be treated so."

Gregory stepped up his direct to the subject of the withholding of food and the supposed motive for the alleged crime—the assets of the sisters.

Webb said that he had fired up the stove and warmed many a meal for the invalid sisters. There had never been a shortage of food.

"I know this, they had plenty; in fact, I used to think more than a sick person should take."

"Mr. Webb, I will ask you if you know anything about what was done with the girls' jewelry while at the Buena Vista apartments?"

The witness had been expecting the question. He did not hesitate.

"One day Claire asked the nurse to get her the box of jewelry; it was taken from a trunk. She brought it to her, I remember, because I wrapped it up afterwards. I remember her looking in it, looking at the different pieces, and she brought out a ring and a case with the ring which belonged to Dora. She closed it up afterward and I took it from her and wrapped it up in paper and tied it with a string. She wanted Dr. Hazzard to place it in her safe—there were plenty of people coming in the rooms, the janitor, and she felt it was unsafe to keep it in the apartments. *She* felt that way."

Frank Kelley found great joy in cross-examination—especially with a witness like Watson Webb. He not only provided ample fodder for impeachment, he also opened the door to areas that otherwise might not have been allowed before the jury. The jewelry testimony was one of those. It put the Williamson sisters' wealth into Dr. Hazzard's hands.

"Was Dr. Hazzard there when you had the jewelry out?"

"Yes sir."

"And she took the package away with her?"

"*I* took the package away," Webb said, correcting the special prosecutor. "I accompanied Dr. Hazzard to the office and saw her put it in the safe, and also advised her to put it in a safe deposit."

Kelley focused on the relationship between the witness and the defendant.

Webb admitted the two had been good friends for several years and as such Dr. Hazzard occasionally called on him for favors—including visiting patients. He paused to search his memory for names. He recalled calling on a Mr. Honnah at his home, and another woman, whose name escaped him, at her residence.

"At Mrs. Hazzard's request?" Kelley asked.

"She asked me if I would call in."

"Anyone else?"

Webb shook his head. "No, I do not remember. I have been to see other patients, but not at her request. I went to see a Mr. Rader at his own request. I called on him personally."

"You do not know whether she suggested it or not?"

"I do not know. I had met him before. It happened to be he was sick when I asked."

Kelley asked why he went to see Rader.

"To help him if I could. I would go there and stay a little while and help him bathe."

"Just the sunshine of your presence?"

"Just, sir."

"You are accustomed to doing that?"

As cross-examination continued, so did Judge Yakey's dissatisfaction with the defense and its witness. Every so often, Webb would pause a long time. Long enough for the defense to rise and tell him to answer the question.

"The court says he does not want you to coach witnesses any further," Judge Yakey said.

Webb admitted that he helped nurse the sisters, but he had done nothing improper.

"You helped the girls move from their room to the bathroom?"

"What do you mean? Yes, I would assist them to the bathroom at their request."

"You would assist them physically did you not?"

"How do you mean?"

"Did you not take hold of them?"

"Yes, the same as you would your mother or your sister."

"Certainly you did." Kelley's voice dripped with sarcasm.

"Of course I did."

"Did you assist in bathing them at all?"

"*Never.*"

"How about those enemas?"

"I *never* assisted them."

The special prosecutor concluded with the witness's loyalty to Dr. Hazzard.

"You have been so much interested in this case that you have attempted to get some of the state's witnesses out of the way?"

"No, sir," he shot back.

Watson Webb had lost his puffed-up demeanor when the questions turned to his visit with Essie Cameron. He denied everything. He neither cajoled, threatened, nor attempted to bribe the former sanitarium worker.

"*No sir! No sir! No sir!*"

As Wattie left the stand, Dr. Hazzard buried her face in her hands. Her body heaved a labored, but quiet sigh. The pure-minded boy had done more damage than good. Frank Kelley was without question a stronger adversary than she had counted on. If he had stayed out of the case, things might have fared differently.

The next two witnesses were called to bolster the defense's assertion that Essie Cameron was a liar. L.E. Rader's already-remarried widow, Emma Rader Gates, was sworn in first. It was a peculiar move for the defense. There wasn't a soul in the courtroom who wasn't aware that her first husband had been rumored to be a victim of the fasting specialist's bizarre treatment. Still, the former Mrs. Rader took the stand and in a loud, certain voice announced that Miss Cameron had a "reputation for untruthfulness."

When Kelley crossed Dr. Hazzard's neighbor, it was learned that the Cameron girl's dishonest reputation went no farther than among members of the Rader Gates household.

"Do you know anything about her reputation outside your family?" he asked.

Emma hesitated. "No, sir. I never talked with anyone."

Her testimony was stricken.

Mary "Mother" Lillie followed. Though it would have hardly seemed possible, the old woman with the rough hands and wearied face was even a poorer witness than Mrs. Gates. After much fumbling with trying to frame a question that the witness could understand and answer properly, lawyer Karr practically threw up his hands before Mary Lillie finally answered that she "knew from reports" she had heard that Essie was untruthful.

Kelley pounced, demanding the source of the gossip.

Mrs. Lillie hemmed and hawed for a few minutes. Finally she conceded that while she had heard it often—in town, or on the *Virginia*—the only specific names she could come up with were her son Frank Lillie and Emma Rader Gates.

She was certain the disparaging words came from others in Olalla, a place where she knew everyone by sight and name, but the names of no others passed her lips.

Not one.

WITH HIS FULL, DARK WHISKERS AND TROUSERS so long they wicked up water on a rainy day, Frank Lillie was an eyeful. He seldom wore shoes—didn't care for the feel of them, preferred to feel the earth beneath his feet. For court, though he didn't like it, he managed to put on a pair. While others had donned their Sunday Best for the trial, this man did not. He was undeniably unkempt. The farmer and sanitarium helper was not schooled in the traditional sense, but Frank Lillie was a reader with broad interests. He was not stupid, only rough around the edges. Whenever it suited him, he played the unsophisticated country bumpkin. It was, of course, a clever act.

Frank Lillie was eager to take the stand as the day came toward its end. Where others had failed, his confidence indicated he fully planned to succeed.

Under Day Karr's direct examination, the witness stated when he first laid eyes on Claire Williamson at the sanitarium, she was not emaciated about the face.

"She looked like an ordinary person does, looked like a woman of a mental temperament, not a fleshy woman."

He insisted her lips did not roll back to expose her teeth and her eyes did not pop from their sockets.

Lillie described Wilderness Heights as a content home, a home without wants. He ran errands for the girls, which involved carrying water and stoking the fire to make their bed bricks hot. And, he said emphatically, he had seen with his own eyes that there was plenty of food given to the girls. He told the jury of a larder stocked with everything from pineapples and rice, peas and butter, olive oil and tomatoes, English walnuts. Everything was the best.

The defense lawyer asked for a description of Dr. Hazzard's bedside manner as it related to Miss Claire and Miss Dora.

"She treated them just as I would appreciate being treated myself if I was in a person's home, very considerate of their wishes. She treated them nice, a little better than I ever expect to be treated."

When queried about the baths and the enemas, Frank Lillie denied ever being present during the procedures. He had only carried the water.

When it came his turn, Frank Kelley picked up where the defense had left off.

"You never saw Claire in the tub?" he asked.

"No, sir."

"And you never saw Dora in the tub?"

Again, a denial.

"Don't you remember after Miss Conway came one time when Dora was in the bathroom and you wanted to get into the bathroom, you referred to some part of the plumbing you were putting in there then and Miss Conway told you you could not come in there because Dora was in there?"

The witness nodded yes, he remembered.

"And didn't you say 'that doesn't make any difference to me. She is just the same as cabbage to me, I have seen her many times when she was taking a bath.' "

"No, sir!"

Kelley tried to affirm the prosecution's thesis that the sisters were held under Dr. Hazzard's complete control.

"Isn't it true that if Mrs. Hazzard told them to do anything, they followed her instructions implicitly?"

"I didn't know that."

The next questions had been awaited by many observers who had heard the rumors of collusion between defense witnesses. An irritated Lillie said he and Miss Sherman were "ordinary friends."

"You have a greater feeling of friendship for Miss Sherman than for anyone else?"

Frank Lillie stretched his neck and raised his voice to such a degree it startled many in the courtroom.

"Do you mean there is a love affair between us?"

"No, no," Kelley said backing off. "I did not even intimate that. I simply asked you if there was a feeling of friendship between you?"

Kelley moved on once a connection, even though riddled with denial, was made between the witness and Miss Sherman.

"Were you and she interested together in any particular cult in Olalla?"

"I would like to know what a cult is?"

"I am referring to your general interest in a spiritualistic matter?"

"What is a spiritualistic matter?"

"I will talk in common garden terms. You and Miss Sherman are both Spiritualists, are you not?"

"No, I am not."

IT CERTAINLY WAS NOT MERE RUMOR THAT LED Frank Kelley to question Frank Lillie about a possible interest in matters of the occult. It was well-known the Hazzards and the Lillies shared more than a passing interest in Spiritualism and Theosophy. Watson Webb was one who practically wore a sandwich board sign promoting his belief in communicating with life in the hereafter. Years later, other clues would turn up.

Frank Lillie's grandson, Marvin, born on May 2, 1923, would recall a couple of things that indicated Frank and Nellie were, in fact, involved in the realm of the supernatural. One item was a pair of school slates, another was an old photograph.

"I was told at one time—these little slates they used to use in school, your own little blackboard—they'd take them, wash them clean, take two of them, nail them together, wrap them in wire anyway you wanted to seal them shut. Then they'd have this reading or whatever it was. Then you could open up these two blackboards again and there would be writing inside."

"They (the slates) used to be in our house for ages. We used to play with them when we were kids.

"We also have a picture if it hasn't disappeared. It's a picture of Grandpa Frank and Nellie . . . the picture was taken of the two of them. When the film was developed there was a third person standing behind them. By the records this third person had been dead for a hundred years. It was a woman who was standing there . . ."

And long after Frank and Nellie had died, a letter from an astrologer known as Professor Edward Whipple was discovered among the papers of a great-granddaughter who had assembled the bric-a-brac of what remained of the family's history. The letter written to Nellie Sherman was dated March 28, 1910.

The man the astrologer referred to was, of course, Frank L. Lillie.

Now, regarding the advisability of your marrying native born September 4, 1867, I have cast his birth chart and will enclose it to you. There are several things to consider. Your respective figures harmonize fairly well, though not completely. Saturn rises in both horoscopes. Ordinarily he would be of even temper and very agreeable; but is easily irritated and then his temper is difficult to control . . . But in his own horoscope conditions will improve and some doors will open about 1912 and these better conditions will last four or five years . . . looks quite favorable for marriage in 1912.

Frank Lillie and Nellie Sherman were married on December 20, 1912, in Los Angeles.

FORTY-ONE

FROM THE FIRST TIME SHE LEARNED OF IT, Dora had felt a little disheartened to see Sarah Robinson's name typed on the list of defense witnesses. Of any of the staff at Olalla, Dora felt Nurse Robinson had shown considerable compassion for the terrible state the fasting treatment had wreaked upon herself and her sister. Miss Robinson was kindly, where others were harsh. Miss Robinson, after all, had helped her sneak mail out. Miss Robinson, Dora had wanted to believe, had been on the side of good, not evil.

And there she was—on the other side.

Unlike Miss Sherman, this witness did not dress in a nurse's uniform. She chose an unassuming chestnut-colored suit fastened with a gleaming row of ebony buttons and a matching handbag. It was a nice ensemble, plainly stretching the limits of her young means. It was an outfit for which the nurse had undoubtedly saved her money.

Mr. Gregory handled the Robinson direct examination. He did so methodically and without the histrionic timbre in his voice that had marred some of his partner's examinations.

Sarah Robinson did not speak to the gallery of spectators, but turned her head at each answer to direct her words to the twelve men deciding the case. She testified she had only known Linda Hazzard a short time before coming to work alongside Nellie Sherman on the Williamson cases at the Buena Vista. Though there was food there, she could only recall serving hot milk to the sisters. She had only been there a little more than a day.

She recalled a conversation she had with Miss Claire while there.

"She was talking to me about her general health, and I told

her I was surprised to think she would have an osteopath treat her. If she had this stomach trouble, why she did not have a medical doctor look over her. She said she had not treated with a medical doctor for some time and did not believe in medicine."

Miss Robinson said she went to Olalla on the evening of April 28, 1911. It was there, she testified, that the sisters were given foods other than hot liquids. They were fed small quantities of asparagus, tomatoes, rice, and cream. Salt and butter seasoned their meals.

"What effect did the food have on Claire?" the lawyer asked.

"Well, she was still very ill with the trouble I first found her with—she did not seem to digest her food. She seemed to have flatulency. In my opinion she was not able to digest what she got."

She said she urged Claire to seek a medical doctor.

"She said she did not want one. She seemed to think she knew her own business best. She told me she had been ill for years with some stomach trouble, and she had come to Dr. Hazzard as a last resort."

"Do you remember her saying anything about what Dr. Hazzard had told her at the time?"

"She told me Dr. Hazzard had said that she had organic trouble and could not possibly live very long with it."

When Frank Lillie's name was brought up Miss Robinson denied anything improper had taken place at Olalla in regard to baths or enemas.

"He certainly did not. I am capable of giving my own enemas!"

The baths, she said, were not overly warm.

"Did Miss Claire ever faint while in the bath?"

"No, sir."

The rest of the morning the nurse told the jury that the sisters were allowed to have as much food as they wanted. She had tried to get them to eat more, but neither had any interest in food. Dr. Hazzard had not restricted the sisters. Their lack of nourishment was their own doing.

The defense witness also had a different take on Claire Williamson's final hours.

"Did Dr. Hazzard go up to the bed and press on Claire's stomach?"

"No, I did not see her do that. She was standing in the door and in a little while I came in again and Claire was trying to say something to Dora and I asked her what it was and Miss Dora said, 'Miss Robinson, let us save her from that.' "

"Did Dr. Hazzard try to prevent Claire from saying anything to Dorothea at that time?"

"No, she did not say anything."

IT WAS A DIFFICULT BEGINNING FOR FRANK KELley and Sarah Robinson when the prosecution took over the questioning. The nurse in the chestnut suit was slow to answer. Reluctance stammered out of each response.

"Everything that you saw at Olalla was above reproach, is that true?" he asked her.

"Everything that I saw."

The lawyer probed deeper.

"Nothing there which you saw caused any uneasiness, anything to excite suspicion or anything to meet your disapproval, is that right? Yes or No?"

The witness sank in her chair and turned to Judge Yakey.

"Can I explain?"

The judge nodded.

"I did not like the feeling existing between Dora and the doctor."

"Now who was it you disapproved of in that matter?"

George Gregory objected, and though the judge overruled it, Sarah Robinson could not find an answer. She did not know the cause of the trouble, and could not fix blame.

"Anything else that met your disapproval?"

"Well, yes."

"What?"

She paused for a long time before answering. "I do not believe in this dieting and osteopathic treatments."

She felt the sisters needed more nourishment, but Dr. Hazzard preferred to keep them on the strict vegetarian diet.

Kelley backtracked a bit, asking the nurse about her connection with Dr. Hazzard.

"You never knew Dr. Hazzard before you went on this case?"

"I never said that."

"Had you met her in a case before?"

"Yes sir."

"What case was that?"

"The Erdman case."

"Where is Erdman now?"

"He is dead."

A swarm of whispers buzzed around the courtroom as spectators made comment. Many wondered if there had been a defense witness who hadn't met Dr. Hazzard during a case that had *not* ended in death. Linda Hazzard's attention drifted to the noise behind her before she studied the faces of the jurors.

Sarah Robinson was losing them from her side, too.

As her cross-examination continued, it was clear that what had been the most perfect defense witness had been reduced to rubble like all the others. Each question was an ax swung at the spindly legs holding up the defense.

According to Miss Robinson, Nellie Sherman, in fact, had been frightened about the sisters' downward spiraling health. When a medical doctor was finally called at the Buena Vista, it was Stephen Olmstead, who came for a cursory review of the sister's dire conditions.

Kelley moved in for the kill with his final question for the nurse.

"If you were to assume for the purpose of the question that Dr. Olmstead who was called up that night, is an eye and ear specialist, will you tell me what there was about the condition of Claire and Dora, which in your opinion and Miss Sherman's, as employed nurses, impelled you to call an eye and ear specialist to look over the girls?"

The witness was not only flustered, she was embarrassed and humiliated as she tried to spit out a response. Finally, it came.

"I did not know I was calling an eye and ear specialist."

AFTER LUNCH WITH A GIRLFRIEND at the Owl Restaurant, Sarah Robinson returned to the stand to endure question after question about what she had fed the sisters at

Olalla. The nurse remained steadfast. Claire and Dora had not been starved. They had not been on a fast, even. It was a diet. As she was questioned on how many servings had been given Claire, Sarah Robinson looked toward the defendant.

As if to suppress a yawn or stem the discharge from a cough, Linda Hazzard held her hand to her face. She slowly rolled her fingers over her mouth.

One. Two. Three. Four . . .

It was just after two in the afternoon, and in a swift instant, Kelley's questions were halted by Thomas Stevenson.

"We would like the jury to be excused," the Kitsap County prosecutor said.

Kelley turned around to see what was happening. He looked as surprised as the judge.

"What is the matter?"

"They are signaling witnesses."

Defense lawyer Gregory rose like a marionette, so quickly he was slightly unsteady. He denied the insinuation. The jury should stay right where they were. Linda Hazzard also stood up and denied doing any such thing.

"*I never . . .*"

Judge Yakey slammed the gavel to its black walnut base. His face now hot with anger.

"I am controlling this jury, and I say the jury shall retire to the jury room!"

Stevenson spoke once the men cleared the room.

"Mrs. Hazzard was counting the number of times with her finger over her mouth. To the last question, for the affirmative I noted that she signaled at least three or four times to the questions asked and responses made, to their witness."

"Ask Miss Robinson if anyone signaled her," Gregory directed toward the bench.

Judge Yakey would have none of that. He had quite enough already. He had enough of the defense.

"There have been times when it is perfectly true that the defendant has showed disapproval of what the witnesses have been testifying to. I have seen that myself. When one witness testified upon the stand Mrs. Hazzard shook her head to the jury. Whether she has been signaling to this witness I do not know, but if there has anything like that been done it is very improper. I do not think it proper to speak of this before the jury."

The judge paused for a moment to catch his breath. He stared hard at Linda Burfield Hazzard.

"I hope this will stop if it has been done, and I want to caution the defendant now that it must not be done or else she will be in contempt of court."

Dr. Hazzard stood and indicated her desire to make a statement to clear her name, but the judge told her to sit down and be quiet. If it were a civil case and not a criminal proceeding, he announced that he'd have had the defendant barred from the courtroom.

The jury returned and the court instructed the men to ignore what took place in the moments before their sudden departure. What happened, if anything had indeed transpired, was not evidence.

And though she was on the stand for another half hour, Sarah Robinson's testimony had been tainted to such a degree that it was a waste of time for either side. Nothing she could say could erase the suspicion that her answers had been directed by the woman on trial.

STEPHEN OLMSTEAD WAS A BONA FIDE DOCTOR. No one disputed that. He proudly displayed an 1884 sheepskin from the Department of Medicine and Surgery of the University of Michigan on the wall of his Seattle office. The fact that he was an ear and eye specialist was the source, however, of much prattle among case watchers. Not because he wasn't any good at his specialty. He might have been more than competent when it came to ears and eyes. It was ludicrous that he would be called in to care for patients in the condition of the Williamson sisters. And the autopsy, that was another story. A couple of snickers broke through the courtroom as he took his place before the court.

Questioning Dr. Olmstead, Day Karr covered ground from the autopsy the defense believed proved Claire Williamson could not have died from starvation. Her skin was soft and pliable, a starved person's was somewhat "rough and scurvy," tight and brown. Fat is completely absent in cases of starvation; Claire Williamson's body retained some subcutaneous fat. In cases of starvation bladders are empty. Claire had water in hers.

The defense directed the witness to a diagram affixed to an easel to show the jury the location and the condition of each of Claire's organs.

Her liver, he pointed out with a penciled mark on the chart, was reduced in size, but it was hard and dry.

The witness said death caused by starvation often showed a liver reduced in size, but otherwise normal.

"What is the condition of the stomach in cases of death by starvation?"

"The stomach is usually contracted, the walls are thin, and it sometimes, or usually, contains a small amount of slimy liquid."

"What was the condition of Claire Williamson's stomach?"

"As regards to size, it was small. The walls were very much thickened, rigid. It did not collapse as the normal stomach would, or one in a case of starvation."

Her stomach, the doctor said, was so small it could only hold three or four ounces of liquid. A healthy stomach could hold a couple of quarts.

So close to mealtime, the detailed dissection of Claire Williamson literally turned stomachs in the courtroom. Dr. Olmstead was steady and sure, and his remarks brought little objection from Frank Kelley. Plenty of note-taking, but few objections.

In this doctor's opinion, Claire had died of lesions on her colon and intestines, which secondarily, led to inanition, the inability to *digest* food. She died of inanition—not starvation. No matter what treatment had been prescribed, he insisted with lofty certainty, Claire Williamson was headed to Death's door. There was no stopping it.

On cross-examination, Frank Kelley did his best to draw the kind of testimony that while not impeaching, was clearly detrimental. Dr. Olmstead said he had known the defendant for two or three years and had been called on by her to attend "three or four" postmortems.

"Who were they?" the lawyer asked.

"We object to the question being incompetent, irrelevant, and immaterial!" Karr called out.

Judge Yakey overruled it.

"I object to that myself," the witness said, blinking his wide eyes up at the bench.

"You are not in a very good position to object," the judge said.

"I haven't any notes with me upon these postmortems, and I have not refreshed my memory."

The special prosecutor sighed and continued.

"You do not recollect the names?"

The witness said he did, though only a few.

"Go on with them."

"Mr. Rader."

"Give me another."

"The name of Whitney."

Dr. Olmstead could not recall the others, though he admitted there were more.

"As many as five in all?"

"Yes, sir."

"Have you ever been called upon by any physician in Seattle to attend any postmortem except Mrs. Hazzard?"

"I don't recall any."

Kelley asked the doctor to search his memory.

"Isn't it true you have not?"

A long pause choked the life from the man's face. Finally, he answered.

"I think it is."

AS DEFENSE WITNESS STEPHEN OLMSTEAD FIN-ished his testimony, the doctor left the jury with a more disturbing picture of what kind of nutrition the sisters were getting than any of the prosecution witnesses had. If they were receiving vegetable broth and orange juice as Dora had maintained when she testified at the beginning of the trial, they would need to take at least fifty quarts of the liquid a day.

Just to survive.

Karr tried to patch up his witness on redirect, but his efforts proved futile. The ear and eye specialist could not backtrack on what he said.

The case stumbled from there. As the next witness, another doctor, had not arrived from Seattle, the court—though not happy about it—allowed the defense to postpone until the following morning.

"This case is costing us several hundred dollars a day and we cannot afford any delays," Judge Yakey said.

THAT TUESDAY AFTERNOON, BEFORE THE PORT Orchard trial was dismissed for the day, the *Tacoma Daily Ledger* stretched a banner across the front page:

> *SENSATIONS ARE EXPECTED IN DYNAMITING CASE*
> *ONE OF MRS. HAZZARD'S WITNESSES TESTIFIES*
> *AGAINST HER*
> *NURSE OPPOSED TO STARVATION,*
> *SHE SAYS*

At the same time, in Australia, the *Melbourne Age* published another update on the Hazzard case.

> *DEATH BY STARVATION*
> *INCIDENT IN SEATTLE COURT*

> *A peculiar incident took place in connection with the giving of evidence yesterday regarding the charge of murder by starvation which has been laid against Mrs. Hazzard, the keeper of a sanitorium at Seattle. Her alleged victim was a wealthy Australian girl named Claire Williamson.*
> *Nurse Robinson was being examined when Mrs. Hazzard signaled to her. The attention of the judge was called to the matter, and he reprimanded the prisoner, declaring that he would deal unmercifully with her if she repeated the offense . . .*

FORTY-TWO

IT WAS NEARLY OVER. FOR THE PROSECU-
tion the feeling that the end was near brought relief and a little
bit of worry. Had they proven the case? For Linda Hazzard and
her supporters the end brought a volcano of ire. Neither Sam
nor Linda could let go of their bitterness over Judge Yakey's
ruling that the patients who had benefited from the fast cure had
been barred from testifying. It was an outrage beyond compre-
hension. The Hazzards' united front had always been that Linda
was not on trial so much as was her method of treatment. It was
unfair. It was outrageous. As the Hazzards saw it, the judge's
ruling was further evidence of the conspiracy of those against a
better way of healing.

The stress had come to the breaking point.

Wednesday morning pure-minded Watson Webb was fit to
be tied. He stomped his feet and cursed like a navy-yard worker
outside the courtroom. It was a tantrum, a spectacle the likes of
which seldom had been seen in a such a staid venue.

"Judge Yakey and the prosecution are in league against Dr.
Hazzard! This trial is a sham! An utter travesty!"

His speech forced mouths agape, eyes unable to blink.

"The jury—if you can even call them that—ought to be hung
for what they conspire to do!"

Frank Kelley was outraged by the flagrant disrespect.
Moments later, as court was about to convene, he informed
Judge Yakey of what had transpired outside. The judge sum-
moned Watson Webb and both teams of attorneys into chambers.

Throughout the outburst, the defendant sat next to her husband wearing the concerned and wary look of a mother whose
boy had been called into the principal's office for some minor

transgression. Linda Hazzard bore such obvious signs of stress and fatigue that a new nickname made the rounds of those who disparaged her.

"*Look! It's Dr. Haggard!*"

When the angry young man emerged a few minutes later he made no comment. Wattie Webb had said too much already, and he knew it. He smiled faintly, but defiantly, as he passed by the defense table. Dr. Hazzard's face was stone. She stared straight ahead.

Word leaked out later that the prosecution was considering taking the unruly fellow on charges.

The *Vancouver Columbian* headlined a story about Webb's run-in with Judge Yakey:

> *JUDGE SEVERELY*
> *CHASTISES FAMOUS*
> *"PURE MINDED" YOUTH*

CHARLES LITTLEFIELD, A HOMEOPATH FOR twenty-seven years who knew the defendant only by sight, was called first thing Thursday. The witness's credentials were established and lawyer Karr posed the hypothetical question which relied on Claire's biographical letter from Riverside to Dr. Hazzard. He detailed the defense's version of the treatment given Claire at the Buena Vista and Olalla.

"Assuming at the end of this time the patient died, would you or would you not say death was due to the fact that food had been withheld or to starvation?"

"I should say no."

Frank Kelley's cross was designed to undermine the doctor's ability to make a judgment based solely on the dead sister's letter. Perhaps she exaggerated? Perhaps she dwelled unduly on physical ailments that were not so severe?

"I think her letters showed her a woman in a clear state of mind," Dr. Littlefield said.

The special prosecutor was skeptical.

"And if you made an examination, assuming sir, that you are a man of ordinary skill and experience, you would have discovered whether or not these conditions were true or not?"

"I think so," the man answered.

The doctor also agreed that in his course of practice he would examine a patient thoroughly. He would make a diagnosis after doing so—not based on the patient's description of her ills.

Dr. Littlefield was followed by Dr. Elbert Lessing. Dr. Lessing also practiced in Seattle, and had been doing so for five years. He was a graduate of the Medical Department of the University of Illinois—a "regular" school. He had met Dr. Hazzard only once—the previous Sunday.

Karr put forth the same hypothetical question.

The witness believed peritonitis had been the cause of death. Claire Williamson was unable to assimilate food.

Kelley scored a big win for the prosecution when he covered Dr. Hazzard's autopsy report.

Dr. Lessing didn't believe that a physician "of common ordinary ability, skill and care" would have reported such ludicrous findings as "*liver cirrhosed, stomach elongated . . . small intestine of infantile appearance.*"

BY THE TIME ERNEST MEHNER, SIXTY-SIX, WAS sworn in, it was a foregone conclusion that the testimony of the father of the Bremerton mayor would not be heard by the jury. Judge Yakey had cut the defense so little slack throughout the trial, that they knew most of their witnesses—fully fifty of them—would not make the grade. Mehner, like the others, was a patient of Dr. Hazzard's.

"Are you qualifying him as an expert?" Yakey asked Karr.

"No, this is simply to show the system used on these girls is not different from the system used in other cases."

The judge shook his head.

"This comes to the question," Judge Yakey said, "as to whether or not you are going to introduce every patient she has treated, in this case."

"We are going to try to do that."

The judge ruled against the defense and the man on the stand was told to step down. To save the record for future appeals, if need be, Day Karr was allowed to call one more such witness.

Retired farmer Max Vetter was called and dismissed in short order.

The defense lawyer said he had one more witness before resting his case, but because the day had gone so quickly, the man was not in Port Orchard.

It was time for rebuttal.

"Call Nellie Sherman!"

The bailiff left for the witness room, but returned a few moments later without the nurse.

"She is out walking," he announced.

Judge Yakey slammed his gavel again.

"Issue a bench warrant and send the sheriff after her!"

IT SEEMED AS IF THE ROOMS HAD BEEN SAVED for them—and considering their importance to the Hazzard case—it was likely that was exactly what had happened. Wednesday afternoon Dora and Margaret checked into the same rooms they had held earlier at the Navy View Hotel. Some odds and ends they had left behind were in place on a dressing table. Dora thought the staff was so very thoughtful. She didn't stop to think that it was because of the trial that Port Orchard hotels and restaurants had experienced a windfall, the likes of which had never been seen in Kitsap County.

Agassiz had escorted the ladies from Tacoma, for what he promised would be their last appearance before the court trying Linda Hazzard for Miss Claire's murder. Both women would be put on the stand—the last two—as rebuttal witnesses.

All three were relieved it was nearing the end.

AND STILL, JUST WHEN MARGARET THOUGHT IT would soon all pass, the memories rushed back. More than anything, it was the manner and sound of Dr. Hazzard's voice that continued to send chills dropping breakneck down her tailbone.

Just the thought of it . . .

It was a voice, Margaret Conway figured, that could cause a soldier to cringe. It cut violently through the air like a blade through a salmon gut. Quick. Sharp. The old nursemaid could still hear the doctor's cowing voice. Talking, long pause. Talking, long pause. Margaret would never forget Linda's tirades when they were directed at Sam. His name was used to punctuate the end of her sentences.

". . . *SAM!*"

Margaret had wondered if the long pause between what the doctor said, indicated whether Sam didn't respond or if his words were merely inaudible. She was never sure. She almost felt sorry for Mr. Hazzard.

"You know," she declared later, "on the other side of the Atlantic they say the American husband's place in the home is the most contemptible on earth. I always knew that was an exaggeration, of course, but the Hazzard home was the first American one in which I began to wonder if the European joke had not a large grain of truth to it."

Margaret also never forgot a bitter exchange between Sam and Linda Hazzard one evening not long after she arrived in Olalla.

"Samuel! You lazy good-for-nothing loafer! Where are you? What are you doing now? There is wood to be chopped, and I won't wait a moment longer for you to get it done!" Linda had yelled from their bedroom.

"I'm in here," came Sam's voice from the dining table, where he liked to do his work. "I'm finishing up paperwork from yesterday."

"Sam! You lout! You should have taken care of it then! I want you to get outside and chop me the wood now. *Now!*"

Margaret Conway would never forget standing on the veranda, stunned by the discourse between the wife and her husband. The stout little Australian woman with the swirl of grey hair could never make sense of it. It seemed otherworldly. No man, no decent man, would stand for such treatment. Why did he?

What was her power?

FORTY-THREE

IF THERE HAD BEEN A HIDING PLACE beneath the courtroom floorboards, Nellie Sherman would have clawed her fingers to a shredded bloodiness to get there. If only she could escape somehow. She despised Frank Kelley and hated being in that courtroom more than anyone, including the defendant. But Nellie was back bright and early on Thursday morning, a guest of the Kitsap County sheriff. Her responses were clipped. Gone were the yammerings of support for Linda Hazzard's "glorious" treatments at Olalla. Gone were the inflections of indignation and surprise. Her tone was flat. Nellie Sherman had been a handy punching bag for the prosecution once before, and she was not a glutton for punishment. She wanted out of there.

So did Lucian Agassiz. For the first time in several days, the vice-consul who had engineered the case took a seat at the prosecution table. He wanted it over, too. The pressure of the waiting had taken a toll. Even though no advocate of *The No Breakfast Plan*, Agassiz had still passed on a plate of eggs and kippers that morning.

"My stomach is turning cartwheels," he said.

"Mine is as well," Dora replied.

As if he needed any reminder, Frank Kelley unfolded several sheets of notepaper before standing to make inquiry. He required no chits from Agassiz to remind him of anything. There were only a few key points to be discussed in rebuttal with Miss Sherman.

He first quizzed her on statements made to Mrs. Keck.

Nellie denied telling the store proprietress Claire and Dora would not eat anything without the implicit instructions of Dr

Hazzard. She denied saying the sisters lived on tomato and celery broths, that they were so light she could carry them about the apartment like children.

She denied everything.

"I am absolutely positive I did not."

Nellie also rejected the prosecution's theories about her conversations with her friend Dr. Brewer. She had never told the osteopath that the sisters subsisted on vegetable juices.

"I told you before if I—if she says I made a statement like that, she misunderstood me."

Nellie Sherman had told herself over and over . . . *do not let Kelley get the best of you* . . .

"Did not Dr. Brewer upon the occasion of these conversations urge you to give the girls more food?"

"She may have. I cannot be absolutely positive as to every word she said to me."

"Did you not in reply say the girls would not take any more food unless Mrs. Hazzard told them to do so?"

Nellie Sherman's eyes flashed a cold look. She stumbled for a reply.

"I did not say it that way."

Kelley moved on to the conversation with Miss Corrigan over the enema pail brimming with strange white matter. Nellie's recall seemed vague. Barely a handful of particles floated in the water, she insisted.

Finally, she denied telling Miss Corrigan that she was worried about the girls and harbored grave doubts about the treatment.

"I could *not* have said that," Dr. Hazzard's nurse flatly insisted, before she was excused by the prosecution. The defense had no questions for Miss Sherman. No more cans of worms would be opened by that witness.

One of the spectators noticed something peculiar about Nellie as she hurriedly left the courtroom after her final humiliation. No one else had remarked on it. But for the first day since she had been part of the Port Orchard proceedings, Miss Sherman had not worn her uniform.

"Maybe she was fired?" a woman asked another seated adjacent to her.

"Might have quit on her own. If she has any sense, she did."

In rapid succession Dorothea Keck and Augusta Brewer took turns as rebuttal witnesses to contradict Nellie Sherman. And, somewhat oddly, they seemed disappointed in Miss Sherman. Throughout their testimony it seemed clear: they liked her. They had no axes to grind.

Claire Corrigan also returned to the stand that afternoon.

"And what was the extent of those white milky like substances?" Frank Kelley asked her.

"The water seemed pretty thick with them," she said.

Miss Corrigan also remained firm in her recollections of Miss Sherman's doubts about the fasting cure.

The defense, though they mercilessly tried, could not shake the young woman.

By then a minor celebrity because her name had been invoked so often, "the beautiful" Miss Cameron followed Miss Corrigan. Though still a teenager, Essie had a beguiling and womanly presence that brought her many, many admirers. The room went quiet when she took her seat. In a halting voice, she confirmed the prosecution's questions about her encounters with Watson Webb first in Portland and, more recently, at the Navy View. He had, in fact, tried to silence her with offers of money and jobs. His directives came from Linda Burfield Hazzard.

Essie's traveling companion, Mae Midgley, came next and backed up her friend. She had seen Watson Webb offer the bribe with her own eyes.

IT WAS LOST ON VERY FEW WHO SAW HER. BUT there in the midst of one damaging rebuttal witness after another, Linda Burfield Hazzard seemed so happy. She smiled. She even appeared to make a little joke at her husband's slightly increasing girth.

"Sam, another piece of cake and I might have to fast you just so you can wear that vest again!"

The reason for her joy was not the case. Though she maintained her belief she would gain an acquittal, the whole affair had been quite taxing and distressing. The longer the case went the more certain the fasting specialist was that vindictiveness and jealousy had been the impetus for the ordeal. The conspiracy of doctors had infiltrated Kitsap County to a degree that even she had not thought possible.

There was nothing to do about that. Not now. Not with the letter she had received from Los Angeles.

She showed it to members of the press. It was from the fasting world's icon: Dr. Tanner. Though the case was almost over, he made an offer to come to her aid.

I am ready to respond to your call to appear in Port Orchard to assist you on receipt of your orders to do so. Keep up your courage. I think I can puncture the gasbag of this expert testimony which has come out in your trial. You know I did this in 1880. I am aching for an opportunity to again hold up the medical fraternity to the derision of the world.

A JAPANESE BOY NAMED FRANK KANEOYA made his way from the witness room. He was barely five feet tall and weighed little more than a hundred pounds. Everyone watched as he nervously walked to the front of the courtroom, seemingly unaware where to sit.

Young Kaneoya was not one of the familiar players in the drama. No one had heard mention of him. Yet, there he was, put on by Thomas Stevenson to rebut the testimony of the lambasted Miss Sherman.

With only four years in America, the boy's command of the English language was shaky enough that an interpreter was contemplated, until the defense objected that if the prosecution had an interpreter, they should as well.

"We don't want to cast any reflections upon the interpreter at all," Karr said sardonically.

Judge Yakey thought the boy could get along without such a bother.

Frank Kaneoya told the jury that he had been hired by Claire and Dora to act as their porter boy at the Buena Vista.

"I will ask you at the time Nellie Sherman was there if you saw any butter, milk, cereals, corn flakes, or puffed rice in the pantry?"

"I never saw those things in the pantry while I was working in there."

Never did. Never. Never.

The defense tried to confuse the witness, making it appear that he had worked in other apartments and could not be certain that the pantry in the Williamsons' was the empty one he described to the jury. The cross-examination failed.

Frank Kaneoya even smiled when he stepped down. And if he had trouble finding his way to the witness stand, he had no problem getting out of the courtroom. He was a streak to the door.

MARGARET CONWAY LUGGED HER CUMBERSOME black satchel through the sea of spectators to the front of the courtroom. She had purchased some little gifts for her sisters in Australia earlier in the day and hadn't had time to get things back to the Navy View. Frank Kelley smiled warmly at her. She was there to refute statements made by Sarah Robinson.

"At the time you arrived at Olalla, which was about June 1, was it not a fact that Dora at that time was afraid of Dr. Hazzard and that there was ill feeling between her and Dr. Hazzard?"

"Mrs. Hazzard herself—before I ever reached Olalla—gave me to understand she disliked Dora because she said to me, she hoped Dora would die first; and as soon as I arrived Miss Robinson—"

The defense cut her off. Judge Yakey told the jury to disregard the answer.

And though he tried to rework his question about the animosity between the defendant and the witness, Frank Kelley was unable to frame the questions in a manner the judge would allow.

It really didn't matter. The jury who had leaned as far forward as they could without tipping chairs did not miss a word of what they were not supposed to hear. Margaret Conway left the stand, leaving it for Dora.

It was fitting that Dora Williamson would have the final word in the matter of her sister's death. She was put on the stand to refute Nellie Sherman and Watson Webb and to support testimony given by Miss Cameron.

No, she told the jury, she and her sister did not have lima

beans, peas, carrots, olive oil, or anything of the kind. They only had vegetable broths as a meal. The broths were never served merely as a "hot beverage."

Yes, Essie had served their meals at Olalla.

No, Watson Webb did not provide cheese, potatoes, milk.

"Did not have anything of the kind?"

"No," she said firmly. "No."

FORTY-FOUR

It was like a kettle that had simmered for weeks on a low fire. It had started full to the top, full of all that had been whispered, all that had been truth and lies, and how it had boiled in the courtroom. Now, all that was left was given over to final arguments. It had been distilled to that moment.

The confines of the courtroom were stretched beyond capacity. The double doors had been swung wide open to allow observers to crowd into the hallway to listen.

Dora and Margaret would hear all of it, though it would take two days for both sides to say all they had kept inside throughout the testimony. The two women had come to face the jury to let the world know that the doctor with the iron will and booming voice could not silence them. An empty chair was set out by the prosecution. It was Margaret's idea. She thought it a silent reminder, a tribute of a kind, of a beloved young woman who was only there in spirit. The empty chair was for Claire.

Linda was not alone. Husband Sam and son Rollin were as fixed at her side as tide-pool barnacles. Both men looked dapper and confident. And *united*. They wanted the world to know that despite the nasty innuendos permeating Port Orchard and far beyond, they were a strong family. A close family.

"It would surely be all right soon. Back to Olalla and the sanitarium we'll go . . ."

Linda could not mask her fatigue, but she did manage to project a semblance of confidence. She looked over her glasses and smiled in the direction of the jurors as twenty-four feet plodded into the jury box.

"They won't hang me," she laughed with a reporter. "The muscles in my neck are too strong!"

Thomas Stevenson handled the opening portion of the state's final argument. No one expected anything he would say had been his own creation. Most had come to know that all of the context of the case had been the invention of Lucian Agassiz. It was he, Nurse Conway, Miss Dora, and Frank Kelley who had shaded what happened in Olalla into the sensation it had become.

"This case is of unusual significance. We are not here to avenge the death of Claire Williamson, but to protect the public not only from Mrs. Hazzard but from others like her. There are other Claire Williamsons all over the United States who may fall into the clutches of such a woman as this. Your verdict will be of a far-reaching effect. This case is being watched all over the civilized world. If Mrs. Hazzard is acquitted, consider the effect of your verdict. Then throughout the United States all sorts of faddists will be reaching out for the weak and unprotected.

"When Dorothea and Claire first came to Mrs. Hazzard she thought they were just ordinary patients coming to be plucked. But when she found they were women of great means, and she had them in her power, she developed the criminal intent. She allowed Claire to die friendless and alone. But she could not get rid of Dora. So she did the next best thing. She had herself appointed Dora's guardian. Did your ever hear of such fraud and crookedness?

"Here is a woman who can get others under her control. Are you going to bring in a verdict that will permit her and others like her throughout this entire country to continue such practices with impunity?"

Day Karr opened the arguments for the defense.

"The real reason for this prosecution is that Mrs. Hazzard is not a college graduate," he said. "Her office consists of having been educated in the school of hard knocks. She has only the common garden variety of intelligence and because of this the doctors with degrees cannot stand her competition. She has lost some patients, but where is the physician who has not? She has lost just eight in the last twelve years. If she is not losing more than that, why not let her alone? You don't need to put her in the penitentiary. If she isn't doing good, her practice will dwindle, and she will have to go back to the garden."

Allusions that Dr. Hazzard had been the victim of medical persecution were not allowed. Frank Kelley interrupted several times.

"Counsel needs to keep within the testimony before the jury!"

It was Kelley who would have the last word. He called the defendant a "financial starvationist" who preyed on the Williamson sisters.

"The defendant is a serpent who trod sly and stealthy, yet, with all her craft left a trail of slime."

As he went over each piece of evidence, each bit of testimony, Frank Kelley turned toward the defendant and jabbed his finger in her direction. It was so abrupt, it caused the woman to flinch.

"This defendant is a menace to public safety and humanity!" he shouted.

Dr. Hazzard, so overcome by the harsh accusation, put her hands to her face and sobbed an audible cry.

JUDGE YAKEY INSTRUCTED THE JURY THAT LINDA Burfield Hazzard need not have *personally* withheld the food to make her acts a crime. If she advised abstinence from food, acting as physician having gained the trust and confidence of Claire Williamson, and if Claire followed her instructions and death resulted, it was a crime. Claire's agreeing to take a treatment was not a defense. But if she was of sound mind and refused nourishment, then Dr. Hazzard should go free.

The next morning, the *Seattle Daily Times* reporter covering the case considered by many to have "stood alone in the history of American or in the world criminology" wrote of its near end:

> No matter what prejudice may have existed in the minds of anyone who beheld the defendant in the courtroom there could not be excited a feeling, perhaps slight, of pity for the woman to whom has been accredited such mental power and who has been admired by her worst enemies for her pluck and her steady demeanor in the first days of the trial. Tonight she presented the picture of a hunted ani-

*mal—not one at bay, but more one that has run its last
race and fought its last fight and awaits destruction. The
look of half malice and half cunning which has characterized her so much during the trial was gone. She was
merely a woman who was robbed of her masculine mask.*

SATURDAY SLIPPED INTO SUNDAY. THOUGH DORA
and Margaret had returned to the lake near Tacoma that afternoon, Agassiz and Kelley stayed in Port Orchard. So did more
than two-hundred others interested in the outcome. Few desired
to miss being there when word came from the jury. Dora and
Margaret felt they had done their part and couldn't bear the nervousness that would consume them during a long wait at the
Navy View Hotel.

It was just before six in the evening, February 4, that word
blew through town a verdict had been reached. It had been twenty
hours since the jurors had received the case. Within a half hour,
Judge Yakey was at the bench, and the courtroom was packed to
overflowing. Linda Hazzard was the last to arrive. She bit her
lips together as she sat, betraying scant emotion or concern for
her fate.

As the foreman stood with the verdict for the clerk, a strange
noise was heard. Like a buzz, or a heavy breath, it rose up and
then down to silence. The lights trembled and pulsated in their
yellow intensity. Then it went completely black. The gas plant
serving the courthouse had failed. A thunder-loud gasp from
the spectators was followed by complete stillness.

"Mrs. Hazzard's light is going out!" a voice called out in the
darkness.

The room was pitch-black. Quiet. Deathly so. The irony of it
was not lost on Agassiz. His pupils enlarged to take in whatever
light there was. He looked in the direction of the defendant. He
could only make out the shape of a woman bent over the
defense table.

Agassiz knew Linda Hazzard was afraid of the dark. He
imagined the force with which her heart heaved beneath her
dress when the lights went black.

Foreman F.T. Ryan passed the verdict in case #2659 to the
clerk. As he did so, the bailiff struck a match against the floor

in a wide sweeping motion. The light from the flame rose, reaching over to illuminate the defense table. It bounced and flickered on the walls.

Linda Hazzard's lower lip stayed clamped by her upper teeth as the words were read:

> *We, the jury in the case of the State of Washington, plaintiff, against Linda Burfield Hazzard, defendant, do find the defendant Guilty of Manslaughter.*

Nellie Sherman gasped. *Her spirit guides had been wrong!* Sam Hazzard held his wife's hand. Rollin Burfield slid his chair closer to his mother. No one said a word. Most peculiarly, Linda didn't react. As the flame undulated in the draftiness of the courtroom, the defendant's face stayed stony. Resolve. *Resolve.* She was going to be all right.

Attorney Day Karr demanded the jury be polled.

"Is that your verdict?" Judge Yakey began.

"It is," the foreman answered. And each man that followed, one after another, in the blackness, stood and answered the same.

More matches burned until the bailiff was out, the last one burning his fingers and falling to the floor. The defense argued for a new bond to be fixed at $5,000—not $10,000 as had been the amount that had secured the woman's freedom pending the outcome of her trial. Karr told the court the Hazzard's financial reserves had been all but depleted by the costly proceedings. Judge Yakey immediately refused and, just as quickly, the defense announced the case would be appealed.

"So I expect it will," the somewhat annoyed judge said as he sat in the dark.

IN THE COMPANY OF THE KITSAP COUNTY SHERIFF, Dr. Hazzard was escorted from the courtroom. Even in the few minutes that had elapsed, much was known about the jury's decision. The verdict had been a compromise. At the first ballot, five had voted for first-degree murder, four for second-degree murder, one for manslaughter and two refused to express opinions. She was guilty, but to what degree had been the great question from the beginning. Manslaughter allowed the men to send her to prison and go home. The hotel had worn out its welcome.

Dr. Hazzard stayed quiet until she got outside and was met by a pack of newspaper reporters.

"I am the victim!" she started to scream. "This is the result of misrepresentation and the persecution of—"

Sam grabbed his wife's arm and yanked—*hard*. Sheriff Howe would have let her have her little soapbox. He didn't mind for one moment to be photographed dragging the convicted woman off to Mrs. Breed's little makeshift jail one more time. But Sam would not let Linda do this to herself. For the first time since it all began, a few detected affection between the dishonored West Pointer and the disgraced doctor. It was almost as if Sam cared for Linda. He was protecting a woman so many felt needed the help of no one.

"Sam! Let me speak of this injustice!"

"*Shut up, Linda!*"

The words were like a wallop. Linda was astonished. Sam had never done that in public before. She directed a contentious look in her husband's direction.

"The high and mighty with the diplomas and letters after their names have done this!" she yelled.

With that, she disappeared into Mrs. Breed's front door.

MARGARET CONWAY WAS BRAIDING DORA'S HAIR when a boy who worked around the Agassiz lake home excitedly announced that a reporter was there to see Miss Dora.

Dora cried when she heard the verdict. She rushed to Margaret and the two women held each other and sobbed. The feeling was bittersweet: a curious mixture of relief and satisfaction born of vengeance. Though Dr. Hazzard had been the enemy and there was joy at the jury's verdict, it would never bring back Claire. Nothing would fill the void of a sister so loved gone forever.

Dora composed herself. She did not wipe away the streaks of wetness that stained her face. They were badges of honor and tribute. For her sister.

"All I can say at present is that I am very glad that Dr.

Hazzard had been convicted. I really cannot see how the state or its citizens could have felt they were delivering justice by doing anything else," she said.

Margaret echoed her sentiments. Now that it was over, the strange American justice having been done, she could share her tears and get on with the business of living. She hoped the civil suits would progress more rapidly now and she could forget about the place at Olalla called Starvation Heights.

"I doubt I shall be able to. Some nightmares attach to the memory forever."

SUNDAY NIGHT AT THE BREED RESIDENCE, DR. Hazzard collapsed. She could barely speak, her legendary nerves of steel had frayed, pulling her into an abyss of near unconsciousness. Nellie Sherman put a cool cloth to her head. Sam drained the flask in his breast pocket. Rollin wondered how he and his stepfather would get along while his mother was in prison.

A reporter for the Associated Press called on the quasi jail. The door was answered by Samuel Hazzard.

"My wife is not in any condition to speak with anyone," he said. "She had been so sure that she would be acquitted that the guilty verdict was an unbearable shock."

Sam stepped outside and stood with the reporter on the porch. The sweet scent wafted from his breath.

"The most unfortunate thing," he said, putting his hand on the man's shoulder, "was the statement made in court tonight that Mrs. Hazzard is at the end of her rope financially. She has ample funds as soon as she can get at them. We will appeal to the Supreme Court."

The next day headlines like one in the *Tacoma Times* appeared throughout the world:

FAST FIEND IS GUILTY;
NO VOTE FOR ACQUITTAL

Frank Kelley gave his perspective in an interview with the *Seattle Daily Times* moments after the verdict:

"This case will, I believe, be a death blow to quack medical and healing individuals and institutions throughout the country. There is not and never was a basis for the statement that the practitioners of legitimate schools of medicine were in any way connected with this prosecution. The prosecution was instigated by Dorothea Williamson, the sister of the girl who met death at Mrs. Hazzard's hand, and C. E. Lucian Agassiz, the British vice-consul who did his duty in protecting the rights of British subjects."

And, even though the trial was over, the inky headlines went on. The *Tacoma Times* had its own little postscript to the Hazzard case. It ran a front-page story about evidence that *didn't* make it before the jury.

MRS. HAZZARD SOLD DEAD
CLAIRE WILLIAMSON'S TEETH

That Dr. Linda Burfield Hazzard, convicted of manslaughter for starving Claire Williamson, sold the teeth from Claire Williamson's mouth for a few paltry dollars after death had come . . .

IT WAS DRIZZLY AND FIFTY DEGREES WHEN MARgaret Conway invited a group of reporters camped outside into the Agassiz bungalow. She told them Dora and she would be staying in Tacoma a few weeks longer, then perhaps on to California, before they returned to Australia. There was a reason for the return to Australia. Rumors had run rampant among trial followers that Dora had accepted a proposal from her batch of letters. Her betrothed was reportedly a wealthy Australian.

"And you are really going back to Australia to be married?" a reporter asked as the pack of news hounds crowded in the doorway.

Dora acted surprised and touched her fingers to her lips. A little blush crossed her face.

"Oh, I haven't accepted him yet," she said.

Margaret Conway brushed the men into the front room.

"It's the very best thing for her. Besides, it's the very thing that made her hang on to life," Miss Conway said.

After a bit more probing, the reporters threw up their hands. The mystery man's name was not going to be revealed by either lady.

A newsman from a Tacoma daily changed the subject.

"It was your simple, straightforward story that practically brought Mrs. Hazzard's conviction," he told Dora.

Before Dora answered Margaret Conway spoke up.

"We only did what we thought was our duty to others. Dora felt that if she could not win the case fairly and honestly, she did not wish to win. We believed that the matter was in higher hands than ours."

"Yes," Dora finally broke in. "It would have been selfish, would it not, just to think of my own personal feelings? Even after all I suffered, that would be nothing, if I could do something to prevent others from going through what I did . . .

"Oh, it was terrible," she continued. "I am not fully recovered from the strain of it all yet. Sometimes I feel weak and tired. The very memory of it is terrible to recall, and then the strain of the trial was hard. I kept up while I was on the witness stand, but afterward came the reaction and now that the verdict has come another reaction."

Margaret spoke up once more.

"We are glad of the justice that has been given to us, but then not all the punishment in the world will bring back to life the one that is dead."

Neither woman ever revealed the would-be suitor's name. Some wondered if there had been one after all. Maybe it was the way out for a broken heart, for the man she could not have? Maybe it was what was needed for the happy ending that could never be. Never without Claire.

ALMOST AS THE MATCH WENT OUT IN THE COURTroom, there was a cry for justice among the followers of nature cures, the fast in particular. If Linda Hazzard had sought to be a martyr for a great cause, with her conviction came the achievement of her goal. A Seattle lawyer, J.W. Bryan, summed up the feelings coming from the fasting specialist's camp. He wrote a letter decrying the outcome of the Port Orchard trial and affixing the blame for it:

In the first place this abominable Lucian Agassiz, British minister at Tacoma, had done everything he possibly could do to poison public sentiment. The Times *at Seattle tried the case before the issues were made up. The jurors had read the* Times. *The most bitter articles had appeared at the greatest length and with most frequent recurrence.*

Her lawyers were good, you might say goody-goody, men. They were and are men of the highest character, but they were not fitted in temperament or make-up for the trial of a case of this kind. The state was represented by the notorious Kelley of Tacoma, who was playing the game solely to take the tricks. He was absolutely unscrupulous about stacking the cards, so as he did not offend the judge who was delighted to see the preference all go to Kelley and against the woman. Kelley simply put it all over the defense. There was no chance for the poor woman. I went into the courtroom and witnessed the proceedings. It seemed to me like a slaughter house. All could see what was happening.

ON WEDNESDAY, FEBRUARY 7, 1912, JUDGE YAKEY told Linda Burfield Hazzard to rise before he passed sentence upon her.

"What, if anything, have you to say?" he asked.

Linda looked greatly surprised and slowly lifted herself from her chair.

"Have I the right to make a statement?" she asked almost timidly.

"You have."

"I can only say that I have not had a thought of doing anything wrong and that a great injustice has been done me. It only takes time, of course, to right all these matters."

With the slam of Judge Yakey's gavel, sentence was pronounced. The fasting specialist would serve not less than two nor more than twenty years of hard labor at the penitentiary at Walla Walla.

For observers who didn't know Linda Burfield Hazzard, it seemed over.

EPILOGUE

A WOMAN LIKE LINDA BURFIELD HAZZARD never surrenders. Nothing in her character, her very soul, would allow the abandonment of her will or ambition. While on bond pending an appeal before the Washington State Supreme Court, the fasting specialist showed the world she was not a quitter. She had frequently told herself there was always the chance for victory if one was willing to wage the fight. Dr. Hazzard had always been more than willing. She would remain so for the rest of her life. And though despised by her enemies, she had a residual of goodwill from women who respected her iron-rigid stance against the male bastion of medicine with their cherished sheepskin diplomas and holier-than-God posturing. In a time when women were seeing rights and freedoms come within their grasp, Linda Hazzard was an inspiration.

That a jury had deemed her a killer was inconsequential.

On February 10, 1912, the ever-critical *Town Crier* turned her gender into the reason she *escaped* the gallows.

> *It is interesting to note that not one of the jurors who tried Mrs. Hazzard believed her innocent. The sole question was on the degree of guilt, and there is no doubt that her sex alone saved her from the verdict of murder.*

Two days later, her most venerated supporter fired back a shot of his own in the war over whether Dr. Hazzard was a murderess or a martyr. United Press International reported from Los Angeles that the great "faster" Henry Tanner announced he would submit to a forty-day fast under Dr.

Hazzard's supervision. He had one proviso. If he was alive at the end of the fast, his convicted colleague should be awarded another trial.

"My fast is to be used as new evidence," the aging doctor said.

At the same time, a thousand miles to the north, Linda offered one better. She telephoned Seattle reporters with the declaration she would fast herself and invited members of the King County Medical Association to monitor the results of her experiment for "the good of science."

As could have been predicted, the medical men laughed at her offer. They responded that they cared "not one tiny continental ejaculation if 'Dr.' Linda Burfield Hazzard ever eats again"—to say nothing of her intended fast.

THE MONTHS SPUTTERED BY AS LINDA AND SAM Hazzard faced more court dates, more subpoenas, and more innuendo. On July 1, 1912, the Washington State Board of Medical Examiners revoked Linda's license at their annual meeting in Tacoma. They cited the need to protect society from her heinous and malicious crimes.

To the public, in spite of it all, Linda presented her still-unflinching face. She denounced the board's action as further proof of the conspiracy that had landed her in trouble in the first place. At home in Olalla, she presented a different picture, however. Tears fell from her tired eyes. Dishes crashed to the floor. She would not give up, but admitted the defeat ripped at her. She had fought to the State Supreme Court to get that license. It was so unfair that those men should take it away from her. She had won the right fair and square.

Dr. Hazzard was not without support. Letters and cables came from all over the world. Lloyd Jones of Wanganui, New Zealand, was among the contingent who responded when the Hazzard conviction threatened the worldwide support of natural cures. Jones, a publisher and owner of the oldest bookshop in New Zealand, drafted a testimonial for the doctor while she awaited word from the courts. He published it in his 1912 book, *Health Reform: Evidence and Testimony in Favour of The No-Breakfast Plan and the Fasting Cure*:

*. . . this lady has been condemned for the manslaughter
of a patient and sentenced to imprisonment. An appeal is
now pending, from which I sincerely hope Dr. Hazzard
will emerge triumphant. If not, a gross miscarriage of
justice will have been perpetrated. Dr. Hazzard has been
practicing the 'fasting cure' for 15 years, and out of several thousands of patients that she has dealt with, there
have been only 15 deaths. In each of these cases there
has been malignant persecution and prosecution, the cli-
max being reached over the present case of Miss
Williamson . . .*

*It will be noted that Miss Williamson was treated at her
own request and was never fasted. The worst that can be
said is that the treatment failed to save her. Great capital
is being made of this case by the opponents of the fasting
cure, but I submit that even if the charge were true it could
not undo Dr. Hazzard's successful practice of the past 15
years, nor affect the real merits of the fasting cure, which
is being also successfully carried on by Dr. Eales, Mr.
Haskell, and many others. A sympathizer writes me thus:
"Even if all that has been said of Dr. Hazzard were true,
she has still done more for suffering humanity than any
'other living doctor.'"*

Linda was not idle. She gave speeches on the fast cure, continued her writings, and tried to figure out a way to live on the
dwindling money she and Sam had hidden away at Olalla. She
hated to answer the door for fear it was another court summons.
She kept an apple crate near Sam's desk to stockpile the deluge
of legal papers that arrived with her name on them.

Sam, as had been his escalating habit, drank himself to sleep
nearly every night. In the mornings, he threw bottles into the
gulch with the hope his maligned wife wouldn't discover the
full extent of his drinking problem. He could hear the little
brown bottles clink against each other after hurling them over
the edge. Of course, deep down he figured, his wife knew what
he was up to. Nothing really escaped Linda. She knew everything that went on.

Son Rollie talked of resuming his acting career—he had to

do something. His mother had few resources left to squander. Rollin Burfield needed a job.

And, while many couldn't fathom why, the patients still came. So did the trouble.

MARY BAILEY WAS A SIXTY-ONE-YEAR-OLD believer. In the fall of 1911, she had seen the news accounts of the pending Hazzard trial over the murder of Claire Williamson. Despite the overtly negative slant the papers carried in the weeks before the trial, Mary Bailey decided anyway that the fast cure might be her answer. It might, she considered, put her on the road to perfect health. Before the trial, she left her home in Tacoma and moved to the Home Colony on the Key Peninsula.

It was a good fit. The anarchist settlement welcomed the newcomer with unorthodox views. Mrs. Bailey took residence with Kingsmill Commander, one of the colony's leaders. As it turned out, Ontario-born Commander had taken Dr. Hazzard's fast treatment and assured Mary Bailey and others that the treatment had cured him of his ills. In twenty-five days, he dropped from 225 to 112 pounds—and never felt better. Because of Dr. Hazzard, he said, he was "in perfect health."

On November 11, 1911, at the height of the pretrial publicity, Mary Bailey made the trip from Home to Olalla to call on Dr. Hazzard at Wilderness Heights. It didn't faze her that others called the fasting specialist a murderer—or at least intended to prove so in court. She disregarded everything but the positive that she read or heard.

Mrs. Bailey, a widow, was a most unusual woman.

A newspaper reporter wrote of her:

> Even at Home Colony, where customs and beliefs are somewhat at variance with those of the ordinary family, Mrs. Bailey was regarded as a person of eccentricity. She was a devoted student of occultism at the colony.

IDA ANDERSON WAS ANOTHER STORY. SHE WAS A woman who simply could not get relief. She was the wife of Stanwood, Washington, banker H.C. Anderson. After her husband suffered from a serious case of ptomaine poisoning, a nurse named June Oakes was called to the Anderson residence to eliminate the poisons and help the man regain his health. The young nurse prescribed a severe diet.

As it turned out, June Oakes was the sister of Watson Webb. Unbeknownst to either Anderson, Miss Oakes was also a follower of fasting specialist Linda Burfield Hazzard. None of that would have mattered had it ended there. But shortly after Mr. Anderson was pronounced cured, Mrs. Anderson discovered she was in a delicate condition—with child. She told her husband to send for Nurse Oakes, to whom she had grown exceedingly fond. Sadly, when the baby was born, it was sickly.

"Babe's none too lively, would you say?"

Though—or because of it—June Oakes "dieted" the infant and gave it frequent mud baths in a nearby creek, the baby died.

The husband and his in-laws blamed the nurse and her strange hold over Ida as the cause of the nightmare. The more they urged Ida to dismiss her, the tighter the nurse's grip became. The family speculated the nurse's ulterior motive was to cause a divorce between the Mister and Missus and gain control of the Anderson assets. When Ida gave birth to the second baby, her husband finally put his foot down. He was not about to have a repeat of what had happened. And he was very worried; he did not want his wife to die.

Mr. Anderson dismissed Miss Oakes and Ida was admitted to a Catholic hospital in Seattle. Under a physician's care, she improved rapidly. Family members' relief was short-lived, however. One day, when no one was watching, Ida Anderson picked up her baby and slipped out of the ward. She checked into a room at the Raleigh Hotel.

Within a few weeks, both were nearly dead; victims of the fast cure. Mrs. Anderson was fed broths, and her baby was given warm water flavored with fruit coloring every other day. Both had wasted away to skin and bones.

On March 20, 1913, Ida Anderson died and her body was taken to Butterworth & Sons. The baby's grandmother took the emaciated infant and nursed it back to health.

While she denied any involvement with the deceased's diet,

Linda Hazzard admitted she had been giving Mrs. Anderson osteopathic treatments almost daily, for about two weeks.

An angry and suspicious Mr. Anderson demanded an investigation. He alleged the use of extreme amounts of funeral home makeup on his wife's face had been an attempt to obscure the true cause of her death. The King County coroner responded by removing the woman's body from Butterworth & Sons to the public morgue. A postmortem was held, though it was greatly hindered because the body had been embalmed. Even so, the exam turned up significant traces of alum in the woman's constricted stomach. Alum, an astringent, could cause the membrane of the stomach to shrink and prevent digestion.

A coroner's inquest on March 23, 1913, determined Mrs. Anderson had been starved to death.

British Vice-consul Lucian Agassiz pounced on the latest disclosure.

"The analysis which showed an unusual quantity of alum in the stomach of the dead woman opens up a peculiarly interesting feature in the case. On Mrs. Hazzard's own statement the stomachs of Ivan Flux and Claire Williamson were both shriveled at the time of their deaths and it is possible that this latest analysis will clear up some of the mystifying features of the deaths of Miss Williamson and Mr. Flux.

"The Miss Oakes, who is mentioned as the nurse, belonged to a family that supported Mrs. Hazzard during her trial. Her brother made an attempt to kidnap Essie Cameron, who was a servant in the Hazzard home and who was a witness against her."

Agassiz vowed to stay on top of each development.

Linda Hazzard, still on bond pending the supreme court ruling, drew plans for the sanitarium building she would erect one day.

THE SAME DAY A CORONER'S JURY IN SEATTLE determined Ida Anderson had died of starvation, the Kitsap County Coroner made a visit to Starvation Heights to investigate the reported death of yet another patient.

It was Mary Bailey, the true believer in the benefits of therapeutic fasting. Her grotesquely emaciated body was found in a bundle of smelly coverings on a cot in the little cabin next to Cabin Claire. A cursory examination held on the spot revealed several large, rectangular burns on her body—the wrappers had burned off the bricks that had been used to keep her warm. In her impossibly weakened condition before her death, Mary Bailey had been unable to tell anyone of her agony.

Gus Weise, a friend of the dead woman's from the Home Colony, told the coroner that nurse June Oakes and Dr. Hazzard had been caring for the patient. Dr. Hazzard, in fact, had been in to see the victim "three or four times" during the night she died.

On March 26, 1913, the *Tacoma Daily Ledger* ran a story on the case headlined:

ANOTHER PATIENT OF
MRS. HAZZARD DIES
DEATH AGAIN PAYS VISIT
TO OLALLA

The *Melbourne Argus* covered the case in its March 31 edition:

"STARVATION HEIGHTS"
MRS. HAZZARD'S "CURE"
ARREST FOLLOWS INQUEST

By the end of the week, the beleaguered fasting specialist was once again in a Kitsap County courtroom, defending her treatment and theories for the cure of disease. This time, as in the Anderson case, the proceeding was a coroner's inquest. Rumors flew with abandon throughout Port Orchard that Mrs. Bailey's diamonds, jewelry, and cash were missing.

"Just like the case of that English heiress!"

Linda Hazzard testified she and Mrs. Bailey were only friends. They did not have a patient-doctor relationship of any sort. Dr. Hazzard denied that remarks made in Mrs. Bailey's diary about taking a "fast cure from Dr. H." had any connection to her. They were "hallucinations" born of an old, feeble mind. There had never been a fast. Mary Bailey, whom Dr. Hazzard referred to as "Polly," was able to eat anything she liked. She would not allow her to fast to a dangerous degree.

"In view of past events," she said, alluding to the trial for

Claire's murder, "I have been very careful of late, and I wouldn't have allowed her to do that while she was there."

Nurse Oakes informed jurors that just after Mrs. Bailey's death, the deceased's pocketbook and other valuables were given to Gus Weise in the cabin.

Weise, however, had a different recollection. When it came his turn to testify, he said he had given the pocketbook to Dr. Hazzard.

"*What?*" Linda called from her place at the defense table.

The witness looked startled. "Didn't I?"

"No," the defendant answered.

Miss Oakes's voice rose from across the courtroom.

"I think you put it—"

"Stop!" yelled Coroner Fred Lewis, finally putting an end to the exchange. For the second time, he admonished the ladies that when they were not on the witness stand they were to remain absolutely quiet.

Whatever Dr. Hazzard had to say made no difference to the jury. Her story that Mrs. Bailey's internal organs were in such poor condition the woman could not assimilate food was seen as pure bunk. Three doctors testified that Mary Bailey had died of starvation.

Since prosecutors in King and Kitsap Counties felt certain the convicted woman would be checking into a cellblock at the prison in Walla Walla before the end of the year, nothing more was done with the Bailey and Anderson cases.

Linda Hazzard laughed it off.

"Maybe those against me are tiring of their little game?"

AND YET THE GAME CONTINUED. IN MID-AUGUST, only six months after the Bailey case receded from the front page, Linda Burfield Hazzard was back where newspaper editors figured she belonged. This time it involved the case of Robert Graham, the self-styled "British Bread King." The London man with a flowing white beard and bakeries all over the British Isles turning out 100,000 loaves a day, reportedly invented a health bread and traveled to Olalla to see if Dr. Hazzard could incorporate his recipe into her treatment for stomach ailments.

He ended up taking the fast cure himself. When concerned business associates contacted authorities, Agassiz led the charge to Starvation Heights once more.

The first visit resulted only in the confirmation that the man had been staying in a cabin and was taking the fast cure. Dr. Hazzard said Mr. Graham was given to taking sunbaths and was likely out in the woods somewhere. She showed the authorities the man's baggage. He was fine, she said.

A few weeks later, Mr. Graham, thin and still rich, left Olalla. The British Bread King's recipe remained in his pocket. A deal was never made.

ON OCTOBER 24, 1913, THE *TACOMA DAILY LEDGER* reported a catarrh sufferer named Fred Ebbeson died after a forty-nine-day fast administered by a disciple of Dr. Hazzard's. The follower had tried to administer the starvation treatment by reading *Fasting for the Cure of Disease*.

Dr. Hazzard had refused to treat Ebbeson because he "had no money," the paper reported.

IT SIMPLY COULDN'T BE. LIKE THE CHAIN PULLED to turn on a lamp, Linda Burfield Hazzard went into a sudden state of shock just before Thanksgiving 1913. For once in her life, she had nothing to say. She couldn't speak. The Washington State Supreme Court had rejected her appeal. Her conviction and sentence for causing Claire Williamson's death would stand. The fasting specialist's legs buckled beneath her. Samuel propped up his wife and dragged her to an upholstered chair in the living room. Linda looked terrible. She was so frail, so wan, he would not have known her if he hadn't been there to witness the transformation when the news came to Starvation Heights.

The authorities allowed Dr. Hazzard a month to close out her affairs before incarceration. All the while, the words stung at her.

"*. . . not less than two nor more than twenty years of hard labor.*"

Just after Christmas 1913, a woman with a single suitcase showed up at the prison in Walla Walla and identified herself to officials as Linda Burfield Hazzard. She was there without escort, without family, and most astonishingly, without prison commitment papers. She had done what she had resolved to do: she took her medicine like a man. She did not suffer the indignity of arriving under guard in shackles. Her enemies would never see her that way.

It took a couple of days to straighten things out. No one had ever done what she had. But then no one was like the fasting specialist.

Kitsap County prosecutors were befuddled and wary. They cabled the warden for a photograph of the inmate *"in order that there shall be absolutely no possibility of an error."* They did not want one of the woman's fanatic followers to step in and take the place of the self-proclaimed medical martyr.

On December 29, Linda Hazzard turned over her gold wedding band with a large glass stone—the one Sam had given to her when he commited bigamy in Minneapolis—a silver pin from her ne'er-do-well son, and her purse. She crossed out the word "convict" in the place for her signature on the documents that itemized her personal effects. On the final question of a prison survey to which she was to give her account of her crime, arrest, and conviction, she displayed her characteristic defiance:

> *"As I did not commit any crime, (it was by persecution of the medical profession that I am here) I cannot give any account of it."*

She was locked up in the women's ward, of course, though she had expected something more fitting for someone of her professional stature. In an odd way, it was. The women's ward was formerly the prison hospital. Warden Henry Drum endeavored to give his most famous woman prisoner as many extra writing privileges as possible, but "cannot have different rules for different prisoners."

For the first few weeks she was confined to her bed, talking with the matron about the rigors of prison life. She confided she had suffered unbelievable "mental strain" from the ordeal that stole her from Olalla and stalled her dreams. In time, she was sure, all of it would return to her, all that she had lost. When she fasted for a few weeks to prove the value of her regimen, Linda Burfield Hazzard once again made the news.

AT THE SHINGLED BUNGALOW IN OLALLA, SAMUEL Hazzard sat alone at his typewriter. The patients had gone. The followers had scattered to the wind in search of other, more accessible, curists. Rollie had left for Seattle to resume his stage career. Sam pulled up a sheet of Wilderness Heights letterhead and tapped out a note for the warden at Walla Walla. He felt the need to do some explaining on his wife's behalf. He imagined that she would be among the most difficult prisoners they ever had.

> She is a woman of most positive nature and conviction. She believes thoroughly in her method and her mission. She has gone to Walla Walla with no exact idea of the conditions she will meet, and with a burning sense of the injustice of courts and the incompetency of lawyers. The latter opinion I share with her to the extent of believing that she was furnished by her trial attorneys with perhaps the 'rottenest' defense ever put up in a criminal case of importance. I am not alone in this opinion, but, while individual lawyers say as much to me in confidence, you cannot get them to commit themselves as against each other.
> She is at this time passing through the menopause, or 'change of life,' and has been subject to severe hemorrhagic discharges lasting for days. This, with the suspense of the past two years, has not been conducive to patience in her disposition. She may say things that will tend to make your matron think that she would like to overturn all penological rules, but these remarks should be taken as that outcome of her reform spirit, and not as criticism upon the present management or surroundings.

IT WAS A COMFORT TO DORA, MARGARET, AND Lucian that their nemesis was finally behind bars. And though it had been three years since the ordeal began, none could put it out of their minds. They expected it would always be that way. Agassiz had continued to work with authorities to see that the woman would be punished for *all* her crimes, and more importantly, stopped from preying on the weak and nervous again. Dora and Margaret sent frequent letters to their friend, the vice-consul. Postmarks came from all over the world.

On March 14, 1914, the British vice-consul made two announcements to the *Tacoma News*.

The first was very good news, indeed. Lucian told reporters Dora Williamson would marry that spring in England. The lucky man was not the wealthy Australian whose proposal she had contemplated just after the trial. He was a clergyman, Rev. W.A. Chaplin, Hill Vicarage, Falfield, Gloucestershire. The wedding was set for April 25. Agassiz said he had business in London at that time, making it possible for his attendance at the ceremony. The second announcement was perhaps the most far-reaching reaction to the entire Hazzard case. To protect its citizens from the notorious American fasting quack, the Australian government refused to allow any mail to leave its shores addressed to Linda Burfield Hazzard, U.S.A.

Dr. Hazzard busied herself painting, reading, and writing. She became one of the editors of the prison newspaper, *Our Viewpoint*. She maintained a lively correspondence with hundreds of supporters throughout the world. A few even came to visit her in prison.

In December of 1915, almost two years since her incarceration, the word came down from the state parole board that Linda Burfield Hazzard would be released in time to spend Christmas with her family in Seattle. Upon hearing the news, Sam Hazzard sobered up enough to dash off a letter addressed to warden Henry Drum.

> *Matters at this end are in such a shape that it would be most inconvenient for Mrs. Hazzard to attempt to live on the home place. She will understand this is due to the financial difficulties that came about through her trial. The place is now in the hands of tenants who were put there by the holders of the mortgage at the time of its foreclosure.*

With Linda gone, it hadn't been easy for Samuel. Money was tighter than it had been in his whole life. Alcohol had expunged some of his charm, withered some of his good looks. While women were still available to him, he no longer could draw the attention of the youngest, the most beautiful. At forty-six, he was already an old man. He plugged along, drumming up whatever business he could, selling insurance, tutoring languages, but the truth was, he was barely making a living.

Sam doubted he could support his wife and asked if she could be granted a "roving parole" so she could temporarily move to California. The milder climate, he suggested, might do her some good.

The parole board didn't agree. The ex-con with the enema bag would remain in Washington where officials could keep an eye on her.

ON DECEMBER 19, 1915, THE FASTING SPECIALIST walked from the gates of Walla Walla a free woman. In her arms were the books she had written, some she had read, paintings she had made, and the iron will that had not been stolen from her by her incarceration. The following week, pale and noticeably tired, she gave her first postprison interview with the *Seattle Post-Intelligencer*. The article appeared two days after Christmas.

> *"I'm learning to walk, which is no easy task. Yes, it is really necessary to learn all over again, when one has been shut up in a little room for a year and a half. I find myself quite weak.*
> *"I feel a thousand years older. The psychology of prison life is strange and interesting. Prisoners know, instinctively, everything that goes on about the prison. At present there are nearly 800 men in Walla Walla and only 100 women; among the men are only three college graduates. The average prisoner is ignorant, usually their studies haven't carried them past the seventh grade. After my release I was allowed to go all through the prison and to talk with the men, and I found that their greatest need is*

*some quiet, gentle woman who may go about among them
exerting a motherly influence."*

THEN IT HAPPENED. FINALLY, A VICTORY. SIX
months after her return to Seattle, Governor Ernest Lister
granted Linda Burfield Hazzard a pardon with the condition
that she live up to her bargain of leaving America. She was glad
for it, though the feeling was bittersweet. While a pardon
restored all her rights as an American citizen, it could not bring
back statutory rights. The medical license would stay out of her
grasp.

She and Sam sailed from Vancouver to New Zealand, where
they were welcomed by supporter Lloyd Jones. Over the course
of the next several years, the fasting specialist took residence in
a house on Mt. Eden Road in Auckland and occupied two suites
of offices in New Zealand Insurance Buildings, where she hung
her shingle variously as a "physician, dietician, osteopath."
Business was brisk and the future looked better than it had since
Dora Williamson left Olalla. Lloyd Jones even acted as publisher of another of Dr. Hazzard's books, *Diet in Disease and
Systemic Cleansing.*

BY 1920 SHE WAS BACK IN OLALLA. NEW ZEALAND
had been financially successful to the degree that the Hazzards
were not only able to resume the ownership of Starvation
Heights, they had amassed enough money and support to build
the great sanitarium that had been the dream since Minneapolis.
Even though she was not allowed to practice medicine, Linda
identified herself to the 1920 census-taker as a physician. Sam
was no longer the institution's promoter, but an agent for
wholesale firms.

Dr. Hazzard slipped back into the community with the kind
of stature befitting of a physician, a leader. What had happened
in the past was of no matter to most who lived in the tiny community. Details were foggy, anyway, and the nearly impossible
business of trying to make a living in the country put the past
out of most minds. Linda and Sam became involved with the
Olalla school, even awarding academic scholarships (the
widow of one recipient of a $25 Hazzard Scholarship still has

the seventy-five-year-old check—it bounced). Linda was also a booster for the community when it came to road improvements, and a major force in the push for electricity to reach Olalla. She was an advocate for whatever it was that would help Olalla. For that, she was admired.

And, of course, there was the great building erected in the field north of the house.

No expense was spared on the sanitarium. For its time and rural location it was an extraordinary and undeniable achievement. It was the kind of place Olallans brought out-of-towners to see when they showed them the local sights.

Years later, Hugh Buchanan recalled the grandeur of the Hazzard sanitarium.

It was the most impressive and beautiful building in the whole community. I can see it in my mind's eye, I think it was three stories. It had a long porch the entire width of the sanitarium. The dormer windows were very well designed and architecturally built. It seemed everything on the inside was the best. The flooring, always highly polished oak. The stairway was the finest. Everybody took great pride in the sanitarium. It was one of the spots to see in the community. No one had anything bad to say about Dr. Hazzard. But I was a kid then. How would I know? There may have been a lot of things.

The great building notwithstanding, Dr. Hazzard's brushes with the law continued, as they would until the day she died. In April 1922, while taking charge of a case in Los Angeles, Linda Hazzard was arrested there for violating California's medical practice act. Three years later, she was arrested for practicing medicine without a license in connection with the death of Leonard Ritter. Ritter, who had been feeling poorly, had sold his farm in Chehalis, Washington, to pay for treatment at the sanitarium, now promoted as a "school of health." After an eighty-four-day fast which saw his weight plunge from 168 to a cadaverous 100 pounds, Ritter went to his great reward. The authorities, gleeful as ever, pounced.

But again, the doctor stood tall.

"You bet I'm going to fight! Because I am suffering for a cause, not for crimes. Think of it! Being called a murderess for trying to help people!"

Two-inch letters in the *Bremerton Daily News Searchlight* blared the verdict on March 27, 1925:

JURY FINDS FOOD SPECIALIST GUILTY

She was fined $100. No jail penalty was imposed.

ALFRED GANGNESS WAS FIFTEEN YEARS OLD THE day the old lady's dream went up in smoke.

It was the end of May 1935, in the forenoon, when a succession of five short rings chimed on the family's crank telephone. It was a primitive system, but for a town served by only two phone lines, it was a necessity. Olallans with phones—and there weren't many—had individual rings that told them that the call on the shared line was for their household. Long Short. Long Short Long. Short Short. So the rings went.

Five short rings, however, indicated a call for everyone.

It was a message from Gladys Fein, who operated the central line in Olalla. The rings were a command to run for the telephone. All across the community, farmers and their wives and children did as Alfred's father, Andrew, did.

"Where is it?" Mr. Gangness asked.

"Fire at Wilderness Heights!" Mrs. Fein called over and over.

The Gangnesses grabbed buckets and shovels and jumped into their car and drove north from their chicken farm in Fragaria toward the smoke and the commotion at Starvation Heights.

Art Buchanan and his teenage son, Hugh, also proceeded to the sanitarium as quickly as they could.

Hugh Buchanan never forgot what he saw:

> When we got there there was smoke issuing from the windows on the front, from the side, from the roof. I wished I had timed it by the clock, but I would almost say that this beautiful building seemed to have reduced itself to ruins in less than a half an hour. It seemed so fast.

When Mr. Gangness approached the north driveway, he and his son could see the flames coming through the roof at the north end of the building.

"She's gone," Andrew said as they drove in. Despite a water source—the concrete pool—a bucket brigade would not be enough to save it. It was such a pity.

The decision was made to get everything out of the building as quickly as possible. A loose chain of neighbors started on the top floor, taking out the furniture piece by piece. Hospital beds, mattresses, bed tables, were pitched from open windows. Over and over. Though no one counted, as many as two dozen little rooms occupied each floor. Some things shattered into smithereens as they fell.

An old man yelled to draw the younger Buchanan's attention to a second-floor window.

"Boy! Catch this!"

Hugh looked up to see an enormous suitcase teeter from a window ledge, before falling and crashing to the ground.

To catch it, would have squished him like a slug.

Almost seventy-years old, white-haired and wearing a sooty white uniform, Dr. Hazzard gathered a few raggedy, thin patients to keep them out of the fray. She pulled them in a circle and told them to remain calm.

It was something she also told herself.

No one went to the area on the third floor where it was believed the fire had started. The room in question was Rollin Burfield's.

Furniture was stacked in a garage adjacent to the main house. Piled to the rafters, all of it was out of harm's way, out of view.

Andrew Gangness was a carpenter and a great admirer of wood craftsmanship. The entry to the structure was set off by hand-carved solid oak double doors. None he had ever seen were more beautiful. At the end of the day, the wood panels caught the last beams of sunlight and gleamed like a mass of copper and bronze.

Through the chaos of smoke, fire, and people, Mr. Gangness searched out Sam Hazzard with a suggestion. He found the old man standing off to the side, alone. Could have been Sam was so upset he didn't know what to do. Could have been Sam flat out didn't want to help, for some reason.

"Sam," the neighbor said, "these are gorgeous doors. Can we take them off?"

Sam, who had been oddly quiet for most of the fire, answered without skipping a beat.

"No! They're insured."

Andrew and Al Gangness later wondered if Linda Hazzard's husband would have preferred that all furniture had been left inside the blazing sanitarium. Maybe the doctor's husband had gotten more help than he really wanted?

"They're insured."

As everything began to tumble in a heap, Dr. Hazzard wandered around the burning building wringing her hands and wailing.

"Oh Lordy, this is happening to me!" she cried. In a dramatic display of angst, she put her hand up to her forehead.

And how she complained, how she blamed. She stood in the smoky air and barked out words disparaging Mrs. Fein, the phone operator. The woman running the central phone line had taken her sweet time in answering the call for help. Linda blamed her for the delay in getting men and equipment out there in time to stop the blaze from consuming her grand sanitarium.

"She just wouldn't answer, I tell you."

Hugh Buchanan later recalled how the fasting specialist endured the terrible circumstance of the fire.

> When the fire had burned itself down, I remember Dr. Hazzard just walking around, I just don't think she was really in her right mind. It just destroyed her. I remember her words to my father were, "Art, it's all gone. Everything's gone. Everything I worked for, it's all gone." That's a sad thing . . . I do remember the human emotion there. 'It's all gone. It's all gone.'

THREE YEARS AFTER THE INFERNO, WITH HER fasting practice having dwindled to a very few staunch disciples, Linda Burfield Hazzard took to her bed ill. It had been two years since her last—her *final*—arrest for practicing medicine and osteopathy without a license. Weakened, but still determined, she called her followers to Olalla to apply the fasting technique and all of its accompaniments. She would save herself. She would prove to the world once and for all. The enema, of course, had to be administered. Dr. Hazzard's bowels had long since been unable to function on their own. She had been dependent on the internal bath for decades.

Propped up in a bed cushioned by a half dozen pillows, she sipped watery broths and barked orders at her husband, who slept on a sofa as he had since their return from New Zealand in 1920. Sam was attentive. He read to his wife and made daily trips to the post office on the bay for "the mail."

"Sam, you heathen! You better not be drinking!"

Linda lay in her bed for weeks, talking, planning, yelling.

And maybe even remembering.

Directly above her bed was the little sunroom where Claire Williamson had died of starvation twenty-seven years before.

And finally it came. Finally, the light went out for Dr. Hazzard. When death came for his wife, it did so so silently that Samuel Hazzard did not know it until the morning he found her grotesquely thin corpse. The great fasting specialist was cold and alone when she died.

Dr. Hazzard's body was carried out of the bungalow on a gloriously sunny morning in June 1938. Sam Hazzard made funeral arrangements from the house, boxed up some of his wife's things, and moved back into the bedroom that night.

The doctor's last therapeutic fasting case had been her own.

IN 1946, HAROLD AND SALLY HARPER ANSWERED AN ad for a parcel of property for sale in Kitsap County, Washington. At the time, the Harpers were living in Los Altos, California, not far from the campus at Stanford. The woman who placed the ad told them she was a teacher at the university, maybe a professor, could have been just an instructor. The Harpers didn't pay much mind to the seller's credentials. They were more interested in her land. The lady said she had some acreage and an old home for sale in a little town called Olalla. The old man who lived there—Samuel C. Hazzard—had just died and left the property to her.

Five decades later, Sally Harper recalled the California woman and the circumstances that brought her family to Olalla.

"*She was a tall woman, not thin, not heavyset. She was very pretty. She had a very nice figure. I may have known her name at the time, but why should I remember it? She told us to meet here in the state of Washington with the Hansens. They lived up the valley road. We drove up in our old Chevrolet—the kids stayed home with their grandmother. We went up there and spent the night with the Hansens. Every time I drive the valley road, I still can see that window, and I think, 'I used to sleep in that bedroom.'*

"*The next day the Hansens took us up to see 'Starvation Heights,' and back then it looked just like it does now. We thought it needed too much work, had too much that needed to be done to it. Well anyway, Mr. Hansen said there was another piece for sale, some people working at the Navy shipyard but they wanted to go back to Oklahoma.*"

Harold and Sally drove their Chevy to the old Culver place, fell in love with the two-story house with the view of the Sound, and made plans to make it their home.

"*After we came back here that's when I heard the whole story of what happened up at that old place. Mrs. Hansen told us. She was the only one who ever spoke about it. She told us the patients were starved to death. Dr. Hazzard got their money just like people do now, I guess. It was Hazzard's illegitimate daughter who had the place for sale. When we came back, that's when Mrs. Hansen told us that the Hazzard girl married a blind man. He was from Stanford University, too. And that was the end of her. Just think, we were the only ones from Olalla to see the daughter.*"

ALL GONE. THE GREAT SANITARIUM BURNED TO the ground more than sixty years ago. The smoke and flames signaled the end of everything Linda Burfield Hazzard had stood for, and everything that had ruined her. All of it, she thought, was gone forever when the place burned to the ground.

Gone, but not forgotten.

Some things never are. Especially the bad history, the kind

that makes folks shudder as they remember. Bad things are always better.

On summer nights when the sky over Puget Sound turns from blush to indigo, young families roast marshmallows with ruddy madrona sticks on the bluff that careens to the edge of Olalla Bay. The light from the fire flickers over their faces as they glance toward the woods. Before a rusty pail of water douses the embers, some tell the story. They recall the tale of the two English ladies, the ambitious doctor with the great sanitarium and the horror that seized the world's attention so many years ago. It all happened at that place at the crest of Orchard Avenue, the place they still call Starvation Heights.

They tell it as their grandfathers, Scout buddies, or the widow next door had once told them.

"Listen! Did you hear it? Did you hear the scream?"

AUTHOR'S NOTES AND ACKNOWLEDGMENTS

THE BOXES HAD BARELY BEEN UNLOADED when a cabinetmaker from up Banner Road slowed his pickup to a halt in the middle of the lane to welcome my family to Olalla. He was a friendly sort, with a steel wool-wiry beard that would have put Papa Hemingway to shame. When neighborly conversation turned to what I did for a living, I told him I was a nonfiction crime writer.

"Have I got a story for you," Bill Murphy confided as he waved a car around his truck. "It happened here in Olalla nearly a hundred years ago."

I smiled with polite interest. It happens all the time. New acquaintances always know of a family member or friend who would make the basis for a true crime book. It comes with the territory.

"They call the place where the murder happened Starvation Heights. A woman doctor killed her patients up there."

"Sounds kind of interesting," I offered as I shrugged toward the house indicating I had other work to do.

Murphy said he'd take me up to see the old place.

"Opal Jones lives up there. She's a great gal . . . kind of an old hippie."

A day or two later Murphy called and drove me up the hill to Starvation Heights.

And so it began. It was the start of a three-year search for the bits and pieces of a story that had nearly slipped into oblivion.

THE JOURNEY TO *STARVATION HEIGHTS*, THE BOOK, that is, has been remarkable for the generous help of the many people who assisted me in assembling my research materials. Two who stand out are Beverly Simpson and Clifford Cernick.

I owe a tremendous gratitude to Beverly Simpson. No author has ever been more fortunate to find such a talented and driven researcher. Over the course of more than a year's time, flight attendant Bev made dozens of visits to New Zealand and Australia. Each time she returned home, she had a packet of information from libraries, government offices, and friends she enlisted to help search out any possible nugget about the Williamson sisters and Dr. Hazzard. Without Bev's astonishing finds, it is fair to say this book would not be half what it is. She will never know how much I appreciate every bit of the material that she brought back for me or that she discovered here in the States.

Her messages often ran to the end of the tape.

"Famous author? Bev here," she would begin before launching into an idea or suggestion on another way to overcome a research stumbling block. I hated to erase those messages from my answering machine. Her enthusiasm was a motivator when frustrating miles of census reels gave nothing but eyestrain.

I thought I knew how to research something. That was before I met Ms. Simpson.

WHAT COULD I SAY ABOUT CLIFF CERNICK? HE and I are kindred spirits. I saw Cliff's name on a letter written March 25, 1949 seeking information from the Washington State Penitentiary. He was writing an article about Dr. Hazzard. I went to the library to see if a Mr. Cernick ever published a book. He had. Books on aviation and Alaska. When I finally tracked him down, Cliff Cernick, now in his late seventies, knew instantly what I was talking about—even though nearly fifty years had passed.

I asked him why he hadn't completed the project.

"Oh, Mr. Olsen," he said, "I was a young man at the time, busy with other things in life, and I just couldn't do the story justice. But I've never forgot it."

"Any chance you have some notes or any source material?" I asked hopefully.

There was a short pause.

"Think I do. I've got a regular rat's nest of boxes around here, but I think I kept that Hazzard stuff. That book will be a best-seller!"

A couple of weeks later a big manila envelope arrived postmarked Anchorage, Alaska. I ripped the package open, knowing that the man who sent it had a five-decade jump on the story. I was not disappointed. Inside I found literally hundreds of slips of paper, scraps of notes, interviews, little bits and pieces that I imagined would likely find their way into *Starvation Heights*. Cliff Cernick, you are my hero. I only hope I did this story—a story that nagged at you for fifty years—justice.

PEOPLE AND PAPER. WHEN IT GETS DOWN TO IT that's what makes a book based on a true story. It was more than a stroke of luck that the fasting specialist had fought her conviction in the Williamson case. Without Linda Burfield Hazzard being true to form and appealing her conviction, I would have been robbed of some of the best material—the basis for critical areas of *Starvation Heights*—the trial transcript and case exhibits. Though no one had asked for it for more than eighty years, I had access to letters Claire and Dr. Hazzard wrote, the diary entries, copies of the doctor's books, and much more. I thank Tyler Williamson of the Archives for the Washington State Supreme Court, Temple of Justice, Olympia, for his help in retrieving the case material for me and ensuring that I got every available page. The transcript from Samuel Hazzard's bigamy trial was also a godsend, discovered among the archives at the Hennepin County Government Center, Minneapolis. Lucian Agassiz's correspondence concerning Dr. Hazzard came by way of Joan McPherson at the Library and Records Department, Foreign & Commonwealth Office, Hanslope Park, Milton Keynes, UK.

THERE ARE SO MANY WHO HELPED WITH *STARVA-tion Heights* (either consenting to interviews or digging through their attics and basements to unearth bric-a-brac like letters, comics, books, even a Wilderness Heights business card), and if I have made an oversight, please forgive and know that you did your part in keeping this story alive.

I thank wonderful new friends Chuck and Opal Abundis for their enthusiastic hospitality as I counted the stairs of their home—the old Hazzard residence—and plundered the ravine for clues to the life that was; Janetta Nelson, for her gorgeous photographs, archival treasures and warm friendship; and Verna Fagerud, Bernice Crouse, Hardis Smith, Cammie Tallman, Irene and Ray Tallman, Bill and Bunny Kuhlman, Cathy Wolfe, Ken Oas, Ray Johnson, Art Banfill, Duke "the Duke of Hazzard" Tanksley, Anne Scott, Ernest Bloomquist, Theresa Heyer, Don Bruer, Marcia Beck, Marvin Lillie, John Smith, Pauline Fein Petersen, Ed Fein, Charlee Glock-Jackson, Becky Beck, Jack Eaton, Cliff and Florence Hurd, Lu Pendarvis, Sandra Ashlock, Ernie Carlson, Bill Burchett, Marie Sheedy, Helen Gage, Hugh Buchanan, Alfred Gangness, Maggie Forsman, Hertha Willock Bancroft, Marie Jessen Bowman, Ethel Olander, Myrtle Nelson, Andy James, Helen Ross, Fredi Perry, Warren B. Anderson, Bill Burchett, Patricia Park, June Wolfe, Paula Bates, Dr. Raj Vasudeva, Tina Marie Schwichtenberg, and quick information specialist Barbara Erickson.

I also wish to thank the contributions of some I never met. Through the generosity of Janetta Nelson, I was able to "meet" Jennie Tuttle, Rose Willock, Ruby Baker, and Myrtle Culver through oral history tapes recorded by Janetta and her late husband Carl in 1972.

RESEARCHING A CASE AS OLD AS THE HAZZARD story took me to museums, libraries, and archives from Washington to Minnesota. Many thanks to the historians who guided my efforts along the way. Chief among them: Charles LeWarne; author and Washington State historian; Richard Engeman, University of Washington Libraries, Special Collections; Brian Kamens, Northwest Room, Tacoma Public

Library; Suzanne Annest, director, Kitsap Historical Society and Museum; Virgil Reames, South Kitsap Historical Society and Log Cabin Museum, Port Orchard; volunteers at the Federal Records Center, National Archives, Seattle; Marty Lukens, Family History Center, LDS, Tacoma; Ivy Larsen, genealogist, Salt Lake City; and the very efficient and always helpful Pat Hopkins, research/archivist at the Washington State Archives, Olympia.

I visited and corresponded with a number of court clerk offices as I sought information on civil or criminal actions concerning the Hazzards or their cronies. I thank the folks at the King County, Kitsap County, Pierce County (Washington) and Ottertail County (Minnesota) clerk offices for their assistance.

I HAVE GREAT RESPECT AND ADMIRATION FOR those who work for historical societies and museums across the country. While thankfully most are paid for their important work, many are volunteers. All I contacted were willing to help. From the following I received copies of Sam and Linda Hazzard's respective prison files, family history, and other material: Paul Maravales, Executive Director and Leanne Brown, Assistant Director, Carver County (Minnesota) Historical Society; the staff at the Ottertail County (Minnesota) Historical Society; Steve Nielson at the Minnesota Historical Society; researchers at the National Archives, Military Records Section and National Archives, College Park, Maryland.

I gratefully acknowledge the following resources in Australia and New Zealand: State Library of New South Wales; General Reference Library, Sydney, Australia; Dawn Melhuish, reference librarian, information services at the National Library of Australia, Canberra, ACT; Alexander Turnbull Library, Wellington, NZ; State Library of Victoria, Melbourne, Victoria, Australia; Australian Archives Central Office, Public Record Office of Victoria, Melbourne; Lynley Fowler, New Zealand Collection librarian, Wanganui District Library; and Victoria-based researcher Louise Wadell.

And the public libraries: Seattle Public Library, Tacoma Public Library, Peninsula and Lakewood Branches of the Pierce County (Washington) Public Library, Minneapolis

Public Library, Nevada (Iowa) Library, photo library at the Museum of History and Industry, Seattle.

Newspapers, of course, were another source for *Starvation Heights*. I reviewed the archives of *Seattle Argus*, *Seattle Times*, *Seattle Post-Intelligencer*, *Sound Views* (Olalla, Washington) *Patriarch* (Seattle), *Town Crier* (Seattle), *West Pass Record* (Olalla, Washington), *Agitator* (Home, Washington) *Port Orchard Independent*, *Bremerton Daily News Searchlight*, *Tacoma Ledger*, *Tacoma Times*, *Tacoma News Tribune*, *Minneapolis Journal*, *Minneapolis Daily Times*, *Minneapolis Tribune*, *New York Times*, *Melbourne Argus*, *Sydney Morning Herald*, *Melbourne Age*, *New Zealand Herald*, *Auckland Weekly News*, *Weekly Times*, (Victoria, Melbourne).

While I looked at every scrap published about Dr. Hazzard and Olalla/Kitsap history, a few books must be noted here for the information contained in each was of great assistance: *Kitsap County: A History*, published by the Kitsap County Historical Society, *South Kitsap County, State of Washington*, pamphlet published by The Port Orchard Chamber of Commerce, July 1922. LeWarne, Charles Pierce, *Utopias on Puget Sound 1885–1915*, University of Washington Press, Seattle, 1995 edition. Hazzard, Linda Burfield, *Fasting for the Cure of Disease*, Hazzard Publishing Company, Seattle, Washington, 1910. Hazzard, Linda Burfield, *Diet in Disease and Systematic Cleansing*, H. I. Jones & Son, Ltd., Wanganui, New Zealand, 1917. LaVene, Radium, *There Was No Place Like Home*, unpublished manuscript, 1945. Jones, Lloyd, *Evidence and Testimony in Favour of the The No-Breakfast Plan and the Fasting Cure*, H. I. Jones & Son, Ltd., 1912, Wanganui, NZ. M.S. Kline, *Steamboat*, *Virginia V*, Documentary Book Publishers Corporation, 1985, Bellevue, Washington.

MY DEEPEST GRATITUDE ALSO TO LITERARY agent Susan Raihofer at David Black, Inc., for her support, keen eye for detail, and enthusiasm over each discovery. Also many thanks to Rob McMahon, editor at Warner Books, and the copy editor Sara Schwager for their conscientious care with this project.

On a personal note, I wish to acknowledge the contributions of my family; my wife Claudia and our daughters Marta and Morgan; my mother and father, Gladyce and Don Olsen. All books start and end with them. And to Jamie and Jessica Schwichtenberg who joined me and my girls one damp Father's Day as we poked around in the mud of the gulch and the bottom of the sanitarium incinerator looking for bones—only to find scads of Samuel Hazzard's vanilla bottles, a cracked enema can, and a 1920s bottle of Phillips Milk of Magnesia.

Girls, I am almost positive if we dig just a little deeper, we'll find some teeth . . . maybe even a skull.

Gregg Olsen
Olalla, Washington

THE AUTHOR

GREGG OLSEN IS ALSO THE AUTHOR OF *Mockingbird: A Mother, a Child, a Tragedy* (Warner Books, June 1995); *Bitter Almonds: The True Story of Mothers, Daughters and the Seattle Cyanide Murders* (Warner Books, December 1993) and *Abandoned Prayers: The Shocking True Story of Murder, Obsession and Little Boy Blue* (Popular Library, December 1990). The author is the recipient of numerous writing and editing awards, including citations from the Society of Professional Journalists (Sigma Delta Chi), the International Association of Business Communicators, Washington Press Association, and a national first place award from the National Federation of Press Women.

The author and his family live in Olalla, Washington.

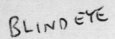
BLIND EYE

THERE ARE CRIMES OF PASSION . . .

CRIMES OF THE HEART . . .

AND THEN THERE ARE THOSE
CRIMES TOO UNSPEAKABLE TO
UNDERSTAND.

ABANDONED PRAYERS
(0-445-21076-1, $4.95 USA) ($5.95 Can.)

BITTER ALMONDS
(0-446-36359-6, $5.50 USA) ($6.99 Can.)

MOCKINGBIRD
(0-446-60095-4, $5.99 USA) ($6.99 Can.)

STARVATION HEIGHTS
(0-446-60341-4, $6.50 USA) ($8.50 Can.)

Available from
WARNER BOOKS

553-C